May 31–June 2, 2012
Milwaukee, Wisconsin, USA

**Association for
Computing Machinery**

Advancing Computing as a Science & Profession

SIGMIS-CPR'12

Proceedings of the 2012
Computers and People Research Conference

Sponsored by:
ACM SIGMIS

Supported by:
**Marquette University, SIM, University of Wisconsin-Parkside,
and University of Wisconsin-Whitewater**

**Association for
Computing Machinery**

Advancing Computing as a Science & Profession

The Association for Computing Machinery
2 Penn Plaza, Suite 701
New York, New York 10121-0701

Notice to Past Authors of ACM-Published Articles

ISBN: 978-1-4503-1110-6

Additional copies may be ordered prepaid from:

ACM Order Department
PO Box 30777
New York, NY 10087-0777, USA

Phone: 1-800-342-6626 (USA and Canada)
+1-212-626-0500 (Global)
Fax: +1-212-944-1318
E-mail: acmhelp@acm.org
Hours of Operation: 8:30 am – 4:30 pm ET

ACM Order Number: 433120

Printed in the USA

Foreword

It is our great pleasure to welcome you to the 50th Annual Computers and People Research Conference - *ACM SIGMIS CPR 2012.* For the past 50 years, ACM SIGMIS CPR has engaged the academic and practitioner communities in understanding issues pertaining to supply of information technology (IT) professionals, demand for their skills and talents, and their readiness for the workplace.

Many issues have evolved and matured with changes in technology, organizational valuation of IT, globalization, and economic downturns and upswings. During the past 50 years of CPR, several generations of IT professionals have undergone this cycle of preparation, recruitment, and retention. As baby boomers retire, a new generation of IT professionals presents yet another set of opportunities and challenges for continued research. These transitions beg the questions: what have we learned in the past 50 years and what do we envision as emerging issues for the next 50?

On this 50th anniversary, the SIGMIS CPR proceedings reflect upon these contributions to theory and research and identify new and emergent issues. The papers, panels, and posters within the proceedings address themes such as diversity and cultural issues in the attraction and retention of IT professionals, occupational commitment, curriculum issues and trends, and traditional CPR topics such as IT career development practices and the skills and abilities essential for the next decade. We hope these proceedings serve as a valuable reference for computer and people researchers and practitioners in the coming years.

Putting together *ACM SIGMIS CPR 2012* was made possible by the work of many dedicated individuals. We first thank the authors for providing the content of the program, which continues to showcase exemplar work in the field. We are grateful to the program committee who worked diligently in reviewing papers and providing constructive feedback for authors. In addition, we would like to thank Andreas Eckhardt and Mike Gallivan for organizing this year's doctoral consortium, which provides a glimpse of the exciting globally diverse research on the horizon. We also thank Indira Guzman de Galvez for her role as Treasurer, and Nita Brooks for publicity. Special thanks go to Lisa Tolles and her team from Sheridan Proceedings Service for their work in processing the proceedings in a timely manner. We would also like to thank the Milwaukee Visitors Bureau and DCD for the photograph included on the front cover of the proceedings. We are also grateful to the Society of Information Management (SIM), Wisconsin, whose partnership has been critical for launching a synergistic engagement with the practitioner community. Finally, we thank our sponsor, ACM SIGMIS, the leadership of Janice Sipior, and our generous supporters.

We hope that you will find this program interesting and thought-provoking and that the conference will provide you with a valuable opportunity to share ideas with other researchers and practitioners from institutions around the world.

Monica Adya
Marquette University
Conference Co-Chair

Robert Horton
University of Wisconsin-Whitewater
Conference Co-Chair

Haiyan Huang
Michigan Technological University
Program Co-Chair

Jeria Quesenberry
Carnegie Mellon University
Program Co-Chair

Kate M. Kaiser
Marquette University
Local Arrangements Co-Chair

Stephen Hawk
University of Wisconsin-Parkside
Local Arrangements Co-Chair

Table of Contents

Session 3.1: IT Workforce Management–I
Session Chair: Cynthia Riemenschneider *(Baylor University)*

Session 3.2: IT Workforce Management–II
Session Chair: Eileen Trauth *(The Pennsylvania State University)*

Session 4.1: Research Poster Session and Doctoral Consortium Poster Session

Session 5.1: Panel Session–II

Session 5.2: IT, Computers and People–I
Session Chair: Lee Erickson *(The Pennsylvania State University)*

Session 6.1: Global and Cultural Aspects of the IT Workforce
Session Chair: Gaetan Mourmant *(University of Strasbourg)*

Session 6.2: IT, Computers and People–II
Session Chair: Deborah J. Armstrong *(Florida State University)*

Session 7.1: IT Workforce Diversity
Session Chair: Damien Joseph *(Nanyang Technological University)*

Session 7.2: History and Future of the IT Workforce
Session Chair: Conrad Shayo *(California State University, San Bernardino)*

SIGMIS CPR 2012 Conference Organization

General Chairs: Monica Adya (*Marquette University, USA*)
Robert Horton (*University of Wisconsin-Whitewater, USA*)

Program Chairs: Haiyan Huang (*Michigan Technological University, USA*)
Jeria Quesenberry (*Carnegie Mellon University, USA*)

Conference Treasurer: Indira Guzman de Galvez (*Trident University International, USA*)

Doctoral Consortium Chairs: Andreas Eckhardt (*Goethe University Frankfurt, Germany*)
Michael Gallivan (*Georgia State University, USA*)

Doctoral Consortium Mentors: Jo Ellen Moore (*Southern Illinois University Edwardsville, USA*)
Gaetan Mourmant (*University of Strasbourg, France*)
Fred Niederman *(Saint Louis University, USA)*
Greta Polites (*Bucknell University, USA*)
Tim Weitzel (*Bamberg University, Germany*)

Local Arrangements Chairs: Kate M. Kaiser (*Marquette University, USA*)
Stephen Hawk (*University of Wisconsin-Parkside, USA*)

Publicity Chair: Nita Brooks (*Middle Tennessee State University, USA*)

Program Committee: Monica Adya (*Marquette University, USA*)
Oluwole Akinyokun (*Federal University of Technology, Akure*)
Deb Armstrong (*Florida State University, USA*)
Sarah Beecham (*The Irish Software Engineering Research Centre, Ireland*)
Catherine Beise (*Salisbury University, USA*)
Johanna Birkland (*Syracuse University, USA*)
Nita Brooks (*Middle Tennessee State University, USA*)
Stephan Böhm (*Hochschule RheinMain, Germany*)
Diana Burley (*The George Washington University, USA*)
Orin Day (*RTI, USA*)
Thomas Dillon (*James Madison University, USA*)
Patrick Donohue (*University of Limerick, Ireland*)
Andreas Eckhardt (*Goethe University Frankfurt, Germany*)
Randy Eckhoff (*RTI, USA*)
Harvey Enns (*University of Dayton, USA*)
Lee Erickson (*The Pennsylvania State University, USA*)
Barbara Felts (*RTI, USA*)
Thomas Ferratt (*University of Dayton, USA*)
Valerie Ford (*The George Washington University, USA*)
Kimberly Furumo (*University of Hawaii at Hilo, USA*)
Indira Guzman de Galvez (*TUI University, California, USA*)

Program Committee (continued):

Tracy Hall (*Brunel University, United Kingdom*)
Andrea Hester (*Southern Illinois University Edwardsville, USA*)
Brian Janz (*The University of Memphis, USA*)
Damien Joseph (*Nanyang Technological University, Singapore*)
Janet Kourik (*Webster University, USA*)
Sven Laumer (*Otto-Friedrich-University Bamberg, Germany*)
Diane Lending (*James Madison University, USA*)
Chuck Litecky (*Southern Illinois University, USA*)
Christian Maier (*University of Bamberg, Germany*)
Jo Ellen Moore (*Southern Illinois University, Edwardsville, USA*)
Gaetan Mourmant (*University of Strasbourg, France*)
Fred Niederman (*Saint Louis University, USA*)
Susanne J. Niklas (*RheinMain University of Applied Sciences, Germany*)
Lorne Olfman (*Claremont Graduate University, USA*)
Irene Petrick (*The Pennsylvania State University, USA*)
Norah Power (*University of Limerick, Ireland*)
Ijaz Qureshi (*Iqra University, Pakistan*)
Cindy Riemenschneider (*Baylor University, USA*)
Sherry Ryan (*University of North Texas, USA*)
Sureerat Saetang (*University of South Australia, Australia*)
Rahmath Safeena (*Taif University, Saudi Arabia*)
Xiqing Sha (*National University of Singapore, Singapore*)
Janice Sipior (*Villanova University, USA*)
Derek Smith (*University of Cape Town, South Africa*)
Mary Sumner (*Southern Illinois University Edwardsville, USA*)
Stefan Tams (*HEC Montréal, Canada*)
Eileen Trauth (*The Pennsylvania State University, USA*)
Karthikeyan Umapathy (*University of North Florida, USA*)
Faith-Michael Uzoka (*University of Botswana, Canada*)
Susan Yager (*Southern Illinois University Edwardsville, USA*)

SIGMIS CPR 2012 Sponsor & Supporters

Sponsor:

Supporters:

Chief Information Officer (CIO) Panel
How to Groom IT Leadership as Change Agents

Colin Boyd
Johnson Controls

Denis Edwards
ManpowerGroup

Philip Loftus, Ph.D.
Aurora Health Care

Timothy G. Schaefer
Northwestern Mutual

Categories and Subject Descriptors
K.1 The Computer Industry; K.7 The Computing Profession

General Terms
Management

Keywords
Industry, IT profession, IT workforce, executive, leadership

1. PANEL MEMBERS

1.1 Colin Boyd

Colin Boyd joined Johnson Controls as Vice President Information Technology and CIO in 2008. He is responsible for all Johnson Controls IT activities. Previously Colin was Corporate Vice President and CIO for Sony Ericsson based in London, General Manager of IS Operations for Sony Europe, British Telecomm, and Logica. Colin holds an M.S. in IT from the University of London and a B.S. in Manufacturing Engineering from the University of Nottingham.

1.2 Denis Edwards

Denis Edwards is Global CIO leading and coordinating IT functions across ManpowerGroup in 80 countries and territories. He was Vice President Global Solutions and Architecture for Cadbury-Schweppes and held senior IT roles with PWC, and Marriott, and served as CTO for several start-ups. Denis holds a M.S. in IT from the University of Maryland and a B.S, from Nova Southeastern University. Denis also holds a Masters Certificate in Six Sigma & Black Belt from Villanova University.

1.3 Philip Loftus, Ph.D.

Dr. Loftus joined Aurora Health Care in 2006, as CIO and VP Information Services. He is responsible for developing and implementing the IT strategy supporting Aurora's strategic plan. Philip was SVP and CIO at Caremark, SVP Global IT Strategy and Applications at GlaxoSmithKline, Executive Director of Research IS at Merck, and VP International R&D IS at Zeneca. He received his PhD from the University of Liverpool and was a Fulbright Hays Postdoctoral Fellow at the California Institute of Technology.

1.4 Timothy G. Schaefer

Tim Schaefer became CIO and head of IS for Northwestern Mutual in 2008. Prior to CIO, he was responsible for development and support of applications covering insurance products and operations, retail and institutional investments, field technology, compensation, and corporate functions. He was Director of Policyowner Services, Systems, and Vice President of Life Benefits. Tim joined NM in 1988 as a programmer. He has a B.B.A. from the University of Wisconsin-Milwaukee and an M.S. Management and Organizational Behavior from Silver Lake College.

SIGMIS-CPR'12, May 31–June 2, 2012, Milwaukee, Wisconsin, USA.
ACM 978-1-4503-1110-6/12/05.

How CPR is Like Madonna: 50 Years of Reinvention
A Discussion Reflecting on the Past, Present, and Future

Monica Adya
Marquette University
Department of Management
Milwaukee, WI 53201
01-414-288-7526
monica.adya@marquette.edu

Catherine Beise
Salisbury University
Perdue School of Busiiness
Salisbury, MD USA
01-410-548-4034
cmbeise@salisbury.edu

Bob Bostrom
University of Georgia
MIS Department
Athens, GA USA
01-706-548-9185
bostrom@uga.edu

Paul Licker
Oakland University
Rochester, MI 48309
01-248-370-2432
licker@oakland.edu

Lorne Olfman
Claremont Graduate University
SISAT
Claremont, CA USA
01-909-621-8209
Lorne.Olfman@cgu.edu

Maung Sein
University of Agder
Department of Information Systems
4604 Kristiansand, Norway
47-38141617
maung.k.sein@uia.no

ABSTRACT
The purpose of this panel is to provide a formal forum and opportunity to reflect on the past, discuss the present, and provide direction and inspiration for the future of what we now call Computers and People Research (CPR). To what extent have these early concerns and themes endured? How have they been transformed over five decades of changes in technology, changes in the workplace and global business context, and IT worker demographics? What progress has the CPR community made in addressing these concerns? What new issues has CPR brought forward that were not envisioned by the early CPR pioneers?

Categories and Subject Descriptors
K.6.1 [**Project and People Management**]; K.7 [**Computing Profession**]

General Terms Management

Keywords Computer Personnel

1. BACKGROUND
The first meeting of the Computer Personnel Research Group took place in 1962 at the Rand Corporation in Santa Monica, California [1]. The participants included representatives from employers of "computer personnel" such as Rand Corporation and Sandia Labs, as well as researchers from institutions such as the University of Southern California and Johns Hopkins University. A review of the transcript of the 2-day meeting identifies several issues of concern to the participants. Their discussion topics touch on themes that have been transformed numerous times over the past five decades in scope and terminology.

Their themes can be mapped to the three major issues laid out in the 2012 Call for Papers.

1.1 Supply of IT Workers
Implicit in the concerns of the 1962 participants is an apparent shortage of computer personnel, primarily programmers, although they also mention systems analysts. One major purpose of the meeting was ostensibly to discuss how to identify and increase the number and quality of these personnel.

1.2 Demand for Skills and Talents
A significant portion of the meeting was spent trying to identify the explicit skills and talents of programmers and analysts. They spent a considerable amount of time on how to distinguish good programmers from not so good programmers, speculating as to the importance of IQ, communication and cooperation skills, independence and ability to work alone, logical reasoning, and critical thinking, among others. An emerging awareness of the importance of job preferences, motivations, and socio-emotional states was also evident from this early CPR meeting.

1.3 Readiness for the Workplace
Another lengthy discussion centered on candidate testing, including aptitude, IQ, and personality, as a way of identifying good candidates and also evaluating performance once in the workplace. There was considerable agreement on their concern for the lack of validity of the test and lack of evidence that any of these tests were good predictors of performance, even though they were widely used. Likewise, there was little consensus on how to reduce the subjectivity of performance evaluations of employees. Another major goal of this early meeting was to encourage more research and coordination of efforts across institutions, and how the group should organize in order to accomplish that.

2. PANEL FORMAT
This panel will be highly interactive. The panelists will not give presentations but instead will engage in a conversation with each other and with the audience. After brief introductions, the panel moderator will ask the panelist a series of structured questions. Each panelist will have an opportunity to respond to the question

as well as to each other, and then audience responses will also be solicited. Questions will include:

- What is different about early CPR research and the challenges we have in the future?
- What contributions of past research have had the greatest impact on practice?
- Given the increasing ubiquity of IT in work and life, what will distinguish IT professionals from other workers? How will this influence the next transformation of CPR?
- How has CPR transformed your own research agenda and methods?
- What is your most memorable CPR story?
- What have we as a community done well over the years? What have we not done well?

4. REFERENCES

[1] Proceedings of the June Meeting of the Computer Personnel Research Group, RAND Corporation, Santa Monica, CA, USA, June 28-29, 1962, p. 1-130.

5. PANELIST BIOGRAPHIES

Monica Adya is an Associate Professor of Management at Marquette University. She received her PhD in MIS from Case Western Reserve University. Monica's research encompasses – (a) IT workforce with themes related to diversity, and offshore team management, and (b) design and use of forecasting support systems. Her work has been published in *Communications of the AIS, Decision Sciences Journal of Innovative Education, Human Resource Management, IT & People, International Journal of Forecasting, Information Systems Research, Journal of Forecasting,* and *Journal of Global Information Management* among others. Monica has been co-investigator on several grants and serves on editorial boards of *Communications of the AIS, International Journal of Forecasting,* and *Journal of Forecasting.*

Bob Bostrom is a Professor Emeritus in Management Information Systems Department at the University of Georgia. He is also President of Bostrom & Associates, a training and consulting company focusing on the effective integration of people and technology. He still teaches part-time in Management Information Systems (MIS) and Leadership areas. Bob has over 150 refereed publications in leading academic and practitioner journals, 14 of those in SIGCPR Proceedings and 1 in *Computer Personnel* Journal. He has also has served on SIGCPR program committees, appeared on panels and chaired sessions. He was Conference Chair in 1985. His current research and consulting interests are focused on business process management, technology-supported learning, and effective design of organizations via integrating human and technological dimensions.

Paul Licker (PhD, University of Pennsylvania) has been a social scientist, information systems professional, software entrepreneur, communication consultant and university lecturer in Thailand, Britain, the USA, Canada, and South Africa. He has authored over eighty published research papers, three textbooks, two monographs, and numerous refereed and invited conference papers. Research interests include IT-user relations, user responsibility in IT and strategic deployment of IT. He is Professor of MIS at Oakland University. He is President of the Global Information Technology Management Association.

Lorne Olfman is a Professor in the School of Information Systems and Technology. Lorne's research interests include: how software can be learned and used in organizations, the impact of computer-based systems on knowledge management, and the design and adoption of systems used for group work. Along with Terry Ryan, Lorne co-directs the Social Learning Software Lab ([SL]2). A key component of Lorne's teaching is his involvement with doctoral students; he has supervised 51 students to completion and has served on more than 60 other dissertation committees. As an active member of the Information Systems community, Lorne has co-authored more than 130 refereed articles and has been a regular participant in the SIGCPR/SIGMIS community. He published his first journal article in *Computer Personnel* and his first conference paper in the 22nd *SIGCPR Proceedings* (along with Bob Bostrom and Maung Sein). Lorne was the Program Chair of the 1995 SIGCPR/SIGMIS conference and Conference Chair in 1996.

Maung K. Sein is a professor of Information Systems at University of Agder, Norway. A Ph.D. from Indiana University, he has led a nomadic life geographically, academically and scholarly. He has previously served at universities in the U.S. His current research focus is on ICT for development and e-Government but started with end-user training. He has published in all manner of journals in IS, eGovernment and Construction Management (gasp!). His wide editorial experience includes a spell on the editorial board of the late lamented *Computer Personnel*. His first publication was in the Proceedings of the 1986 SIGCPR conference at Calgary (the first of 18 tri-authored papers with Lorne Olfman and Bob Bostrom). As conference chair in 2002, he wooed the CPR community to cross the Atlantic to Norway for the first CPR conference outside the comforting confines of North America. His proudest honor is the inaugural Magid Igbaria Outstanding Paper award he received (with Maren Simonsen) at the 2004 CPR conference in Tucson. To relive his past life as a hardware and software professional, he finds time to break bread with practitioners. His work, academic tourism, and sheer wanderlust has taken him to all the continents except Antarctica and he is within striking reach of being a Full member of The Century Club.

Catherine Beise (Moderator) is a tenured full professor at Salisbury University. She received her PhD in MIS from Georgia State University and an MS in Information & Computer Science from Georgia Institute of Technology. In addition to holding academic positions at several universities, she has worked professionally as a programmer, systems analyst, and eLearning project manager. Her enduring interests include ICT support for collaboration and learning, IS education, and diversity in the IT workforce. She has published in *Computer Personnel* and *The Database for Advances in Information Systems* (among other outlets), has presented papers at numerous SIGMIS/CPR conferences, and served as an officer of SIGCPR. She serves on the Editorial Board of the *Journal of Information Systems Education.*

Legacy Job Titles in IT: The Search for Clarity

Patrick Donohue
University of Limerick
Limerick
Ireland
+353 61 208832

patrick.donohue@ul.ie

Norah Power
University of Limerick
Limerick
Ireland
+353 61 202769

norah.power@ul.ie

ABSTRACT

The use of Information Technology (IT) job titles is problematic. Titles may have different meanings depending on context, with job descriptions and responsibilities varying from one organization to another. This paper investigates the causes of this issue by examining the historical context; a comparison is made with three other established professional groupings and differences determined. The ramifications from current recruitment practices are identified, highlighting the potential conflict between business needs and for IT as a profession. An empirical approach towards job title discovery is suggested, utilizing the body of knowledge already available.

Categories and Subject Descriptors

K.2 [**History of Computing**], K.3.2 [**Computers and Education**]: Computer and Information Science Education, K.7.1 [**The Computing Profession**]: Occupations

General Terms

Human Factors, Theory.

Keywords

IT job titles, professionalism, IT career.

1. INTRODUCTION

1.1 Jane: The IT Job Seeker

Jane is a twenty one year old Information Technology (IT) graduate. She has just completed a Degree in IT and has sent many resumes to different organizations seeking employment, but to date, has had little luck with interviews or job offers. She finds that many companies are looking for specific certifications and experience; in some cases with no requirement for a degree in an IT related discipline.

As an alternative, she turns to the Internet as another avenue for her quest. There are many websites offering IT related jobs, both domestic and abroad. After registering, she starts to search based on what she considers to be suitable job categories. This in itself, turns out to be problematic.

She begins to run into difficulties primarily because the job titles are both confusing and specific, but also because her IT education is generic. In many cases she is not certain whether or not she qualifies for many available positions. She does, however, notice that many employers are looking for specific technical skills, with a requisite amount of experience required. Eventually, although uncertain as to whether or not she is qualified from an experiential point of view, she applies for a number of positions based on technical skills she feels she will be comfortable with, acquired through her formal education.

1.2 The Dilemma

Jane's situation is not uncommon. Having graduated with a general degree in IT, she is faced with the task of finding a position based on specific search criteria. She finds an abundance of positions available, but is not certain which positions to apply for. Employers are looking for specific skills, as opposed to positions based on generic job titles. This in general terms, is not the case in other professional groups, who tend to qualify based on their formative education.

1.3 The Research Question

The purpose of this paper is to establish why, when compared to other professional groups, job titles in the IT sector appear to be problematic even to insiders. It compares the IT profession with other groups to establish the need for clarity. It further makes recommendations as to an empirical approach to establishing a framework of appropriate job titles for the IT sector. To summarize, the research question is: "IT job titles: how can we clarify their meaning and skill implications"?

2. THE HISTORICAL CONTEXT

2.1 The birth of modern computing

In order to understand why IT job titles are problematic the modern evolution of computing needs to be examined. It is generally accepted that the birth of modern computing took place in the late 1930's [12, 52].

The history of computing is well documented. Timeline starting points vary, depending on context, covering the discovery and use of mathematics by early civilizations [41, 49] through the Industrial Revolution [9] to the emergence of modern computers in the 1930's [38, 52] and 1940's [12]. Indeed, the Institute of Electrical and Electronics Engineers (IEEE) has a journal dedicated to the subject, namely Annals of the History of Computing [25].

In the context of IT jobs, job titles and their meaning, the development of modern computing has been taken as the starting point for the purposes of this research. If the timeline of modern computing is taken as being from the 1930s [38] to the present day, it is possible to examine the roles of IT personnel through this evolution.

The availability of computer programming languages and supporting software development methodologies began in the early 1950's and remained static until the late 1960's [27]. As time progressed, new technologies began to emerge, allowing new ways of interacting with computers through hardware interface improvements. As predicted by Moore's Law [39], computers continued to increase in power at an exponential rate. Increasingly, computers could be manufactured more cheaply, allowing for the development of personal computers in the 1970's.

From the early 1950's to the early 1990's, roles began to develop and were relatively well-defined. Systems analysts, computer programmers, hardware engineers and computer operators were very specific job titles, with firm demarcation between roles, particularly in large organizations with a data processing (DP) function [2].

2.2 A clarity of computer job titles

As hardware and associated technologies progressed, the availability of computer programming languages and supporting software development methodologies remained static, however, until the late 1960s [27]. This is reflected in the relatively small number of job titles that were used at the time. Barnes and Gotterer [2] identify 11 computer job titles as reflected in Table 1. The research, undertaken in 1971 highlights the small amount of computer job titles in use at the time.

Table 1. Job titles identified by Barnes and Gotterer [2]

Title	Number
Junior/Trainee Programmer	13
Programmer	8
Systems Programmer	5
Technical Staff Member	3
Instructor	2
Systems Engineer	2
Assistant Systems Analyst	1
Systems Analyst	1
Systems Manager	1
Sales	1
Military Service Grades	3

2.3 Job titles and the expansion of roles

As technology developed and methodologies changed, the roles of IT staff expanded. This coupled with the adoption of the Object-Oriented (OO) paradigm and the advent of the Internet [10] changed and expanded the role of the IT developer considerably. The number of programming languages [42, 53] and software development methodologies [43] grew to capitalize on these advances. Tools became cheaper; in many cases they were free and some methodologies became automated to a certain extent.

This abundance of tools contributed to the skill requirements demanded of the IT developer.

As software development methodologies matured, it became unclear as to the definition of various tasks. Businesses, with their on-going need to be competitive, looked for faster means of getting products to market. The skills [32, 40] required by development teams and individual practitioners expanded, resulting in more obscure titles for specific jobs.

2.4 The open-source phenomenon

The open source model, as described by Wu and Lin [54] adds further complexity to the skill requirements of software developers and IT professionals generally. Before the advent of this phenomenon, the IT skills requirement was to a degree limited, based on proprietary tools and languages, limiting their availability. Madey et al. [36] observe that when applied to open source, traditional project management techniques are not used, coupled with a lack of accountability.

Many practitioners view aspects of software development as being an engineering discipline [45, 46]. If this is the case, Collins et al. [14, pp. 37-39] suggest that accountability is a key factor in the professionalization of engineering as a whole.

2.5 The Job Titles Legacy

The rate and expansion of the IT industry has resulted in an abundance of job titles. The causes are multi-faceted, stemming from a technology explosion, coupled with the introduction of new programming languages, tools, software development paradigms, work practices and job requirements. There may also be, however, underlying factors, particularly when treating IT as a profession.

3. IT AND OTHER PROFESSIONAL GROUPS

3.1 A comparison

There is greater clarity when it comes to job titles within other professional groups. This can be demonstrated by examining work undertaken by the British Council [8]. The Council, an organization that deals with international cultural relations and diversity has, as part of its remit, the role of encouraging international students to study in the United Kingdom. Information sheets have been produced covering a wide spectrum of careers and professions as an aide to course selection. An examination of some of these sheets can show that, for the prospective student, the educational and other requirements are clearer for some careers than others.

Medicine [7], accountancy [4] and engineering [6] were examined and compared with computing [5, 20]. Table 2 is derived from these information sheets; the mature profession model, as suggested by Ford and Gibbs [20] is applied to the four groupings for comparison. Computing is deemed a professional grouping for comparison purposes.

An examination of each of the groupings clearly shows a lack of clarity when examining computing/IT in terms of a professional career. The other professions have specific, undergraduate courses. IT as a profession, on the other hand, has no formal educational requirements (although expected), for many IT jobs. In particular, there is no legal requirement for certification or licensing. In terms of a formal undergraduate education; the

Category	Medicine (UK) [7]	Accountancy [4]	Engineering (UK) [6]	Computing [5,20]
Initial Professional Education	5 years undergraduate degree in medicine or 4 years graduate entry program	Professional body examinations Academic route or professional route	Undergraduate or Master's degree in Engineering	Varied
Accreditation	General Medical Council (UK)	The professional bodies	The professional bodies	ABET-USA CSAB-USA BCS-UK The Engineering Council (UK)
Skills Development	Post Graduate specialisms	Programs organized by the professional bodies	Professional bodies	Skills Framework for the Information Age (SFIA-UK
Certification	General Medical Council (UK) Specialist colleges	Professional bodies	Professional bodies	Discipline based (optional)
Licensing	General Medical Council (UK)	Professional bodies	The Engineering Council (UK)	None
Professional Development	Specialist colleges	Organized by the professional bodies	Organized by the professional bodies	SFIA-UK
Code of Ethics	General Medical Council (UK)	Professional bodies	Professional bodies	BCS-UK ICS-IRE ACM
Professional Society	By specialism	ACCA, AIA, CIMA, CIPFA, ICAI	Depending on discipline	BCS-UK ICS-IRE ACM, IEEE
Legal Requirements	Licensing	Licensing	Varied	None

myriad of qualifications available [5] reflects the lack of a recognized formative, general education in IT.

The computing/IT information sheet does not compare favourably with the other career categories. Formative educational and further requirements are quite specific in the comparators. For example, medical doctors undergo many years of training at undergraduate level, graduate as medical doctors and then participate in an internship. Further study can be achieved at postgraduate level in specific areas of medicine, One of these, a consultant anaesthesiologist, is a doctor with undergraduate education (pre-med and med), postgraduate training and professional registration in both medicine and anaesthesiology. There is a legal requirement for registration with various medical councils and similar bodies in order to practice [7, 50]. Although medicine has little resemblance to IT, it is important to recognize that the formality and structure culminate in medicine being recognizable as a profession, with job titles, for the most part, being universally understood.

It is clear that for each of the other groups, a formative, general undergraduate education in the discipline area is required (although for some areas of accountancy an apprenticeship model is adopted with a requirement to pass professional examinations).

A license to practice is also necessary. A key difference between many other professions and IT generally is the legal requirement to be appropriately registered after undertaking a specific education with relevant, certified experience. There is also a requirement to maintain competence, although this is not as well-defined.

When compared to other professions, IT practice needs to be improved through formal education [33] as a minimum requirement for entry.

3.2 Protean career paths

In 2005 Joseph et al. [28] identified three potential career paths for IT professionals, namely technical, professional and protean. Protean paths are not as common in other professions, reflecting the low threshold of entry to IT in general. Through the boom years, demand for IT staff remained high. This has continued through to recession times, with little effect on the demand for IT personnel [35]. Organizations have IT business needs that must be met by human resources; if these resources are not forthcoming from traditional IT staff sources, they will be met by other means. In particular, task-oriented, operational needs can be, in many cases, met by protean staff. Furthermore, Lash & Sein [30] point out that many organizations are meeting their needs outside the IS department leading to implications for IT as a profession.

3.3 Job titles

If IT is to be considered a profession it must have similar characteristics to other professional groups. These groups are more specific in their job titles; they require formative general education in their respective fields with, in many cases, a legal requirement for licensing. Because of the legal requirement to be generally competent, job titles within other professional groups can be defined more easily, with a higher threshold of entry. The professional title is, in itself, a statement of competency.

This begs the question as how to effectively structure IT (generally) as a profession. Clearly there are formative educational and skill requirements necessary to establish IT as a profession. Considering the breadth and diversity of IT roles a suitable research instrument is necessary to successfully extrapolate and identify the necessary empirical data to create a theoretical model for IT job titles.

4. RECRUITMENT PRACTICES
4.1 Task-oriented job titles and certification
Many organizations base job titles on narrow tasks undertaken. This is further reflected in the literature, where researchers categorize jobs based on task groupings [15, 22]. It is a growing practice for many organizations to resort to the use of certifications [24]. Certifications are task-oriented, allowing organizations recruit for specific needs. This approach does not, however, recognize the need for a broader education in the IT field. The Skills Framework for the Information Age (SFIA-UK) [44] reflects this increasing trend in industry, suggesting certification paths across the spectrum of skill requirements.

4.2 Meeting short-term needs
Short-term needs are regularly met using certifications or limited training; quite often the recipients of these certifications will have no other IT qualifications. The protean career path of many IT staff is also a means of some organizations meeting their short-term needs. This approach can be effective, but is a key element of there being a low threshold of entry. This low threshold allows businesses to meet short-term needs, but is a barrier to the professionalization of IT.

5. CURRENT PRACTICES IN THE LITERATURE
5.1 Categorizing job titles
The literature reflects the lack of clarity in job title usage. Research in the area of job titles and related skills explains the need for categorizing for research purposes [13, 15, 18, and 22]. It is common for researchers to put job titles into categories because it is not clear what the jobs actually are. This is not a reflection on the research but on the necessity due to the use of a wide range of job titles. It is done as there are no other means of defining jobs for the purposes of the research.

Researchers, out of necessity, are required to categorize various jobs in order to undertake any meaningful analysis. Analyses are also undertaken establishing skill requirements of employers, as this is a common approach used by employers for job advertisements.

5.2 Information and Communications Technology Job Ontology
Chin and Chang [13] recognise that job titles are not well-defined and suggest Information and Communications Technology (ICT) job ontology as part of an overarching ICT ontology framework. They further suggest that examining current skills should be used to create the ontology. This approach is suggested in order to map skills with educational requirements as part of an education ontology in the same framework.

6. INVESTIGATING JOB TITLES
6.1 Adopting a research approach
The challenge for researchers in identifying IT job titles is their subjective nature. Generic titles are needed, reflecting specialisms as with other professional groups. Considerable research has been undertaken in identifying IT and other related skills [1,3,11,16,17,19,21,22,23,31,32,34,37,40,47 and 48]. This body of knowledge is predominantly qualitative in nature and could be further utilized using qualitative methods.

6.2 Discovery from the research already undertaken
There are common trends in skill requirements identifiable through qualitative methods. These requirements could be used to form a professional skills framework, encompassing formal undergraduate IT education, internship requirements, experience, continuing professional development, post-graduate specialisms and professional registration. Such a framework would compare directly and favourably with the traditional professions. It would serve to establish the long-term skill requirements for IT professionals and their potential specialisms, rather than fulfilling short-term business needs based on specific technical certifications.

6.3 Professional specialization
The concept of specialization is well-established in the literature [26]. This approach has merit insofar as it identifies the need for specific job roles. Using the grounded theory approach, a specialization could be viewed as an abstract category of IT professional based on the coding of skills-concepts. These specializations would therefore directly reflect long-term human resource needs of the IT function to meet ever changing business requirements.

6.4 Ideal Types
The identification of ideal types can be traced back to the works of Max Weber. Weber suggests an abstract view of a work type that does not exist in the real world [51]. Although this theory was developed in the early 20th century, the approach is still valid [29], particularly when applied to a research methodology. The concept of an abstract type could be used to develop an appropriate theory for job types, reflecting IT specialisms. The content of these types could be established from the empirical data, discovered from identified skills.

7. CONCLUSIONS
Job titles in the IT sector are subjective in nature. The number of titles has grown over time, reflecting the rate of advancement in the sector generally. This paper compared IT to three other professional groups. The comparison highlighted the lack of formality in the IT sector, reflecting a low threshold of entry with a lack of formative, general IT education with no legal requirement for licensing or registration. It was further highlighted that other professional groups have and use recognised generic titles.

Organizations use task-oriented recruitment practices, to meet short-term operational needs. This practice is undertaken out of necessity, as generic titles do not exist, when compared to other professional groups. This is further reflected in the need for researchers to categorize in general terms when examining job titles, usually by task or specialism.

It was shown that a theory of IT job title discovery should be developed and such a theory could be based on a qualitative approach. This could be achieved utilizing research already undertaken combined with grounded theory methods to develop a theoretical model for job titles. These titles could then be used to reflect the specialisms, as with other professional groups. The established research would, however, need to be viewed through a different colored lens, reflecting the jobs-focus rather than a skills-oriented approach. This would be achieved by identifying the relevant empirical data, with a view to establishing specialisms in line with other professions.

If the IT requirements of organizations continue to be met by short-term operational needs, the true development of a professional IT framework will be hindered. Such a framework is needed if generic job titles are to be achieved. However, putting the needs of the IT profession before business requirements may be self-defeating.

The lack of a legal requirement for IT staff to be licensed or registered will hinder the professionalization of IT generally. It will only happen if there is a significant increase in litigation due to faults in IT systems [14, pp.116-145].

8. REFERENCES

[1] Bailey, J.L. and Stefaniak, G. 2002. *Preparing the information technology workforce for the new millennium.* ACM SIGCPR Computer Personnel, 20(4), 2002, 4-15.

[2] Barnes, B.H. and Gotterer, M.H. 1971. *Attributes of Computer Professionals.* Proceedings of the Ninth Annual SIGCPR conference, 167-179.

[3] Bassellier, G. and Benbasat, I. 2004. *Business Competence of Information Technology Professionals: Conceptual Development and Influence on IT-Business Partnerships.* MIS Quarterly, (28), 4, 673-694.

[4] The British Council. 2005. *Accountancy Learning Information Sheet.* The British Council. Available at: http://www.britishcouncil.org/learning-infosheets-accountancy.pdf. Accessed Sept. 15th 2011.

[5] The British Council. 2006. *Computing Learning Information Sheet.* The British Council. Available at: http://www.britishcouncil.org/learning-infosheets-computing.pdf. Accessed Sept 14th 2011.

[6] The British Council. 2006. *Engineering Learning Information Sheet.* The British Council. Available at: http://www.britishcouncil.org/learning-infosheets-engineering.pdf. Accessed Sept. 14th 2011.

[7] The British Council. 2006. *Medicine Learning Information Sheet.* The British Council. Available at: http://www.britishcouncil.org/learning-infosheets-medicine.pdf. Accessed Sept. 15th 2011.

[8] The British Council. Website available at: www.britishcouncil.org. Accessed Sept. 10th 2011.

[9] Campbell-Kelly, M. and Aspray, W. 1996. *A History of information machine.* Harper Collins Publishers Inc.

[10] Cash, E. et.al. 2004. *The Impact of E-commerce on the Role of IS Professionals.* ACM SIGMIS Database, 35(3), 50-63.

[11] Castelli, A. 2004. *ICT Practitioner skills and Training: banking and Financial Services.* Cedefop Panorama Series; 95, Office for Official Publications of the European Communities.

[12] Ceruzzi, P.E. 2003. *A History of Modern Computing.* The MIT press.

[13] Chin, K.L. and Chang, E. 2011. *A Sustainable ICT Education Ontology.* Proceedings of the 5th IEEE International Conference in Digital Ecosystems and Technologies, 350-354.

[14] Collins, S. et al. 1989. *The Professional Engineer in Society: A Textbook for Engineering Students.* Jessica Kingsley Publishers.

[15] Davis, D.C. 2003. *Job Titles, Tasks and Experiences of Information Systems and Technologies Graduates from a Midwestern University.* Journal of Information Systems, 14(1), 59-68.

[16] Dixon, M. 2002. *Information Technology Practitioner Skills in Europe.* Council of European Professional Informatics Societies, 2002.

[17] Downey, J. 2005. *A Framework to Elicit the Skills Needed for Software Development.* Proceedings, SIGMIS CPR '05, 122-127.

[18] Education Development Center Inc. 2000. *IT Occupations Framework.* Data Communications, Education Development Center Inc., 2000.

[19] Expert Group on Future Skills Needs. 2008. *Future Requirement for High-level ICT Skills in the ICT Sector.* Expert Group on Future Skills Needs Secretariat.

[20] Ford, G. & Gibbs, N. 1996. *A Mature Profession of Software Engineering.* Software Engineering Institute, Technical report CMU/SEI-96-TR-004, Carnegie Mellon University.

[21] Gallagher, K.P. et al., 2010. *The Requisite Variety of Skills for IT Professionals.* Communications of the ACM, 53(6), p.144.

[22] Gallivan, M.J. et al. 2004. *Changing Patterns in IT Skill sets 1988-2003.* ACM SIGMIS Database, 35(3), 64-87.

[23] Goles, T. et al. 2008. *Information Technology Workforce Skills: The Software and IT Services Perspective.* Information Systems Frontiers, Springer, 10, 179-194.

[24] Hunsinger, D. et al. 2011. *A Framework of the Use of Certifications by Hiring Personnel in IT Hiring Decisions.* ACM SIGMIS Database, 42(1), 9–28.

[25] The IEEE, Annals of the History of Computing, website.available at: http://www.jstor.org/stable/3377761, Accessed Sept. 17th 2011.

[26] Jackson, M. 1994. *Problems, methods and specialization.* Software, IEEE, 11(6), 57–62.

[27] Jiang, L. & Eberlein, A. 2009. *An Analysis of the History of Classical Software Development and Agile Development.* IEEE International Conference on Systems, Man and Cybernetics, 3733-3738.

[28] Joseph, D. et al. 2005. *Identifying the Prototypical career Paths of IT Professionals: A Sequence and Cluster Analysis.* Proceedings of the 2005 ACM SIGMIS CPR conference on Computer personnel research. ACM, 94–96.

[29] Koshul, B.B. 2005. *The Postmodern Significance of Max Weber's Legacy.* Gordonsville, VA, USA: Palgrave Macmillan.

[30] Lash, P.B. & Sein, M.K. 1995. *Career Paths in a Changing IS Environment: A Theoretical Perspective.* Proceedings of the 1995 ACM SIGCPR Conference on Supporting Teams, Groups, and Learning Inside and Outside the IS Function Reinventing IS, 117–130.

[31] Lee, C.K. 2005. *Transferability of Skills over the IT Career Path.* Proceedings, SIGMIS CPR '05, 85-93.

[32] Lee, D.M.S., et al. 1996. *Critical Skills and Knowledge Requirements of IS Professionals: A Joint Academic/Industry Investigation.* MIS Quarterly, 19(3), 313.

[33] Lethbridge, T.C. et al. 2007. *Improving Software Practice through Education: Challenges and Future Trends.* Future of Software Engineering (FOSE '07), 2, 12-28.

[34] Litecky, C. et al. 2010. *Mining for Computing Jobs.* IEEE Software, IEEE Computer Society, 78-85.

[35] Litecky, C. et al. 2006. *The IT/IS Job Market: A Longitudinal Perspective.* Proceedings, SIGMIS-CPR '06, 50-52.

[36] Madey, G. et al. 2002. *The Open Source Software Development Phenomenon: An Analysis based on Social Network Theory.* Americas Conference on Information, 1806-1813.

[37] Marks, A & Scholarios, D. 2008. *Choreographing a System: Skill and Employability in Software Work.* Economic and Industrial Democracy, 29(1), Sage, 96-124.

[38] Metropolis, N. (editor) et al. *1980. A History of Computing in the Twentieth Century: A collection of Essays.* Academic Press.

[39] Mollick, E. 2006. *Establishing Moore's Law.* IEEE Annals of the History of Computing, 28(3), 62-75.

[40] Noll, C.L. and Wilkins, M. 2002. *Critical Skills of IS Professionals ⁇: A Model for Curriculum Development.* Journal of Information Technology Education, 1(3), 143-154.

[41] O'Regan, G. 2008. *A Brief History of computing.* Springer-Verlag.

[42] O'Reilly Media Inc. 2004. History of Programming Languages poster available at: http://oreilly.com/news/languageposter_0504.html, O'Reilly. Accessed: Aug 15th 2011.

[43] Rodríguez-Martínez, L.C. et al. 2009. *A Descriptive / Comparative Study of the Evolution of Process Models of Software Development Life Cycles (PM-SDLCs).* Mexican International Conference on Computer Science, (ii), 298-303.

[44] SFIA Foundation, Framework reference SFIA version 4. Available at: http://www.sfia.org.uk. Accessed: Sept 1st 2011.

[45] Shaw, M. 1990. *Prospects for an Engineering Discipline of Software.* IEEE Software, Nov. 1990, 15-24.

[46] Shaw, M. 2009. *Continuing Prospects for an Engineering Discipline of Software.* IEEE Software, Nov. /Dec. 2009, 64-67.

[47] Stucky, W. et al. 2003. *Information technology practitioner skills in Europe: Current status and challenges for the future.* Computer Science in Perspective, Springer-Verlag, 304-317.

[48] Sukhoo, A. et al. 2005. *Accommodating Soft Skills in Software Project Management.* Issues in Informing Science and Information Technology, (2), 691-703.

[49] Swedin, E.G. & Ferro, D.L. 2005. *Computers: The Life Story of a Technology.* Greenwood Publishing Group.

[50] University of Illinois. 2005. *Steps to Becoming a Physician,* University of Illinois.

[51] Weber, M. 1947. *The Theory of Social and Economic Organization. (*Translated by AM Henderson & Talcott Parsons). Oxford University Press.

[52] Winegrad, D. 1996. *Celebrating the Birth of Modern Computing: The fiftieth Anniversary of a Discovery at the Moore School of Engineering of the University of Pennsylvania.* IEEE Annals of the History of Computing, 18(1), 5-9.

[53] Wired magazine. 2010. *Mother Tongues: Tracing the Root of Computer Languages, Through The Ages.* Poster, available at: http://www.quicklycode.com/infographics_posters/computer-programming-languages-chart, Wired Magazine.

[54] Wu, M.-W. & Lin, Y.-D. 2001. *Open Source Development ⁇: An Overview.* IEEE Computer, (June), 33-38.

Are We in the Right Profession? – Comparing Information Systems, Computer Science and other Disciplines' Professional's Perceptions of the Job Market

Sven Laumer
Centre of Human Resources Information Systems
University of Bamberg, Germany
+49 951 8632873

sven.laumer@uni-bamberg.de

Andreas Eckhardt
Centre of Human Resources Information Systems
Goethe-University of Frankfurt, Germany
+49 69 79834659

eckhardt@wiwi.uni-frankfurt.de

Christian Maier
Centre of Human Resources Information Systems
University of Bamberg, Germany
+49 951 8633919

christian.maier@uni-bamberg.de

Tim Weitzel
Centre of Human Resources Information Systems
University of Bamberg, Germany
+49 951 8632871

tim.weitzel@uni-bamberg.de

ABSTRACT
Based on an empirical analysis with 2,887 professionals with different educational backgrounds, this research shows that Information Systems and Computer Science professionals are more optimistic toward the labor market and available job alternatives than other disciplines such as General Business Management, Engineering, or Social and Humane Science. The results underline that professionals in the IT field have a bright future for their further career. In times of shrinking information systems and computer systems enrollments, this promising prospect can support both undergraduate and graduate schools activities to promote their courses. Several implications for this issue will be discussed in the paper.

Categories and Subject Descriptors
K.7.1 [THE COMPUTING PROFESSION] Occupations

General Terms
Management, Measurement, Human Factors

Keywords
IT Personnel, Job Perception, Job Alternatives, Turnover Intention, IS Enrollments

1. INTRODUCTION
During career information days for potential students at high schools, where several universities introduce their different kind of course degrees, and where potential employers present their potential entry jobs for high school graduates, one of the authors of this paper experienced that other disciplines' round of talks are better attended than his own for the Information systems field.

Even popular organizations like the police or those with a well-known product are able to convince high school graduates to start a career in their organization without studying at a university or college. While talking to the visitors of career information days, one central argument evolves as many high school graduates indicate that they expect that the Information Systems (IS) and Computer Science (CS) disciplines are rapidly changing environments, where a life-long job cannot be guaranteed. One student put it this way: "*When I join the police the state guarantees me an attractive job for my whole life, and if I would join your discipline I do not know, if those skills will be necessary and demanded by organizations in 20 years as well, and if the jobs are interesting*". A 17-year old one argued that "*Marketing or Finance have mattered during the last decades and will matter for business in future as well. If IT will still matter in 10 years, I cannot anticipate*".

These examples and experiences can be seen in the enrollment statistics of IS or CS, which declined or at best have been on constant level over the last ten years. Figure 1 illustrates enrollment statistics for several disciplines from Germany and indicates that IS and CS are, compared to other disciples, on a very low level since 1999. However, organizations report extreme challenges to recruit CS or IS graduates compared to graduates from other disciplines [12]. Although the career expectations are promising, the enrollment numbers in IS or CS programs in Germany do not increase.

In this context and as a potential explanation, Panko [18] discusses that there is a deep belief among both IS and non-IS students that the career outlook for IS professionals is poor. In his point of view, students are concerned about the employment opportunities caused by the dotcom bust and long-term issues caused by job offshoring to less-developed countries. Panko also points out that beliefs about career prospects have to be addressed with high priority as it is one of the major reasons preventing more students from selection IS as a course of study. In addition Panko provides evidence that there is a lot of misinformation about what happened to the IT job market during the dotcom bubble as many believe that unemployment among IS professionals rose to very high levels [18].

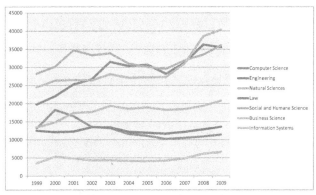

Figure 1: Enrollment Statistics in Germany[1] [2]

In 2009, the global economy experienced again a crisis which continues to some extent until today. The crisis called *"sub-prime crises"* started with financial problems of one particular bank, continued as an essential issue for financial institutions and finally reached almost every company in every industry sector worldwide. Even today, the crisis of the EURO countries is one extension of this global economic development. Especially, between the dotcom and the sub-prime crisis the IT industry had to face the challenge of hiring suitable IT personnel and retaining them within their organizations [14]. However, in the 2009 SIM survey, recruiting, developing, and retaining IT talent left the ranking of CIO's ten most important concerns as *"companies have experienced IT budget and salary reductions, projects and purchases put on hold, and hiring freezes"* [15]. As a consequence, potential students might perceive again that the number of jobs in the IT industry is still declining. Although, the situation especially in Germany seems to be improving as the economy is growing again and is reporting promising business opportunities in 2011 [12]. Nonetheless, the enrollment numbers of IS programs are still on a low level and one of the major reasons might be the low IS career expectations, due to misleading information about the IS or CS job market [18].

Therefore, as Hirschheim and Newman conclude "there also appears to be major problem – not of a technical nature but rather a perceptual one" (p. 358, [3]). A common belief is that there are few jobs for IS graduates available on the job market [23]. Hirschheim and Newman discuss the year 2000 remediation, the dotcom collapse, the "IT doesn't matter" debate, offshoring and the 2008/2009 economic recession as potential explanations for the general public perception of the IS job market.

Therefore, this research builds upon the results of [3, 18] in order to discuss the perceptions of the job market by IS, CS, and other disciplines' personnel in 2011. The research is intended to extend Panko's discussion of the dotcom crisis and Hirschheims and Neuman's reasons by a discussion of the subprime crisis of 2009/2010 and the current EURO crisis. Based on an empirical analysis, the objective of the paper is to show differences between academic disciplines, and how professionals of each discipline perceive the current job market and the respective career expectations. Based on the results, IS programs can present an

accurate picture of potential IS careers and career paths, and what is likely to happen in the future, in order to address potential students concerns regarding the IS job market.

Therefore, the remainder of this paper is as follows. First, the research background of our approach will be discussed, in order to investigate different perceptions of the job market. Afterwards, the research method will be explained, how we gathered and evaluated our data. In section 4, the results will be presented. A discussion of the results concludes the paper.

2. RESEACH BACKGROUND

Research on employees' perceptions of the job market is strongly related to research on voluntary turnover. In this context, [4] indicate that an employee's turnover intention is influenced by job satisfaction, job alternatives, and search intentions.

For the context of IT professionals, Joseph et al. [6] identify job satisfaction as the most examined determinant of IT personnel turnover [6], and [9] provide a basic model of Western IT professionals, explaining turnover by job satisfaction (JS), organizational commitment (OC), and perceived job alternatives (PJA). PJA are defined as *"the employee's perceived availability of equal or better jobs in other organizations"* (pg. 228, [9]) and refer to *"workers' beliefs that they can find a comparable job in another organization"* ([21], p.236). Theory suggests that PJA have a direct effect on OC, and a mediated effect on turnover intention [16]. In addition, IS research and referent fields have found that PJA has a direct effect on turnover intention [6-8, 21]. When employees perceive many employment alternatives, they will express lower levels of organizational commitment and, consequently, higher levels of turnover intention [21].

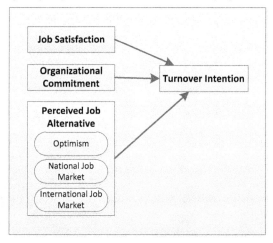

Figure 2: Model of Turnover (based on [6, 9])

For actual turnover rates of German professionals, Figure 3 indicates that the highest actual turnover rate in Germany can be attributed to IS professionals followed by computer science and law. Lower turnover rates are observed for engineering, natural science, social and humane science and business management [11].

---

[1] Since 2006 the numbers indicate enrollment statistics for both bachelor and master degrees. Before, only Diplom degrees are listed. As consequence the numbers are increasing as first semester master students are also counted.

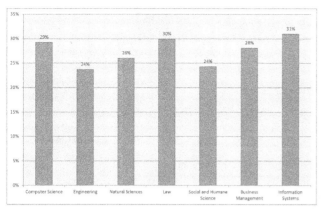

Figure 3: German Professionals Turnover Rates in 2011 [11]

According to the observed correlation between perceived alternatives and actual turnover rates [6-8, 21], we assume that IS and CS personnel perceive the job market much more optimistic (and consequently show higher turnover rates) than other disciplines' personnel. In order to control for these assumed differences, we conducted an empirical study as described in the following paragraph.

3. RESEACH METHOD

As this research aims at providing information of perceived job alternatives of professionals of different disciplines and from different companies, age, gender, and tenure, an online survey was evaluated as the most appropriate form of data collection. The surveyed personnel were registered users of the job platform Monster, and got an e-mail invitation to take part in the online study. Demographic information about the participating personnel is summarized in Table 1.

Table 1. Demographic information of survey participants (N=2,887)

Gender	Male	72.9%
	Female	27.1%
Age	<25	2.7%
	25-29	17.1%
	30-34	24.6%
	35-39	16.6%
	40-44	16.4%
	45-49	12.1%
	>50	10.4%
Degree Course	Computer Science	10.7%
	Engineering	22.4%
	Natural Sciences	7.5%
	Law	4.2%
	Social and Humane Science	3.1%
	Business Management	46.5%
	Information Systems	5.5%
Tenure*	Young Professional	15.7%
	Professional	38.4%
	Manager	19.1%
	Other	26.8%
* Young Professional (<5 years), Professional (>= 5 years)		

Based on Information Systems and organization science literature, different measures were selected to measure job-related factors (e.g., PJA). The used measurement items can be seen in the construct result tables in the results section. To measure PJA, different items are available as used by prior research. However,

these measurement models include limitations [5, 20]. For the research presented in this paper, the perceived job alternatives measurement items as developed by Thatcher et al. [21] were used to control for PJA of IT personnel.

Based on data of 2,887 participants, we performed eight ANOVA.

4. RESULTS

Based on the survey we conducted, we will present the results regarding different perceptions of the job market and perceived alternatives of each discipline observed in the following paragraphs structured by each measurement item used within the survey. For each item an ANOVA has been conducted to control for significant differences of the perception by each discipline. Based on [21] different measurement items were included in the survey and the results of each item for different disciplines will be presented in the following paragraphs.

How optimistic are you about the development of the labor market for you in person? Regarding the personal optimism, Table 2 shows that IS personnel indicate the highest personal optimism for the development of the labor market (mean (m)=4.98) followed by computer science personnel (m=4.60). Engineering is ranked third (m=4.58). According to the ANOVA analysis, IS personnel's optimism regarding the individual personal development of the labor market is significantly better than those of natural science, law, social and humane science, and business management professionals. No differences can be observed for computer science and engineering. In addition, CS personnel's optimism is significantly better than those of law and social and humane science professionals.

Table 2: Personal Optimism

Degree Course	Mean	Sig (ANOVA	Multiple Comparison					
			2	3	4	5	6	7
1 = Computer Science	3.59		1.000	0.970	0.000**	0.722	1.000	0.135
2 = Engineering	3.59			0.958	0.000**	0.680	1.000	0.57*
3 = Natural Sciences	3.50				0.023*	0.984	0.849	0.019**
4 = Law	3.09	0.000**				0.565	0.000**	0.000**
5 = Social and Humane Science	3.38						0.525	0.012**
6 = Business Management	3.61							0.069*
7 = Information Systems	3.88							

How optimistic are you about the further progess of your professional career in your current job? Regarding career optimism, Table 3 indicates that IS personnel perceive the progress of their own professional career as more optimistic than the other disciplines observed (m=5.12). On the second rank is computer science (m=4.99) followed by engineering (m=4.82) on rank three. According to the ANOVA analysis, IS and CS personnel's optimism is significantly different from those of social and humane science, as well as law.

Table 3: Career Optimism

Degree Course	Mean	Sig (ANOVA	Multiple Comparison					
			2	3	4	5	6	7
1 = Computer Science	3.21		0.914	1.000	0.274	0.798	0.998	0.105
2 = Engineering	3.32			0.870	0.015**	0.273	0.970	0.422
3 = Natural Sciences	3.19				0.472	0.904	0.989	0.101
4 = Law	2.90	0.000**				0.999	0.048**	0.000**
5 = Social and Humane Science	2.99						0.487	0.014**
6 = Business Management	3.55							0.104
7 = Information Systems	3.55							

How do you regard the chances to find your dream job. Another item for an individual's perception of the job market is one's perception of the chances to find the dream job. According to Table 4, the highest degree of agreement can be observed to the group of IS (m=3.25) and engineering (m=3.14) personnel. CS personnel is ranked third (m=3.07) followed by natural science (m=3.04). Based on the ANOVA analysis, significant differences can be observed for IS and social and humane science, as well as law personnel, and for CS and law.

Table 4: Chances for Dream Job

Degree Course	Mean	Sig (ANOVA	Multiple Comparison					
			2	3	4	5	6	7
1 = Computer Science	3.07		0.990	1.000	0.023**	0.322	1.000	0.785
2 = Engineering	3.14			0.944	0.001**	0.076*	0.980	0.958
3 = Natural Sciences	3.04				0.095*	0.124	0.072*	0.102
4 = Law	2.67	0.000**				0.999	0.003**	0.001**
5 = Social and Humane Science	2.76						0.165	0.032**
6 = Business Management	3.09							0.721
7 = Information Systems	3.25							

There are many options to find a job doing satisfying work. Beside the chances of finding an individual's dream job, the chances of finding a job, where one can do satisfying work is another measurement for PJA in turnover research. Again, IS personnel are ranked first (m=3.80), followed by natural science (m=3.66), engineering (m=3.65), and computer science (m=3.65). Based on the ANOVA analysis, differences can be observed for IS and CS personnel and law, as well as social and humane sciences.

Table 5: Chances for Satisfying Job Alternatives

Degree Course	Mean	Sig (ANOVA	Multiple Comparison					
			2	3	4	5	6	7
1 = Computer Science	3.65		1.000	1.000	0.000**	0.080*	0.999	0.837
2 = Engineering	3.65			1.000	0.000**	0.045**	0.997	0.765
3 = Natural Sciences	3.66				0.001**	0.101	0.999	0.896
4 = Law	3.15	0.000**				0.983	0.000**	0.000**
5 = Social and Humane Science	3.28						0.078*	0.005**
6 = Business Management	3.62							0.470
7 = Information Systems	3.80							

It is easy to get a new job offer. Besides the general optimism for the personal development and the chances of finding a job, the following Table 6 indicates the results for the perceived ease of getting a new job offer. The highest degree of agreement that it is easy to get a new job offer can be observed for IS (m=4.69) and CS (m=4.28) personnel. Engineering (m=4.08) is ranked fourth, followed by natural (3.93), and business management (3.92). Significant differences based on ANOVA analysis can be evaluated for IS personnel with business, social and humane, natural science, law, and engineering, and for CS personnel with law, social and human science, and business management.

Table 6: Ease of Getting a New Job Offer I

Degree Course	Mean	Sig (ANOVA	Multiple Comparison					
			2	3	4	5	6	7
1 = Computer Science	4.28		0.802	0.454	0.001**	0.016**	0.062*	0.391
2 = Engineering	4.08			0.967	0.014**	0.128	0.641	0.009**
3 = Natural Sciences	3.93				0.306	0.618	1.000	0.004**
4 = Law	3.42	0.000**				1.000	0.130	0.000**
5 = Social and Humane Science	3.48						0.467	0.000**
6 = Business Management	3.92							0.000**
7 = Information Systems	4.69							

Due to my current job situation it is promising to find a new job. The results for another item for capturing an individual's perceived ease of getting a new job offer are illustrated by Table 7. IS personnel agree at the highest degree that it is promising due to an individual's current job situation to find a new job (m=4.98). On the following ranks are CS (m=4.60), engineering (4.58), natural science (m=4.37), and business management (m=4.35). Significant differences can be observed for IS personnel and business, social and human, natural science, and law. The level of agreement of CS personnel is significantly different from those of law, and social and humane science professionals.

Table 7: Ease of Getting New Job Offer II

Degree Course	Mean	Sig (ANOVA	Multiple Comparison					
			2	3	4	5	6	7
1 = Computer Science	4.60		1.000	0.856	0.002**	0.003**	0.416	0.439
2 = Engineering	4.58			0.839	0.001**	0.002**	0.176	0.241
3 = Natural Sciences	4.37				0.150	0.139	1.000	0.040**
4 = Law	3.81	0.000**				1.000	0.050*	0.000**
5 = Social and Humane Science	3.73						0.061*	0.000**
6 = Business Management	4.35							0.001**
7 = Information Systems	4.98							

There are attractive opportunities on the national job market. Beside the perception of the job seeking process and the ease of getting a new job offer, Table 8 indicates the general perception of the national job market of each discipline. IS personnel perceives the national job market in Germany better than the other disciplines (m=5.12). On rank two are CS personnel (m=4.99), followed by engineering (m=4.82), business management (m=4.69), and natural science (m=4.61). Significant differences can be evaluated using ANOVA for IS personnel and business, social and human science, and law. In addition for CS personnel, differences can be observed for law, and social and humane science.

Table 8: National Job Market

Degree Course	Mean	Sig (ANOVA	Multiple Comparison					
			2	3	4	5	6	7
1 = Computer Science	4.99		0.872	0.300	0.017**	0.003**	0.152	0.992
2 = Engineering	4.82			0.837	0.123	0.028**	0.780	0.551
3 = Natural Sciences	4.61				0.852	0.480	0.999	0.134
4 = Law	4.32	0.000**				0.996	0.439	0.007**
5 = Social and Humane Science	4.15						0.137	0.001**
6 = Business Management	4.69							0.078*
7 = Information Systems	5.12							

There are attractive opportunities on the international job market. In addition to the national German job market, Table 9 indicates the perception of the international job market. IS personnel (m=4.93) are ranked first with the highest degree of agreement that there are attractive opportunities on the international job market. Engineering (m=4.88) and computer science (m=4.82) are the follow ups. In addition, the degree of agreement of IS personnel is significantly different from business and social, and humane science. For CS personnel, differences can be observed with social and humane science based on an ANOVA analysis.

Table 9: International Job Market

Degree Course	Mean	Sig (ANOVA	Multiple Comparison					
			2	3	4	5	6	7
1 = Computer Science	4.82		0.999	0.999	0.106	0.007**	0.179	0.998
2 = Engineering	4.88			0.973	0.020**	0.001**	0.001**	1.000
3 = Natural Sciences	4.74				0.329	0.041**	0.765	0.971
4 = Law	4.26	0.000**				0.970	0.824	0.061*
5 = Social and Humane Science	4.00						0.203	0.004**
6 = Business Management	4.52							0.142
7 = Information Systems	4.93							

The presented results of perceived job alternatives and perceptions of the job market for the seven degree courses indicate that for all measurement items used, IS personnel show the highest degree of agreement and perceive the alternatives available on the job market as more promising than other disciplines such as engineering, natural science, law, social and humane science, and even business management. Moreover, the results reveal that CS personnel are the second most optimistic disciplines in our data sample. Therefore, we can state that professionals of diverse disciplines have different perceptions of the current job market and the respective career expectation. Implications based on these results for the initial objective of our approach will be discussed in the concluding paragraph.

5. DISCUSSION

After the dotcom bubble, Panko [18] shows that even in times of high unemployment rates the employment rate of IS or CS personnel is far above the general one. In his analysis for the US, Panko concludes for the dotcom crisis that even in times of economic downturns IS and CS personnel can be optimistic. With our results from Germany, we can conclude for the subprime crisis that in 2011, IS and CS are those disciplines, which perceive the job market more promising and optimistic than other disciplines. Therefore, based on our results and on the results of [18], IS or CS programs can present an accurate picture of career paths and developments of IS or CS jobs, in order to address potential students' concerns regarding the IS job market [18]. In addition, Hirschheim and Newman discuss several reasons why there is a misleading perception of the IS job market [3].

The results indicate that turnover is still a major challenge for IT executives, as on the one side the turnover rate of IS or CS personnel is higher compared to other disciplines, and on the other side IS or CS professionals perceive better job alternatives on the job market. Therefore, new approaches for retaining IT staff over a long period are necessary. Literature suggests different approaches, which could be useful in future as well; however organizations might focus on retaining IT talent again [1, 10, 17, 19]. Furthermore, it is also essential to hire new qualified IT staff. For this purpose, literature contains diverse suggestions, strategies, and frameworks [13, 22].

Contrary to the implications for organizations, employees and potential students have good prospects for the future. If the demand of organizations for IT personnel remains on a high level, and enrollment numbers are continuously declining, IS or CS employees will represent an extremely scarce group of talent, getting more job offers, and with a better position for employment negotiations. Therefore, the trend on the job market as perceived by German IS and CS personnel reveals that IS and CS are the right professions for an interesting, satisfying professional career.

The results have to be discussed, while acknowledging some limitations of our study. Due to the data collection procedure, we are not able to control for different business majors and their perception of the job market, which might be an additional interesting comparison to IS personnel. With our data, we are only able to control for differences to business management as a degree course in general. Furthermore, our results are limited as we only surveyed those individuals, who are registered Monster users. On the one side, this procedure enables us to reach different professionals of different organizations at the same time. However, on the other side it also limits our results as we can only research professionals, who are online and are not able to include offline professionals as well. Furthermore, one might argue that those professionals, who are member of an online platform for business purposes might have a higher turnover intention than non-members as the membership in those platforms might be an indicator for potential turnover behavior. Nonetheless, an active participation in those platforms might provide additional information about the job market and potential career opportunities, as recruiters or headhunter use these platforms for active sourcing [22], so the surveyed personnel might have different perceptions compared to non-members of these platforms. Therefore, the data collection procedure is a limitation of our results. In addition, we make no claim to be representative.

Future research might address this limitation and extend our analysis by surveying further groups of professionals regarding turnover intentions and perceived job alternatives. Moreover, future research might develop more detailed strategies, how organizations could fulfill the challenges of economic fluctuations in the IS or CS discipline. Moreover, the descriptive analysis of the perception of the job market can be analyzed in another way like structural equation modeling to reveal, if turnover intentions can be determined by perceived job alternatives to the same extent for the different disciplines observed. Furthermore, the EURO crisis in Europe offers the possibility for future research to investigate, whether this new crisis will have an impact in IS or CS professional expectations for the future, and if these expectations and especially the perception of the job market will change during and after the EURO crisis. In addition, it might be interesting to compare the longitudinal perceptions of IS and CS personnel with others disciplines. Especially, a comparison between those professionals, who have studied at a university and those who entered the job market after high school graduation directly might be interesting.

The message that IS or CS personnel are according to our results in the right profession can be used by IS programs to increase the number of students going into IS or CS courses. One has to spread the message that there are a lot of good jobs available for IS and CS personnel and that the talent shortage on IS and CS job markets will potentially remain for a long time. IS or CS programs need to contact potential students, news media, parents, and especially school counselors to explain that an IS or CS course is still extremely relevant to the job market and might be even better than other ones. Using the results, the talks at respective information days and high school job fares might be a bit easier to convince high school graduates to join IS programs, as we are able to say: *IS is the right profession*.

6. REFERENCES

[1] Ferratt, T.W., Agarwal, R., Brown, C.V., and Moore, J.E. IT Human Resource Management Configurations and IT Turnover: Theoretical Synthesis and Empirical Analysis. Information Systems Research, 16, 3 (2005), 237-255.

[2] Genesis. Genesis-Online Datenbank Des Statistisches Bundesamt. 2011; Available from: https://www-genesis.destatis.de/genesis/online.

[3] Hirschheim, R. and Newman, M. Houston, We've Had a Problem ... ... Offshoring, IS Employment and the IS Discipline: Perception Is Not Reality. Journal of Information Technology, 25, 4 (2010), 358-372.

[4] Hom, P.W., Caranikas-Walker, F., Prussia, G.E., and Griffeth, R.W. A Meta-Analytical Structural Equations Analysis of a Model of Employee Turnover. Journal of Applied Psychology, 77, 6 (1992), 890-909.

[5] Igbaria, M. and Greenhaus, J. Determinants of MIS Employees' Turnover Intentions: A Structural Equation Model,. Communications of the ACM, (1991), 34–49.

[6] Joseph, D., Kok-Yee, N., Koh, C., and Soon, A. Turnover of Information Technology Professionals: A Narrative Review, Meta-Analytic Structural Equation Modeling, and Model Development. MIS Quarterly, 31, 3 (2007), 547-577.

[7] Judge, T.A. Validity of the Dimensions of the Pay Satisfaction Questionnaire: Evidence of Differential Prediction. Personnel Psychology, 46, 2 (1993), 331-355.

[8] Kim, S.W., J.L., P., Muelier, C.W., and Watson, T.W. The Determinants of Career Intent among Physicians at a U.S. Air Force Hospital. Human Relations, 49, 1 (1996), 947-976.

[9] Lacity, M., Iyer, V., and Rudramuniyaiah Turnover Intentions of Indian IS Professionals. Information Systems Frontiers, 10, 2 (2008), 225–241.

[10] Laumer, S. Non-Monetary Solutions for Retaining the It Workforce. 2009.

[11] Laumer, S., Eckhardt, A., Maier, C., Stetten, A.V., Westarp, F.V., and Weitzel, T. Bewerbungspraxis 2012. 2012 (forthcoming), Centre of Human Resources Information Systems: Bamberg, Frankfurt am Main, Germany.

[12] Laumer, S., Eckhardt, A., and Weitzel, T. Electronic Human Resources Management in an E-Business Environment. Journal of Electronic Commerce Research, 11, 4 (2010), 240-250.

[13] Lee, I. An Architecture for a Next-Generation Holistic E-Recruiting System. Commun. ACM, 50, 7 (2007), 81-85.

[14] Luftman, J. and Kempaiah, R. Key Issues for IT Executives 2007. MIS Quarterly Executive, 7, 2 (2008), 99-112.

[15] Luftman, J., Kempaiah, R., and Rigoni, E.H. Key Issues for IT Executives 2008. MIS Quarterly Executive, 8, 3 (2009).

[16] Mobley, W.H., Griffeth, R.W., Hand, H.H., and Meglino, B.M. Review and Conceptual Analysis of the Employee Turnover Process. Psychological Bulletin, 86, 3 (1979), 493–522.

[17] Murray, J.P. Successfully Hiring and Retaining IT Personnel. Information Systems Management, (1999).

[18] Panko, R.R. IT Employment Prospects: Beyond the Dotcom Bubble. European Journal of Information Systems, 17, 3 (2008), 182-197.

[19] Pare, G., Tremblay, M., and Lalonde, P. Workforce Retention: What Do It Employees Really Want? 2001.

[20] Steel, R.P. and Griffeth, R.W. The Elusive Relationship between Perceived Employment Opportunity and Turnover Behavior: A Methodological or Conceptual Artifact? Journal of Applied Psychology, 74, 6 (1989).

[21] Thatcher, J.B., Stepina, L.P., and Boyle, R.J. Turnover of Information Technology Workers: Examining Empirically the Influence of Attitudes, Job Characteristics, and External Markets. Journal of Management Information Systems, 19, 3 (2002), 231-261.

[22] Weitzel, T., Eckhardt, A., and Laumer, S. A Framework for Recruiting IT Talent: Lessons from Siemens. MIS Quarterly Executive (MISQE), 8, 4 (2009), 175-189.

[23] Zwieg, P., Kaiser, K.M., Beath, C.M., Bullen, C., Gallagher, K.P., Goles, T., Howland, J., Simon, J.C., Abbott, P., Abraham, T., Carmel, E., Evaristo, R., Hawk, S., Lacity, M.C., Gallivan, M., Kelly, S., Mooney, J.G., Ranganathan, C., Rottman, J.W., Ryan, T., and Wion, R. The Information Technology Workforce: Trends and Implications 2005-2008. MIS Quarterly Executive (MISQE), 5, 2 (2006), 47-54.

Information Technology Security Task-Technology Fit Based on the Technology-to-Performance Chain Theory

Carole C. Angolano
Trident University International
carole.angolano@trident.edu

Indira R. Guzman
Trident University International
indira.guzman@trident.edu

Michael Garmon
Trident University International
Michael.garmon@trident.edu

Carlos J. Navarrete
California State Polytechnic Univ. Pomona
cjnavarrete@csupomona.edu

ABSTRACT

This research study explored the information security technologies that are currently being used within organizations; attempted to determine if, according to information technology security professionals, these technologies are performing the security tasks they were designed to perform; and evaluated the survivability of the infrastructure network after the infrastructure has been attacked or penetrated. The Technology-to-Performance Chain and the fit between tasks, technologies, and individual characteristics (Task-Technology Fit) are the theoretical basis for this study. This study incorporated the methodology of previous studies, but added the evaluations of security technologies and tasks by the IT professionals, which contributes to the existing knowledge base of information security. Structural equation modeling was used to determine the strength of the relationships between Task-Technology Fit, perceived performance impacts, and utilization of security technologies. Not all hypotheses were supported due to the re-specification of the original model.

Categories and Subject Descriptors

C.2.3 [**Computer Systems Organization**]: Computer-Communications Networks – *Network Monitoring.* K.6.5 [**Computing Milieux**]: Management of Computing and Information Systems – *Security and Protection.*

Keywords

Information Technology Security.

1. INTRODUCTION

Computer networks have become a critical element in modern society since their modest beginning over 35 years ago. They have had an impact on virtually every aspect of human life, have achieved global reach, and have become the principal enabling agents in business, industry, government, and national defense.

Major economic sectors depend on a vast array of networks operating locally, nationally, and globally. This has created societal dependency on networks which has magnified the consequences of intrusions, accidents, and failures, and amplified the critical importance of ensuring network survivability, as was emphasized by Ellison, Fisher, Linger, Lipson, Longstaff, and Mead (1999).

With these advancements in technology came the proliferation of individuals who are determined to illegally gain access into these infrastructures for nefarious purposes, personal entertainment, financial gains, and more recently, attacks on the United States national security.

The main purpose of this study was to evaluate the information security control technologies that are currently being used to protect infrastructure networks and attempt to determine if these technologies are actually performing the tasks they were designed to perform. This process evaluated the fit between Information Technology (IT) professionals and the security control systems they utilize on a daily basis. Security control systems/tools, or technologies, are utilized to intercept, identify, remediate, prepare for disaster recovery, prevent future attacks, and ensure business continuity of an organizations infrastructure network; and include hardware, software, and personnel to support the organization's functionality. To sustain this functionality or survivability, network security features must be placed throughout the infrastructure to ensure data integrity, and protect proprietary information and trade secrets. Data is an organization's most valuable asset and protecting this data is the function of the IT professionals.

The research questions for this study:

1. Do the system-level security control technologies that are currently being utilized by IT professionals, perform security tasks to positively affect perceived performance impacts?

2. Do higher evaluations of security technologies (Task-Technology Fit) by IT professionals result in higher perceived performance impacts for the individuals?

3. How do the individual skill levels and certifications of the IT professionals' impact ITSEC utilization and ITSec performance impacts?

4. Does the utilization of specific security control technologies, whether mandatory or optional, affect perceived performance impacts?

2. LITERATURE REVIEW

2.1 Task-Technology Fit and Technology-to-Performance Chain

The Task-Technology Fit (TTF) and the Technology-to-Performance Chain (TPC) are the theoretical foundations for this study. There is a linkage between information technology and individual performance that has been a concern in information systems (IS) research. Goodhue and Thompson (1995) present and test this linkage "by drawing on insights from two complimentary streams of research (user attitudes as predictors of utilization and task-technology fit as a predictor of performance)" (p. 213). The technology must be utilized and must fit the tasks it supports to have a positive impact on individual performance, as described by the TPC.

2.2 Components of the TTF and TPC Model

Each component that forms the basis of the TPC model is described below. The model is then reduced to a smaller model that is capable of being tested empirically. As defined by Goodhue and Thompson (1995, pp. 216-219):

1. Technologies: tools used by individuals in carrying out their tasks (in relation to IS research) that consist of hardware, software, data, security control tools, and IT support systems.

2. Tasks: actions carried out by individuals in turning inputs into outputs such as IT professionals relying more heavily on certain aspects of IT and answering unpredictable questions on organizational operations or database administration.

3. Individuals: ability to use the technologies to assist in the performance of their tasks (training and skill levels, IT experience, motivation, social norms, and cultural beliefs).

4. TTF: the degree that a technology assists individuals in performing their range of tasks, i.e., the correspondence between task requirements, individual abilities, and the functionality of the technology (interactions between task, technology, and individual: certain tasks require specific technological functionality from varying organizational units).

5. Utilization: behavior of employing the technology in completing the task such as the frequency of use or the diversity of the applications used. Beliefs about the consequences of use, affect toward use, and social norms would lead to the individual's decision to use or not use the specific system (theories about attitudes and behavior based on voluntary and involuntary utilization).

6. Impact of TTF on utilization: link between TTF and beliefs about the consequences of using a system which is based on the determinant of whether systems are believed to more useful, less useful, or provide relative advantage.

7. Performance impact: accomplishment of a range of tasks by an individual. Higher performance is characterized by improved efficiency, improved effectiveness, and/or higher quality.

Note that because of the model reduction, Goodhue and Thompson (1995) did not use the construct of "individuals" that was referring to the individual skill levels of the IT professionals that assist in the performance of the tasks. In this study, I expanded and operationalized the use of this variable under this theoretical approach and within the information security context. Later, Goodhue and Thompson updated the model based on more empirical evidence, but still without taking the variable of individual characteristics. Below, I present a summary of the follow up studies conducted by Goodhue and Thompson.

2.3 Studies Conducted by Goodhue and Thompson (1995) and Goodhue (1995, 1998)

The goal of the first study by Goodhue and Thompson (1995) was to test across the core components of the model, from task and technology to performance impacts, with a particular emphasis on the role of task-technology fit. The propositions were based on professional evaluations of TTF being affected by task characteristics and technology characteristics; evaluations of TTF will influence the utilization of IS by individuals; and evaluations of TTF will have additional explanatory power in predicting perceived performance impacts beyond that from utilization alone.

The overall results suggest that task and technology characteristics influence professional user ratings of TTF. Users who utilize the IS more frequently and are more dependent on the IS may be more frustrated with system downtime and experience negative performance impacts. It was determined that performance impacts are a function of both TTF and utilization (TPC).

A second study conducted by Goodhue (1995) expanded on the TTF model by adding professional evaluations of IS as a measurement technique. As suggested by Goodhue (1995), the TTF perspectives must be applied to a specific task domain at a detailed level and, for his study, used quantitative information in managerial tasks. The task domain consists of three interacting steps. The first is identifying the needed data. The second step is accessing identified data. The third step is integrating and interpreting accessed data.

In elaborating propositions from the TTF perspective, Goodhue (1995) developed four propositions as (1) technology, (2) task, (3) individual, and (4) interactions.

The results of the Goodhue (1995) study indicate that the professional evaluations of TTF are a successful measure of IS. The value of a technology is dependent on the professional user's tasks and it was indicated that professional users are capable of evaluating the TTF of their technologies.

An additional study conducted by Goodhue in 1998 addressed measurement validity of TTF for evaluations of information systems. This study describes the conceptual development of the instrument with special emphasis on a task model which focuses on information in management decision making and provides the basis for the key subconstructs in the instrument.

Goodhue (1998) defines the logical sequence of steps in developing the theoretical framework. What do we wish to measure? The subconstructs are locatability, authorization, compatibility, ease of use, training, reliability, assistance, confusion, detail, meaning, accessibility, accuracy, currency, presentation, right data, and flexibility. The next step is to develop questions to measure the defined constructs. This TTF model leads to four propositions. As implied by Goodhue (1998), three of the four propositions are information systems/technologies and service characteristics, task characteristics, and individual characteristics will each influence user evaluations of IS. The fourth most critical proposition for the TTF is that task and individual characteristics of skill level, education, and experience interact with or moderate the relationship between IS/services and professional user evaluations. It is suggested that higher TTF will lead to higher individual performance. Using the above defined theoretical framework, this study applied the theory in the information technology security context and elaborated more on the variables related to skill levels of IT professionals and its influence on ITSec performance impacts.

3. INFORMATION TECHNOLOGY SECURITY (ITSec)

3.1 ITSec Technical Knowledge

One of the most important security concerns for organizations is a false sense of security in the field of ITSec. Firewalls, anti-virus software, intrusion detection systems (IDS), and other technologies are only a small portion of the overall solution to control cyber attacks and abnormalities on infrastructure networks. No single source technology solution is effective. According to Jenson and Romo (2005), a major weakness in security is untrained IT professionals. Jenson and Romo (2005) make the following suggestions to handle these ITSec issues. Management should (1) know in what areas the ITSec staff is weak, (2) know where the network/physical security is weak, and (3) make sure the IT professionals get the training and experience they require to secure the network.

Measuring the capabilities of the IT professionals and the technologies they utilize to perform their tasks of securing an infrastructure network is paramount for an organization's survivability in an environment that is evolving with cyber attacks, insider threats, and a host of other vulnerabilities.

3.2 ITSec Task Characteristics

Task characteristics are the actions carried out by individuals in turning inputs into outputs and are identified as the use of information technologies that are utilized to protect the infrastructure network from abnormalities. More specifically, the task is to protect the infrastructure network by detecting, remediating, and reducing or eliminating the amount and magnitude of attacks on the network infrastructure. This is performed by the IT professionals through educating users on security awareness issues, monitoring the ITSec technologies, and utilizing the generated data from these technologies to complete their tasks.

An example of the more common abnormalities are described as insider threats, sabotage, and espionage; misuse of Web access and e-mail by clients/users; malicious code attacks; denial of service; and penetration attacks. This is not representative of all possible system attacks or abnormalities.

3.3 ITSec Technology Characteristics

Technology characteristics are the security control tools used by the IT professionals in carrying out their tasks of securing the infrastructure network and include hardware, software, data, and user support systems. Each of these controls alone will not adequately secure a network. They must be used in conjunction with other tools offering multi-layered security protection and must be supported by management policies and funding. The type and scope of technologies used by any organization will be determined by the size, mission, IT functionality, budget, level of outsourcing, and demographics of users within the organization. Examples of these technologies are described as IDS; firewalls; anti-virus and anti-spyware software; access control lists; encryption/decryption; login authentication; smart cards; public key infrastructure; biometrics; redundant systems; security audits; penetration testing; Web/-mail and log/event file monitoring;

password management; data backup systems; information security policy; and configuration management.

3.4 ITSec Professional's Individual Characteristics

Individual characteristics are identified by the IT professionals who use the technologies to assist them in performing their tasks and are represented by training, computer experience, motivation, beliefs, social norms, and attitudes. Enhanced individual abilities lead to better performance impacts which result in greater network survivability. Training should include technical expertise, soft skills, business applications knowledge, certifications (Cisco, MicroSoft, etc.), and information assurance.

3.5 ITSec Professional's Testing of Technologies

ITSec professional's testing of technologies are defined as "an assessment made by a user, along some continuum from positive to negative, about certain qualities of information systems" (Goodhue, 1995, p. 1827). The evaluations discovered if the ITSec technologies fit the needs of the IT professional's tasks and their individual abilities. The evaluation of the performance of information systems has appeared as a priority for businesses and as a major research direction for IT. The behavior of IT professionals, as individuals who use the technologies, will determine the effectiveness of the ITSec technologies. Leclercq (2007) suggests that certain factors influence the processes and performance of information systems, and the contribution of the measurement models used for these factors are perceptions and attitudes (perceived values), measures of information systems technical functionality (quality of information), and measures of the impact of information systems on task accomplishment (performance impact of securing an infrastructure network).

3.6 ITSec Utilization

Utilization is measured as the proportion of times IT professionals choose to utilize specific ITSec technologies. This is defined as which system provides the most information and is determined to be the most effective in performance. The IT professional's attitudes and beliefs about a particular technology, the IT professionals experience and knowledge, and the social norms or status quo of using a technology will affect the utilization of that specific technology. Combining utilization and positive task-technology fit should provide positive IT professional's evaluations than either of these constructs alone. Properly utilizing technologies will lead to higher individual performance, which will ultimately lead to securing the infrastructure network from attacks, thus providing positive performance impacts.

3.7 ITSec Performance Impacts

Performance impacts are determined by maintaining and sustaining infrastructure network survivability, and are measured by perceived performance impacts of the IT professionals. If the IT professionals are capable of utilizing the appropriate IT technologies to identify, locate, and remediate a security breach on the infrastructure network, they will evaluate the TTF of the technologies higher. IT professionals who have difficulties selecting the appropriate technology due to lack of training or insufficient experience will evaluate the TTF of the technologies lower. Higher individual performance will ultimately lead to maintaining and sustaining the survivability of the infrastructure network.

Performance impacts are affected by utilization and task, technology, and individual characteristics. Performance impacts should be positive, thus supporting network survivability under all conditions. Combining the characteristics provides a means of measuring specific variables to determine the effectiveness of accomplishing the tasks, with the given technologies, using trained IT professionals who utilize the technologies to support positive performance impacts.

3.8 Combining the Characteristics

Figure 1 is a graphical representation of the theoretical foundation of the ITSec task, ITSec technology, and ITSec professional's individual characteristics; ITSec TTF; ITSec utilization; and ITSec performance impacts, as described above. This model has been adapted from Goodhue and Thompson (1995) to depict the TTF and the TPC of Information Technology Security, as described throughout this research study. It reflects the measurement variables that are defined for each of the ITSec TTF and TPC constructs.

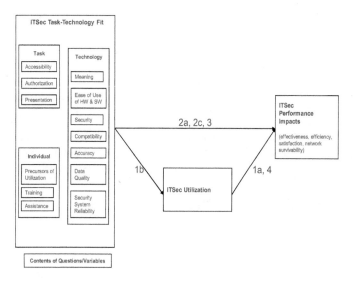

Figure 1. Theoretical Foundation and Measurement Variables for ITSec TPC derived from Goodhue and Thompson (1995, p. 220).

3.9 Role of the IT Professional

Network managers, systems administrators, network engineers, and network security officers (IT professionals) have the responsibility to monitor critical infrastructures to prevent, detect, and counteract attacks on their systems. Thus, technologies, their effectiveness in reducing attacks on an infrastructure, and the skill level of the IT professionals must be evaluated continuously to determine the security posture and ensure the infrastructure network is protected from abnormalities and attacks.

The link between TTF, utilization (TPC), and performance impacts must be researched to assist IT professionals in performing their duties. "A person seeking to harm a business in this day and age does not aim his attacks at the company's physical assets; instead he takes aim at its computers" and security breaches have been on the rise in the past year between 25% and 50%, according to recent surveys (Yang and Hoffstadt, 2006, p.

201). Cyber-crime tools are also becoming more available to those who are willing to invest in this activity.

4. METHODOLOGY
4.1 Population and Sample
The study utilized a survey design. Participants were selected using USADATA and the data was collected using Survey Monkey. A total of 4, 054 invitations to participate were emailed or mailed to perspective participants. Of the invitations sent, a total of 401 were returned with 328 usable, which is a return of 9.8% of the recipients responded. The target was organizations that do not outsource their IT functions

4.2 Data Analysis
Descriptive statistics with Predictive Analytics Software (PASW) was used to determine the demographics of the study population and the basic features of the data, i.e. most commonly used security devices, types of cyber-attacks, etc. The replace missing values tool was performed on the usable responses/data to compensate for missing values.

Exploratory factor analysis (EFA) was used to test the factor loadings, and included Pearson correlation and Cronbach's alpha; Bartlett's test of sphericity; Kaiser-Meyer-Olkin (KMO); Individual Measures of Sampling Adequacy (MSA); stage 1 factor analysis (FA) to determine the number of constructs being measured; stage 2 FA to select 10 initial components; and Varimax rotation to maximize the variances of the loadings. During this process, factors were dropped leaving Security, Reliability, Accessibility of Data, Ease of Use, Perceived Performance Impacts, and IT Utilization for further analysis.

Structural equation modeling (SEM) with Linear Structural Relationships (LISREL) 8.8 was used to estimate the fit of the model to the collected data. The SEM process includes 2 steps; validating the measurement model and fitting the structural model. Validating was accomplished through Confirmatory Factor Analysis (CFA) and fitting was accomplished through path analysis with latent variables. Four initial models were tested and one was selected to continue with the CFA process. After numerous iterations and re-specifications of the selected model, including cross loading and non-cross loading, a final model met the acceptable fit specifications of SEM. The model is illustrated in Appendix A.

5. RESULTS
5.1 Hypothesis 1a
H1a: The utilization of system-level security control technologies will be associated with decreased network intrusions. Nine questions from Section 2 of the survey focused on PPI and ITUtil. The coefficient of the LISREL run was a path of 0.57, which is acceptable, but at a moderate level of correlation. H1a is supported (reference Figure A1).

5.2 Hypothesis 1b
H1b: Higher Task-Technology-Fit will be associated with the utilization of system-level security control technologies. ITUtil and TTFit were used to test this hypothesis. There were no significant correlations and the LISREL run did not generate a good model fit for ITUtil and TTFit, therefore H1b was not supported (reference Figure A3).

5.3 Hypothesis 2a

H2a: Increased training and experience of IT professionals will be associated with decreased network intrusions. There were no statistically significant correlations between education, tenure, IT certifications, and attempted and successful attacks. H2a was not supported (reference Tables B2 and B3).

5.4 Hypothesis 2b

H2b: Increased training and experience of IT professionals will be associated with higher Task-Technology-Fit. There were no significant correlations between technical certifications and the constructs that comprise the TTF after the best model fit was generated using LISREL. H2b is not supported (reference Table B1).

5.5 Hypothesis 2c

H2c: Increased training and experience of IT professionals will be associated with increased perceived performance impacts. Relating to correlation coefficients, there were no statistically significant correlations between PPI and education/certifications of IT professionals. All coefficients were calculated at the slight inconsequential level. H2c is not supported (reference Figure A2).

5.6 Hypothesis 3

H3: Higher Task-Technology-Fit will be associated with increased perceived performance impacts. The correlation matrix and the LISREL run generated an acceptable model fit and a moderate correlation. H3 is supported (reference Figure A2).

5.7 Hypothesis 4

H4: The utilization of system-level security control technologies will be associated with increased performance impacts. The variables ITUtil and PPI are correlated with a path of 0.57 which is acceptable, but with a moderate level of correlation. H4 is supported (reference Figure A1).

6. DISCUSSION AND IMPLICATIONS

6.1 Summary of Major Findings

The literature reviewed for this study support research question 1, but the results of the statistical analysis in this study partially supports this question. The identified and tested system-level control technologies currently being utilized by IT professionals perform security tasks that are capable of decreasing network intrusions; positively affecting perceived performance attacks. This is a calming discovery taking into consideration the number of "fatal" attacks on our infrastructures throughout the United States and the amount of proprietary information and finances that have been stolen.

All referenced literature positively supported that higher TTF resulted in higher perceived performance impacts. This result was unexpected, and may be attributed to the hackers always being "one step ahead" of IT professionals when it involves hacking into networks.

The literature throughout this study and the results from this study supports that higher Task-Technology-Fit affects the utilization of security control technologies and perceived performance impacts. Research question 3 is fully supported. The task of securing a network must be completed using a variety of technologies with the IT/IS professional customizing the technologies to accomplish the task of IT security. Task complexity influences the tool

reliability and the perceived performance impacts of each tool to accomplish each task.

The utilization of security control technologies leads to perceived performance impacts. By the effective use of security control technologies, IT professionals believe that the network infrastructure will be protected from hackers and any other type of network intrusion. This may give IT professionals a false sense of security with IT protection. This may ultimately lead to a host of issues relating to infrastructure attacks and damages. IT professionals must remain diligent in their efforts in obtaining and maintaining IT security at all levels of the infrastructure. Research question 4 is supported by the literature review and the results of this study.

6.2 Contributions

By studying IT professionals and the security control technologies, additional information was obtained regarding protecting an infrastructure network from attacks. This research study generated the development of a new measurement scale which can be used to analyze data collected from IT professionals. Through rigorous and extensive data analysis with SEM and CFA, the original measurement scale used by Goodhue (1995, 1998) was reduced and modified specifically for IT security research.

7. Recommendations for Future Research

There are numerous possibilities for future research on the topic of IT security. It is very difficult for a single instrument to meet all the needs of a research study. Because of the strong conceptual background and its strong measurement validity, the TTF and the TPC instruments, with the newly developed measurement scale that was designed in this research study, should be considered for researchers who are seeking to measure the effectiveness of organizational information systems. Due to the fast paced evolution of the technologies and hacker abilities, the TTF and TPC will have to be modified to accommodate new technologies and the practical application of these technologies. Currently, cloud computing has become a dominant technology for private organizations and government agencies. To measure the security, utilization, and effectiveness of cloud computing, many of the questions and measurable varia

bles that are currently used will require modifications to provide accurate measures.

8. ACKNOWLEDGMENTS

Thanks to all the participants in this survey.

9. REFERENCES

[1] Belsis, P., Kokolakis, S., and Kiountouzis, E. 2005. "Information system security from a knowledge management perspective", Information Management and Computer Security, 13(2/3), 189-202.

[2] Ellison, R.J., Fisher, D.A., Linger, R.C., Lipson, R.C., Longstaff, T., and Mead, N.R. 1999. Survivable network systems: An emerging discipline. http://www.cert.org/10.1145/archive.

[3] Goodhue, D.L. 1995. "Understanding user evaluations of information systems", Management Science, 41(12), 1827-1844.

[4] Goodhue, D.L. 1998. "Development and measurement validity of a task-technology fit instrument for user evaluations of information systems", Decision Sciences, 29(1), 105-138.

[5] Jenson, B.K. and Romo, J. 2005. "The expert opinion", Journal of Information Technology Case and Application Research, 7(2), 49-52.

[6] Leclercq, A. 2007. "The perceptual evaluation of information systems using the construct of user satisfaction: Case study of a large French group", The Data Base for Advances in Information Systems, 38(2), 27-60.

[7] Raykov, T. and Marcoulides, G.A. 2006. A First Course in Structural Equation Modeling. Mahwah, NJ: Lawrence Erlbaum Associates.

[8] Yang, D.W. and Hoffstadt, B.M. 2006. "Essay: Countering the cyber crime threat", The American Criminal Law Review, 43(2), 201-215.

Appendix A

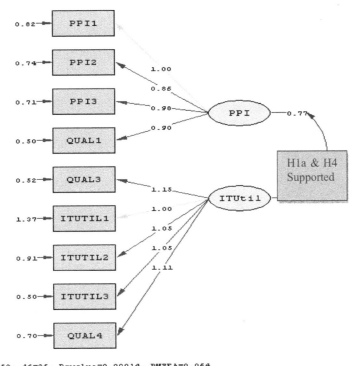

Chi-Square=60.62, df=26, P-value=0.00014, RMSEA=0.064

Figure A1. Measurement Model: PPI and ITUtil Construct Diagram.

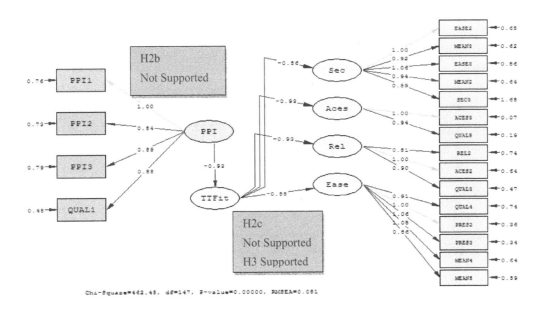

Chi-Square=462.45, df=147, P-value=0.00000, RMSEA=0.081

Figure A2. Measurement/Structural (CFA) Model: TTFit and PPI Construct Diagram

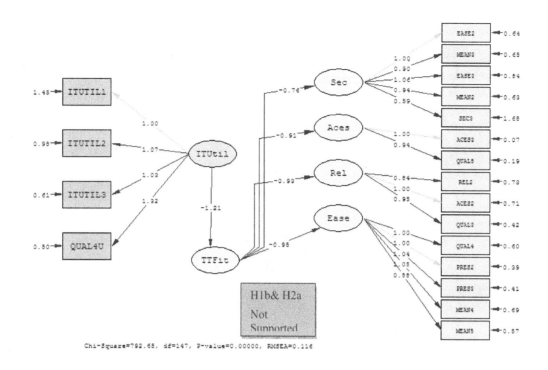

Chi-Square=792.65, df=147, P-value=0.00000, RMSEA=0.116

Figure A3. Measurement/Structural Model: TTFit and ITUtil Construct Diagram.

Appendix B

Table B1.

Correlation Matrix for Certifications and Final Constructs/Variables of TTFit.

		MS	Cisco	IA	S+	N+	A+
Pearson Correlations							
Security	EASE2	.191**	.122*	.053	.108	.134*	.112*
	MEAN3	.188**	.106	.031	.082	.093	.090
	EASE3	.144**	.077	.040	.078	.099	.123*
	MEAN2	.182**	.087	-.074	.044	.118*	.062
	SEC3	.028	.000	-.099	-.042	-.023	-.004
Accessibility	ACES3	.170**	.109*	-.056	.114*	.106	.077
	QUAL5	.184**	.103	-.037	.107	.067	.059
Reliability	REL2	.088	.035	-.032	.074	.042	.072
	ACES2	.063	.033	-.016	.076	.083	.103
	QUAL3	.133*	.070	-.031	.072	.067	.121*
Ease of Use	QUAL4	.123*	.035	-.018	.094	.033	.069
	PRES2	.134*	.021	-.044	.052	.040	.053
	PRES3	.201**	.125*	-.024	.130*	.125*	.111*
	MEAN4	.158**	.076	.043	.124*	.109*	.066
	MEAN5	.186**	.119*	.006	.166**	.090	.117*

Table B2.

Correlation Matrix for IT Professionals Training and Amount of Successful/Attempted Attacks.

Pearson Correlations								
Education Certifications Attacks/Damages	Education	MS	Cisco	IA	S+	N+	A+	Attempt
MS	.040	1						
Cisco	.152**	.623**	1					
IA	-.008	.420**	.601**	1				
S+	.077	.567**	.659**	.735**	1			
N+	.124*	.558**	.736**	.607**	.704**	1		
A+	.051	.530**	.558**	.539**	.710**	.766**	1	
Attempt	.193**	.324**	.290**	.116*	.229**	.173**	.310**	1
Success	.187**	.228**	.383**	.276**	.281**	.347**	.332**	.351**

Table B3.

Correlation Matrix for IT Organizational Demographics and Types of Attacks/Damages.

Pearsons Correlations								
	Gender	Tenure	Education	Type Org.	Size of Org.	Size IT Division	# Emp. ITSec	Occupation Title
System Penetration	-.115*	.101	.087	.008	-.017	.006	-.024	-.102
Downtime	.025	.121*	-.011	.047	-.052	-.006	-.035	-.024
Damage to OS	-.031	.129*	-.003	.050	-.052	-.044	-.029	-.103
Damage to Files/ File Corruption	-.031	.099	.003	.081	-.019	-.065	-.033	-.101
Malicious Code	-.091	.117*	.047	.040	-.005	-.015	-.036	-.104
SPAM	-.019	.094	.035	.080	-.068	-.101	-.034	-.111
Trojans/Worms	-.046	.113*	.027	.053	-.018	.033	-.031	-.133*
Phishing Scams	-.030	.127*	.025	.088	-.070	-.036	-.026	-.121*
DoS	-.083	.137*	-.005	.095	-.018	.011	-.027	-.142*
Misuse Web Access/E-Mail	.022	.113*	.016	.022	-.080	-.044	.010	-.026
Loss of Proprietary Information	-.056	.148**	-.011	.137*	.000	.026	-.029	-.070
Loss of Data	-.059	.161**	.003	.071	-.024	.028	-.031	-.142*

The Role of Informal Control in PMO Lite Environments

Jo Ellen Moore
Southern Illinois University
Edwardsville
Campus Box 1106
Edwardsville, IL 62026-1106
618-650-5816

joemoor@siue.edu

Clay K. Williams
Southern Illinois University
Edwardsville
Campus Box 1106
Edwardsville, IL 62026-1106
618-650-2504

cwillaa@siue.edu

Mary Sumner
Southern Illinois University
Edwardsville
Campus Box 1106
Edwardsville, IL 62026-1106
618-650-2504

msumner@siue.edu

ABSTRACT

The Corporate Executive Board Company PMO (Project Management Office) Executive Council's report on the *State of the PMO: 2010* identified six key findings, one of which was: "A Trend Toward Reduced Methodology" [18]. In line with this trend, 47% of the PMOs in the CEBC study indicated "Establishing a 'PMO Lite' function" as a top priority for 2010. PMO Lite is a configuration that has minimal staff and no direct control over the management of individual projects, but supports project managers by creating standards and serving as a project information repository.

Viewed through the theoretical lens of control theory, the recently reported trend of cutting mandatory deliverables, making some of them optional deliverables, and moving toward a standards and repository type of PMO implies a reduction of formal controls. If organizations aim to maintain or continue to improve project management outcomes while shrinking formal controls, control theory suggests informal controls will play a vital role in achieving desired outcomes.

This in-progress research involves a quantitative field study to examine the extent and nature of informal controls in PMO Lite environments. To ascertain whether informal controls play a more significant role in PMO Lite environments, we also will collect data from project managers in "PMO Heavy" organizations. Participating companies will be drawn from our School's Project Management Advisory Board and a web-based survey will be administered to 200-300 project managers.

Data will be analyzed using structural equation modeling. We will relate insights gleaned on informal controls present in PMO Lite environments to the extent to which their organization meets key project management goals. We will also examine antecedents to informal controls in these organizations, to gain insights into how managers can spark and nurture informal controls that contribute to the achievement of organizational project management goals.

Categories and Subject Descriptors

K.6.1 Project and people management.

General Terms

Management.

Keywords

Control theory, informal control, PMO, project managers, managerial behavior.

1. MOTIVATION AND RESEARCH QUESTIONS

The Corporate Executive Board Company PMO (Project Management Office) Executive Council's report on the *State of the PMO: 2010* identified six key findings, one of which was: "A Trend Toward Reduced Methodology" [18]. The report states that, for the PMOs participating in their study, the median number of mandatory and optional deliverables in the standard PM methodology is 30. Over the next two years (2011-2012), 35% of those PMOs want to reduce the number of mandatory deliverables, and 50% expect to increase the number of optional deliverables.

In line with this trend, 47% of the PMOs in the CEBC study indicated "Establishing a 'PMO Lite' function" as a top priority for 2010. PMO Lite is a PMO configuration that has minimal staff and no direct control over the management of individual projects. In a PMO Lite environment, the PMO plays a supporting role to project managers by creating standards for project management and serving as a project information repository [19].

The recent CEBC findings beg researcher attention to this trend toward reduced methodology, or PMO Lite, and critical success factors associated with such a move. Control theory provides theoretical guidance for our study – and a fresh perspective on the use of PMOs. In control theory terminology, all types of PMOs facilitate the implementation of "formal" controls [15]. By definition, formal controls are management-initiated mechanisms that utilize formal documentation to state expected performance along with rewards to influence the probability that personnel will behave in ways that support objectives [2,7,8]. There are two types of formal controls: behavioral and outcome. With behavioral controls, management seeks to influence the means of achieving the organizational objectives [7]. Outcome controls involve the specification of desired outputs and rewards for their achievement [8,9].

Control theory also recognizes "informal" controls, which are social or people strategies, usually undocumented, that focus on influencing employee behaviors [7,8,9].

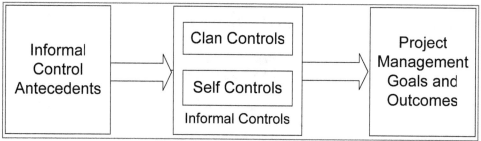

Figure 1. Conceptual Research Model

The two types of informal controls are clan control and self control. A clan is any group sharing common goals [14] and clan control is largely a group socialization process that influences the behavior of individuals, encouraging common values, beliefs, and problem solving approaches [8,9]. Clan control involves a deep level of agreement on what constitutes proper behavior and a strong commitment to those behaviors [14]. Finally, self control addresses how and when individuals in organizations control their own actions, i.e., set goals, monitor work, and reward or sanction another [9].

Viewed through the lens of control theory, cutting mandatory deliverables, making some of them optional deliverables, and moving toward a support/standards/repository type of PMO implies a *reduction of formal controls*. If organizations aim to maintain or continue to improve project management outcomes while shrinking formal controls, control theory suggests *informal controls will play a vital role* in achieving desired outcomes [7].

To investigate the role of informal controls in relation to PMO Lite environments, we will examine informal controls (both clan and self) in several PMO Lite organizations in multiple companies. In regard to clan controls, the focus of our study is the "clan" of project managers supported by the PMO Lite. We will relate the data gleaned on informal controls to the extent to which these PMO Lite organizations report that they meet key project management goals, including the extent to which common project problems occur. We will also examine antecedents to informal controls (both clan and self) in these organizations, to gain insights into how managers can spark and nurture informal controls that coalesce with PMO Lite structures to contribute to achievement of organizational project management goals. Finally, we also will collect data from "PMO Heavy" organizations to ascertain whether informal controls have a more significant impact on project outcomes in the PMO Lite environments.

Research Questions:

RQ1. In a PMO Lite environment, does extent or type of informal controls utilized by project managers relate to achievement of organizational project management goals?

RQ2. In a PMO Lite environment, what are key contributors to informal controls? i.e., elements of the workplace that contribute to the clan and self controls observed?

2. SUPPORTING LITERATURE
2.1 Streams of Research
As implied by our conceptual research model shown in Figure 1, we draw upon two primary streams of research: control theory,

and project management. Key elements from these two streams of research are reviewed in the sections that follow.

2.2 Control Theory
By definition, controls are various types of mechanisms used to encourage individuals to act in ways that support achievement of organizational objectives [5,10]. Controls are the specific ways a controller attempts to influence the behavior of a controllee. The controller and controllee may be an individual dyad or groups of individuals [2].

Formal controls (behavioral, outcome) are mechanisms that management uses to encourage desired behaviors by clearly defining the required behaviors or the desired outcomes [2,7,8]. Project management methodologies that include mandatory deliverables are examples of formal behavioral controls, as these define the activities, rules and procedures that are the accepted means for completing a project. Performance targets associated with the project, such as acceptable error rates, schedule compliance and person-hour over-run rates, are examples of formal outcome controls.

Informal controls (self, clan) seek to influence behaviors through social strategies that align controller and controllee goals or promote acceptable behaviors through peer influence [7,8]. Desired self controls in a PMO Lite environment may include making an effort to identify truly tangible milestones and a dedication to daily follow-ups with action item owners. Where self control is inherently intrinsic and a product of the individual's objectives and personal standards [8], clan control is a group phenomenon, and our study focuses on the clan of project managers supported by a PMO Lite. Clan controls can support or run counter to an organization's goals. For example, clan controls relevant to the PMO Lite environment may include consistent utilization (or non-use) of a particular risk management technique, a common pattern of using (or not using) optional deliverables, a collaborative (or non-collaborative) culture [4], and normative socialization encouraging clan-accepted behaviors through peer-to-peer signaling [5].

The general thrust of our hypotheses will be that informal controls have more effect on project outcomes in PMO Lite environments (where formal controls in the form of mandatory deliverables and required project management practices are reduced) than in PMO environments with extensive formal controls (i.e., PMO Heavy). The control literature provides general support for this [7]. We will further examine our data to ascertain specific clan controls and self controls that are associated with positive outcomes and also with negative outcomes in PMO Lite environments. Finally, we will utilize the control theory literature to identify antecedents to informal controls to be examined in our study

[5,10,13], as well as contextual factors that should be assessed and possibly controlled.

2.3 Project Management and PMOs

A PMO is an organizational body or entity assigned various responsibilities related to the centralized and coordinated management of multiple projects under its domain. The responsibilities of a PMO can range from providing project management support to directly managing projects [16]. Singh, Keil, and Kasi [19] define two ends of the PMO spectrum as PMO Lite and PMO Heavy. A PMO Lite creates and maintains standards and serves as a project information repository, but has no direct control over the management of individual projects and does not contribute to portfolio management. A PMO Heavy also creates and maintains standards and serves as a project information repository but, unlike the PMO Lite, the PMO Heavy has direct control over projects and contributes to portfolio management.

In addition to defining characteristics of the PMO Lite structure, we turn to the project management literature to identify project goals commonly stated by organizations, as well as project problems commonly experienced by organizations. Project management goals center around the triple constraints of schedule, budget, and functionality [3,12,18]. In addition to those traditional outcome variables, information on the occurrence of common project management problems will be collected from the PMO Lite (and PMO Heavy) environments. We have identified these common problems by drawing on the PMBOK [16], Singh et al. [19], and members of our PM Advisory Board:

- High project manager workload
- Lack of stakeholder commitment to PM methods
- Lack of project manager commitment to PM methods
- Lack of project team member commitment to PM methods
- Failure to capture and utilize lessons learned
- Lack of prioritization of projects across organizational units
- Poor definition of project scope
- Poor estimating of time and resources
- Poor change control
- Poor management of project or product quality
- Poor project risk management
- Poor project communication

Finally, we expect the project management body of literature to aid in interpreting and learning from our results. For example, major typologies of PMOs imply a particular progression from one type to another. The Gartner Group classifications [11] and PMI's OPM3 model [17] generally presume that PMOs start out as "Lite" (standards and repository) and progress into a "Heavy" type of PMO (contributing to portfolio management). Recent studies, however, suggest a more dynamic evolution that can involve an "emptying" or dissolution of the PMO [1,15]. Hobbs and Aubry [6] contend that it is natural for PMOs to be formed, disbanded, and then potentially re-formed. This is in line with Pellegrinelli and Garagna [15] who view PMOs to be created by organizations in response to a perceived need – and as the PMO progressively addresses that need, then relevance and value of the PMO decreases.

In other words, recent theory and research suggest that effective dissemination of project management tools and techniques can lead to the demise of the PMO within an organization. Our study of informal controls relative to PMO Lite may shine important new light on this matter. For instance, we may find that regressing back to PMO Lite can be effective for an organization if project managers have adopted certain informal controls.

3. METHODOLOGY

We will conduct a quantitative field study to examine informal controls in real-world PMO Lite environments. The primary data will be collected via an online survey completed by project managers who are supported by a PMO Lite. We also will collect the data from project managers in PMO Heavy organizations to ascertain whether informal controls have a more significant impact on project outcomes in the PMO Lite environments. Data will be analyzed using structural equation modeling.

From our project supporter within each organization, we will collect organizational demographics (e.g., industry, firm size, number of PMs supported by each PMO) and organization-level information regarding the extent to which project goals are achieved and project problems are experienced.

Data collected from project managers via the survey instrument will include:

- PMO characteristics (as a secondary check to ensure the PM is operating with a PMO Lite or a PMO Heavy)
- Control variables specific to control theory studies (to be determined through literature review)
- Independent variables (to be refined through literature review):
  - Clan controls
  - Self controls
  - Antecedents to clan controls
  - Antecedents to self controls
- Dependent variables
  - PM's perception of extent to which project management goals are achieved
  - PM's perception of extent to which project management problems are experienced

4. RESEARCH-IN-PROGRESS

This work is ongoing, as indicated by the research-in-progress designation of our submission. At the time of the conference, we will present the foundation of our study as put forth in this paper, as well as the detailed research model (specific constructs, relationships, hypotheses) that we are developing.

5. REFERENCES

[1] Aubry, M., Muller, R., Hobbs, B., and Blomquist, T. (2010). Project management offices in transition. *International Journal of Project Management*, 28, 766-778.

[2] Choudhury, V. and Sabherwal, R. (2003). Portfolios of Control in Outsourced Software Development Projects. *Information Systems Research*, 14(3), 291-314.

[3] Dai, C.X., and Wells, W.G. (2004). An exploration of project management office features and their relationship to project performance. *International Journal of Project Management*, 22, 523-532.

[4] Gopal, A. and Gosain, S. (2010). The role of organizational controls and boundary spanning in software development outsourcing: Implications for project performance. *Information Systems Research,* 21(4), 960-982.

[5] Harris, M.L., Collins, R.W., and Hevner, A.R. (2009). Control of Flexible Software Development Under Uncertainty. *Information Systems Research*, 20(3), 400-419.

[6] Hobbs, B., and Aubry, M. (2007). A multi-phase research program investigating project management offices (PMOs): The results of phase 1. *Project Management Journal,* 38(1), 74-86.

[7] Jaworski, B. J., Stathakopoulos, V., and Krishnan, H.S. (1993). Control combinations in marketing: Conceptual framework and empirical evidence. *Journal of Marketing,* 57, 57-69.

[8] Kirsch, L.J. (1996). The Management of Complex Tasks in Organizations: Controlling the Systems Development Process. *Organization Science,* 7(1), 1-21.

[9] Kirsch, L.J. (1997). Portfolios of Control Modes and IS Project Management. *Information Systems Research,* 8(3), 215-239.

[10] Kirsch, L.J., Ko, D.G., and Haney, M.H. (2010). Investigating the Antecedents of Team-Based Clan Control. *Organization Science*, 21(2), 469-489.

[11] Light, M. (2000). *The project office: Teams, processes, and tools.* Stamford, CT: Gartner Research.

[12] Martin, N.L., Pearson, J.M., and Furumo, K. (2007). IS project management: Size, practices, and the project management office. *The Journal of Computer Information Systems,* 47(4), 52-60.

[13] Maruping, L.M., Venkatesh, V., and Agarwal, R. (2009). A Control Theory Perspective on Agile Methodology Use and Changing User Requirements. *Information Systems Research*, 20(3), 377-399.

[14] Ouchi, W.G. (1979). A Conceptual Framework for the Design of Organizational Control Mechanisms. *Management Science*, 25(9), 833-848.

[15] Pellegrinelli, S., and Garagna, L. (2009). Towards a conceptualization of PMOs as agents and subjects of change and renewal. *International Journal of Project Management*, 27, 649-656.

[16] PMI (2008a). *A Guide to the Project Management Body of Knowledge, 4th Edition.* Newtown Square, PA: Project Management Institute.

[17] PMI (2008b). *Organizational Project Management Maturity Model: OPM3 Knowledge Foundation.* Newtown Square, PA: Project Management Institute.

[18] Project Management Solutions (2010). *The State of the PMO 2010: A PM Solutions Research Report.* Glen Mills, PA: PM Solutions.

[19] Singh, R., Keil, M, and Kasi, V. (2009). Identifying and overcoming the challenges of implementing a project management office. *European Journal of Information Systems,* 18, 409-427.

Research-In-Progress: Reframing a Knowledge Level Framework

Maung K. Sein
University of Agder
Post Box 422
4604 Kristiansand S, Norway
+47 3814 1617

Maung.K.Sein@uia.no

Stig Nordheim
University of Agder
Post Box 422
4604 Kristiansand S, Norway
+47 3814 1610

Stig.Nordheim@uia.no

Tero Päivärinta
Luleå University of Technology
Department of Computer Science
97 187 Luleå, Sweden
. +46 (0)72 - 532 0530

tero.paivarinta@ltu.se

ABSTRACT

In this paper, we present a research-in-progress study where we are revisiting a well known knowledge-level framework of understanding (i.e. knowledge) of a system proposed by Olfman et al. [1]. The catalyst for this relook was the anomalies and incongruencies that surfaced when we tried to apply this framework in another study whose aim was to examine how hermeneutic reflection helps in learning. While the framework proved a useful vehicle to carry out hermeneutic analysis, it also proved inadequate in accounting for some significant aspects of what constitutes understanding of a system. A closer look at the data revealed that other theoretical premises could not only provide a better interpretation but also that these premises can potentially enhance the knowledge level framework. We are currently reinterpreting the data using three interpretive lenses, namely, practice lens, socio-materiality and genres. Our goal is to reconceptualize what constitutes understanding or knowledge of a system and propose a revised knowledge level framework.

Categories and Subject Descriptors

K.6.1 [Project and People Management]: Training

General Terms

Human Factors

Keywords

User training, hermeneutics, learning processes, training process.

1. BACKGROUND

This study is part of a program of research that we are conducting to examine the role hermeneutics can play in user training. In the interest of brevity and given that this is a research-in-progress contribution, we will not elaborate on the arguments for hermeneutics in this context. Instead, we refer the reader to a previous paper presented at an earlier CPR conference [2] and to Prasad [3] for an explanation of how hermeneutics is a good mechanism to understand text or any other artifact. The more curious reader is referred to Gadamer [4] for a thorough treatment of hermeneutics itself. In short, in our earlier paper, we explained succinctly the hermeneutic process and through an analysis of the training materials used in a course on e-Collaboration tools at a large multinational company, demonstrated the usefulness of hermeneutics as a basis for training. We used the Olfman et al. [1] framework, shown in Figure 1, to base our analysis. In summing up the implications of the findings, we proposed that a sterner test of our propositions would require an empirical study where the actual hermeneutic processes of trainees could be traced. That led to a second study.

In that second study, we asked students enrolled in a 13-week semester long master's course in eCollaboration and enterprise content management to keep diaries with their reflections. These were based on the procedure devised by Mathiassen and Purao [5] and written in a wiki which also contained comments by the course instructor. At the end, these diaries consisted of 118 pages in total, including guidelines and comments. On average each student wrote 10 pages of reflections. Then we conducted a document analysis of these diaries where we traced the hermeneutics process of the students' reflection. To do this tracing in such analysis, we need a "whole", which has "parts" which will be the basis for reflecting and iterating between understandings of the parts and then use this understanding to enhance their understanding of the whole. This new understanding (termed "horizon of understanding" in hermeneutics) is then used back to reflect on the "parts". Each such reflection occurs when an "encounter" takes place. An encounter in the context of the course would be a class meeting, or the use of the e-Collaboration tool suite. The cycle recurs when the next encounter takes place. The process continues until a certain level of understanding is achieved. In our case, the process ended at the end of the semester in which the course was run. As explained above, we used the Olfman et al. framework [1] in our analysis. The higher levels of the e-Collaboration tool suite represent the whole which is composed of parts which are the lower levels. In some cases, a lower level can also be viewed as a "smaller" whole with its own component parts (levels lower than that". For example, level 4 (Tool conceptual) is a whole with all the lower levels being its parts. However, level 2 (Tool procedural) is also a whole whose parts are the syntax and semantics of level 1 (Command-based).

While analyzing the data, we ran into a problem. While the framework proved to be a useful starting point for tracing the hermeneutic process, many of the reflections in the diaries did not map to any level. One specific illustration of this inadequacy was that socio-organizational aspect around the use of a tool was not accounted for in the framework. Our first action was to make some simple revisions to the framework to fit the data. We divided levels 6 (motivational), 5 (Business conceptual) and 3

(Business procedural) into three contexts (course context, business context and other contexts). This eased the problem to some extent and we used this revised framework to do the analysis. Table 1 summarizes our mapping.

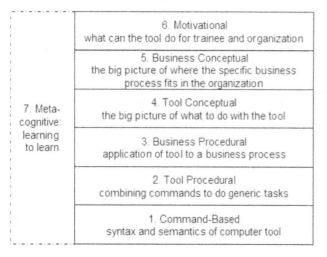

Figure 1: Knowledge level framework, from [2]

Table 1. Levels and total number of reflections

Level	Total No. of reflections
7. Meta-cognitive	33
6. Motivational	45
5. Business conceptual	17
4. Tool conceptual	28
3. Business procedural	29
2. Tool procedural	13
1. Command-based	10
0. Unable to map	55

The findings from our analysis can be summarized as follows.

• The big picture of the diaries appears well balanced, with daily (or for some: weekly) reflections on most of the knowledge levels

• There were considerably fewer reflections on levels 1 and 2 than the higher levels

• In many of the daily reflections, reflections on one theme spanned several levels, moving up and down in the knowledge levels

• The degree of hermeneutic reflection is related to understanding, as reflected in the students' exam grades. Those who scored higher grades reflected regularly, with no large time gaps in their diaries.

• The better students had the highest number of reflections, specifically at level 7 (meta-cognition). On an average the students who got A and B grades had twice as many reflections in total compared to the students who got C (or lower).

• More interestingly, the better students also had twice as many reflections outside the levels in the framework compared to the other students.

2. DISCUSSION

The main insight from the findings reported in brief above is that a knowledge level framework can be a useful mechanism to perform hermeneutic analysis. The Olfman et al. framework [1] was a good basis but an inadequate one. We surmised that the fundamental shortcoming of the framework is that it is primarily "tool-centric" in terms of the conceptualization of the IT artifact proposed by Orlikowski and Iacono [6]. It does not take an ensemble view. The social and organizational aspect that is in the nomological net around the artifact is missing. Using a tool has socio-organizational aspects. To illustrate, we present an extract from the diary of a student "A". Given the option of attending the class either in person or on-line, he decided to use the tool to attend the class on-line and not to come to class unless at least another student was present. Looking at it another way, he would use the system if he would otherwise be the only one in a F2F session. This "horizon of understanding" of the tool has little to do with any of the levels in the framework but can be accounted for if we consider the tool as an ensemble. Another shortcoming is that it does not fit very well a "tool set" such as eCollaboration which has a number of component software. So, we would need another level (or redefine tool conceptual to mean how a set of tools can be combined to accomplish a task). In short, there is a need for a more expansive framework.

3. ONGOING RESEARCH-IN-PROGRESS

The objective of the research-in-progress that we report here is to do precisely that - develop an enhanced knowledge level framework. We are using the framework of Olfman et al. [1] as a point of departure to build this enhanced framework. We are re-analyzing the diaries using three lenses: anticipated practice lens, genres, and socio-materiality. The practice lens perspective places the understanding of a system in the situated context of its use [7]. A change of context changes this understanding. In a training context the practice lens is necessarily anticipated because the trainees had not used the tool before. The genre theory of organizational communication can also be used to contextualize the understanding based on the genres of communication involving the tool [8], [9]. Socio-materiality [10] emphasizes the dual nature of a tool and intertwines the "material" (i.e. a physical tool) in the "social" context of use. All three lenses, singly and in combination, have the potential to enrich and enhance our understanding of what "understanding of a tool" means. Initial results are encouraging. We have been able to map the hitherto unmapped levels to concepts in these theories. At the conference, we plan to present the results of our analysis and an initial revised knowledge level framework.

4. REFERENCES

[1] Olfman, L., Bostrom, R P. and Sein, M. K. (2006). Developing training strategies with an HCI Perspective. In P Zhang and D Galletta (Eds): Human-Computer Interaction and Management Information Systems: Foundations. Advances in Management Information Systems (5), 258–283.

[2] Sein, M.K. and Nordheim, S. (2010). Learning processes in user training: The case for hermeneutics. Proceedings of ACM SIGMIS CPR Conference, May 20-22, 2010, Vancouver, BC, Canada.

[3] Prasad, A. (2002). The contest over meaning: Hermeneutics as an interpretive methodology for understanding texts. Organizational Research Methods (5:1), 12-33.

[4] Gadamer, H.G. (1989). Truth and Method, 2nd revised edition. Continuum, New York.

[5] Mathiassen, L. and Purao, S. 2002. Educating reflective systems developers. Information Systems Journal (12), 81–102.

[6] Orlikowski, W. J. and Iacono, C. S. (2001). Research commentary: Desperately seeking the "IT" in IT research – A call to theorizing the IT artefact. Information System Research (12:2), 121-134.

[7] Orlikowski, W. J. (2000). Using technology and constituting structures: A practice lens for studying technology in organizations. Organization Science (11:4), 404-428.

[8] Yates, J. and Orlikowski, W. (1992). Genres of organizational communication: A structurational approach to studying communication and media. Academy of Management Review (17:2). 299-325.

[9] Päivärinta, T. (2001). The concept of genre within the critical approach to information systems development. Information & Organization (11:3), 207-234.

[10] Orlikowski, W. J. and Scott, S.V. (2008). Sociomateriality: Challenging the separation of technology, work and organization. The Academy of Management Annals (2:1). 433-474.

Skills in the Management Oriented IS and Enterprise System Job Markets

Chuck Litecky
Southern Illinois University Carbondale
College of Business
Carbondale, IL 62901
618-453-7892

clitecky@business.siu.edu

Amy J. Igou
Southern Illinois University Carbondale
College of Business
Carbondale, IL 62901
618-453-7891

ajigou@business.siu.edu

Andrew Aken
Northeastern State University- Broken Arrow
Broken Arrow, OK 74014
618-924-5805

Andrew.aken@nsuok.edu

ABSTRACT

With turmoil in the U.S. and world economies, it is more necessary than ever to ensure that graduates and employees have the skills necessary to compete in the job market. Some of the previous research on job skills has looked at job advertisements in print and online media to determine skills that employers were seeking; other research interviewed or surveyed employers to determine employers' needs. Results were often conflicting as previously summarized in Litecky [1], Zwieg [2] and Huang [3]. Now web content data mining techniques allow for much greater sampling and specific analysis of current MIS (simply defined as Management oriented Information Systems types of skills) oriented job ads. In this approach over two million advertisements were filtered to over one half million U.S. job advertisements for MIS degree graduates from various job websites. Management-oriented IS skills were compiled in a thesaurus and then those skills were extracted from the selected job ads. These skills were compared to the job advertisements for subsequent analysis. Results suggest much more concordance between disparate job advertisements and survey-based research. These results reinforce much of the desired uniqueness of MIS curricula as compared to other computing degree curricula. Results herein are limited to U.S. and are also contrasted with the similar content and analysis of job skills in the Australian IS job market. In addition an analysis is performed on the cross disciplinary data on Enterprise System/SAP jobs which were not limited to MIS graduates.

Categories and Subject Descriptors

K.3.2 Computer and Information Science Education –Curriculum, K.6.1 Project and People Management – Staffing

General Terms

Management, Human Factors

Keywords

MIS, job skills, careers, job markets, SAP, enterprise systems

1. INTRODUCTION

Continuing turmoil in the U.S. and global economies implies considerable uncertainty for the job market as many organizations have continued to limit their hiring to specialists [4]. Faced with the possibility of limited hiring, it is even more important for MIS professionals, students, and academic curriculum planners to carefully consider the portfolio of skills required to fill these positions. A thorough enumeration of the skills in current job openings can help to tailor skill portfolios. Aasheim et al. [5] surveyed 600 IT managers and workers and found 49% were hired from job advertisements. Aasheim et al.'s results illustrate that job advertisements are crucial for both recruiting and job searches. Moreover, a new web site tracking service by the Conference Board publishes data on the number of job advertisements in the U.S. for ease in tracking economic conditions [6] further emphasizing the importance of job ads.

The purpose of this paper is to provide an analysis of the job skills required to fill MIS positions. Along with this purpose, the paper strives to shed further light on the controversies between soft and hard skills and continued application of unobtrusive measures methodologies. Simply stated, the hard skills, such as math and logic, are often assumed to underlie the technical skills. Often the terms technical and hard skills are synonymous. Job skills terms are especially important as applicant screening and tracking software are widely being used by employers to reduce the flood of applicants [7].

Persistently weak economic conditions mean that both organizations and professionals need to sharply focus their recruiting and job searches. As a result, there is increased competition among searchers and reduced distinctiveness between applicants. Organizations and computing professionals have many job search and recruitment tools at their disposal to connect available jobs to talent. These tools range from professional career placement services to job search websites such as Monster.com [8], CareerBuilder.com [9] , and SimplyHired.com [10]. Kennan et al. [11] studied these tools for the Australian job market and their research calls attention to the benefits of the unobtrusive nature of content analysis research based on web job ads. A similar discussion of IT jobs is embedded in Litecky et al. [12] which was written without knowledge of the Kennan et al. research. This article merges the concepts from Litecky et al. (2010) with the results of Kennan et al. [11] and adapts them to high demand job skills in the U.S.

As already mentioned, this paper reports the results of a study of the most highly demanded job skills in the MIS job market to include technical (hard), business and soft skills and contrasts those skills to the demand for more narrow technical skills previously reported for IT jobs as in Prabhakar et al. [13]. Also included in this study is ES (Enterprise Systems) job data for U.S. positions which is compared with the global shortages of SAP skills cited by Hawking [14].

The rationale for the focus on MIS (simply defined as management oriented IS) types of positions versus IT positions was a recognition that CIOs are "increasingly demanding business acumen as well as technical skills. [3]" Although, Huang et al. [3] concentrated on synthesizing job skills from academic studies, practitioner publications, and job ads, they only found Enterprise Systems (ES) skills specifically referenced in the practitioner literature. This paper hopes to remedy this situation by integrating ES jobs advertisements into the analysis of MIS and related positions. The urgency of this is given by an example from Prabhakar [15], where he states that at Proctor and Gamble, thousands of IS employees have been reduced to a few hundred and those jobs have migrated to the user areas. He also indicates that former IS functionality has been replaced with an interface to a set of skills such as in accounting and finance modules in SAP. Influenced by Prabhakar and others, a working assumption explored in this paper is that position requirements in Enterprise Systems, defined by Hawking [14] to include ERP, are currently much more cross-disciplinary than those of other IT or MIS positions [16, 17].

2. PRIOR RESEARCH ON MIS JOB SKILLS RELATED TO COMPUTER PERSONNEL

Prior research on IS job skills has offered conflicting findings. Some research has indicated more importance for soft skills while others have found more importance should be given to technical skills. Technical skills or hard skills are defined as "those skills acquired through training and education or learned on the job and are specific to each work setting," while soft skills are defined as "the cluster of personality traits, social graces, language skills, friendliness, and optimism that mark each one of us to varying degrees [18]". Others would also define the soft skills as being at least in part acquired through managerial or communications training. As for initial hiring, research using data gathered from job advertisements offers evidence that technical skills are predominantly required for IS positions [5]. Yet more traditional empirical research using data gathered from surveys on IS career development and job skills has offered conflicting evidence, often emphasizing the importance of soft skills.

A more analytical look at the conflicting evidence in prior career development and job skill research in IS can be obtained by classifying the research as normative, traditional empirical, unobtrusive empirical (position advertisement research) and other approaches, mainly practitioner opinion based. Alternatively, Lee et al. [19] offer alternative classifications of IS job skills. Herein, normative studies are characteristically aimed at producing authoritative pronouncements on IS career development and are generally issued under the aegis of academic and professional societies. Normative approaches are not included in this paper.

Traditional empirical studies are usually directed toward describing what exists in IS job skills related to career development. Traditional empirical studies contrast with normative studies in their emphasis on academic rigor and in their suggested implications from the findings. These studies do not issue pronouncements with the authoritative force of the normative studies. Unobtrusive empirical studies are similarly concerned with describing what exists in IS job skills and career development and use unobtrusive methods of data collection [20]. These methods were selected over interviews and survey as they require no effort from subjects who might not even be aware of the study [21]. The unobtrusive studies mainly use data gathered from position advertisements from newspapers, search engines or corporate websites. This means that these studies are using the counts in job advertisements of job skills as an indicator of the demand for that job skill. Unfortunately, this is an indirect measure and has the weakness of not directly validating expert opinion from actual interviews. For example, some job advertisements are written by human resources, rather than subject matter experts. Other approaches characteristically use less formal research methods and many of these are practitioner-oriented. As a summary of the prior research, Tables 1A and 1B are organized around the above research approaches, except most practitioner studies are not included.

Table 1A. Prior Studies Using Traditional Empirical Methods

Study	Empirical Approach	Source of Data	Type of Skills
Green [22]	Survey	System Analyst	Soft skills
Khan and Kukalis [23]	Survey	DPMA Members	Both, although soft skills deemed more important
Leitheiser [24]	Survey	IS Managers	Soft skills more important than hard skills
Trauth et al. [25] Lee et al. [26]	Focus Groups and Survey	IS Professionals and IS professors	Soft skills more important than hard skills
Cappel [27]	Survey	Recruiters	Hard skills more important than soft skills
Aasheim et al. [5]	Survey	IT managers and workers	Soft skills more important than hard skills
Gallagher et al. [28]	Interview	IT managers	Soft skills

Table 1B. Prior Studies Using Unobtrusive Measures

Study	Empirical Approach	Source of Data	Type of Skills
Athey and Plotnicki [29, 30]	Unobtrusive Measure	Newspaper want ads	Hard skills
Arnett and Litecky [31]	Unobtrusive Measure	Newspaper want ads	Hard skills
Litecky et al. [32, 33]	Unobtrusive Measure	Newspaper want ads	Hard skills
Prabhakar et al [34]	Unobtrusive Measure	Newspaper want ads	Hard skills
Todd et al. [35]	Meta-analysis Historical	Newspaper want ads	IS managers require soft skills; computer programmers need hard skills
Trower [36]	Unobtrusive Measure	Newspaper want ads	Hard skills
Prabhakar [13]	Unobtrusive Measure	Online Job boards	Hard skills
Webb [37]	Unobtrusive Measure	Internet job board	Balance of skills with IS development high
Kennan et al. [11]	Unobtrusive Measure	Online Job boards	Entry-level need balanced skills with IS development high
Lee et al. [38]	Unobtrusive Measure	Corporate websites	Hard skills slightly more important than soft skills for programmers
Huang et al. [3]	Meta-analysis	Academic literature, practitioner literature, job ads	Balance of skills
Litecky et al. [12]	Data Mining and Cluster Analysis	Online Job boards	Combinations of skills required for job definitions

2.1 Traditional Empirical Research on Job Skills

As shown in Table 1, under traditional empirical research, there was substantial activity. For a review of research prior to 2004, see Litecky [1]. This type of research has continued through the present. In 2009, Aasheim [5] et al. surveyed 600 IT managers and workers and found that soft skills were more important than hard skills. Similarly the findings of studies such as Gallagher et al. [28] and Zwieg [2] stressed the importance of interviewing IT managers to determine their opinion on the critical skills for long range career success. Practitioners are strongly influenced by long-range career success factors in their hiring decisions [1]. Nonetheless, the lack of agreement and less than universal adoption of the results of traditional empirical research on IS jobs

may lend credence to the MIS job skills data are described later in this paper.

2.2 Unobtrusive Measures-based Empirical Studies

Early research on position advertisements from 1982 to 2004 is also summarized in Litecky [1]. The research on these unobtrusive measures after 2004 started with a traditional study by Prabhakar et al. [13] with improved methodology for the scope of the data but with similar results showing the importance of hard skills as required for more technical IT jobs, not MIS jobs. About that time, the findings of studies such as Gallagher et al. [28] and Zwieg et al. [2] were published stressing the importance of interviewing IT managers to determine their opinion on the critical skills for IS hiring rather than the skills advertised in job ads. Often these interview based studies have results which stress the relative importance of non-technical skills over technical skills. In fact these contradictory findings have become known as a hard versus soft skills controversy. One researcher [39] even lamented that managers base their decision on soft skills but still mainly advertise requirements for hard skills. Previously but motivated by early versions of this controversy, Litecky et al. [1] drew upon Beach and Mitchell's image theory [40] to theorize a two-stage hiring process in which technical skills are evaluated first as filtration criteria and then typically communication and soft skills are evaluated in face to face interviews. This image theory work was further critiqued in Kennan et al. [11]. Yet based upon these studies and controversies, this study of job advertisements includes specific skills appropriate for management information systems and the results may bridge some of the controversy between results of interviews versus results of unobtrusive measures, such as job ads. Huang et al. [3] may be considered to have performed similar research, but their results may be dependent upon their meta-data sources.

This study is in contrast to that of Prabhakar et al. [13] which reported narrow technical skill requirements non-specialist IT jobs. Their findings were an indication of the technical skills in demand in the IT job market but not the MIS job market. At that time, the limited sampling methodology did not allow specific focus on MIS. The current research is based on a much more comprehensive sampling methodology using data mining and syntactical parsing which enables a focus on what skills are sought in the MIS job market. A classification scheme based on the skills advertised on the Internet during the study period was developed based upon much of the prior research cited in Table 1. These skills were further tuned from a taxonomy of Internet job advertisements from Monster.com in 1998 [13], and an earlier taxonomy by Trauth et al. [41].

In contrast to Webb [37] and Kennan et al. [11], this paper uses a thousand times more data than Webb and is not solely based on entry level jobs like Kennan et al. [11]. The larger database has the advantage of a finer focus on specific job skills in the MIS field. Also multiple sources from U.S. job sites were studied so that this paper covers the entire U.S. and spans multiple years. Consequently this study may be regarded as confirmatory research which partially replicates earlier research without some of the prior limitations. A smaller portion of the database used cluster analysis to define IT jobs [12] and is not repeated here. Finally the database is posted on the web for others to use [42].

3. DATA COLLECTION METHODOLOGY FOR MIS JOB SKILLS

A custom spider [12] crawled five large U.S. job web sites including Monster.com [8], CarrerBuilder.com [9], Dice.com [43], and SimplyHired.com [10]. . Only advertisements which specified computing program degrees, such as CS (Computer Science), MIS/CIS, and IT, were retained. During the study period of 2007-2011, more than 2.7 million computing job advertisements were collected from these sites. The data used in this program of research is believed to be representative of the U.S. advertisements for employees with computing program degrees due to the voluminous sources and the extent of the sample. The primary concern in this paper, however relates to the skills sought by employers of MIS graduates. Similar to Kennan et al.'s study of Australian job advertisements [11], and other traditional uses of data mining techniques, the advertisements specifically requesting MIS degrees, such as those specifying degrees in "MIS", "CIS", "Management Information Systems", "Management of Information Systems", or "Computer Information Systems", in the U.S. were extracted, restricting the sample size to approximately 640,000 job ads. Also after building a first pass thesaurus of job skills, our thesaurus included MIS technical, programming, business, and soft skills [12]. The thesaurus was further pared by only keeping skills which appeared in at least 2% of the ads. A complete list of the skills, their frequencies, and other data is available on the companion website [42].

This paper differs from Litecky et al. [12] since the objective in that research was to define specific IT jobs utilizing a statistical technique called cluster analysis. This paper segments the database into MIS jobs and then analyzes the frequency of job skills in MIS positions as contrasted to previous research on more general IT positions. There has been substantial discussion of the potential differences in MIS positions and except for the Kennan et al. [11] paper there has been little quantitative differentiation of MIS skills. The Kennan et al. [11] database of job advertisements contained only 400 entries. This study reviews more than a thousand times that amount for better evaluation of terms and an exhaustive representation of the large U.S. MIS job market.

4. SKILLS DEMANDED IN MIS JOB ADS

The skill in the MIS job advertisements were grouped into three broad categories: Business skills, Soft skills, and General Technical skills. Technical skills were further broken down into: Application development skills, Database management Skills, Programming skills, and System and Network Administration skills. These classifications are based on job definitions in Litecky, et al. [12]. Business skills included such items as strategy, project management, finance, accounting, marketing, etc. Soft skills included terms such as leadership, responsibility, communications, and initiative. General technical skills included security, programming, certification, and software development.

4.1 Business Skills

As shown in Table 2, Business skills, a wide range of business skills for MIS employees is sought. Skills which appeared in over five percent of advertisements are shown. All percentages in tables are the percent of advertisements which require that skill. The percentages add up to more than 100 due to multiple skills listed in advertisements. The most important of these skills, measured by frequency, is the Managing/Supervision skill. This skill was required in 48% of the advertisements (closely followed

asTable 2. Business skills for MIS

Skill	Percentage
Managing/Supervision	48%
Administration	29%
Quality	29%
Financial	28%
Analyst	25%
Project Management	23%
Customer Support	23%
Business Strategy	21%
Accounting	15%
Monitoring	13%
Troubleshooting	12%
Marketing	10%
Auditing	9%
Contracting and Legal	7%
Business Analyst	7%
Coordination	7%
Human Resources	7%
Workflow	5%
Calendar and Scheduling	5%

by Administrative and Quality). This high level of importance matches the skills identified by prior interview-based research [39] which expressed opinions voiced by industry leaders and is consistent with the emphasis placed on these skills for developing professional MIS personnel.

Financial skills were also of high importance and appeared in over 27% of ads. Perhaps the importance of this skill is prescient of or related, to the regulatory environment put into place in the early part of this decade and can be expected to continue in light of the current financial market turmoil that has highlighted the need for additional financial controls. With the breadth of its occurrence across a wide variety of job advertisements, inclusion of fundamental financial knowledge remains an important need for practitioners.

An additional set of skills had considerable importance including Business Strategy (21%), Accounting (15%) and Marketing (19%). These skills, along with financial skills, seems to re-iterate the need for MIS professionals to have a broad knowledge of fundamental business concepts. On the IS development and management side of the business skills, Analyst (25%) and Project Management (23%) were frequently required. Many more technically-oriented MIS professionals may not possess these skills and might consider retooling in these areas.

4.2 Soft Skills

Table 3. Soft skills for MIS practitioners

Skill	Percentage
Leadership	23%
Problem Solving Skills	19%
Written Communications	15%
Initiative/Motivation to Work	13%
Integrity/Honesty/Ethics	12%
Responsibility	12%
Innovation	7%
Judgment & Decision Making	7%
Mathematics	6%
Presentations	6%
Teamwork	5%
Learning	5%

As shown in Table 3, Soft Skills, 23% of the jobs demanded Leadership followed by Problem Solving, Written Communications, Initiative, Integrity/Honesty/Ethics, Responsibility, and Innovation. The overall demand for soft skills in these advertisements is significantly higher than in previous studies of more technical and perhaps more narrowly focused IT jobs [44] illustrating their particular importance in the MIS job market. When MIS managers are consulted in interview-based research studies, many of them have indicated the importance of such soft skills [39] even though it is often less frequently mentioned in research based on ads.

4.3 General Technical Skills

Table 4. General Technical skills

Skill	Percentage
Security	50%
Testing	30%
Certification	23%
Programming	22%
Office Applications	20%
Software Development	20%
Security Clearance	17%
Systems Analysis	13%
SDLC	11%
Backup & Recovery	10%
Software Testing	9%
Systems Integration	9%
Software Engineering	9%
Statistical analysis software	8%
ERP Software	8%
Enterprise Resource Planning	7%
Customer Relationship Management	7%
Graphic Software	7%
Object Oriented Programming	7%
GPS/GIS/Survey software	6%
CASE Tools	5%

Table 4, General Technical Skills, illustrates general technical skills mentioned in at least five percent of the ads. Within this category, Security (50%) is the most frequent skill specified in the job ads. An important factor in the general technical skills is security knowledge and traditional software development. An interesting note is that although there is a significant emphasis in software development techniques and skills, the specific software development languages (other than SQL and HTML) are not nearly as important for MIS personnel and are not very frequent compared to the other skills required. This may indicate less demand on MIS personnel for traditional programming roles. With relatively high frequencies within this category for Web-oriented skills (e.g., HTML), it seems that many employers expect MIS personnel to be able to perform some website development or maintenance. The frequency of requirements for general security skills seems to indicate increasing requirements for security-related knowledge across all functional areas of MIS. Programming is itself less frequently required. Previous research has generally shown programming skills to be the most important of all technical skills among IT jobs [13]. Yet here, with interest restricted to MIS jobs, there is less demand for specific programming skills. Surprisingly, Office Applications are demanded only slightly less frequently than general references to programming which implies that this is a prerequisite skill for

many MIS personnel. Although individually ranking low, together the ERP (Enterprise Resource Planning) Software which includes specific brands of ERP Software and general Enterprise Resource Planning along with Customer Relationship Management are apparently of considerable importance to many employers.

As shown in Table 4, many MIS professionals already have an inventory of skills in these general areas yet the demand for certification illustrates the need to document those skills. Vendors of industry certifications from not-for-profit organizations such as the Institute for Certification of Computer Professionals are all good investments in documentation of skills. In some areas such as Security, industry certification may be required to hold or continue in a position. For example, although only about 23% of the job advertisements mentioned certification, almost 50% of the job advertisements which required security also required certification. Thus, MIS professionals in areas such as Security should consider getting the requisite certifications in order to boost value to their current and future employability. Enterprise Systems are also important not only for MIS but allied disciplines as shown in the next section.

4.4 Enterprise Systems

Table 5. ERP/SAP skills Demanded in Business Disciplines - Chicago

Discipline	Total Number of Job ads	Percentage Requiring SAP
Accounting	8,940	10%
Finance	28,510	8%
Marketing	18,000	3%
MIS Information Systems	705 21,320	8% 11%
Production and Operations Management	11,813	10%

Table 5 shows a small sample of SAP openings restricted to Chicago for selected business disciplines from SimplyHired.com. This data were collected separately from the database discussed previously. Time requirements did not allow wider sampling. The main database showed only a moderate percentage of jobs requiring ERP (See Table 4). Since this result was unexpected, a closer examination was necessary to look more widely than MIS for positions using ES. Previously, Kennan et al.'s survey of entry-level positions [11] showed similarly low levels of frequency of job advertisements for ERP skills which ranked only 16th of 17 suggesting that ERP skills were more appropriate for more experienced professionals. Another possibility is that ES and especially SAP the dominant brand of enterprise systems [45] are actually more demanded by other disciplines than MIS such as Accounting, Operations Management and even Marketing. Of the enterprise-level software packages, Customer Relationship Management (CRM), Enterprise Resource Planning (ERP), and Geographic Information Systems (GIS) software are also important to many organizations. For example, Prabhakar calls attention to the change in personnel using and supporting ESs and that this makes capturing MIS positions in this area of ES more difficult [15].

From Table 5, it can be seen that many fields or disciplines are involved in enterprise systems such as SAP. For example, accounting has as large a requirement as the average MIS requirement, indicating that enterprise systems should be of concern to most business oriented professionals and aspiring entrants. Moreover since this table was generated from SimplyHired.com, the table includes corporate job sites representing a large total of over 5 million job ads. This ameliorates the criticism that online job boards solely focus on small organizations and are ignored by large organizations (Lee et al. 2008).

The percentages in Table 5 are not high, and yet Hannon [46] states that SAP skills are among the most difficult jobs skills to find. Also, the Robert Half [47] survey of 1,600 North American CIO's reported 37% of the CIO's were seeking employees with ES skills of ERP and Business Intelligence. As per Lee and Mirchandani's [48] study and survey of 70 IS managers, the importance of ERP skills is expected to increase in the next five years. Even as early as 2002, pundits theorized ERP jobs were difficult to fill due to the unique combination of technical, business and interpersonal skills required for ES [49].

Despite the demand for difficult to fill ES jobs, MIS collegiate enrollments are declining [50]. This is an opportunity for business programs to provide students with the needed skills to enter the workforce. In our view, teaching ES skills in the framework of business courses will result in better prepared students to fill the positions needed by organizations.

4.5 Application Development – Programming

Table 6. Programming Language and Scripting skills

Skill	Percentage
SQL	27%
HTML/XHTML/DHTML	19%
Java/J2EE/J2P	15%
C/C+	10%
XML	10%
.Net	9%
Visual Basic	9%
ASP	7%
JavaScript	7%
C#	7%

As shown in Table 6, Programming Language Skills, the frequency of demand of specific functional, object-oriented, or procedural programming language skills for MIS personnel is not very high compared to the other skills discussed. This may indicate less demand for MIS personnel for traditional programming roles. With relatively high frequencies within this category for Web-oriented skills (e.g., HTML), it seems that many employers expect MIS personnel to be able to perform some website development or maintenance.

A high frequency requirement for SQL (Structured Query Language) in Table 6 indicates the high relative importance of database work by MIS personnel. Of the functional and object-oriented application development languages, Java is only moderately mentioned. This is in stark contrast to the high importance of programming language skills required for general IT positions [13]. This difference seems to indicate less need for in-depth application development by MIS personnel, but rather a need for a fundamental understanding of programming concepts. Many other programming skills were advertised at relatively low levels, indicating that even relatively scarce programmer skills exist in niche job markets but without any overriding clear

favorite. Yet Kennen et al.'s [11] results for 400 personnel at entry level to three year out job advertisements showed a surprisingly high demand for programming skills, ranking third in specific sub-categories of IS development. They suggested that their results were due to limiting their data to entry level jobs. The current study did not make that limitation so MIS professionals and student aspirants should be aware of these frequency differences and should avoid being type-cast as having a single type of proficiency in order to maintain reasonable levels of marketablility.

4.6 Database Management Skills

Table 7. Database skills

Skill	Percentage
SQL	27%
Oracle Databases	18%
Generic Databases	15%
Microsoft Databases	14%
Database Administration	8%
Database Design Software	6%
Data Warehousing	5%
Data Modeling	3%
IBM Databases	3%
Unified Modeling Language	3%
Database Reporting	3%
Open-Source Databases	2%
Database Programming	2%

In Table 7: Database skills, SQL skills are also the most frequently mentioned and have already been discussed in the context of programming skills, but yet it should be noted this skill's level of demand has increased by a solid ten percent during this research period. Among the vendors, skill with Oracle is still in a commanding level of demand. Generic databases simply represent the term without a vendor indicating a general skill being demanded without specifying a particular brand of database product. Demand for Microsoft databases has increased and is at about three-fourths of that for Oracle. The term "database administrator" or "database administration" without mention of a vendor occurred in almost 8% of the MIS ads. IBM database skills are only at about three percent and are even outscored by data warehousing, database design and data modeling ads. Open-source databases were mentioned in only about two percent of the job advertisements perhaps showing a lack of adoption by enterprises. MySQL is included in the open source databases skill indicating another database that is frequently claimed to have a high level of popularity but apparently not with employers of MIS personnel as it occurred in less than two percent of the advertisements and thus is not included in the figure. The implications for MIS professionals and students are fairly clear: competency is needed in SQL and Oracle along with some level of generic and Microsoft database skills combined with knowledge of database administration.

4.7 System Administration Skills

In Table 8: Network and Systems Administration skills, demand for Microsoft operating systems skills is shown with a commanding lead in frequency over any other OS. UNIX operating systems are shown as much lower at about 14%. Open-Source operating systems (e.g., Linux) occurred slightly less frequently than UNIX but are in more demand that Sun or IBM's specific versions of UNIX. Consequently, experience with both

Table 8. Network and System Administration skills

Skill	Percentage
Microsoft Operating Systems	22%
UNIX Operating Systems	14%
Operating Systems	11%
Voice/Data Telecom	10%
Computer Servers	10%
System Administration	9%
Open-Source OSS	9%
Network Administration	9%
Network Security Software	8%
Web Servers	7%
Network Admin Software	6%
Sun Operating Systems	6%
Helpdesk or Call Center	6%
Cisco	5%
TCP/IP	5%
Web Application Server	5%
Network Hardware	4%
Wireless	4%

Microsoft and UNIX-based operating systems is an important skill set for MIS professionals to possess. Specific networking technologies, however, are less important in the job market, though not insignificant. MIS personnel need at least familiarity if not some capability of supporting other personnel in this area.

5. LIMITATIONS AND CONCLUSIONS

A limitation of this paper is that results of the data mining process may be significantly influenced by the *a priori* terms selected by the researchers. It could be said that since soft skill terms were added to the thesaurus, these skills were going to be reported and the skills are not rigorously defined. They are simply adopted from the job ads and the usage in those organizations. This particular bias of the researchers affected the study results, but this is a limitation of data mining research based upon a thesaurus. Unequivocally, the soft skills are important and different from previous results gathered on technically oriented IT, rather than MIS, job skills research.

The filtration process selected computing jobs for analysis only if the position required a computing type of degree. There may be some computing jobs that were not selected because a degree was not specifically required. Similarly, some MIS positions may not be included as those advertisements did not specify an MIS college degree. In addition, the accuracy of filtration was not separately checked by human judges due to time constraints. Jobs posted on multiple sites may be duplicated if a unique identifier was not included in the ad to exclude the duplicate entry. The ES postings were analyzed separately from the initial database. These listings were not subject to filtration by college degree. Despite these limitations, due to the high volume of job advertisements analyzed, the study is presumed to present the most comprehensive analysis of market demanded skills in MIS currently available.

The use of online job boards has allowed employers to fully list all of the skill requirements for a position, including soft skills. Previous methods, such as newspaper ads, had limitations on the skills listed due to space restrictions. The elimination of this restriction provides an opportunity in this study for a more complete analysis of the skills requested by organizations.

In general these results support educational curricula design and both labor market searches of employers' advertisements along with survey research of employers. Educators can use these results as an aid in developing curricula better attuned to the MIS labor market. Similarly students and displaced IT workers can use the data as an aid in making their choices of strategies to fit labor market demands. Employers might use this data to compare their companies' inventory of job skills to those demanded and popular in the labor market.

The skills needed by organizations are continually changing as the technology available evolves. The intrusion of systems such as ES and ERP into the field has been drastically changing the composition of the information technology workforce. Many of the information technology workforce is now no longer in the IS discipline but is in functional areas, such as Accounting, Finance, and POM (Production Operations Management). The emergence of ES and associated non-MIS workers replacing IS workers has been unprecedented and un-acknowledged in the job skills research, perhaps more than the wave of outsourcing and offshoring. ES shows up as only a small part of the spectrum of IS skills because much of the ES work is performed by others. However, it is unclear what portion of these positions requires SAP skills as an end-user, rather than as an MIS analyst. Further research on this movement of jobs due to the implementation of ES is needed. This may be the first job skills paper to acknowledge this drastic change which more than any other factor, might account for the continued dearth of IS collegiate enrollment. In the main, ES are not positive factors for IS enrollments; however ES can be used to increase MIS enrollment. For example, Case [51] discusses how at least one university was able to triple the IS enrollments by integrating SAP into their MIS curriculum.

The triple threat of outsourcing, adoption of ES and a bad economy needs strong measures to avoid the short-sighted dissolution of IS programs and departments. The results of this study indicate a stronger emphasis on ES and soft skills in our collegiate IS programs may be the answer.

6. ACKNOWLEDGMENTS
Our thanks to SIGMIS and the anonymous reviewers.

7. REFERENCES

[1] Litecky, C., Arnett, K. P. and Prabhakar, B. 2004. The Paradox of Soft Skills Versus Technical Skills in IS Hiring. *Journal of Computer Information Systems*, (45:1), 69-76.

[2] Zwieg, P., Kaiser, K., Beath, C. M., Bullen, C., Gallagher, K. P., Goles, T., Howland, J., Simon, J. C., Abbott, P., Abraham, T., Carmel, E., Evaristo, R., Hawk, S., Lacity, M., Gallivan, M., Kelly, S., Mooney, J. G., Rangathan, C., Rottman, J. W., Ryan, T. and Wion, R. 2006. The Information Technology Workforce: Trends and Implications 2005-2008. *MIS Quarterly Executive*, (5:2), 101-108.

[3] Huang, H., Kvasny, L., Joshi, K. D., Trauth, E. M. and Mahar, J. 2009 Synthesizing IT job skills identified in academic studies, practitioner publications and job ads. In *Proceedings of the The 47th annual conference on Computer personnel research - SIGMIS-CPR '09* (Limerick, Ireland, 2009). ACM Press, 121-129.

[4] Beer, S. 2010 IT Salaries to Rise as CRM, CMS, and ERP skills shortages loom. IT Wire.

http://www.itwire.com/it-people-news/recruitment/40982-it-salaries-to-rise-as-crm-cms-and-erp-skills-shortages-loom Accessed on 17 September 2011.

[5]   Aasheim, C. L., Lixin, L. and Williams, S. 2009. Knowledge and Skill Requirements for Entry-Level Information Technology Workers: A Comparison of Industry and Academia. *Journal of Information Systems Education*, (20:3), 349-356.

[6]   The Conference Board 2011 Help Wanted Online. *http://www.conference-board.org/data/helpwantedonline.cfm* Accessed on 10/7/2011.

[7]   Weber, L. 2012. Career Jounal: Your Resume vs. Oblivion - - Inundated Companies Resort to Software to Sift Job Applications for Right Skills. *Wall Street Journal*, 24 January 2012.

[8]   Monster.com Monster Job website. *www.monster.com* Accessed on 17 September 2011.

[9]   CareerBuilder.com 2011 Career Builder Job site. *http://www.careerbuilder.com/default.aspx?cbRecursionCnt=1* Accessed on 17 September 2011.

[10] SimplyHired.com 2011 SimplyHired Job site. *http://www.simplyhired.com/* Accessed on 17 September 2011.

[11] Kennan, M. A., Willard, P., Cecez-Kecmanovic, D. and Wilson, C. S. 2008. IS Knowledge and Skills Sought by Employers: A Content Analysis of Australian IS Early Career Online Job Advertisements. *The Australasian Journal of Information Systems*, (15:2), 1-22.

[12] Litecky, C., Aken, A., Ahmad, A. and Nelson, J. 2010. Mining for Computing Jobs. *IEEE Software*, (27:1), 78-85.

[13] Prabhakar, B., Litecky, C. and Arnett, K. P. 2005. IT skills in a tough job market. *Communications of the ACM*, (48:10), 91-94.

[14] Hawking, P. 2010 The Dilemma Of Addressing SAP Skills Shortages In Developing Countries. In *Proceedings of the Proceeding of the Sixteenth Americas Conference on Information Systems* (Lima, Peru, 2010), 1-7.

[15] Prabhakar, B. *Interview at SAP Curriculum Conference.* City, 2011.

[16] Hawking, P., McCarthy, B. and Stein, A. 2004. Second wave ERP education. *Journal of Information Systems Education*, (15:3), 327-332.

[17] Boyle, T. A. and Strong, S. E. 2006. Skill requirements of ERP graduates. *Journal of Information Systems Education*, (17:4), 403-412.

[18] Tech Directors. 2003. Career Directions, (10), 22-23.

[19] Lee, S., Yen, D., Havelka, D. and Koh, S. 2001. Evolution of IS Professionals' Competency: An Exploratory Study. *Journal of Computer Information Systems*, (41:4), 21-31.

[20] Babbie, E. R. 2001 *Survey Research Methods.* Wadsworth/Thompson Learning, Belmont, CA.

[21] Marshall, C. and Rossman, G. B. 2006 *Designing qualitative research*. Sage Publications, Thousands Oaks, Calif.

[22] Green, G. I. 1989. Perceived Importance of Systems Analysts' Job Skills, Roles, and Non-Salary Incentives. *MIS Quarterly*, (13:2), 115-133.

[23] Khan, M. and Kukalis, S. 1990. MIS professionals: Education and performance. *Information & Management*, (19:4), 249-255.

[24] Leitheiser, R. L. 1992. MIS Skills for the 1990's: A Survey of MIS Managers' Perceptions. *Journal of Management Information Systems*, (9:1), 69-92.

[25] Trauth, E. M., Farwell, D. W. and Lee, D. 1993. The IS expectation gap: Industry expectations versus academic preparation. *MIS Quarterly*, (17:3), 293-307.

[26] Lee, D. M. S., Trauth, E. M. and Farwell, D. 1995. Critical Skills and Knowledge Requiremnts of IS Professionals: A Joint Academic/Industry Investigation. *MIS Quarterly*, (19:3), 313-340.

[27] Cappel, J. J. 2001. Entry-Level IS Job Skills: A Survey of Employers. *Journal of Computer Information Systems*, (42:2), 76-83.

[28] Gallagher, K. P., Kaiser, K. M., Simon, J. C., Beath, C. M. and Goles, T. 2010. The Requisite Variety of Skills for IT Professionals. *Communications of the ACM*, (53:6), 144-148.

[29] Athey, S. and Plotnicki, J. 1992. A Comparison of Information System Job Requirements in Major Metropolitan Areas. *Interface: The Computer Education Quarterly*, (13:4), 47-53.

[30] Athey, S. and Plotnicki, J. 1998. The evaluation of job opportunities for IT professionals. *Journal of Computer Information Systems*, (38:1), 71-88.

[31] Arnett, K. P. and Litecky, C. R. 1994. Career path development for the most wanted skills in the job market. *Journal of Systems Management*, (45:2), 7-10.

[32] Litecky, C., Arnett, K. P. and Prabhakar, B. 1995 The Educational Implications of Job Market Trends for IS Personnel: A Look at 1992-1995. In *Proceedings of the Proceedings of the 27th Annual Conference of the Decision Sciences Institute* (Boston, MA, November 1995, 1995),

[33] Litecky, C., Prabhakar, B. and Arnett, K. P. 1996. The IS Job Market: Shaken, but not Stirred. *Journal of Systems Management,*, (July/August), 50-54.

[34] Prabhakar, B., Litecky, C. and Arnett, K. P. 1995. Boom Times Ahead! The MIS job market is up, way up! Do you have the skills in demand? *Journal of Systems Management*, (46), 24-24.

[35] Todd, P. A., McKeen, J. D. and Gallupe, R. B. 1995. The evolution of IS job skills: a content analysis of IS job advertisements from 1970 to 1990. *MIS Quarterly*, (19:1), 1-27.

[36] Trower, J. K. 1995 The Impact of Job Skills Requirements on I.S. Curricula. In *Proceedings of the Proceedings of the First Americas Conference on Informaiton Systems* (Pittsburgh, PA, 1995), 597-599.

[37] Webb, G. K. 2006. The market for IS and MIS Skills and Knowledge: Analysis of On-Line Job Postings. *Issues in Information Systems*, (VII:1), 253-258.

[38] Lee, C. K. and Han, H. 2008. Analysis of skills requirement for entry-level programmer/analysts in Fortune 500 corporations. *Journal of Information Systems Education*, (19:1), 17-27.

[39] Goles, T., Hawk, S. and Kaiser, K. M. 2008. Information technology workforce skills: The software and IT services

provider perspective. *Information Systems Frontiers*, (10:2), 179-194.

[40] Beach, L. R. and Mitchell, T. R. *Image Theory, The Unifying Perspective*. Lawrence Erlbaum Associates, City, 1996.

[41] Trauth, E. M. 2003. Cases on global IT applications and management: Successes and pitfalls. *Inf. Soc.*, (19:1), 107-108.

[42] Aken, A. 2011 The Degree-Oriented Guide to Skills in Information Technology. *http://www.dogs-it.org/data/freqs/* Accessed on 17 September 2011.

[43] Dice.com 2011 Dice.com website. Accessed on 17 September 2011.

[44] Litecky, C., Prabhakar, B. and Arnett, K. P. 2006 The IT/IS job market. In *Proceedings of the Proceedings of the 2006 ACM SIGMIS CPR conference on Computer Personnel Research* (Claremont, CA, 2006/04//, 2006). ACM Press, 50-52.

[45] Magal, S. R. and Word, J. 2012 *Integrated Business Processes with ERP Systems*. John Wiley & Sons, Inc, Hoboken.

[46] Hannon, D. 2010 Project Expert - ERP, SAP Skills Remain Hot. *http://www.projectexpertonline.com/article.cfm?id=5495* Accessed on 17 September 2011.

[47] Robert Half Technology 2011 *2012 Salary Guide*. Robert Half.

[48] [Lee, K. and Mirchandani, D. 2009 Analyzing the dynamics of skill sets for the U.S. information systems workforceusing latent growth curve modeling. In *Proceedings of the Proceedings of the special interest group on management information system's 47th annual conference on Computer personnel research - SIGMIS-CPR '09* (New York, New York, USA, 2009). ACM Press, 113-120.

[49] Myerson, J. M. 2002 *Enterprise System Integration*. CRC Press.

[50] Ferratt, T. W., Hall, S. R., Prasad, J. and Wynn Jr, D. 2010. Choosing Management Information Systems as a Major: Understanding the smiFactors for MIS. *Communications of the Association for Information Systems*, (27:1), 265-284.

[51] Case, T. 2011 Public relations and promoting your SAP initiative. In *Proceedings of the SAP Curriculum Congress* (Monterrey, CA, March 2011, 2011),

Developing a Survey to Identify IT Consultant Skills for Incorporating in the IS Curriculum

Diane Lending
James Madison University
Computer Information Systems
Harrisonburg, VA 22807
1-540-568-3480

lendindc@jmu.edu

Thomas W. Dillon
James Madison University
Computer Information Systems
Harrisonburg, VA 22807
1-540-568-3015

dillontw@jmu.edu

ABSTRACT

In this paper, we describe the research questions and methodology for a research project investigating excellent performance in Information Technology consulting, both technical and behavioral attributes. Exploratory qualitative data will be gathered using a multi-city focus group and interviews with IT consultants. Based upon the exploratory data and the IS skills literature, a survey will also be created, validated, and conducted for a large consulting population. In our analysis, we will compare the skills of IT consultants with other IT professionals. We will recommend how IS curriculum should be structured to fill these needs. At the time of the conference, we will be able to report on the qualitative data based upon the focus groups and interviews. We will also share our validated survey.

Categories and Subject Descriptors

K.3.2 [**Computers and Education**]: Computer and Information Science Education – *Curriculum, Information systems education* K.6.1 [**Management of Computing and Information Systems**]: People and Project Management – *Staffing* K.7.1 [**The Computing Profession**]: Occupations

General Terms

Management

Keywords

Job skills, Consultant skills, IS Curriculum, Survey Development.

1. INTRODUCTION

Over the last twenty years the Information Technology (IT) field has migrated from the use of internal employees to the extensive use of external consultants. With this migration, the attributes (i.e. the technical and behavioral skill sets) for a successful Information Systems (IS) graduate have changed. The IT consultant needs to have strong communication and functional skills on top of their technical skills [6].

At our university which is located in the Mid-Atlantic part of the United States, our graduating IS students tend to be hired by consulting companies rather than for in house IT jobs. In particular, almost all of our best graduates are hired by consulting companies. When we ask people from these companies why they hire our students they talk about graduates having skills in talking to clients, working well in groups, and understanding business functions. When pushed, they acknowledge that they take for granted the excellent technical skills that the students have learned in our program. However, our IS curriculum focuses on the technical skills with courses in programming, database, IT architecture, and telecommunications. Does our IS curriculum serve these companies well? What changes should be made to the curriculum to serve our hiring audience? And will these changes also serve the companies that hire for in house IT jobs?

In our research, we will compare and contrast IT consultant attributes with other IT professionals (technical skills, behavioral skills, entering the work force skills and established professional skills). We will study behavioral variables such as the identification of "top performers," the attributes and attitudes of excellent performance, ethical principles, and the practical implications for career socialization, management, and decision making.

2. PRIOR RESEARCH

In both the research and practitioner literature in IT, the importance of technical and "soft" behavioral skills to career success are a commonly addressed issue. Huang et al. [5] conducted a meta-analysis of the skills identified in academic research, practitioner publications, and job advertisements. They grouped IT skills into three categories: technical, business (e.g., business function knowledge and problem-solving skills), and humanistic skills (e.g, teamwork, leadership and communications skills). They found that the academic research tended to focus on all three areas but humanistic skills were the least frequently cited. The importance of the softer skills is occasionally shortchanged in academic research, for example, they are lumped into a single measure called "project management and other relevant business skills" in Lee & Mirchandani [10]. Other researchers recognize the importance of the softer skills and focus on them, e.g., Purao & Suen [11]. For example, Lee et al. [8] identified knowledge of human relations as a critical skill to be covered in the IS curriculum. In summary, the academic research over the years includes all three sets of skills.

Much of the research in this area addressed the relative importance of various skills and how they are incorporated into the hiring or performance process. Other research identifies the relative importance in career advancement (e.g., Bassellier, et al.,

[1] which identifies the skills needed by IS managers or Lee [9] which looks at skill transferability as one advances in an IT career.)

Huang et al. [5] indicated that practitioner publications focus on a rich set of technical skills but do not emphasize business and humanistic skills. Job skills in recent job advertisements did focus on all three sets of skills [5]. This was not necessarily true in earlier IS job advertisements, for example Gallivan, et al. [4] found that job advertisements between 1988 and 2003 focused on technical skills, and Todd, et al. [13] found similar results between 1970 and 1990.

There is not much academic research on IT consulting skills specifically. Joshi, et al. [6] looked at what it meant to be an excellent IT consultant which they associate with being a top performer in an IT role. They found that all stakeholders found it of high importance that an entry-level top-performer have the ability to deliver, be committed, be cooperative, and be analytical. Some of their raters also found it to be high importance that this entry-level person be a quick learner and be able to manage relationships. Most academic research includes IT consulting as one of many possible jobs and does not investigate whether there are differences in needs for that job specifically. We plan to fill that gap.

Typically, the hard technology skills are the topics of the IS curriculum with courses designed to produce them. Soft skills such as problem solving, critical and creative thinking, oral and written communications, and team skills should be taught in all IS courses [2]. Students in a consulting class suggested that negotiating skills, communications skills, and teamwork were critical [7]. From a practitioner's perspective, customer communication, relationship management, and issue resolution skills were stressed [3].

3. RESEARCH METHODOLOGY

3.1 Qualitative Study
In January and February 2012, we plan to hold focus group sessions with consultants in some of the largest and most successful consulting companies in New York, Philadelphia and Washington D.C. We will also interview senior officials at consulting firms in Northern Virginia and the North East Corridor of the Mid-Atlantic States (Maryland, Pennsylvania, New Jersey, & New York). The focus of the qualitative research will be on IT consultant attributes such as technical skills, behavioral skills, entering the work force skills and established professional skills. The behavioral skills that we will ask about will include the identification of "top performers," the attributes and attitudes of excellent performance, ethical principles, and the practical implications for socialization in the firm and profession, management, and decision making.

3.2 Survey Design
Based upon the focus groups and interviews, we will design a survey instrument to measure the importance of each of these skills in the IT consulting profession. Based upon Straub [12], we will validate the instrument. The steps we follow will be to use already validated measures where possible from the IT skills literature. Where not possible, we will create our own measures. These measures will be validated through structured interviews with IT Consultants. We will pilot test the survey and perform

reliability and validity tests using Cronbach's alphas and factor analysis. We anticipate that this pilot test will occur in late spring 2012.

3.3 Quantitative Study
The fully validated survey will be sent to IT consultants and to workers in other types of companies. The survey will be a web-based survey using Qualtrics. We plan to analyze the two populations and check for differences between the skills wanted for a recent graduate. Based upon the quantitative and qualitative analysis, we will recommend an IS curriculum that provides IT consulting skills.

4. CONFERENCE PRESENTATION
We plan to present our research plan in more detail at the 2012 SIGMIS CPR conference. At the time of the conference, we will have conducted the focus groups and interviews, developed the survey, and field-tested the survey. We will share the qualitative results with the conference attendees and the survey. Any preliminary quantitative results will also be presented.

5. REFERENCES
[1] Bassellier, G., Reich, B. H. and Benbasat, I. (2001) "Information Technology Competence of Business Managers: A Definition and Research Model," *Journal of Management Information Systems*, 17(4), pp. 159–182.

[2] Downey, J.P., McMurtrey, M.E., and Zeltmann, S.M. (2008) "Mapping the MIS Curriculum Based on Critical Skills of New Graduates: An Empirical Examination of IT Professionals," *Journal of Information Systems Education*, 19(3), pp. 351-363.

[3] Djavanshir G.R. and Agresti, W.W. (2007), "IT Consulting: Communication Skills are Key," *IT Professional Magazine*, 9(1), pp. 46-50.

[4] Gallivan, M. J., Truex, D. P. and Kvasny, L. (2004) "Changing Patterns in IT Skill Sets 1988–2003: A Content Analysis of Classified Advertising," *Databases for Advances in Information Systems*, 35(3), pp. 64–87.

[5] Huang, H., Kvasny, L., Joshi, K. D., Trauth, E., and Mahar, J. (2009) "Synthesizing IT Job Skills Identified in Academic Studies, Practitioner Publications and Job Ads," *Proceedings of SIGMIS CPR 09, May 28-30, 2009, Limerick, Ireland*, pp. 121-127.

[6] Joshi, K. D., Kuhn, K.M. and Niederman, F. (2010) "Excellence in IT Consulting: Integrating Multiple Stakeholders' Perceptions of Top Performers," *IEEE Transactions on Engineering Management*, 57(4), pp. 589-606.

[7] Komarjaya, J., Huifang, L, and Bock, G.-W. (2004). "Consulting from students' perspective," *Consulting to Management*, 15(2), pp. 29-33.

[8] Lee, D., Trauth, E. and Farwell, D. (1995) "Critical skills and knowledge requirements of IS Professionals: A joint academic and industry investigation", *MIS Quarterly*, 19(3), pp. 313–338.

[9] Lee C. K. (2005). "Transferability of skills over the IT Career Path," *Proceedings of SIGMIS CPR 05, April 14-16, 2004, Atlanta, Georgia*, pp. 85-93.

[10] Lee, K. and Mirchandani, D. (2009). "Analyzing the dynamics of skill sets for the U.S. information systems work force using latent growth curve modeling," *Proceedings of SIGMIS CPR 09, May 28-30, 2009, Limerick Ireland*, pp. 113-120.

[11] Purao, S. and Suen H. (2010) "Designing a Multi-Faceted Metric to Evaluate Soft Skills," *Proceedings of SIGMIS CPR 10, May 20-22, 2010, Vancouver, BC, Canada*, pp. 88-90.

[12] Straub, D.W. (1989) "Validating Instruments in MIS Research," *MIS Quarterly,* 13(2), pp. 147-169

[13] Todd, P.A., McKeen, J.D. and Gallupe, R.B. (1995) "The evolution of IS job skills: a content analysis of IS job advertisements from 1970 to 1990," *MIS Quarterly*, 19(1), pp. 1-26.

What Should I Understand?

The Concept of Shift of Understanding, a Quote-Based Analysis

Gaëtan Mourmant
HuManiS (EA 1347)
Humans and Management in Society
École de Management Strasbourg
Université de Strasbourg
Bureau PE9- Bâtiment B.
61, avenue de la Forêt-Noire
f-67085 Strasbourg Cedex
Tel. : +1 604 781 9698
Gmourmant@gmail.com

Katerina Voutsina

National Technical University of Athens
School of Applied Mathematical and Physical Sciences
Polytechneioupolis
GR 157 80 Zografou, Athens, Greece

Tel.: +30-210-772 1869

Voutsina@central.ntua.gr

ABSTRACT

In this paper, we address an under-investigated thematic area of Information Technology (IT) personnel turnover literature: IT Entrepreneurial Turnover. Following a Grounded Theory Methodological approach, we introduce the following concept: 'Shift of Understanding' (SoU). We develop this concept through the analysis of 57 interviews, completed by the analysis of over 200 famous quotes from authors/entrepreneurs. A SoU occurred after a shock, an entrepreneurial event or when a gradual evolution of a condition (e.g. accumulation of information or experience which at some point turns into knowledge) has come to its completion phase. In such cases, the inertia governing human behavior is interrupted and the individual perceives things under a new lens: a shift of understanding has just happened. A newly formed desire towards entrepreneurship, the realization of the urgency and immediacy of action, the reconsideration of both pragmatic and existential concerns such as the risk reduction, the capability to seize opportunities, or the meaning of life in general, the re-evaluation of one's prospects, propensities and needs are some of the manifestations of SoU which are found to be directly or indirectly linked to the actual IT entrepreneurial turnover behavior.

Categories and Subject Descriptors

K.7.1 Occupations

General Terms

Management, Human Factors, Theory

Keywords

Turnover, IT Entrepreneurial Turnover, Shock, entrepreneurial event, cognition.

1. INTRODUCTION

Understanding the circumstances under which an Information Technology (IT) employee decides to leave salaried employment in order to start his or her own venture is a critical issue for IT managers, future IT entrepreneurs and policy makers. For IT and non-IT companies, retaining IT employees may prove to be a source of competitive advantage [1], while for policy-makers, the nurturing of entrepreneurship is considered a source of technological innovation and economic development [2 , 3, 4]. Future IT entrepreneurs can also benefit from this topic by becoming more aware of the potential and risks embedded in the IT Entrepreneurial Turnover process.

Although much research has been conducted on the circumstances that explain IT turnover [5-9] and the fostering of entrepreneurship [10-13], research on IT Entrepreneurial Turnover has been rather disjointed (i.e. few cross-citations). Apart from a few exceptions [14, 15], current research treats the issue of IT turnover and IT entrepreneurship as two distinct research agendas. The paper builds upon the research tradition which brings the two research streams together, and aims at deepening our understanding of the circumstances that support IT Entrepreneurial Turnover.

Initially our research question focused on the exploration of the conditions and mechanisms which explain "how and why an IT employee decides to quit her job and start a business". Yet, adopting a Glaserian Grounded Theory Methodology (GTM), the research question displays a dynamic process- it is expected to evolve overtime. More specifically, the understanding of IT Entrepreneurial Turnover process is deepened by exploring a new emerging conceptual category: 'Shift of Understanding' (SoU). To do that we present the concept of SoU -The notion of SoU refers to a change in the individual's perception about the context within which he/she lives and works, the meaning of life, his/her personal image and lifestyle. In addition, SoU is linked with various types of disrupting events which precede it. The contribution of the paper lies in changing the focus of studying *intention* to "quit and start a new business" to the actual IT Entrepreneurial Turnover behavior, through the study of real-life *contingencies* which are directly or indirectly involved in the actual IT Entrepreneurial behavior. Awareness of these contingencies can be of great interest to all stakeholders, -IT managers, future IT entrepreneurs and policy makers- who may anticipate certain benefits or threats related to the IT entrepreneurial turnover behavior.

The paper is structured as follows. First, we review the literature on entrepreneurship, IT turnover and shock/entrepreneurial event. We then introduce the theoretical construct of 'shift of understanding'; and analyze its constituting components. We conclude by discussing the new construct and the emerging paths to consider for future research.

2. LITERATURE REVIEW
2.1 Entrepreneurship and IT Turnover

In the entrepreneurship area of research, we can highlight several definitions and categorizations of entrepreneurs according to i) the degree and length of their engagement in the entrepreneurial field [16], ii) their entrepreneurial status and length of entrepreneurial experience [17], iii) their entrepreneurial goals [18], etc. In this paper, we are interested in the first categorization of entrepreneurs. First, the nascent entrepreneurs (i.e. "are actively involved with the idea of a business start-up, but who have not yet completed the formal launch of the start-up" [16], then the new entrepreneurs (i.e. have come into the entrepreneurial field quite recently) and established entrepreneurs (i.e. show a lengthy entrepreneurial career). Nascent entrepreneurs are the most pertinent to the notion of Shift of Understanding which is the focus of the study. More accurately, a nascent entrepreneur can be seen as an entrepreneur-to-be, a person who is at the early stages of the process of establishing a new organization, [19]. In this study, we are focusing on IT professional who decides to leave salaried employment in order to start his or her own company, i.e. a 'future' nascent IT entrepreneur.

In the relevant literature, several studies have proposed theoretical models or identifies antecedents of entrepreneurial behavior or IT turnover intention. In particular, significant effort has been made to model parts or the whole of the pre-start-up process [20 , 21, 22 , 23] by focusing mostly on the individual as a nascent entrepreneur. The studies belonging in this literature can be separated into three major streams: personality traits and knowledge capital, cognitive characteristics of entrepreneurial behavior and motivation linked to entrepreneurial behavior.

Research on *personality traits* and nascent entrepreneurship attributes the emergence of entrepreneurship to factors that affect an individual's disposition, such as the need for recognition, role models [10], propensity to battle the status quo [17], locus of control, risk-taking and innovativeness [24] and alertness to opportunities [25]. Research on knowledge capital suggests that variables such as knowledge, breadth of education, balance of skills, and experience [26 , 27-29] as better predictors of entrepreneurial behavior, leading to the Jack-of-all-trades model.

Cognitive approaches to nascent entrepreneurship [21 , 30 , 31] asserts that entrepreneurial behavior is related to ways that individuals draw on their perceptual and reasoning skills in order to comprehend themselves and their environment. Two main streams of research can be identified within this literature [31, p.433]: the study of cognitive structures and the study of cognitive processes. In the first stream, researchers describe and analyze the knowledge structures that entrepreneurs draw upon to form judgements or decisions as they attempt to evaluate opportunities and create their business [32 , 33]. In the second stream, researchers assume that the individual's thoughts, speech and actions are influenced by the cognitive processes employed to acquire, use and process information [34]. Perceived self-efficacy [17, p.7, 24] and counterfactual thinking (thinking about what might have been) [35] are found to be cognitive variables distinctive of entrepreneurs.

Motivational approaches [23, 36] to nascent entrepreneurship focus on the various types of motives which seem to trigger entrepreneurial behavior. Internal vs external (internal need for autonomy vs. recognizing an opportunity in the market), push- vs. pull (reason that force people to entrepreneurial paths vs. reasons that attract people into entrepreneurial paths) and economic vs. social are some types of motives commonly found in the relevant literature.

By the same token, a large body of IS turnover research has highlighted individual level factors that are related either in a positive (e.g., role ambiguity, role conflict, threat of professional obsolescence, work exhaustion, emotional labor constructs, personnel anchors), or negative way (e.g. affective commitment, job satisfaction, boundary spanning activities, autonomy, fairness of reward) to the turnover intention [6-9, 37-39, 40 , 41 , 42 , 43]. The models supporting IT Turnover research (see [40] for more details), include i) the Organizational Equilibrium Theory [44], ii) Met Expectations Theory [45], iii) Linkage Model [46], iv) the Unfolding Model of Turnover [47] and v) the Job Embeddedness Theory [48].

It is worth noticing that some of the articles found in the literature discard the examination of static factors and proposes *process models* in order to explain the gradual -i.e. over time- creation of entrepreneurial ventures [20, 49-52] or the gradual maturation of IT turnover decision [53, 54]. Yet, they are used either to explain entrepreneurial behavior or IT turnover behavior. The study of the SoU follows the research trajectory of the process model of IT entrepreneurial turnover [14] which brings the two streams of literature together and aspires to bring to the fore the conditions that underpin decisions of entrepreneurial turnover. Additional work along this line of research introduced the concept of IT Entrepreneurial Epiphany [15], as a "critical moment when the IT employee/future entrepreneur realizes that some or all of the necessary conditions for her to quit her job and start her own business have been met". The present study is an extension of this work, as SoU is closely linked to an IT Entrepreneurial Epiphany.

2.2 Shapero's Notion of "Entrepreneurial Event" and Lee and Mitchell's Notion of "Shock"

In the entrepreneurship literature, Shapero's model [55] assumes that inertia guides human behavior until an event interrupts or displaces that inertia. The observed departure from the current state, or displacement, can be negative (e.g. a job loss) or positive (e.g. increase in the salary) and usually precipitates a change in behavior. Krueger Jr. et al. [56, p.93] commenting on Shapero's model explain that "The entrepreneurial event thus requires the potential to start a business (credibility and propensity to act) to exist prior to the displacement (along with the disposition to act after being displaced)"; after the occurrence of the event, individuals remain the same. What it has changed is their perceptions about the new circumstances which can be either subjective (e.g. getting older) or objective (e.g. financial turmoil). "The potential to be entrepreneurs was clearly there, but it required some sort of displacement for that potential to surface" [56, p.93] . Alternatively, several studies show that the intention or the decision to act is triggered as the result of the interaction between the situational factors or precipitating events with individual variables [56, 57].

In IT Turnover literature, a similar concept to the entrepreneurial event emerges under the name of the 'shock'. The shock is considered to be "a particular jarring event that initiates the psychological analyses involved in quitting a job" [54, p.451] and in the context of the current paper in starting her one's business. To the best of our knowledge, only the studies by Holtom et al. [58] and Morrell et al. [59] elaborate on the notion of shocks which have been initially described in Lee and Mitchell's unfolding model of voluntary employee turnover, by testing specific hypothesis regarding the nature, content and role of shocks in turnover decisions. Yet, in both studies the types of shocks examined refer to the employee's general turnover behavior, and subsequently the prospect of entrepreneurial careers has been briefly described and related to just one type of shock : "Start own business", p. 342 [58, p.342].

Assuming that the initiation of change in the status quo of the individual can come from a shock, it is not clear that all such shocks create the same dynamics by which results follow. Questions about different dynamics following different types of shocks are difficult to address without first considering the range of types of shocks that are possible as well as the pre-shock situation (conditions, context, etc). After the shock is experienced, individuals re-assess their current position regarding their values, goals and plans for goal attainment [54, 60] and they adjust their behavior accordingly: they decide (or not) to leave. A shock may trigger the enactment of a pre-existing plan of action, based on past experience or cultivated expectations and thus directly enforce the individual's decision to leave; it may prompt the employee to re-evaluate her 'fit' with the organizational values; or "it may create a misalignment between the individual's values, goals and strategies for goal attainment and those of the employing organization", (Lee et al, 1999, p. 451-452).

As we will show in the following sections, this paper will focus on the description and the analysis of the 'shift of understanding'. The 'shift of understanding' is observed after an event happens and interrupts or displaces that inertia underlying the usual behavior of the individual. This displacing event can be either a shock or the completion of a gradual saturation process of an 'x' condition which can be either subjective or objective. We imply that this 'shift of understanding' influences the intention which in its turn influences the attitude which finally results in the choice of the particular behavior. Yet, in the context of this paper, we will solely introduce and analyze the concept of 'shift of understanding'. Let us be more specific.

3. SHIFTS OF UNDERSTANDING

The epistemological position of this study embraces the tradition of critical realism while its research approach is grounded theory methodology [61]. "If we were to follow a "purist" rendition of interpretive research [...], the theory would normally appear *after* the data presentation" (Anonymous, in Suddaby 2006, p. 637). Yet, following Suddaby's suggestion [62] for advanced clarity in the presentation of our arguments, we "employ the more traditional presentational strategy of providing a theoretical overview first, to preview the major findings and resulting model" (2006, p.637). It is important to keep in mind, however, that the concept of SoU actually emerged from the data itself, as an open code and a category.

3.1 Definition

The notion of 'Shift of Understanding' (SoU) refers to a change in the individual's perception about the context within which one lives and works. Additionally, change in the individual' s views and beliefs about his or herself, general lifestyle and his or her perceived meaning of life are also included in the notion of SoU.

Additionally, we observed that once a sudden, jarring event happens or a gradual evolution of a condition (e.g. accumulation of information or experience which at some point turns into knowledge) has come to its completion phase, a SoU is observed. The individual starts perceiving things under a new lens. An example of a SoU could be a shift in the individual's perception about his or her 'fit' in the corporate world, another SoU could be the perceived level of risk inherent in the uptake of new entrepreneurial endeavour vs. the perceived level of risk accompanying salaried employment.

The aim of this paper is to thoroughly describe the particulars of the SoU by studying IT workers who decided to quit their job in order to start their own business. Such a rich description is expected to shed light to the overall process of IT Entrepreneurial Turnover behavior, a research domain of increased interest for managers and nascent entrepreneurs, as well as policy makers.

4. METHODOLOGY

We followed a Glaserian Grounded Theory (GT) approach [61, 63, 64], to study the initial general question : "How and why do IT employee decide to quit their job and start a business". We used the following tools related to the Glaserian approach of Grounded Theory Methodology : open, selective and theoretical coding, constant comparison, 'memoing', theoretical saturation and theoretical sampling [61, 63].

The initial objective of the study was to build a typology of shock. However, while we were doing, we noticed the emergence of a new concept: Shift of Understanding. In table 1 and 2, we present several examples of how this concept is grounded in the data. SoU emerged by a set of questions related to the classification of the consequences of the shocks: What is the impact of the shock itself? How can we classify those impacts? Can we reproduce those consequences without reproducing the shock itself (in case of external shocks)? Thereupon, the concept of SoU came forward during the open coding process. We then decided to pursue the consolidation of this concept through theoretical sampling centered on SoU., During this phase, the data revealed that several entrepreneurs were citing published quotes from famous or less famous authors/entrepreneurs and they were considering them as instrumental in their decision to quit and start a business. Those quotes fitted our concept of SoU. Therefore, we decided to consider the knowledge derived by the analytical description of SoU as a new type of data: quotes (from famous or less famous authors/entrepreneurs) that would inspire future entrepreneurs to start their business . We follow here Glaser's famous sentence "all is data".

In regard to data description, we started our analysis with 57 cases of future and/or current IT entrepreneurs collected through one or several interviews. These were collected using both retrospective and longitudinal approaches, i.e. following future IT entrepreneurs overtime. The aim of the data collection has been to maximize the variation among the sample[1] (e.g. age group, gender, type of entrepreneurs, software/hardware industry, company size, country). While coding for the purpose of the identification/classification of shocks, the core category Shift of Understanding started emerging. We then continued the theoretical sampling by looking at entrepreneurial quotes. We collected quotes following (1) the analysis of our interviews, (2) a

---

[1] Due to space constraints, we did not include the details on the demographics of the sample. Those are available upon request.

Google search on entrepreneurial quotes (3) a Google search on Steve Jobs's quotes who was often cited by our entrepreneurs (possibly due to the timing of the data collection, close to his death).

We strongly believe that those quotes will be of importance to entrepreneurs as (1) interviewed entrepreneurs mentioned that specific quotes played an important role in their decision to quit their job and start a business, (2) the ranking of a website is partially linked to popularity and referrals, so the collected quotes were of some importance for other webmasters and (3) the analysis of the comments on each page of quotes illustrated the importance and relevance of the quotes for future and present entrepreneurs. For example: "Quotes can be really powerful." (http://juniorbiz.com/40-entrepreneurship-quotes).

Reflecting upon our data, i.e. our respondents' testimonies that new knowledge, or a gradual accumulation thereof, regarding a specific field of experience made them perceive things differently, and thereafter they quit their job in order to start a business, we consider entrepreneurial quotes as a useful agent of potential change (SoU) for all the stakeholders interested in the IT Entrepreneurial Turnover behavior. Moreover, famous quotes resonate with the experience' of the entrepreneurs and can be seen as a synthesis of those experiences. We coded all the collected quotes (over 200) and used this coding to saturate the core category Shift of Understanding (SoU). During the coding process, we had to exclude a large part of the quotes linked to success and not starting a business. For each quote, in addition to classic coding, we also coded the understanding before and after the quote (see table 1 for some examples).

As far as the reference back to the literature is concerned, because the topic of IT Entrepreneurial Turnover has already been well known by the authors, we had to distance ourselves from it as much as possible. Once the concept Shift of Understanding (SoU) emerged, we consolidated it, and then looked at the literature on that specific topic, following a typical Glaserian Grounded Theory approach.

5. FINDINGS

In this section, we introduce the properties of the concept of SoU and we present the emerging concepts composing this category.

5.1 Propositions

An event which interrupts or displaces the inertia which then characterized an individual's behavior, can be either a shock or an accumulation of knowledge.

In that sense, one does not necessarily need to create the conditions of the shock in order to trigger a SoU which in turn prompt entrepreneurship. The entrepreneur-to-be can shift his/her perception regarding his/her ability/desire to quit his/her job and start his/her own business by reading a book, or discussing the project, or attending a seminar or just thinking (i.e. reflecting on her experiences and current needs). For example, one can understand that he/she can make more money by being self-employed than by being a salaried employee without necessarily experiencing a shock. We therefore suggest the following propositions (synthesized in Figure 1).

- Proposition 1: in this proposition, we study the relation between a Shift of Understanding and an IT

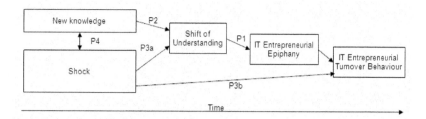

Figure 1 : Conceptual Framework

Entrepreneurial Epiphany.
   One or several Shifts of Understanding lead to an IT Entrepreneurial Epiphany

- *Proposition 2: In this proposition, we suggest that new knowledge such as new data, a new pattern identified in existing data, new concept, new relationship may lead to a SoU. Therefore :*
   New knowledge may lead to a Shift of Understanding

- In proposition 3a and 3b, we describe two possible paths that could lead to an IT entrepreneurial Turnover decision.

   o Proposition 3a: the first path is linked to a shift of understanding triggered by a shock; for example, watching a co-worker being fired due to the recession, will trigger a Shift of Understanding related to a deeper understanding of the current work crisis.
   A shock may lead to a Shift of understanding

   o *Proposition 3b:* An emerging category of shocks has been a specific type of shock which triggers a change mostly in the reality itself rather than in the individual's understanding of this reality. This type of shock may trigger the decision to quit, but it will not trigger a shift of understanding. For example, an inheritance or the acceptance of a loan by the bank can be perceived as a shock triggering an entrepreneurial adventure, but it will not trigger a shift of understanding. Thus, we suggest the followings:
   A shock may lead to an IT Entrepreneurial Turnover behavior

- *Proposition 4: In this situation, a shock will impart new knowledge to the future IT entrepreneur, for example, by successfully handling a new situation resulting from the shock as explained in table 1.*
   New knowledge could lead to a shock, and vice-versa, a shock could lead to new knowledge.

Following this list of propositions, we also analyzed the properties of SoU that emerged from our data. The next section will describe these properties.

5.2 Properties of Shifts of Understanding

We detail here various properties related to SoU.

- Conditions triggering the decision to quit one's job in order to start one's own business
   According to our data, the necessary conditions for an event to trigger the decision to leave vary among individuals. They also depend on the timing of the

event. The same event may generate a SoU for one person, whereas it would have no impact for another. However, because a SoU can be translated into knowledge, it then becomes less context-independent and therefore such SoU can be triggered more easily.

- SoU as an ontological position
  The Shift of Understanding may vary according to the ontological (i.e. the nature of reality) stance of the

Table 1 : Illustrations of the different propositions

Propositions	Examples from interviewees
Proposition 1: Shift of Understanding and IT Entrepreneurial Epiphany	- "For some time I felt nice not to be the one who has the final responsibility in anything which could potentially go wrong. I liked the idea that my boss would supervise my work minimizing the possibility of a mistake. Soon I realized that I was the one to be blamed for any mistake made and he was the one to be praised when the project which I had fully undertaken was a success. It was then I realized that I need to be boss. I need to own my own company."
Proposition 2: New knowledge and Shift of Understanding	- "After attending an executive seminar on "marketing skills for successful entrepreneurs", I understood that managing customer relations was not as unattainable as I initially believed." - After discussing a French administrative procedure to start a business, the future entrepreneur decreased his or her perception of the administrative complexity
Proposition 3a: shock and Shift of understanding	- "Once my boss was fired, -not because he didn't meet the performance criteria of his job position, but because of the recession- I understood that the job security traditionally associated with very big companies is no longer the case."
Proposition 3b: shock and IT Entrepreneurial Turnover Decision	- "my wife got a job" => the financial risk has decreased - "I inherited some money" => the financial risk has decreased - End of a project, for example, a new version of a software has been released => A time slot is available to launch the company - "The bank agreed to lend me $200,000 for my business" => enough money is now available - Severance package available => enough money is now available - Your first client is ready to sign with you => the market is ready for you product
Proposition 4: Shock and Knowledge	When at some point my boss was out of the country and I had to handle a crisis moment with a client by myself, to my great surprise, I realized that I am much better at interpersonal relations than I initially thought.

future entrepreneur. For example, the idea of risk for an entrepreneur is to be compared to the risk an IT employee may take longer staying in her salaried job (see for example the fact that an employee has only one customer - her employer while an entrepreneur could potentially have hundreds or thousands of customers). However, such risk may very well be related to an ontological position of what is risk. If one were to compare the fact that we all die, risk is relative : See for example, Steve Jobs's quote: "Almost everything–all external expectations, all pride, all fear of embarrassment or failure–these things just fall away in the face of death, leaving only what is truly important. Remembering that you are going to die is the best way I know to avoid the trap of thinking you have something to lose. You are already naked. There is no reason not to follow your heart."

- Acceleration of the process
  By using SoU, one can accelerate the process of starting a business, as key elements of knowledge will be brought in and therefore triggers the IT Entrepreneurial Turnover decision, without having to necessarily experience the corresponding shock.

5.3 Type of Shifts of Understanding

While coding the different SoU, we reached the following types of SoU. We illustrate each concept with some quotes and a vignette telling the story of a fictional entrepreneur, Ramesh. We first list the different categories of quotes that emerged from our coding.

5.3.1 The Desire for Entrepreneurship

First and foremost, the IT employee has to regain control over his/her life (if such feeling of lack of control exists). Realizing that such control is not present may take place through several Shifts of Understanding.

(a) "The cover-your-butt mentality of the workplace will get you only so far. The follow-your-gut mentality of the entrepreneur has the potential to take you anywhere you want to go or run you right out of business--but it's a whole lot more fun, don't you think?", B. Rancic

(b) "If you live for weekends or vacations, your shit is broken", G. Vaynerchuk

Although they are not directly related to employment, a lot of quotes refer to the potential for greatness that each one of us should aim for.

(c) "Keep away from people who try to belittle your ambitions. Small people always do that, but the really great make you feel that you, too, can become great", M. Twain

(d) "Far better is it to dare mighty things, to win glorious triumphs, even though checkered by failure, than to rank with those poor spirits who neither enjoy nor suffer much, because they live in the gray twilight that knows not victory nor defeat.", T. Roosevelt

Once the desire to be a great entrepreneur is there, one needs to work on the potential brakes and fears related to starting a business.

Table 2: Some codes to support the Shift of Understanding

Understanding prior to the shock[1]	Shocks leading to a SoU	New understanding	Emerging concept
I am fairly paid as an IT employee.	I was shocked to learn how much money a friend who has his business is making.	I am not paid enough for my level of competency…	Work or market related environment
I like working for someone or for a company.	I got an argument with my boss.	I don't like working for someone else anymore.	
The company I am working for is doing a great job managing opportunities.	My boss proved that he was not competent enough and disagreed with my strategic vision of the market and the perceived opportunities.	I perceive a very important opportunity in the market.	
I think that being an entrepreneur is risky. I have a job for life. Having only one boss is enough for me and not risky.	Five colleagues just got fired following a merger	I think that being a salaried employee is riskier than being my own boss. My employer can fire me as soon as they want. Instead of having one boss/client, I can have one thousand as an entrepreneur.	IT employee vs. IT entrepreneur
I don't think about death and its possible occurrence in a near future.	One of my relative died in a car accident.	Life is short; there is no more time to waste. I need to start my business now.	Life

5.3.2 To Act or Not to Act

The large majority of the quotes are dealing with action issues. The lower-level concept 'Stop…' embeds several codes such as stop waiting, stop playing small, stop being afraid of risk, stop daydreaming, stop over-thinking, stop over-analyzing, stop having too many ideas, stop anticipating, stop asking permission, stop watching, stop over-theorizing, stop doubting, stop wishing ; do, act, try, "get your butt off", think big ; now, today.

(e) "Well done is better than well said", B. Franklin

(f) "The way to get started is to quit talking and begin doing". W. Disney

(g) "It's easier to ask forgiveness than it is to get permission", G. Hopper

Various ways are used to trigger such change.

5.3.3 Death, Urgency and Risk Reduction

In order to instil a sense of urgency, some quotes are using a change of perspective : instead of looking at what you are doing now, change the perspective and look at it 20 years from now, or from the moment of your death.

(h) "Life is too short to live someone else dream.", H. Hefner

Along the same line, quotes may appeal to greatness, combined with the shortness of life:

(i) "One day your life will flash before your eyes. Make sure it is worth watching", unknown author

(j) "Twenty years from now you will be more disappointed by the things that you didn't do than by the ones you did do. So throw off the bowlines. Sail away from the safe harbor. Catch the trade winds in your sails. Explore. Dream. Discover", M. Twain

Reducing risk could be another result of such a shift of perspective regarding life and death:

(k) "Remembering that you are going to die is the best way I know to avoid the trap of thinking you have something to lose.", S. Jobs

(l) "Almost everything–all external expectations, all pride, all fear of embarrassment or failure–these things just fall away in the face of death, leaving only what is truly important. Remembering that you are going to die is the best way I know to avoid the trap of thinking you have something to lose. You are already naked. There is no reason not to follow your heart." – S. Jobs' Stanford Commencement Address

Reducing risk is linked to a large number of quotes, reflecting different ways to reduce risks, in addition to the comparison with the imminence of death.

5.3.4 Positive Failure and Risk-Reduction

The necessity of failure, seen as part of the entrepreneurial process

(m) "Most great people have attained their greatest success just one step beyond their greatest failure", N. Hill

(n) "The important thing is not being afraid to take a chance. Remember, the greatest failure is to not try. Once you find something you love to do, be the best at doing it.", D. Fields

5.3.5 Difficulty is there, but can be overcome with Perseverance, Work, Drudge and Fight

Having recognized that failure is not necessarily negative, it should still be avoided. In that sense, quotes remind the future entrepreneurs that the entrepreneurial adventure is risky, difficult and may lead to failure. A lot of quotes reflect those aspects, but they also emphasize the importance of overcoming difficulties for various reasons.

- Don't forget the finances,

(o) "Nobody talks about entrepreneurship as survival, but that's exactly what it is and what nurtures creative thinking. Running that first shop taught me business is not financial science; it's about trading: buying and selling.", A. Roddick

- Recognizing that the difficulty of the path is linked to the accomplishment

(p) "To win without risk is to triumph without glory", Corneille

(q) "If you are not willing to risk the unusual, you will have to settle for the ordinary.", J. Rohn

(r) "Every worthwhile accomplishment, big or little, has its stages of drudgery and triumph; a beginning, a struggle and a victory", M. Gandhi

- Learning to be persistent

(s) "Entrepreneurs average 3.8 failures before final success. What sets the successful ones apart is their amazing persistence", L. M. Amos

(t) "I'm convinced that about half of what separates the successful entrepreneurs from the non-successful ones is pure perseverance.", S. Jobs

- Having a life

(u) "The brave may not live forever, but the cautious do not live at all!", Sir R. Branson

- Learning from mistakes and growing with them

(v) "The most valuable thing you can make is a mistake – you can't learn anything from being perfect.", A. Osborne

(w) "A man must be big enough to admit his mistakes, smart enough to profit from them, and strong enough to correct them." – J. C. Maxwell

- Seeing opportunities in mistakes, and viewing that not being in control as a positive thing.

(x) "If everything seems under control, you're just not going fast enough." – M. Andretti

---

Vignette: from IT employee to IT Entrepreneur, the typical case of a quote-based path

Before starting his business, Ramesh was an IT employee. He has been employed for 4 years by an IT company, however, he was tired with the "cover-your-butt" mentality of the workplace (a), the lack of fun in his work (b) and seriously considered to start his business and create a new type of software. Two elements played an important role in his decision. First, he realized that his co-workers were not helping him to improve his IT skills, but rather belittling him (c) . Second, he also remembered all those great goals that he had for his life, which are now far different from his current life (d)(h)(j).

However, Ramesh was still very unsecure about his entrepreneurial ideas, and this insecurity was very powerful. Upon reflection, he soon realized that death may happen anytime and that 20 years from now, he should be proud of his life (i)(j)(k)(l). Therefore, he understood that it is urgent to act, and more importantly that the risks of his venture were nothing compared to death (k). In addition, realizing that success is very likely to follow a failure, he gradually lost his fear of failure (m)(n). Indeed, he understood that this is part of the game of success (m)(p)(q)(r)(s)(u) and that not trying (n) or lacking perseverance (s)(t) or courage (u) is the real failure. Indeed, he realized that failure in itself is a valuable thing in term of learning (v) and if failure does not happen, it may even indicate that he is not going fast enough (x).

He then started to do an in-depth analysis of the situation in order to carefully assess the risks and moreover the importance of having a profitable business (o). He also quickly realized that risks cannot be all planned in advance; it may even be a trap of overanalyzing (ff) , however, the process of planning is still crucial (y). In that sense, he went through several business courses (e.g. marketing, finance) to complement his IT skills.

At the same time he was reducing the risk and its associated fear, he was also looking for the right opportunity. This is where dreams, visions, and ideas became increasingly important (bb)(gg). However, he constantly reminded himself that an entrepreneur is a "doer", not a dreamer (cc). Therefore he focused his energy on acting on his dream and visions (hh), while keeping alive the sense of urgency (dd).

Ramesh never had difficulties spotting opportunities, which is one of the reasons he has always been attracted by entrepreneurship (ii), feeling that spotting an opportunity is not the difficult part (jj), but selecting the right one is (ii). Even if he couldn't see an opportunity, he knew that he could always made one (nn) without thinking about the difficulty of the task (ll)(mm).

Ramesh was also very passionate about his new business idea (oo)(pp) and how his software could change the world. In fact, he hardly made his decision based on money (ss); yet he kept in mind its importance (tt) and never abandoned the idea that one day he might well become a millionaire (uu). Indeed, his motivation was toward a greater goal, not only for himself, but also for the community and the world (vv)(ww)(xx)(yy). He even considered that Life, based on his spiritual beliefs is helping him through his path. Indeed, he believe that trusting life is one of the most powerful way to be successful in his endeavor (aaa)(zz).

- The importance of planning

(y)   "In preparing for battle I have always found that plans are useless, but planning is indispensable", D. D. Eisenhower

- Ending doubts with action

(z)   "Doubt, of whatever kind, can be ended by action alone.", T. Carlyle

And to synthesize…

(aa)   "Far better is it to dare mighty things, to win glorious triumphs, even though checkered by failure, than to rank with those poor spirits who neither enjoy nor suffer much, because they live in the gray twilight that knows not victory nor defeat."- T. Roosevelt

5.3.6 Visions are the Triggers for Action

Some codes signify contradictions, or in fact, they reflect a more complex construction. For example,

(bb)   "When you cease to dream you cease to live", M. Forbes

which is a good complement to quotes such as

(cc)   "The true entrepreneur is a doer, not a dreamer.", N. Bushnell and C. E. Cheese's.

Such apparent contradiction could be resolved looking at quotes likes this one:

(dd)   "A goal is a dream with a deadline.", N. Hill

The same type of contradiction exists when we compare those two quotes:

(ee)   "What We Think, We Become", Buddha

and

(ff)   "I was thinking for many years to start my own business. But every time I was playing all the possible scenarios in my head I was getting overwhelmed and ended up doing anything. My best friend told me it is time for you to stop thinking and analyzing and start acting.", quote from one of our interviewee.

(gg)   "It's really hard to design products by focus groups. A lot of times, people don't know what they want until you show it to them.", S. Jobs

Of course, this is related to the balance between thinking and acting:

(hh)   "Many great ideas go unexecuted, and many great executioners are without ideas. One without the other is worthless.", T. Blixseth

5.3.7 Identifying, Catching and Transforming Opportunities

Opportunity recognition is considered as the core topic of entrepreneurship research. In this specific work, we focus on how opportunities are perceived through quotes, and how SoU related to opportunities are generated.

Interestingly, opportunities seem to be easily recognized for some entrepreneurs, while difficult to select. By contrast, discussions with aspiring entrepreneurs show that opportunities are difficult to spot. This is illustrated by this quote:

(ii)   "The entrepreneur in us sees opportunities everywhere we look, but many people see only problems everywhere they look. The entrepreneur in us is more concerned with discriminating between opportunities than he or she is with failing to see the opportunities", M. Gerber

(jj)   "Business opportunities are like buses, there's always another one coming", R. Branson

You have to be ready to grasp the opportunity

(kk)   "The secret of success in life is for a man to be ready for his opportunity when it comes.", B. Disraeli

Or you have to create it, from the impossible, from problems or from nothing

(ll)   "They didn't know it was impossible, so they did it" M. Twain

(mm)   "A pessimist sees the difficulty in every opportunity; an optimist sees the opportunity in every difficulty". W. Churchill

(nn)   "I had to make my own living and my own opportunity! But I made it! Don't sit down and wait for the opportunities to come. Get up and make them!", C.J. Walker

5.3.8 Pleasure and Passion

Passion and pleasure are a driving force for entrepreneurs and future entrepreneurs. The importance of fun is linked to the idea of great work, perseverance and success.

(oo)   "Your work is going to fill a large part of your life, and the only way to be truly satisfied is to do what you believe is great work. And the only way to do great work is to love what you do. If you haven't found it yet, keep looking. Don't settle.", S. Jobs

(pp)   "Find a job you love and you'll never work a day in your life." –Confucius

5.3.9 Money is Not a Good Reason!

Interestingly, it seems money is not a strong enough motivator for becoming an entrepreneur. Although some quotes from our interviews clearly points out money as an important element, it is not the main element as reflected by those quotes (from very rich people).

(qq)   "Being the richest man in the cemetery doesn't matter to me … Going to bed at night saying we've done something wonderful… that's what matters to me.", as quoted in The Wall Street Journal (Summer 1993), S. Jobs

(rr)   "I was worth over $1,000,000 when I was 23, and over $10,000,000 when I was 24, and over $100,000,000 when I was 25, and it wasn't that important because I never did it for the money", S. Jobs

(ss)   "If you do it for love, money come anyway" R. St. John.

That said, money still needs to be on the top priority list, but not as the main motivation.

(tt)   "The longer you're not taking action the more money you're losing" - C. Wilkerson (uu) "Set a Goal to be a Millionaire for What it will Make of you to Achieve it.", J. Rohn

5.3.10 Towards a Greater Goal

Another set of quotes are related to changing the world and doing something meaningful.

(vv) "Giving is better than receiving because giving starts the receiving process.", J. Rohn

(ww) "The best reason to start an organization is to make meaning - to create a product or service to make the world a better place", G. Kawasaki

(xx) "I want to put a ding in the universe.", S. Jobs

(yy) "Do you want to spend the rest of your life selling sugared water or do you want a chance to change the world?" – S. Jobs

5.3.11 Believing in Life and Spirituality

Maybe the latest statement for entrepreneurship (and life in general) would be to trust life (or anything else). This is an interesting statement, as it is also an act of faith.

(zz) "Again, you can't connect the dots looking forward; you can only connect them looking backwards. So you have to trust that the dots will somehow connect in your future. You have to trust in something — your gut, destiny, life, karma, whatever. This approach has never let me down, and it has made all the difference in my life." , S. Jobs

(aaa) "When God takes something from your grasp, He's not punishing you, but merely opening your hands to receive something better". Unknown author

We now discuss the general contributions of this paper.

6. CONTRIBUTIONS

In this paper, we hope to contribute to the IT Entrepreneurial Turnover research in the following fundamental ways: the goal of the paper has been to introduce the conceptual lens of 'Shift of Understanding' as a way for the researcher to focus on actionable (and therefore practical) knowledge items which describe the particulars of the change observed in the individual's perception, a change which often leads to the decision to quit one's job in order to start one's own business. By linking the different shifts of understanding to various shocks, we provide a useful tool for investigating the shocks that a future entrepreneur may want to trigger (or an IT manager may want to avoid) in order to quit his job and start his business. By providing a deeper understanding of those shifts of understanding, a future IT Entrepreneur may avoid having to experience such shocks, but rather cognitively process those Shifts of Understanding (e.g., through education or reading). Additionally, by focusing on SoU, we shift the attention from the study of the behavioral *intention* to "quit and start a new business" to the actual IT Entrepreneurial Turnover behavior. Finally, with this study, we answer Joseph et al.'s call for elaborating on process perspectives of IT Turnover research [40], such as the unfolding model of voluntary turnover [47, 53, 65]. While at the same time, we respond to similar calls made by the entrepreneurship literature studies, [24, 27, 28, 29].

7. CONCLUSION, LIMITATIONS AND FUTURE RESEARCH

In this paper, we addressed an under-investigated thematic area of IT turnover personnel literature: IT Entrepreneurial Turnover. We introduced the concept – Shift of Understanding – to describe the jarring of the individual's well-established perceptions about her surrounding environment, either in the sphere of personal or working life, the meaning of life, his/her personal image and lifestyle. After a shock is experienced or an entrepreneurial event happens, the inertia governing human behavior is interrupted and the individual perceives things under a new lens: a shift of understanding has just happened. A newly formed desire towards entrepreneurship, the realization of the urgency of immediacy and action, the reconsideration of both pragmatic and existential concerns such as the risk reduction, the capability to seize opportunities, or the meaning of life in general, the re-evaluation of oneself prospects, propensities and needs are some of the manifestations of SoU which are found to be directly or indirectly linked with the actual IT entrepreneurial turnover behavior.

We support the view that quotes constitute data which should be considered as an insightful source of important information regarding human behavior, independently of their potential of wide applicability in large populations and at times their contradictory or twofold character. The same quote can be interpreted differently by various individuals and may have varied or unspecified effects on the way their perceptions are formed. Yet, they are still very good indicators of what entrepreneurs think as important or distinguishable factor in their decision to quit their job and start their own business.

Future research should further elaborate on the properties and dimensions of SoU. Questions related to the possible inhibitors in the possibility of shift of understanding, the amount of information transmitted by the new knowledge, the degree of transformation of the individual, the relation with personality[2], [66 , 67] are expected to be investigated in the future. In addition, the role of new ICTs, such as social networking technologies, e.g. Twitter, should be investigated as channels through which SoU happens. Indeed, analysis of tweets (short messages which are destined to convey a whole idea in 140 characters) from famous IT entrepreneurs may be exactly the expression of a SoU, introducing a new relations between two concepts, or introducing a new concept in itself. Finally, further research on SoU might be valuable for the study of IT turnover in general, without necessarily considering the option of an entrepreneurial path, or even the opposite– a SoU leading to stop being an entrepreneur and becoming an IT employee- could be probably worth undertaking.

8. ACKNOWLEDGMENTS

This study benefited from the financial support of the foundation CIGREF.

9. REFERENCES

[1] Andrew, R. and Ciborra, C. *Organizational learning and core capabilities: the role of IT.* John Wiley, City, 1998.

---

[2] In particular the MBTI dimensions, and the exploration of its inferior functions

[2] Schumpeter, J. *The theory of economic development.* Harvard University Press, Cambridge, MA, 1934.

[3] Birley, S. New ventures and employment growth. Journal of Business Venturing1987), 155-165.

[4] Kumar, S. and Liu, D. Impact of globalization on entrepreneurial entreprises in the world markets. *International Journal of Management and Entreprise Development*, 2, 1 2005), 46-64.

[5] Agarwal, R., Ferratt, T. W. and De, P. An experimental investigation of turnover intentions among new entrants in it. *The DATA BASE for Advances in Information Systems*, 38, 1 2007), 8-28.

[6] Igbaria, M. and Greenhaus, J. H. Career orientations of MIS employees: An empirical analysis. *MIS Quarterly*, 15, 2 (1991/06 1991), 151-169.

[7] Igbaria, M. and Greenhaus, J. H. Determinants of MIS employees' turnover intentions: a structural equation model. *Communications of the ACM*, 35, 2 1992), 34-49.

[8] Igbaria, M. and Wormley, W. M. Organizational Experiences and Career Success of MIS Professionals and Managers: An Examination of Race Differences. *MIS Quarterly*, 16, 4 (1992/12 1992), 507-529.

[9] Moore, J. E. One Road to turnover: An Examination of Work Exhaustion in Technology Professionals. *MIS Quarterly*, 24, 1 (2000/03 2000), 141-168.

[10] Carter, N. M., Gartner, W. B., Shaver, K. G. and Gatewood, E. J. The career reasons of nascent entrepreneurs. *Journal of Business Venturing*, 18, 1 2003), 13-39.

[11] Davidsson, P. and Honig, B. The role of social and human capital among nascent entrepreneurs. *Journal of Business Venturing*, 18, 3 2003), 301-331.

[12] Delmar, F. and Davidsson, P. Where do they come from? Prevalence and characteristics of nascent entrepreneurs. *Entrepreneurship & Regional Development*, 12, 1 2000), 1-23.

[13] Giacomin, O., Guyot, J.-L., Janssen, F. and Lohest, O. *Novice creators: personal identity and push pull dynamics.* City, 2007.

[14] Mourmant, G., Gallivan, M. and Kalika, M. Another road to IT turnover: the entrepreneurial path. *European Journal of Information Systems*, 18, 5 2009), 498.

[15] Mourmant, G. and Voutsina, K. *From IT Employee to IT Entrepreneur: the Concept of IT Entrepreneurial Epiphany.* City, 2010.

[16] Brixy, U., Sternberg, R. and Stüber, H. From potential to real entrepreneurship. *IAB Discussion Paper*, http://doku.iab.de/discussionpapers/2008/dp3208.pdf2008).

[17] Davidsson, P. *Nascent Entrepreneurship: Empirical Studies and Developments.* Now publishers inc, Hanover, MA, USA, 2006.

[18] Stewart Jr., W. H. and Roth, P. L. *Risk Propensity Differences Between Entrepreneurs and Managers: A Meta-Analytic Review.* American Psychological Association, City, 2001.

[19] Reynolds, P. D., Bygrave, W. D., Autio, E. and Hay, M. *GEM Global Entrepreneurship Report, 2002 Summary Report.* Babson, Wellesley, MA and London Business School, London, 2002.

[20] Bhave, M. P. A process model of entrepreneurial venture creation. *Journal of Business Venturing*, 9, 3 1994), 223-242.

[21] Busenitz, L. W. and Lau, C.-M. A cross-cultural cognitive model of new venture creation. *Entrepreneurship: Theory & Practice*, 20, 4 (1996///Summer 1996), 25.

[22] Larson, A. and Starr, J. A. A network model of organization formation. *Entrepreneurship: Theory & Practice*, 17, 2 (1992///Winter 1993), 5.

[23] Naffziger, D. W., Hornsby, J. S. and Kuratko, D. F. A proposed Research model of entrepreneurial motivation. *Entrepreneurship: Theory & Practice*, 181994), 29-42.

[24] Chen, C. C., Greene, P. G. and Crick, A. Does entrepreneurial self-efficacy distinguish entrepreneurs from managers? *Journal of Business Venturing*, 13, 4 1998), 295-316.

[25] Arenius, P. and Minniti, M. Perceptual variables and nascent entrepreneurship. *Small Business Economics*, 24, 3 2005), 233-247.

[26] Deakins, D. and Whittam, G. *Business start-up: theory, practice and policy.* Pearson Education, City, 2000.

[27] Wagner, J. Are nascent entrepreneurs 'Jacks-of-all-trades'? a test of Lazear's theory of entrepreneurship with German data. *Applied Economics*, 38, 20 2006), 2415-2419.

[28] Lazear, E. P. Balanced skills and entrepreneurship. *American Economic Review*, 94, 2 2004), 208-211.

[29] Lazear, E. P. *Entrepreneurship.* National Bureau of Economic Research, City, 2002.

[30] Mitchell, R. K., Busenitz, L. W., Bird, B. J., Gaglio, C. M., McMullen, J. S., Morse, E. A. and Smith, J. B. The Central Question in Entrepreneurial Cognition Research. *Entrepreneurship: Theory & Practice*, 31, 1 2007), 1-27.

[31] Sánchez, J. C., Carballo, T. and Gutiérrez, A. The entrepreneur from a cognitive approach. *Psicothema*, 26, 3 2011), 433-438.

[32] Gaglio, C. M. and Katz, J. A. The Psychological Basis of Opportunity Identification: Entrepreneurial Alertness. *Small Business Economics*, 16, 2 (2001/03// 2001), 95.

[33] Mitchell, R. K., Smith, B., Seawright, K. W. and Morse, E. A. Cross-Cultural Cognitions and the Venture Creation Decision. *Academy of Management Journal*, 43, 5 2000), 974-993.

[34] Baron, R. A. and markman, G. D. *Cognitive mechanisms: Potential differences between entrepreneurs and non-entrepreneurs.* City, 1999.

[35] Baron, R. A. Counterfactual thinking and venture formation: The potential effects of thinking about "what might have been". *Journal of Business Venturing*, 151999), 79-91.

[36] Gatewood, E. J., Shaver, K. G. and Gartner, W. B. A longitudinal study of cognitive factors influencing start-up

behaviors and success at venture creation. *Journal of Business Venturing*, 101995), 371-391.

[37] Guimaraes, T. and Igbaria, M. Determinants of turnover intentions: comparing IC and IS personnel. *Information Systems Research*, 3, 3 1992), 273-303.

[38] Igbaria, M., Parasuraman, S. and Badawy, M. K. Work Experiences, Job Involvement, and Quality of Work Life Among Information Systems Personnel. *MIS Quarterly*, 18, 2 (1994/06 1994), 175-201.

[39] Ferratt, T. W., Agarwal, R., Brown, C. V. and Moore, J. E. IT human resource management configurations and IT turnover: theoretical synthesis and empirical analysis. *Information Systems Research*, 16, 3 2005), 237-255.

[40] Joseph, D., Ng, K.-Y., Koh, C. and Ang, S. Turnover of information technology professionals: a narrative review, meta-analytic structural equation modeling, and model development. *MIS Quarterly*, 31, 3 2007), 547-577.

[41] Trauth, E., Quesenberry, J. and Huang, H. Retaining women in the U.S. IT workforce: theorizing the influence of organizational factors. *European Journal of Information Systems*, 18, 5 2009), 476.

[42] Rutner, P., Riemenschneider, C., O'Leary-Kelly, A. and Hardgrave, B. Work exhaustion in information technology professionals: the impact of emotion labor. *SIGMIS Database*, 42, 1 2011), 102-120.

[43] Chang, C. L.-H., Chen, V., Klein, G. and Jiang, J. J. Information system personnel career anchor changes leading to career changes. *European Journal of Information Systems*, 202011), 103-117.

[44] March, J. G. and Simon, H. A. *Organizations*. Wiley, New York, 1958.

[45] LW Porter, R. S. Organizational, work, and personal factors in employee turnover and absenteeism. *Psychological Bulletin*, 80, 2 1973), 151-176.

[46] Mobley, W. H. Intermediate linkages in the relationship between job satisfaction and employee turnover. *Journal of Applied Psychology*, 62, 2 1977), 237-240.

[47] Lee, T. W., Mitchell, T. R., Wise, L. and Fireman, S. An unfolding model of voluntary employee turnover. *Academy of Management Journal*, 39, 1 1996), 5-36.

[48] Mitchell, T. R. Why People Stay: Using Job Embeddedness to Predict Voluntary Turnover. *Academy of Management journal*, 44, 6 2001), 1102.

[49] Shaver, K. G. and Scott, L. R. Person, process, choice; The psychology of new venture creation. *Entrepreneurship: Theory & Practice*, 16, 2 (1991///Winter 1991), 23-45.

[50] Carter, N. M., Gartner, W. B. and Reynolds, P. D. Exploring start-up event sequences. *Journal of Business Venturing*, 11, 3 (1996/05// 1996), 151-166.

[51] Bygrave, W. *The entrepreneurial process*. John Wiley and Sons, City, 1994.

[52] Hayton, J. C., George, G. and Zahra, S. A. National Culture and Entrepreneurship: A Review of Behavioral Research. *Entrepreneurship: Theory and Practice*, 262002).

[53] Lee, T. W. and Mitchell, T. R. An alternative approach: the unfolding model of voluntary employee turnover. *The Academy of Management Review*, 19, 1 1994), 51-89.

[54] Lee, T. W., Mitchell, T. R., Holtom, B. C., McDaniel, L. S. and Hill, J. W. The unfolding model of voluntary turnover: a replication and extension. *Academy of Management Journal*, 42, 4 1999), 450-462.

[55] Shapero, A. *The Entrepreneurial Event*. Lexington Books City, 1984.

[56] Krueger Jr., N. F. and Brazeal, D. V. Entrepreneurial potential and potential entrepreneurs. *Entrepreneurship: Theory & Practice*, 18, 3 (1994///Spring 1994), 91.

[57] Hornsby, J. S. and Naffziger, D. W. An Interactive Model of Corporate Entrepreneurship process. *Entrepreneurship, Theory & Practice*, 17, 2 1993), 29-37.

[58] Holtom, B. C., Mitchell, T. R., Lee, T. W. and Inderrieden, E. J. Shocks as causes of turnover: what they are and how organizations can manage them. *Human Resource Management*, 44, 3 2005), 337.

[59] Morrell, K., Loan-Clarke, J. and Wilkinson, A. The role of shocks in employee turnover. *British Journal of Management*, 15, 4 2004), 335-349.

[60] Beach, L. R. *Image Theory*. Lawrence Erlbaum Associates, Publishers, 1998.

[61] Glaser, B. and Strauss, A. L. *The Discovery of Grounded Theory: Strategies for Qualitative Research*. Aldine Transaction, 1967.

[62] Suddaby, R. From the editors: What grounded theory is not. *Academy of Management Journal*, 49, 4 2006), 633.

[63] Glaser, B. *Theoretical sensitivity: Advances in the methodology of grounded theory*. The Sociology Press, 1978.

[64] Glaser, B. *Doing Grounded Theory: Issues and Discussions*. Sociology Press, Mill Valley, CA, 1998.

[65] Mitchell, T. R. and Lee, T. W. The unfolding model of voluntary turnover and job embeddedness: foundations for a comprehensive theory of attachment. *Research in Organizational Behavior*, 232001), 189.

[66] Gardner, W. L. M., Mark J. Using the Myers-Briggs Type Indicator to Study Managers: A Literature Review and Research Agenda. *Journal of Management*, 221996), 45-83.

[67] Briggs-Myers, I. *Introduction to type*. CPP, 1998

10. APPENDICES

Table 3 : Coding of the quotes and grounding (total: 240)

Code	Count	Code	Count	Code	Count
Action/Practice/Daring/Sthg new/Start	30	Spirituality	3	Conceive	1
Life/Ambition/Glory/Great life/Think Big/Wonderful	30	Stop waiting	3	cover-your-butt	1
Dreams/Ideas/Vision/Imagination/Intuition	17	Thinking	3	Discriminating vs. failing to see	1
Perseverance/Work/Drudge/Fight	12	Stop starting/doing too many things	2	Stop asking for instructions	1
Success/Victory	12	Change the world/Meaning (make)	2	Energy	1
Failure/Mistake	10	Independence	2	Face reality	1
Risk	8	No fear/Brave	2	Giving	1
Death/Limited time	7	Not trying	2	Need a brain	1
Opportunity	7	Self-development	2	Negative thinking	1
Employment	5	Someone else's dream	2	Positive thinking	1
Money	5	Stop asking for permission	2	Receiving	1
Passion/Pleasure	5	Theorizing	2	Solutions	1
Stop talking	5	Try	2	Stop analyzing	1
Fear/Doubt	4	(Voluntary) naivety	1	Stop being afraid to fail	1
Problem/Obstacles	4	20 years from now	1	Stop theorizing	1
Trust life	4	Art	1	Stop thinking	1
Daydreaming	3	Ask forgiveness	1	Stop trying	1
Learning	3	Become an expert	1	Stop watching	1
Life-Changing	3	Begin	1	Survival	1
NOW/Deadline	3	Believe	1	Tell everyone	1
Planning	3	Buying/Selling	1	Unknown	1
Rebel	3	Change the world	1	Mediate	0
Small vs Great people	3	Chaos	1		

Once You Click 'Done': Investigating the Relationship between Disengagement, Exhaustion and Turnover Intentions among University IT Professionals

Valerie F. Ford
The George Washington University
Graduate School of Education and Human
Development
44983 Knoll Square, Suite 391 Ashburn, VA
20147
1-703-726-1924

vford@gwu.edu

Diana L. Burley
The George Washington University
Graduate School of Education and Human
Development
44983 Knoll Square, Suite 391 Ashburn, VA
20147
1-703-726-3761

dburley@gwu.edu

ABSTRACT

Recent studies have shown that turnover is a major issue in IT environments (Armstrong & Riemenschneider, 2011; Carayon, Schoepke, Hoonakker, Haims, & Brunette, 2006; Moore, 2000a; Rigas, 2009). In fact, the research literature in IT and the popular press suggest that IT professionals are particularly vulnerable to burnout (Armstrong & Riemenschneider, 2011; Kalimo & Toppinen, 1995; McGee, 1996; Moore, 2000a). Using the Job Demands-Resources Model of Burnout as a framework, this study investigates the relationship between disengagement, work exhaustion and turnover intentions among IT professionals in a single university in a major metropolitan area. This study employed a non-experimental, cross-sectional survey research design using a Web-based survey questionnaire to collect data from a population (N=287) of university IT employees in a major metropolitan area. Two instruments were employed in the study: the OLdenburg Burnout Inventory (OLBI) measures work exhaustion and disengagement as developed by Demerouti et al. (2001); the Michigan Organizational Assessment Questionnaire Job Satisfaction Subscale (MOAQ-JSS) measures turnover intentions. The findings from this research indicated that disengagement consistently showed a statistically significant, positive correlation with turnover intentions. The most important conceptual implication of the study is that future investigations of disengagement, work exhaustion and turnover intentions among university IT employees must account for the unique work environment and how those workplace characteristics predict disengagement, work exhaustion and subsequent thoughts about quitting.

Categories and Subject Descriptors

K.7.3 The Computing Profession

General Terms

Management, Human Factors, Theory

Keywords

IT profession, burnout, disengagement, exhaustion, turnover intentions, Oldenburg Burnout Inventory (OLBI), MOAQ-JSS

1. INTRODUCTION

Turnover of information technology (IT) professionals is one of the most persistent challenges facing organizations (Allen, Armstrong, Reid, & Riemenschneider, 2009; Armstrong & Riemenschneider, 2011; Carayon, et al., 2006; Joseph, Ng, Koh, & Ang, 2007; 2000a, 2000b). More specifically, turnover of IT employees within institutions of higher education is especially critical as universities strive to keep pace with technology innovation (Glenn & Johnson, 2008). This era of pervasive technology has significant implications for higher education (Glenn & Johnson, 2008). For example, in a 2008 white paper sponsored by the New Media Consortium, institutions of higher education report that with increased demand for technological advancements, they are faced with the challenge of ensuring that universities and colleges have the IT infrastructure and operations in place to support the adoption of new technology (Glenn & Johnson, 2008). With these technological demands, institutions of higher education can ill-afford to have a 'revolving door' approach to managing IT staff.

Although researchers and managers long have explored why people leave their jobs and why they stay, we do not have a complete understanding of the problem. In general, people stay if they are satisfied with their job and committed to their organization and they leave if they are not. A 2006 Gallup poll regarding turnover in 44 organizations and 10,609 business units, reported that most people quit for a few explainable reasons: 32% of employees left for career advancement or promotional opportunities, 22% left for an increase in salary, 20% left for lack of job fit, and 17% left because of management or the general work environment (Harter, 2008). The current study focuses on the 37% who leave their jobs for negative reasons.

2. PROBLEM STATEMENT

Many factors, some related to the work environment and some related to the individual, influence an employee's commitment to the organization and satisfaction with his or her job (Moore, 2000a). Studies have shown that job stress is an important factor in an employee's overall commitment, job satisfaction and decision to leave their job (Sethi, Barrier, & King, 1999). Job burnout, an extreme or advanced form of job stress has been recognized as an occupational hazard for various people-oriented professions, such as human services, education, health care and the public sector and is important to researchers because of its association with critical psychological and behavioral outcomes, including productivity, withdrawal, and employee well-being (Maslach & Goldberg, 1998; Maslach, Schaufeli, & Leiter, 2001).

Burnout is a particularly tragic endpoint for professionals who entered the job with positive expectations and enthusiasm. The key characteristics of burnout are overwhelming exhaustion; feelings of frustration, anger, and cynicism; and a sense of ineffectiveness and failure. The trouble is that although some people may quit their job because they are burned out, others will stay on, and will only do the bare minimum rather than their very best (Maslach & Goldberg, 1998). This decline in the quality of work and in both physical and psychological health can be very costly for the individual worker, for everyone affected by that person and the organization.

Recent empirical studies have shown that burnout is not limited to human services occupations and that IT professionals are particularly vulnerable to job burnout (Moore, 2000b). In their many studies to understand the link between burnout and individual and organizational impacts, IT scholars have considered a wide range of predictors, including personal characteristics, role constructs, job characteristics, and organizational characteristics (Joseph & Ang, 2003). Further, research has linked job burnout to a plethora of ailments, including depression, physiological problems and family difficulties (Cropanzano, Rupp, & Byrne, 2003).

Despite the progress that has been made on defining and measuring job burnout, identifying correlates and understanding its development in the IT domain, (Cooper, Dewe, & O'Driscoll, 2001) to date, there has been little systematic study of burnout among IT professionals in higher education institutions. This study addresses this gap by investigating burnout among IT professionals in one institution of higher education in a major metropolitan area. This particular population also may be of interest to researchers by virtue of its proximity and possible similarity to the public sector and as such it may best mirror what is happening in the public sector. Much research has already been conducted on occupations within the public sector as it relates to burnout.

One reason that job burnout may be particularly important among IT professionals in higher education institutions, is that like their contemporaries in the public sector, these workers may experience an environment where political, economic or administrative realities prevent them from realizing their ideals (Kim & Wright, 2007). In fact, an Educause survey of higher education institutions in the U.S. reported that although higher education's intellectual climate attracts many, its ambiguity or multiplicity of purpose, political nature of leadership, and loose alignment of organizational subcomponents may cause other staff to leave (Katz, et al., 2004). Research on public sector motivation suggests the prevalence of idealistic employees in government who care about their jobs because of the potential to benefit or change society (Perry & Wise, 1990). For this reason, social scientists have suggested that the quality of the work experience for public sector professionals is problematic (Cherniss & Kane, 1987). Furthermore, scholars have proposed that professionals in

the public sector initially approach work with higher expectations concerning autonomy and intrinsic fulfillment but instead find themselves in routinized jobs constrained by close supervision and rigid bureaucratic controls (Cherniss & Kane, 1987).

Similarly, in institutions of higher education, IT professionals go to work for the collegial environment, learning opportunities, the nonprofit mission and the opportunity to contribute to and make a difference in the community (Golden, 2006). As in the public sector, these workers instead find themselves in an environment filled with the constraints of administrative practices that emphasize rules and regulations, control systems, and limited autonomy and flexibility (Golden, 2006). These factors are further compounded by the tendency to purchase packaged solutions that reduce in-house work to basic system maintenance and relatively simple high level programming activities (Coombs, 2009). Also, higher education institutions like the public sector, are in constant competition with private industry for well-trained and experienced IT professionals (Coombs, 2009; Golden, 2006).

3. PURPOSE OF THE STUDY AND RESEARCH QUESTION

Though considerable research has been conducted on job burnout in the management literature among human services occupations, the public sector and in the IT literature across various occupations, we still do not have a clear understanding of burnout and its relationship to turnover intentions. Perhaps the reason for this lack of clarity is because the construct of job burnout is too complex to be studied as a single entity. In order to further our understanding, we may need to deconstruct burnout. In the literature, one theory suggests that the collective burnout construct is comprised of two major constructs: work exhaustion and disengagement (Demerouti, et al., 2001). For example, Schaufeli and Bakker (2004), with a sample of nearly 1,700 workers in four different occupational groups, found support for the two-dimensional construct with the notion that disengagement was related to job resources. However, they found that both demands and resources were related to work exhaustion. Bakker, Demerouti and Verbeke (2004) found a similar effect in their study of job performance, suggesting that the differential main effects predictions of the JD-R may need to be reconsidered and refined. Yet, the two-dimensional construct has not been researched among IT professionals in higher education institutions.

Thus, the purpose of this study is to further our understanding of job burnout by deconstructing this compound, complex phenomenon into the constructs—work exhaustion and disengagement and then to examine each one in relationship to the turnover intentions of IT professionals in one institution of higher education in a major metropolitan area. In addition to contributing to our understanding of collective job burnout and turnover intentions, the current study hopes to provide useful information that may help higher education institutions recognize work-related issues faced by IT staff and better compete for talented IT workers. Thus, the research question for this study is:

RQ: What is the relationship between disengagement, work exhaustion and turnover intentions among IT professionals in one higher education institution in a major metropolitan area?

4. STATEMENT OF POTENTIAL SIGNIFICANCE

Burnout has grown from a specialized occupational hazard to a pervasive workplace hazard and brings enormous costs to both organizations and individuals. Burnout negatively impacts attitudes and leads to undesirable behaviors, such as lower job involvement, reduced task performance and increased turnover intentions (Alarcon, 2011; Allen, et al., 2009; Armstrong & Riemenschneider, 2011; Jackson & Maslach, 1982; Leiter & Maslach, 1988; Schaufeli, Bakker, & Van Rhenen, 2009; Shirom, 1989). A recent Gallup poll published in October 2011 found that 71% of American workers are 'not engaged' or are 'actively disengaged' in their work, meaning they are emotionally disconnected from their organizations and as a result are less likely to be productive (Blacksmith & Harter, 2011).

The existing IT research on the relationship between the turnover intentions of IT workers and collective burnout is limited in scope because it focuses solely on exhaustion and therefore leaves gaps in our understanding of the phenomenon. One area that should be more closely examined is how and whether disengagement is related to turnover intentions. Further, burnout among university IT professionals is a niche that has not been investigated despite the fact that higher education institutions rely on these professionals to help them keep pace with technological advances and the technology demands of students, faculty and administrators. This study is designed to help to begin to fill this void in the research.

4.1 Conceptual Framework

In this study, the JD-R model will be adapted to further our understanding of exhaustion and disengagement and their relationship to turnover intentions among university IT professionals. Specifically, the JD-R model will be recreated as depicted in Figure 1. The antecedents of disengagement and exhaustion will be removed and the focus will be on exhaustion and disengagement and their relationship to turnover intentions.

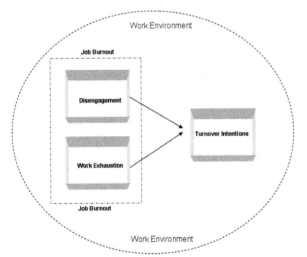

Figure 1: Conceptual framework of the relationship between disengagement, work exhaustion and turnover intentions

The JD-R model posits that to the extent that we can reduce demands and supplement resources for workers, burnout may be reduced (Halbesleben & Buckley, 2004). The current study theorizes that disengagement and exhaustion are two independent constructs that together constitute burnout, and separately may influence turnover intentions.

4.2 Turnover Intentions

Historically, turnover researchers viewed job satisfaction and perceived job alternatives as the most important variables in understanding why employees voluntarily leave organizations (Hulin, Roznowski, & Hachiya, 1985). Over the last 20 years, considerable research has been devoted to developing predictive models of voluntary turnover, with job satisfaction, organizational commitment, and turnover intentions among the most commonly proposed antecedents (Ferratt, Agarwal, Brown, & Moore, 2005; Lee, Mitchell, Wise, & Fireman, 1996; Moore, 2000a). Recent studies support the fact that burnout is a predictor of turnover intentions and turnover (Alarcon, 2011; Allen, et al., 2009; Armstrong & Riemenschneider, 2011; Demerouti, et al., 2001; Kim & Wright, 2007; Moore, 2000a, 2000b; Moore & Burke, 2002; Pawlowski, Kaganer, & Cater III, 2004).

4.3 Disengagement

Two schools of thought on disengagement exist in the literature. One school considers disengagement to be a component of job burnout (Demerouti, et al., 2001), while the other does not specifically isolate disengagement, but instead focuses on the positive perspective of engagement as the direct opposite of burnout (Alarcon, 2011; Maslach & Leiter, 1997; Maslach & Leiter, 2008). Conceptualizations of disengagement tend to confuse and/or combine it with the occurrence of other job attitudes and behaviors, such as engagement, job satisfaction and organizational commitment (Attridge, 2009; Simpson, 2009).

4.4 Exhaustion

Exhaustion is a recurring theme in the IT literature with research that links exhaustion to turnover intentions and turnover (Kim & Wright, 2007; Moore, 2000a, 2000b; Moore & Burke, 2002; Pawlowski, et al., 2004). IT professionals experiencing exhaustion are expected to report a higher propensity to leave the job (Moore, 2000a). It also has been suggested that the first thing most people consider when they encounter exhaustion is changing jobs (Leatz & Stolar, 1993).

4.5 Research Question and Hypotheses

In analyzing the relationship among turnover intentions, disengagement, and work exhaustion as the two dimensions of burnout, one research question and eight hypotheses were tested.

> **RQ1** What is the relationship between disengagement, work exhaustion and turnover intentions among IT professionals in one higher education institution in a major metropolitan area?

> **H1**: There will be a statistically significant, positive correlation between an IT professional's disengagement score and turnover intentions score in a single higher education institution in a major metropolitan area.

> **H1a**: There will be a statistically significant negative correlation between IT professional's disengagement score and turnover intentions score among IT professions in a single higher education institution in a major metropolitan area.

H1o: There will not be a statistically significant relationship between an IT professional's disengagement score and turnover intentions score among IT professions in a single higher education institution in a major metropolitan area.

H2: There will be a statistically significant, positive correlation between an IT professional's work exhaustion score and turnover intentions score in a single higher education institution in a major metropolitan area.

H2a: There will be a statistically significant, negative correlation between an IT professional's work exhaustion score and turnover intentions score in a single higher education institution in a major metropolitan area.

H2o: There will not be a significant relationship between an IT professional's work exhaustion score and turnover intentions score in a single higher education institution in a major metropolitan area.

H3: There will be a statistically significant interaction between disengagement scores and work exhaustion scores on the turnover intentions scores of IT professionals in a single higher education institution in a major metropolitan area.

H3o: There will be no statistically significant interaction between an IT professional's work exhaustion scores, disengagement scores on the turnover intentions scores in a single higher education institution in a major metropolitan area.

5. SUMMARY OF METHODOLOGY

This study used a non-experimental, cross-sectional survey research design using a Web-based questionnaire. The data was collected from a population of IT professionals in a single university. Two instruments were used to capture the data. The OLdenburg Burnout Inventory (OLBI) measures exhaustion and disengagement as developed by Demerouti et al. (2001). The OLBI measures attitudes toward the work task (e.g., uninteresting, not challenging) as well as a devaluation and mechanical execution of work (Demerouti, et al., 2001). Also, the disengagement items concern the relationship between the employee and their job. The sixteen questions in the OLBI address the burnout dimensions of work exhaustion and disengagement from work so that subscales could be formed for multiple regression analysis. The mean score for each respondent's questions was calculated to derive a composite score for each of the burnout dimensions.

The three questions that measure turnover intentions are from the Michigan Organizational Assessment Questionnaire Job Satisfaction Subscale (MOAQ-JSS) and measure the likelihood of an individual to quit his or her job. The questions are: "How likely is it that you will actively look for a new job in the next year?" "How likely is it that you could find a job with another employer with about the same pay and benefits you now have? And "I often think about quitting." Respondents selected from a 7-point Likert-type scale to respond to these items. The three questions were combined to create the dependent variable.

Also, correlational analyses were conducted to answer the research question. The research question for the current study is:

5.1 Proposed sample

The total population (N = 287) of U.S. IT employees in a single university in a major metropolitan area served as the participants for the study. The employees in the IT department are dispersed across three campuses and perform activities related to information technology ranging from customer-facing technology support (they work directly with students, faculty and staff), code development, operational support and maintenance, database administration, project management, administrative support, testing, systems analysis and systems administration.

This study used a comprehensive sampling approach in that every IT employee in the IT department was given access to the survey about their perceptions of their work environment as it relates to turnover intentions, exhaustion and disengagement from work. The survey invitation email was sent to the entire site population of 287 potential study participants. The surveys were strictly confidential and anonymous to protect the identity of the respondents.

5.2 Procedure and Design

Once permission was received from the Office of Human Research Internal Review Board (IRB), human resources and the IT management, the initial survey was pre-tested in a pilot study to test for reliability measures as compared to the psychometric data acquired from the original developers of the surveys and to find any discrepancies.

One IT employee was asked to participate in a voluntary pilot study by completing the online survey and providing feedback to the researcher concerning any errors or questions about the instrument. Since the online survey database recorded the start and finish times of each respondent, the length of time to complete the survey was assessed. This information was used later in the request for participation in the final survey. The feedback received from the respondent in the pilot study was analyzed and incorporated into the final questionnaire, as appropriate, prior to publishing and distributing to the study population. Pilot test responses were not included in the final data analysis.

The final survey data was collected via the online survey tool. An e-mail communication with a hyperlink to the survey was sent to the potential participants and provided the research study details, estimated testing timeframe, and informed consent regarding the survey. Two reminder emails were sent to the respondents during the four-week period.

5.3 Data Analysis

Data collected as part of this study was tabulated and entered into the Statistical Package for the Social Sciences (SPSS) version 17.0 by the researcher. Specifically, SPSS was used to code, record, and analyze the data. SPSS-enabled data was sorted based on similarities or differences, and accuracy in totals was checked. All respondents answered clearly and no surveys were removed from the analysis of the data. Descriptive statistics were conducted on the demographic data. Chronbach's alpha tests of reliability were conducted on the exhaustion, disengagement from work and turnover intentions scales with results ranging from .828 through .837.

To answer the research question, the OLBI and MOAQ-JSS responses were averaged individually and then correlation statistics were calculated. To quantify the strength of the relationship between the variables and to compare results from the OLBI and MOAQ-JSS, the Pearson correlation coefficient was used. For both the OLBI and the MOAQ-JSS descriptive statistics were used to describe disengagement, work exhaustion and turnover intentions. Multiple regression analyses were conducted to further substantiate the findings from the Pearson correlation coefficient calculation.

In addition, qualitative content analyses were used to analyze the themes that were extracted from the open-ended questions about their experiences of work exhaustion, disengagement and turnover intentions.

5.4 Limitations
The delimitations offer important considerations for this and future studies. The limitations for the current study included the following:

1. Any time respondents are asked to self-report, there is the risk that they may mis-represent themselves. Since very little qualitative data will be collected, it will be impossible to determine whether this has occurred.

2. This study used a comprehensive sample rather than a random sample. For this reason, the results can only be generalized to the population of which the sample is representative.

5.5 Research Assumptions
There are three assumptions that are important to the current study. They are that work exhaustion; disengagement and turnover intentions at the individual level can be measured and analyzed using a quantitative approach.

6. PRELIMINARY RESULTS
The Web-based survey was made available to 287 IT employees in a single university. The email with a hyperlink to the online survey was sent out on January 4, 2012 and access to the survey was turned off on February 2, 2012—approximately four weeks after the email containing the hyperlink to the original survey was distributed. Within the span of four weeks, 116 surveys were completed and returned representing a return rate of 40%.

6.1 Demographics of the Sample
The demographic data that were collected through the survey provided information about the characteristics of the sample. The data indicated that 53.1% of the respondents were male and 46.9% were female. Eighteen respondents did not respond to the question about gender. The data further revealed that 64% of the sample ranged in age from 31 to 50. In addition, 58% of the respondents had worked in their current position between one and five years, 30% worked in their position between six and ten years and 11% had worked in their current position between 11 and 15 years. Only 1% of the sample worked in their current role for more than 20 years. No responses were recorded for the timeframe between 15 and 20 years. Also in the sample, 33.7% of respondents had worked in the IT field between 11 and 15 years. Another 14.9% worked in IT between one and five years, 16.8% worked in IT between six and ten years, 15.8 % reported that they worked in the IT field between 16 and 20 years and 18.8% reported that they worked in IT for 21 or more years. The roles represented in the sample included, analysts, developers, database administrators, system engineers, webmasters, project

managers and other IT specialists. 56.3% of the sample self-identified as White, 11.5% self-identified as Black or African-American, 25% identified themselves as Asian, the remaining 7% self-identified as being from multiple races or other. There were 20 participants who did not answer the question about ethnicity.

6.2 Findings
A multiple regression analysis was conducted to assess how well measures for disengagement from work and work exhaustion predicted the turnover intentions of university IT employees. Three predictors were entered simultaneously into the analysis: disengagement, work exhaustion, and the interaction between disengagement and exhaustion (to create the interaction variable). The overall variance explained by the three predictors was 24.3%. Each predictor was positively related to the outcome variable, including disengagement from work ($\beta = .02$, $p = .946$), work exhaustion ($\beta = -.55$, $p = .090$), and the interaction variable of work exhaustion and disengagement from work ($\beta = -.94$, $p = .121$). None of the factors emerged as a significant predictor of turnover intentions.

Particular attention was given to determining the evidence of multicollinearity among the variables since the two dimensions of burnout were the variables of interest to the study. Multicollinearity is a statistical phenomenon in which two or more predictor variables in a multiple regression model are highly correlated (Tabachnick & Fidell, 2007). In this situation the coefficient estimates may change erratically in response to small changes in the model or the data. Multicollinearity does not reduce the predictive power or reliability of the model as a whole; it affects only calculations relating to individual predictors. That is, a multiple regression model with correlated predictors can indicate how well the entire bundle of predictors predicts the outcome variable, but it may not give valid results about any individual predictor or about which predictors are redundant with others (Wiersma & Jurs, 2005).

In the current study, Pearson correlation calculations resulted in all correlations' ranging between .322 and .931. Scores above .90 suggest multicollinearity among the variables. Additionally, the t-ratios for the individual coefficients were not statistically significant, yet the overall F statistic was. According to (Wiersma & Jurs, 2005), the best solution for dealing with multicollinearity is to understand the cause and eliminate it if possible.

Since in the case of multicollinearity the variables basically measure the same thing, the researcher decided to refine the statistical model and retest the hypotheses by measuring the variables separately in the model using a backward deletion, statistical regression. Statistical regression is used to examine the impact of each variable to the model step by step by successively adding and removing variables based solely on the t-statistics of their estimated coefficients (Tabachnick & Fidell, 2007).

The results of the regression analysis indicated that disengagement was consistently and moderately more significant than work exhaustion when the variables were retested without the intercept while work exhaustion and the interaction variable remained non-significant.

6.3 Responses to Open-Ended Questions
The last portion of the survey consisted of three open-ended questions that were constructed by the researcher with the assistance of a quantitative research methodologist. The

questions attempted to provide further insights into how decisions about turnover intentions, disengagement and work exhaustion were related, and to provide further insights into the responses in the survey. All participants were asked the following open-ended questions: "What aspects of your work experience cause you to consider leaving your current position? "What aspects of your current work experience impact your level of engagement?" "What aspects of your work experience impact your energy level?" Qualitative data analysis was used to analyze and code the responses to the open-ended questions. The categories were derived from the variables that are inputs to the demands and resources in the JD-R model. Additional categories were added if the response did not fit into an existing category. Table 3 presents the questions, examples of responses and the categories into which they were coded.

Table 1: Examples of Categorized Responses to the Open-Ended Questions

Question	Participant Responses	Categories
What aspects of your work experience cause you to consider leaving your current position	Poor working conditions. Rigid policies on flex time and telework	Management Issues
	If ever, chances are very bleak. "Salary""... I took a drastic salary cut to work closer from home	Personnel Practices
What aspects of your current work experience impact your level of engagement	Boring work. Trivial work	Work structure
	I do not feel disengaged from my work	NA
	When I have to do a task to ""check a box"" vs. accomplishing anything	Meaningful work
What aspects of your work experience impact your energy level	Too much work in too few hours	Personnel practices
	Tedious activities and redundant work	Work structure

The initial review of the qualitative responses to the open-ended questions suggested that there are a number of variables related to job and work characteristics that influence an individual's disengagement, exhaustion and turnover intentions. Few responses indicated that being located in a major metropolitan area was an important factor in their intentions to quit their job.

7. SUMMARY AND CONCLUSIONS

This study attempted to extend existing research on burnout among IT professionals by focusing on IT workers in a university setting. These IT professionals haves not been studied extensively in the literature. The underlying belief was that university IT workers are similar to IT professionals in the public and private sector and that their turnover intentions would increase as their work exhaustion and disengagement levels increased.

The findings from this research indicated that disengagement consistently showed a statistically significant, positive correlation with turnover intentions. The other two variables (work exhaustion and the interaction variable combining work exhaustion and disengagement) were found to be inconsistently statistically significant in their correlation to turnover intentions. This finding for university IT employees is in direct contrast to the results for IT professionals obtained in other studies in which work exhaustion rather than disengagement was the primary predictor of turnover intentions (Kim & Wright, 2007; Korunka, Hoonakker, & Carayon, 2005; Moore, 2000a). While it is certainly true that the university IT employees in this study experienced work exhaustion, it was a less significant influence on their turnover intentions.

According to McKnight, Phillips and Hardgrave (2009) IT employees' turnover intentions are influenced by workplace characteristics (such as structural fairness, trust in senior management and job security) as well as job characteristics. This was a finding from the open-ended questions in this study.

7.1 Study Limitations

The primary limitation to this research was that the degree to which an employee experiences work exhaustion and disengagement may be attributable to other factors not included in this study. This became evident in the misalignment of and inconsistency between the survey responses and the open-ended questions. The survey responses indicated that the employees' experience of burnout and turnover intentions was neutral. However, when asked about what makes them feel disengaged and exhausted and look for another job, the responses richly described specific negative work and job characteristics in their environment. Other limitations included:

1. Some work exhaustion and disengagement can be attributed to personal traits or characteristics instead of environmental factors.

2. An organization's culture may influence an individual's perceptions of the variables in this study. This study did not take organizational culture into consideration.

7.2 Implications for Future Research

The most important information gained from this study is that turnover intentions among university IT employees cannot be solved by merely reducing disengagement and work exhaustion. The argument is not that burnout is a good thing for employees. But, burnout itself is not always the issue. Perceptions of the workplace characteristics played a major role in how these employees experienced burnout and turnover intentions.

The most important conceptual implication of the study is that future investigations of disengagement, work exhaustion and turnover intentions among university IT employees must account for the unique work environment and how those workplace characteristics predict disengagement, work exhaustion and subsequent thoughts about quitting.

Another implication of this study is to repeat the work and expand the model to include antecedents, incorporating job characteristics and workplace characteristics to see how and whether they influence work exhaustion and disengagement. Also, there should be more research on whether geography (e.g., living in a major metropolitan area) has an influence on turnover intentions. The open-ended questions were only a small portion of the overall study. It would be interesting to conduct a larger qualitative study to see what themes emerge.

8. ACKNOWLEDGMENTS

Our sincere thanks to the IT department who granted us permission to conduct the study with the staff. We also thank our colleagues who provided their thoughts and ideas on this topic, and to the anonymous reviewers who provided valuable suggestions.

9. REFERENCES

[1] Alarcon, G. M. (2011). A meta-analysis of burnout with job demands, resources, and attitudes. *Journal of Vocational Behavior, 79*, 549-562.

[2] Allen, M. W., Armstrong, D. J., Reid, M. F., & Riemenschneider, C. K. (2009). *IT employee retention: employee expectations and workplace environments.* Paper presented at the SIGMIS-CPR, Limerick, Ireland.

[3] Armstrong, D. J., & Riemenschneider, C. K. (2011). *The influence of demands and resources on emotional exhaustion with the information systems profession.* Paper presented at the Thirty Second International Conference on Information Systems, Shanghai.

[4] Attridge, M. (2009). Measuring and managing employee work engagement: A review of the research and business literature. *Journal of Workplace Behavioral Health, 24*, 383-398.

[5] Bakker, A. B., Demerouti, E., & Verbeke, W. (2004). Using the job demands-resources model to predict burnout and performance. *Human Resources Management, 43*(1), 83-104

[6] Blacksmith, N., & Harter, J. K. (2011). Majority of American workers not engaged in their jobs: highly educated and middle-aged employees among the least likely to be engaged. *Gallup Wellbeing.* Retrieved from http://www.gallup.com/poll/150383/majority-american-workers-not-engaged-jobs.aspx.

[7] Carayon, P., Schoepke, J., Hoonakker, P. L. T., Haims, M. C., & Brunette, M. (2006). Evaluating causes and consequences of turnover intention among IT workers: the development of a questionnaire survey. *Behaviour & Information Technology, 25*(5), 381-397.

[8] Cherniss, C., & Kane, J. S. (1987). Public sector professionals: job characteristics, satisfaction and aspirations for intrinsic fulfillment through work. *Human Relations*(40), 125-136.

[9] Coombs, C. (2009). Improving retention strategies for IT professionals working in the public sector. *Information & Management, 46*, 233-240.

[10] Cooper, C. L., Dewe, P. J., & O'Driscoll, M. P. (2001). *Organizational Stress: A Review and Critique of Theory, Research and Applications* CA: Sage Publications.

[11] Cropanzano, R., Rupp, D. E., & Byrne, Z. S. (2003). The relationship of emotional exhaustion to work attitudes, job performance, and organizational citizenship behaviors. *Journal of Applied Psychology, 88*(1), 160-169.

[12] Demerouti, E., Bakker, A. B., Nachreiner, F., & Schaufeli, W. B. (2001). The job demands-resources model of burnout. *Journal of Applied Psychology, 86*(3), 499-512.

[13] Ferratt, T. W., Agarwal, R., Brown, C. V., & Moore, J. E. (2005). IT human resource management configurations and IT turnover: theoretical synthesis and empirical analysis. *Information Systems Research, 16*(3), 237-255.

[14] Glenn, M., & Johnson, L. (2008). *The future of higher education: how technology will shape learning.* The Economist Intelligence Unit. New Media Consortium.

[15] Golden, C. (Ed.). (2006). *Cultivating careers: professional development for campus IT.* Washington, DC: Educause.

[16] Halbesleben, J. R. B., & Buckley, M. R. (2004). Burnout in organizational life. *Journal of Management, 30*(6), 859-879.

[17] Harter, J. K. (2008). Why People Change Jobs? . *Gallup Management Journal.* Retrieved from http://gmj.gallup.com/content/106912/Turning-Around-Your-Turnover-Problem.aspx.

[18] Hulin, C. L., Roznowski, M., & Hachiya, D. (1985). Alternative opportunities and withdrawal decisions: empirical and theoretical discrepancies and an integration. *Psychological Bulletin, 97*(2), 233-250.

[19] Jackson, S. E., & Maslach, C. (1982). After effects of job-related stress: families as victims. *Journal of Occupational Behavior, 3*, 63-77.

[20] Jackson, S. E., & Maslach, C. (1982). After effects of job-related stress: families as victims. *Journal of Occupational Behavior, 3*, 63-77.

[21] Joseph, D., & Ang, S. (2003). *Turnover of IT professionals: a quantitative analysis of the literature.* Paper presented at the SIGMIS Conference, Philadelphia, PA.

[22] Joseph, D., Ng, K., Koh, C., & Ang, S. (2007). Turnover of information technology professionals: a narrative review, meta-analytic structural equation modeling, and model development. *MIS Quarterly, 31*(3), 547-577.

[23] Kalimo, R., & Toppinen, S. (1995). *Burnout in computer professionals.* Paper presented at the Work, Stress and Health 1995: Creating Healthier Workplaces Washington, DC.

[24] Kanwar, Y. P. S., Singh, A. K., & Kodwani, A. D. (2009). Work-life balance and burnout as predictors of job satisfaction in the IT-ITES industry. *VISION --The Journal of Business Perspective, 13*(2), 1-12.

[25] Katz, R. N., Kvavik, R. B., Penrod, J. I., Pirani, J. A., Nelson, M. R., & Salaway, G. (2004). Information technology leadership in higher education: the condition of the community. *1.* Retrieved from www.educause.edu/ecar.

[26] Kim, S., & Wright, B., E. (2007). IT employee work exhaustion: toward an integrated model of antecednets and consequences. *Review of Public Personnel Administration, 27*(2), 147-170.

[27] Korunka, C., Hoonakker, P., L. T., & Carayon, P. (Eds.). (2005). *Towards a universal turnover model for the IT work force – a replication study.* Santa Monica, CA: IEA Press.

[28] Leatz, C., & Stolar, M. (1993). *Career stress/personal stress: how to stay healthy in a high-stress environment.* New York, NY: McGraw-Hill.

[29] Lee, M., Mitchell, T. R., Wise, L., & Fireman, S. (1996). An unfolding model of voluntary turnover. *Academy of Management Review, 39*, 5-36.

[30] Leiter, M. P., & Maslach, C. (1988). The impact of interpersonal environment on burnout and organizational commitment *Journal of Organizational Behavior 9* 297-308.

[31] Maslach, C., & Goldberg, J. (1998). Prevention of burnout: new perspectives. *Applied and Preventive Psychology, 7*, 63-74.

[32] Maslach, C., & Leiter, M. P. (1997). *The truth about burnout* San Francisco, CA: Jossey-Bass.

[33] Maslach, C., & Leiter, M. P. (2008). Early predictors of job burnout and engagement. *Journal of Applied Psychology, 93*, 498-512.

[34] Maslach, C., Schaufeli, W. B., & Leiter, M. P. (2001). Job burnout. *Annual Review of Psychology, 52*, 397-422.

[35] McGee, M. K. (1996). Hot skills in '96: internet, client-server, and networking experts top lists of the most wanted. *Information Week, 560*-564.

[36] McKnight, D. H., Phillips, B., & Hardgrave, B. C. (2009). Which reduces IT turnover intention the most: workplace characteristics or job characteristics? *Information & Management, 46*, 167-174.

[37] Moore, J. E. (2000a). One road to turnover: an examination of work exhaustion in technology professionals. *MIS Quarterly, 24*(141-168).

[38] Moore, J. E. (2000b). Why is this happening? a causal attribution approach to work exhaustion consequences. *Academy of Management Review, 25*(2), 335-349.

[39] Moore, J. E., & Burke, L. A. (2002). How to turn around 'turnover culture' in IT. *Communications of the ACM, 45*(2), 73-78.

[40] Pawlowski, S., Kaganer, E., & Cater III, J. (2004). *Mapping perceptions of burnout in the information technology profession: a study using social representations theory.* Paper presented at the International Conference on Information Systems (ICIS).

[41] Perry, J., & Wise, L. (1990). The motivational bases of public service. *Public Administration Review, 50*, 367-373.

[42] Rigas, P. P. (2009). A model of turnover intention among technically-oriented informatoin systems professionals. *Information Resources Management Journal, 22*(1), 1-23.

[43] Schaufeli, W. B., & Bakker, A. B. (2004). Job demands, job resources, and their relationship with burnout and engagement: a multi-sample study. *Journal of Organizational Behavior, 25*, 293-315.

[44] Schaufeli, W. B., Bakker, A. B., & Van Rhenen, W. (2009). How changes in job demands and resources predict burnout, work engagement, and sickness absenteeism. *Journal of Organizational Behavior, 30*, 893-917.

[45] Sethi, V., Barrier, T., & King, R. C. (1999). An examination of the correlates of burnout in information systems professionals. *Information Resources Management Journal, 12*, 5–13.

[46] Shirom, A. (Ed.). (1989). *Burnout in work organizations.* New York, NY: John Wiley & Sons.

[47] impson, M. R. (2009). Engagement at work: A review of the literature. *International Journal of Nursing Studies, 46*, 1012-1024. doi: 10.1016/j.ijmurstu

[48] Tabachnick, B. G., & Fidell, L. S. (2007). *Using Multivariate Statistics* (5th ed.). Boston, MA: Pearson Education.

[49] Wiersma, W., & Jurs, S. G. (2005). *Research methods in education: an introduction* (Eighth ed.). New York: Pearson.

Work-Life Conflict and Job Mobility Intentions

Damien Joseph
Nanyang Technological University
50 Nanyang Avenue S3-B2C-99
+65 6790 4831

adjoseph@ntu.edu.sg

Christine Koh
Nanyang Technological University
50 Nanyang Avenue S3-01C-96
+65 6790 4831

askkoh@ntu.edu.sg

ABSTRACT

This study takes the first step in IT literature to examine the role of time-based and strain-based work-life conflicts on turnover and turnaway. Prior research on work-life (and work-family) conflicts and turnover typically examines it as a unidimensional construct. This study examines work-life conflict as a multidimensional construct comprising of time-based and strain-based conflicts. In this study, time and strain (i.e. demands on energy) are conceptualized as resources. The Conservation of Resources Theory is utilized to develop two sets of hypotheses relating time and strain to turnover and turnaway intentions. The hypotheses are tested on a sample of IT professionals drawn from a local IT professional association. The results indicate that time-based conflicts are not related to turnover and turnaway intentions. Strain-based conflicts, however, are positively related to turnover and turnaway intentions. This study concludes with a discussion of this pattern of results and presents subsequent research directions, which the authors are pursing.

Categories and Subject Descriptors

K.7.1 [**Occupations**]

General Terms

Management, Theory.

Keywords

Information Technology Professionals, Work-life Conflict, Turnover, Turnaway.

1. INTRODUCTION

The demand for IT jobs continues to outstrip the supply of IT talent [4, 23]. Securing talent remains one of the most critical issues for IT managers [21]. IT managers experience difficulties securing IT talent because such talent is likely to leave organization and the IT profession. A constellation of reasons have been proposed to explain why IT professionals leave their organizations [19] and the IT profession [2]. These reasons include work-life conflict [2, 17, 19].

Work-life conflict refers to the inter-role imbalance arising from the demands of work and non-work-related responsibilities [24, p. 50]. The domains of work and non-work compete for finite personal resources such as time, attention, and energy [8, p.181]. Resources spent in one domain (e.g. work) necessarily mean that

there is less of such resources available for use in the other domain. For example, long effortful hours at work leave little time and energy for non-work activities [8, 32].

Prior IT and management research has extensively examined the role of work-life conflict on turnover intentions [3, 6, 19, 22, 28]. The research is in consensus that work-life conflict is a stressor. The stress of work-life conflict is positively related to the turnover of IT professionals. In other words, IT professionals experiencing work-life conflict tend to leave their organizations, presumably to reduce such stresses.

The extant research in IT and management, however, remains silent on the role of work-life conflict in explaining professionals' intentions to exit from their profession, i.e. turnaway. Understanding the effect of work-life conflict on turnaway is critical to help the IT profession better retain valuable IT talent and prevent further shortages in the supply of IT labor.

Moreover, prior research in IT and management has typically treated work-life conflict as a unidimensional construct [e.g. 3, 13]. Current conceptualizations of work-life conflict in the management literature, however, have been multidimensional, i.e. time-based and strain-based conflicts [7, 33]. Although the theory of work–family conflict [11] included behavior-based conflict as an additional dimension, time-based and strain-based conflict are the most frequently measured and studied conflict dimensions [7]. For example, studies have examined the role of person-environment fit as an antecedent to time-based and strain-based conflict [7]. This study finds that greater person-environment fit is negatively related to both time-based and strain-based conflicts. In another study examining gender differences in time-based and strain-based conflicts [33], the results suggest that females report higher strain-based conflicts than males; but there are no gender differences with time-based conflicts.

Similarly, recent IT research has followed management research in conceptualizing work-life conflict as a multidimensional construct [20, 27, 31]. These IT studies have highlighted time-based and strain-based conflicts as major stressors within IT work [20, 27]. IT professionals tend to experience time-based conflicts because they are required to be on call 24/7 [20]; thus, making it more difficult to plan and devote time to non-work obligations. Likewise, IT professionals tend to experience strain-based conflicts because work pressures such as meeting service level agreements may spillover to non-work domains [27]. These IT research have also examined differences in time-based and strain-based across genders, marital status and IT experience [20, 31]. But, IT and management research has yet to examine the consequences of time-based and strain-based conflicts.

This study fills this gap in the IT and management literature by relating time-based and strain-based work-life conflicts to its consequences - turnover and turnaway intentions. By doing so, this study contributes to research by taking the first step towards offering a nuanced explanation of work-life conflict in relation to job mobility intentions. To the best of our knowledge, this is the first study to examine the consequences of time-based and strain-based conflicts in IT and management research.

2. THEORY AND HYPOTHESES

To explain IT professionals' perceptions of work-life conflict and its consequences, we draw on the theory of conservation of resources [14, 15].

Resources, in this theory, are defined as "entities that are centrally valued in their own right (e.g., self-esteem, close attachments, health, and inner peace) or act as a means to obtain centrally valued ends (e.g., money, social support, and recognition)" [14, p. 307]. Within this theoretical framework, time and energy are resources as they acts as a means to obtain centrally valued ends such as compensation and work-life satisfaction [9].

The theory of conservation of resources proposes that stress occurs when resources are threatened with loss; and that individuals respond to such threats by seeking to conserve those resources [14, 15]. When threatened with time-based and strain-based conflicts arising from competing demands on time and energy, the theory of conservation of resources posits that IT professionals will tend to protect their resources. IT professionals may protect their time and energy by either engaging actively to resolve conflicts or withdraw from stressful environments in which conflicts occur [27].

2.1 Time-based Work-life Conflict

Time-based conflict occurs when the time devoted to work makes it difficult to fulfill the obligations and requirements of non-work responsibilities [25, p. 428]. The basic premise of time-based conflict is that additional time spent in the work domain precludes individuals from investing that time in the non-work domain. For IT professionals, time-based conflicts may arise because unrealistic deadlines for IT projects lead to insufficient time to complete them [1, 22]. Consequently, IT professionals are obliged to spend more time at work to meet deadlines and less time on non-work activities.

The competing demands on time from work and non-work domains threaten to deplete the finite time resources available to IT professionals. The theory of conservation of resources predicts that IT professionals will tend to withdraw from this stressful environment. Hence:

H1a: *Time-based work-life conflict is positively related to turnover intentions.*

H1b: *Time-based work-life conflict is positively related to turnaway intentions.*

2.2 Strain-based Work-life Conflict

Strain-based work-life conflict occurs when work pressures spillover and affects the non-work domain [25, p. 428]. The basic premise of strain-based conflict is that additional energy spent in the work domain precludes individuals from investing that energy in the non-work domain [11]. Strain-based conflicts may arise due to energies spent undertaking shift work or working after office-hours while trying to maintain obligations in non-work domains [20]. Strain-based conflict may also arise when individuals face difficulties in leaving the pressures of work behind when transitioning to their non-work domains.

Technologies today allow IT professionals to continue to work regardless of location and time [30]. Work pressures require IT professionals to remain connected to the office more often and more regularly than their non-IT coworkers [5].

The competing demands on energy from work and non-work domains threaten to deplete the finite energy resources available to IT professionals. The theory of conservation of resources predicts that IT professionals will tend to withdraw from this stressful environment. Hence:

H2a: *Strain-based work-life conflict is positively related to turnover intentions.*

H2b: *Strain-based work-life conflict is positively related to turnaway intentions.*

3. METHOD
3.1 Sample and Procedures

We tested the hypotheses using survey data collected from a sample of IT professionals of a local IT professional association. Data were gathered through a web-based survey, following email invitations to members of this association.

Our final sample comprises 486 IT professionals working in multinational corporations (55%) and public-sector organizations (45%). Respondents were predominantly male (79%), married (62%), and between 25-40 years old (65%).

3.2 Measures

Turnover intent was measured with three items (1 = strong disagree; 7 = strongly agree) adapted from Rusbult et al. [26]. A sample item is "I am thinking about quitting my current job for an alternative ICT job".

Turnaway intent was measured with three items (1 = strong disagree; 7 = strongly agree) adapted from Rusbult et al. [26]. A sample item is "I am thinking about quitting my current job for an alternative non-ICT job".

Time-based work-life conflict was measured with three items (1 = strong disagree; 7 = strongly agree) adapted from Stephens and Sommer [29]. A sample item is: "My work leaves me with less time for non-work activities".

Strain-based work-life conflict was measured with three items (1 = strong disagree; 7 = strongly agree) adapted from Stephens and Sommer [29]. A sample item is: "I come home feeling too tired to do the things I enjoy".

Control variables. We controlled for alternative explanations of turnover [19] and turnaway with age (measured using eight ordered categories: 20 years and below; >20-25 years; >25-30 years; >30-35 years; >35-40 years; >40-45 years; >45-50 years; >50 years); gender (1=male, 2=female), and marital status (1=single, 2=married).

4. ANALYSES AND RESULTS

To assess convergent and discriminant validity of the measures, we conducted a confirmatory factor analysis (CFA) using LISREL 8.80 [18].

Results showed good fit of the hypothesized four-factor model (turnover intent, turnaway intent, time-based worklife conflict, and strain-based worklife conflict): χ^2 (df = 48) = 141.29, $NNFI$ = 0.97; CFI = 0.98; $RMSEA$ = 0.063, p < 0.05); $SRMR$ = 0.035, with all fit indices above recommended values [16]. Composite reliabilities for all constructs were above 0.70 (range 0.76 - 0.94), and standardized factor loadings were all significantly different from zero (*t*-values range 8.40 - 32.68), showing support for convergent validity.

To assess discriminant validity, we calculated the average variance extracted (AVE) for the four constructs. The AVE represents the amount of construct-related variance captured in relation to error variance. Results showed that the AVE of the four constructs were above 0.50 (range $0.53 - 0.85$), indicating that the variance shared between each construct with its own indicators is greater than the variance it shared with the other constructs. In sum, the results demonstrated convergent and discriminant validity [10].

We tested our hypotheses using hierarchical regressions, entering the controls (age, gender, and marital status) in Step 1, and the predictors (time-based and strain-based work-life conflict) in Step 2. The tolerance (all values < 1.0) and variance inflation factors (all values < 2) were well within threshold values, indicating multicollinearity is not an issue in our data [12]. We interpreted results based on the change in F (ΔF) at Step 2, and *t*-values of individual parameters.

Hypotheses 1 predicted that time-based work-life conflict will be positively related to turnover intent (*H1a*) and turnaway intent (*H1b*). Contrary to our expectation, results showed that time-based work-life conflict was not significantly related to turnover intent ($\beta = 0.07$, $p > 0.05$) and turnaway intent ($\beta = -0.08$, $p > 0.05$). Thus, Hypothesis 1 is not supported.

Hypothesis 2 predicted that strain-based work-life conflict will be positively related to turnover intent (*H2a*) and turnaway intent (*H2b*). Hierarchical regression results showed that strain-based work-life conflict was significantly related to turnover intent ($\beta = 0.16$, $p < 0.01$) and turnaway intent ($\beta = 0.30$, $p < 0.01$). Thus, Hypothesis 2 is supported.

Over and above the controls, adding the two forms of work-life conflict in step 2 increased the explained variance of turnover intent by 4% ($\Delta F = 10.84$, p<.001; overall adjusted $R^2 = 0.04$), and of turnaway intent by 7% ($\Delta F = 17.68$, p<.001; overall adjusted $R^2 = 0.07$).

5. DISCUSSION AND CONCLUSION

This study examines the role of time-based and strain-based work-life conflicts on turnover and turnaway. This study finds support for one of two hypotheses. Time-based conflicts appear unrelated to both turnover and turnaway intentions. But, strain-based conflicts, which concern IT professionals stock of energy, are positively related to both turnover and turnaway intentions.

One reason for this pattern of findings is that IT professionals are aware of the expectations on their time resource. IT literature is replete with statements about IT work being long in hours and encroaching into non-work time [e.g. 20]. IT professionals have come to expect a 24/7 work cycle and may be mentally prepared for such stresses. IT professionals may also have acquired and developed support for managing time-based conflicts. Although IT literature also contains statements about shift work or even of bringing work home, IT professionals may not have acquired or developed support for managing strain-based conflict [20].

The findings from this study are a first step towards enriching IT research by conceptualizing time and energy as critical resources for IT work and relating them to withdrawal intentions. Prior IT research on work-life conflict has been silent on the role of time and energy in explaining IT professionals' intentions to exit from the profession. Moving forward, more research with other samples of IT professionals is required, to see if the pattern of results applies in different countries, context, and types of IT professionals. Further work can also explore different mechanisms that IT professionals and their organization can use to reduce the effect of time- and strain-based work-life conflict on turnover and turnaway intentions.

6. REFERENCES

1. Agarwal, R. and T.W. Ferratt, *Crafting an Hr Strategy to Meet the Need for IT Workers.* Communications of the ACM, 2001. **44**(7): p. 58-64.

2. Ahuja, M.K., *Women in the Information Technology Profession: A Literature Review, Synthesis and Research Agenda.* European Journal of Information Systems, 2002. **11**(1): p. 20-34.

3. Ahuja, M.K., et al., *IT Road Warriors: Balancing Work-Family Conflict, Job Autonomy, and Work Overload to Mitigate Turnover Intentions.* MIS Quarterly, 2007. **31**(1): p. 1-17.

4. Bartsch, K.J., *The Employment Projections for 2008–18.* Monthly Labor Review, 2009. **132**(11): p. 3-10.

5. Batt, R. and P.M. Valcour, *Human Resources Practices as Predictors of Work-Family Outcomes and Employee Turnover.* Industrial Relations, 2003. **42**(2): p. 189-220.

6. Beauregard, T.A. and L.C. Henry, *Making the Link between Work-Life Balance Practices and Organizational Performance.* Human Resource Management Review, 2009. **19**(1): p. 9-22.

7. Chen, Z., G.N. Powell, and J.H. Greenhaus, *Work-to-Family Conflict, Positive Spillover, and Boundary Management: A Person-Environment Fit Approach.* Journal of Vocational Behavior, 2009. **74**(1): p. 82-93.

8. Edwards, J.R. and N. Rothbard, P., *Mechanisms Linking Work and Family: Clarifying the Relationship between Work and Family Constructs.* Academy of Management Review, 2000. **25**(1): p. 179-199.

9. Ford, M.T., B.A. Heinen, and K.L. Langkamer, *Work and Family Satisfaction and Conflict: A Meta-Analysis of Cross-Domain Relations.* Journal of Applied Psychology, 2007. **92**(1): p. 57-80.

10. Fornell, C. and D.F. Larcker, *Evaluating Structural Equation Models with Observable Variables and Measurement Error.* Journal of Marketing Research, 1981. **18**(1): p. 39-50.

11. Greenhaus, J.H. and N.J. Beutell, *Sources of Conflict between Work and Family Roles.* Academy of Management Review, 1985. **10**(1): p. 76-88.

12. Hair, J.F., Jr., et al., *Multivariate Data Analysis with Readings.* 4th ed1995, Englewood Cliffs, NJ: Prentice Hall.

13. Hammer, L.B., et al., *Clarifying Work-Family Intervention Processes: The Roles of Work-Family Conflict and Family-*

Supportive Supervisor Behaviors. Journal of Applied Psychology, 2011. **96**(1): p. 134-150.

14. Hobfoll, S.E., *Social and Psychological Resources and Adaptation.* Review of General Psychology, 2002. **6**(4): p. 307-324.

15. Hobfoll, S.E., et al., *Conservation of Social Resources - Social Support Resource Theory.* Journal of Social and Personal Relationships, 1990. **7**(4): p. 465-478.

16. Hu, L.T. and P.M. Bentler, *Cutoff Criteria for Fit Indexes in Covariance Structure Analysis: Coventional Criteria Versus New Alternatives.* Structural Equation Modeling, 1999. **6**(1): p. 1-55.

17. Igbaria, M., S. Parasuraman, and M.K. Badawy, *Work Experiences, Job Involvement, and Quality of Work Life among Information-Systems Personnel.* MIS Quarterly, 1994. **18**(2): p. 175-201.

18. Jöreskog, K. and D. Sörbon, *Lisrel for Windows 8.80*, 2006, Scientific Software International: Lincolnwood, IL.

19. Joseph, D., et al., *Turnover of Information Technology Professionals: A Narrative Review, Meta-Analytic Structural Equation Modeling, and Model Development.* MIS Quarterly, 2007. **31**(3): p. 547-577.

20. Messersmith, J., *Managing Work-Life Conflict among Information Technology Workers.* Human Resource Management, 2007. **46**(3): p. 429-451.

21. Mok, L. and D. Berry, *Survey Analysis: IT Organizations Need to Change Skills Mix and Staffing Models to Fulfill Business Needs*, 2011, Gartner Inc.: Stamford, CT.

22. Moore, J.E., *One Road to Turnover: An Examination of Work Exhaustion in Technology Professionals.* MIS Quarterly, 2000. **24**(1): p. 141-168.

23. National Science Board, *Science and Enginering Indicators 2010*, 2010, National Science Foundation: Arlington, VA.

24. Netemeyer, R.G., T. Brashear-Alejandro, and J.S. Boles, *A Cross-National Model of Job-Related Outcomes of Work Role and Family Role Variables: A Retail Sales Context.* Academy of Marketing Science, 2004. **32**(1): p. 49-60.

25. Quick, J.D., A.B. Henley, and J.C. Quick, *At Work and at Home.* Organizational Dynamics, 2004. **33**(4): p. 426-438.

26. Rusbult, C.E., et al., *Impact of Exchange Variables on Exit, Voice, Loyalty, and Neglect: An Integrative Model of Responses to Declining Job Satisfaction.* Academy of Management Journal, 1988. **31**(3): p. 589-599.

27. Sarker, S., S. Sarker, and D. Jana, *The Impact of the Nature of Globally Distributed Work Arrangement on Work–Life Conflict and Valence: The Indian Gsd Professionals' Perspective.* European Journal of Information Systems, 2010. **19**(2): p. 209-222.

28. Shockley, K.M. and N. Singla, *Reconsidering Work-Family Interactions and Satisfaction: A Meta-Analysis.* Journal of Management, 2011. **37**(3): p. 861-886.

29. Stephens, G.K. and S.M. Sommer, *The Measurement of Work to Family Conflict.* Educational and Psychological Measurement, 1996. **56**(3): p. 475-486.

30. Stokes, S.L., *A Line in the Sand: Maintaining Work-Life Balance.* Information Systems Management, 1996. **13**(2): p. 83-85.

31. Sumner, M., *An Investigation of Work Family Conflict among IT Professionals.* SIGMIS CPR 2008: Proceedings of the 2008 Acm SIGMIS CPR Conference, ed. D.J. Armstrong and C. Riemenschneider2008. 127-133.

32. Valcour, M., *Work-Based Resources as Moderators of the Relationship between Work Hours and Satisfaction with Work-Family Balance.* Journal of Applied Psychology, 2007. **92**(6): p. 1512-1523.

33. van Daalen, G., T.M. Willemsen, and K. Sanders, *Reducing Work-Family Conflict through Different Sources of Social Support.* Journal of Vocational Behavior, 2006. **69**(3): p. 462-476.

Too Much Of and Less Than a Good Thing: Implications for Managing IT Professionals

Thomas W. Ferratt
University of Dayton
300 College Park
Dayton, OH 45469-2130
937-229-2728

tferratt1@udayton.edu

Harvey Enns
University of Dayton
300 College Park
Dayton, OH 45469-2130
937-229-2677

henns1@udayton.edu

Jayesh Prasad
University of Dayton
300 College Park
Dayton, OH 45469-2130
937-229-2286

Jprasad1@udayton.edu

ABSTRACT

The management of information technology (IT) professionals is an important managerial concern. The way that IT organizations manage their IT professionals is essentially manifested in their implementation of human resource management (HRM) practices, such as those related to work environment and career development opportunities, social support, compensation, and employment security. This paper briefly introduces person-environment (P-E) fit theory to explore what an IT professional wants from an employment arrangement and what is supplied by the employer. However, a criticism of P-E fit theory is that it does not specify the form of the relationship between P-E fit and other constructs, such as satisfaction and job search. In order to address this gap, the paper investigates both equity theory and prospect theory as possible explanations. Ultimately, prospect theory is used to develop illustrative hypotheses. The paper then describes the methodology that will be used to test these hypotheses. The results of the tests, when completed, will be used to suggest directions for managing IT professionals and future IT HRM theory development and testing.

Categories and Subject Descriptors

K.6.1 [**Management of Computing and Information Systems**]: Project and People Management – *staffing*

General Terms

Management.

Keywords

Person-Organization fit, Equity Theory, Prospect Theory.

1. INTRODUCTION

Managing IT professionals is a critical issue for CIOs (Luftman, et al., 2009). HRM practices for IT professionals represent the CIO's and other organizational leaders' implementation of a set of levers used to manage IT professionals. Human resource management (HRM) practices have been shown to influence satisfaction and job search behaviors of IT professionals, important outcomes associated with managing IT professionals (e.g., Ferratt, Prasad, and Enns, forthcoming).

Most research in the IT domain has examined the effects of organizational HRM practices without considering the characteristics of the IT professionals (e.g., Ferratt et al., 2005). In the broader HRM literature, much work has examined the effects of both the organizational HRM practices and the values of individuals. This work has been within the stream of person-environment fit research; particularly complementary needs-supplies fit (Kristof, 1996). Recent work has critically evaluated theoretical progress in person-environment fit in organizations (Edwards, 2008). A major conclusion is that:

> "...one of the most significant shortcomings of P-E fit theories is that they do not specify the form of the relationship between P-E fit and other constructs, and any attempt to predict the form of P-E fit relationships depends on the content of the person and environment dimensions involved... P-E fit theories can incorporate content dimensions into the process explanations of P-E fit. Without content, the meaning and implications of P-E fit will remain elusive, and P-E fit theories are unlikely to yield predictions that go beyond simplistic generalizations." (p. 221)

Thus, our goal in this research study is to address this shortcoming of P-E fit theories and determine the form of the relationship between P-E fit and outcomes bearing in mind the specific dimensions of the person and environment. Our perspective of the person is what the person's needs are in terms of what they want from the organization. Similarly, our particular view of the environment is the HRM practices supplied by the organization. For example, one specific dimension, that we refer to later, is work environment and career development. This dimension specifies what a person wants in a work environment (e.g., autonomy, clear role requirements, etc.) and what the organization actually supplies to meet this want. The outcomes (e.g., employment arrangements satisfaction), represent the effects of managing IT professionals via the HRM practices or content dimensions.

Lack of understanding of the form of the relationship between P-E fit and such outcomes raises questions that have practical implications. For instance, is an IT professional's satisfaction maximized only when the degree of autonomy provided (an aspect of work environment) exactly matches the extent of autonomy desired by the individual? That is, can there be too much autonomy so that satisfaction actually decreases, perhaps due to feelings of isolation, if the level of autonomy provided exceeds that which is desired? Even if more autonomy always results in better satisfaction, does increasing autonomy have the same effect irrespective of whether the level provided is less than or more than the desired level? Or, are there diminishing returns to providing more autonomy such that the effect of autonomy is non-linear? Answers to such questions would help organizations marshal their resources in the design of a more effective work environment. Thus, our research question is:

> What forms do the relationships between different content dimensions of P-E fit and outcomes take?

The rest of the paper proceeds as follows. The next section discusses the theoretical background of our research. This section also provides an illustrative hypothesis. The last section discusses the methodology we will use to test the hypotheses and what results can be expected at the conference.

2. THEORETICAL BACKGROUND
2.1 P-E Fit Theory
Periodic literature reviews (e.g., Edwards, 1991; Kristof, 1996; Kristof-Brown, Zimmerman, & Johnson, 2005) highlight the continuing significance of theories of fit between individuals and their work environment in understanding and predicting organizational behavior. These theories of person-environment fit encompass the notion of matching individuals to different levels of their work environment (e.g., jobs, work groups, organizations, and vocations) with good fit being an antecedent to an organization's ability to meet competitive challenges (Kristof, 1996). For instance, a meta-analysis of the literature on fit theories shows that fit at some of these levels (e.g., person-job fit, person-organization fit, etc.) is strongly associated with key outcomes such as job satisfaction, organizational commitment, and turnover intentions (Kristof-Brown et al., 2005). A variety of outcomes such as performance, citizenship behaviors, attitudes, and withdrawal potentially are important in managing IT professionals. To manage scope, we limited this research to attitudes (i.e., employment arrangement satisfaction) and withdrawal (i.e., job search).

We focus on the needs-supplies fit (also referred to as supplies-values or S-V fit in the literature) version of P-E fit theory (Kristof, 1996; Edwards and Rothbard, 1999). Thus, our definition of the person refers to what IT professionals want or prefer from their organizations. This definition is consistent with Locke's (1969) values, which a person seeks to attain, Edwards' (2008) work-related preferences, and Dawis and Lofquist's (1984) preferences for reinforcers. Our definition of environment refers to IT professionals' perception of supplies available from their organization to fulfill their needs. Fit occurs when what the organization supplies is commensurate with what the IT professional seeks to attain; thus fit is assessed on complementary needs-supplies content dimensions.

2.2 Content Dimensions
Prior researchers have identified a number of potential HRM content dimensions that could guide our research. For example, to conduct a meta-analysis of the effects of HRM practices on organizational performance, Combs et al. (2006) identified a set of High Performance Work Practices (HPWPs) examined in at least five studies. Some of these include flexible work, training, internal promotion, compensation level, and employment security. In the IT literature Ferratt, et al. (2005) drew on the work of researchers in Strategic Human Resource Management (e.g., Delery and Doty, 1996, Huselid, 1995 and Pfeffer, 1998) and the IT domain (e.g., Agarwal and Ferratt, 1999, 2002) to identify a theoretically and empirically grounded set of IT HRM practices, which are consistent with HPWPs. From these practices, we select the following dimensions that influence the outcomes – employment arrangement satisfaction and job search behavior – in our study:

- **Work environment and career development**
- Community building (changed to **social support** in this study)
- Incentives (changed to **compensation** in this study)
- **Employment Security**

In terms of HRM content dimensions affecting employment arrangement satisfaction, this study is informed by the "Minnesota Studies" (e.g., Borgen, Weiss, Tinsley, Dawis, & Lofquist, 1968; Dawis, Lofquist, & Weiss, 1968; Dawis & Lofquist, 1978). The HRM content dimensions in those studies are defined as reinforcers of individual needs that the work environment provides, consistent with P-E fit theory. Essentially, if there is a good fit between what the individual needs and what the employer provides, satisfaction occurs. The four HRM practices we use are consistent with a number of reinforcers used in the Minnesota studies, including autonomy, co-workers, compensation, and security.

Price's (2001) model of turnover includes a number of the IT HRM practices mentioned above and incorporates job search behavior in the causal chain. In this model, HRM practices or content dimensions (e.g., promotional chances or "career development opportunities", "compensation", and social support) are antecedents to job satisfaction and organizational commitment, both of which have a negative relationship with job search behavior, an early behavior in the turnover process.

The selected content dimensions are expected to affect the chosen outcomes based on the prior work we cite above. However, our research goal is to investigate the form of the relationship of P-E fit on these dimensions to the outcomes. For this purpose, we draw on equity theory, prospect theory, and related ideas as theoretical bases.

2.3 Form of Relationship between HRM Dimensions' Fit and Outcomes: Theoretical Bases
Equity theory proposes that individuals make assessments of their inputs (e.g., job effort) into an employment exchange and the outcomes they receive (e.g., pay, working conditions, etc.). This assessment is based not only on the inputs and outcomes but also includes a reference source, typically a coworker. Inequity exists when the ratio of a person's outcomes to inputs departs significantly from the perceived ratio for the reference source

(Miner, 2005). For example, someone may consider themselves as a very hard worker, but the compensation they receive is the same as other, less diligent coworkers and therefore is not commensurate with what they perceive to be fair. In this under reward situation, individuals may reduce their work efforts in hopes of still receiving the same pay, especially if the inequity reaches a threshold where the individual perceives that some action is necessary. Other responses consistent with equity theory may be dissatisfaction and increased job search behavior.

Inequity can also exist if a person is over rewarded for the input provided, leading to guilt (Miner, 2005). A strain is created in comparison to the amount of inequity. This strain acts as a motivating force to diminish the inequity. In this case, an individual may increase work effort. However, the thresholds of inequity are higher for over reward situations than under reward since some amount of incongruity can be rationalized as 'good fortune' and does not cause a great deal of strain. Clearly, this has implications for diminishing marginal returns, since higher pay than what is expected can eventually, but not immediately, lead to guilt and reduced effort or dissatisfaction and job search behaviors.

Equity theory, therefore, appears to suggest various possibilities. There may be an optimum, perfectly equitable point at which there is no strain. Deviation from this point causes increased strain due to anger in an under reward situation or guilt in an over reward situation. More likely, there is a zone, rather than a point, of no strain given the discussion of thresholds before strain is felt. Also, following from the notion of thresholds, the strain from guilt is likely to be less than from anger for dimensions such as pay. All of this suggests that the impact of content dimensions on outcomes is likely to be different in under versus over reward situations.

Other mechanisms may be used in conjunction with equity theory to explain such impact. Equity theory also posits that multiple inputs and outcomes exist in an employment context and thus all outcome / input ratios for relevant factors must be included to arrive at an overall ratio. The concepts of carryover and interference (Edwards and Rothbard, 1999) are useful in this regard. Carryover refers to the use of excess supplies on one dimension to satisfy needs on other dimensions, e.g., when excess recognition is used to make up for a deficiency in compensation. Interference refers to the situation where excess supply on one dimension inhibits the supply on another dimension, e.g., when excess challenge makes it difficult to complete tasks successfully, thereby inhibiting a sense of achievement. However, some dimensions, such as pay, may have more salience for a person than others. Therefore, it is also useful to consider the concepts of conservation and depletion (Harrison, 1978) related to a single dimension of an employment exchange. When the outcome is more than anticipated by the input (i.e., "positive" inequity), conservation suggests that the excess is retained for future use in fulfilling values on the same dimension, for example, when excess pay is retained to satisfy future need for pay. Conservation, therefore, serves to reduce the strain associated with an inequitable, over-reward situation. On the other hand, depletion can increase the strain, for example, excess supervisory support may preclude future support.

An alternative theory that provides insights into the form of the relationship for each of the four HRM dimensions and the two outcomes in our work is prospect theory (Kahneman and Tversky

1979). Hunton, Hall, and Price (1998) use prospect theory (Kahneman and Tversky 1979) to explain the relationship between a commodity received (e.g., a reinforcer, such as participation in decision making) and its value (e.g., satisfaction). Price, Hall, van den Bos, Hunton, Lovett, and Tippett (2001, pp. 98-99) state the following about prospect theory:

"Prospect theory (Kahneman & Tversky, 1979) suggests that individuals assess the value of alternative amounts of a commodity (e.g., money and time off from work) in relation to a neutral reference point. The rationale for this assertion is that human perception is attuned to the detection of change in a stimulus rather than to the absolute magnitude of the stimulus. ... Stimulus outcomes that compare favorably to the reference point are perceived as favorable outcomes while stimulus outcomes that compare unfavorably to the reference point are perceived as unfavorable outcomes. Hence, the reference point is the amount of commodity received that the individual would consider as a neutral outcome that is neither a gain nor a loss."

In terms of P-E fit theory, the reference point is the point where values equal supplies. When supplies exceed values, over fit occurs, shown as the gain domain in Figure 1. When values exceed supplies, under fit occurs, shown as the loss domain. As an example, consider the amount of employment security needed by an IT professional and the amount supplied by an employer. Using the amount of employment security needed by the IT professional as the reference point, the amount supplied would be represented on the horizontal axis of Figure 1. Satisfaction is represented as "Value" on the vertical axis. The more that employment security is less than or to the left of the reference point (which is the loss domain or under-fit condition); the lower is the IT professional's satisfaction. The opposite occurs when supplies exceed or are to the right of the reference point (which is the gain domain or over-fit condition). Price et al. (2001) further state the following about prospect theory:

Another important feature of the prospect theory value function is that as the amount of the commodity received moves further away from the reference point, the marginal significance or value associated with unit increments in the amount of the commodity received declines. ... The presence of diminishing marginal returns means that the value function is concave above the reference point and convex below the reference point.

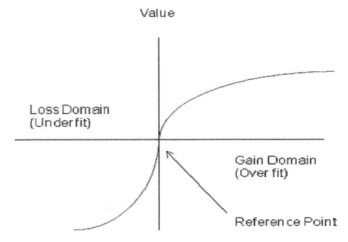

Figure 1: Hypothetical Value Function of a Commodity
(Adapted from Price et al. 2001)

Prospect theory, therefore, suggests that increasing supplies always improves outcomes but at a diminishing marginal rate. Further, this rate is different for comparable changes in the under fit and over fit domains. A change in supplies beyond the point of perfect fit has a lesser effect on outcomes than a comparable change before the point of perfect fit.

2.4 Hypotheses

For illustrative purposes in this work-in-progress we have selected one dimension – work environment[1] – to illustrate the development of our hypotheses. At this point we assume that hypotheses about other dimensions conform to similar explanations.

Equity theory and prospect theory (as well as P-E fit theory in general) would suggest that improvements to an inadequate work environment (i.e., where the environment is less than desired), which would move it toward better fit, would improve the IT professional's satisfaction. While it is unlikely that a work environment that offers more than that desired would create any strain that would cause a reduction in satisfaction, there may be diminishing returns as predicted by prospect theory. Some aspects of work environment, such as training may reflect these mechanisms. Excess training may develop skills that meet future needs. However, this effect may be offset if excess training deprives an IT professional of future training opportunities because the organization attempts to be equitable in offering training opportunities to all its employees. A work environment that is better than expected may have some carryover effect, albeit indirectly. For instance, such a work environment may increase productivity and performance leading to better pay and job security, thus increasing supplies on other dimensions that affect satisfaction. A more direct and realistic effect in the face of ubiquitous resource constraints is that of interference. Resources allocated to developing a better than expected work environment, e.g., providing more training than desired, reduces the resources that are available for supplying other needs such as pay. On balance, therefore, we believe that an excess of work environment would improve satisfaction but with diminishing returns. Thus:

H1: For work environment, satisfaction will increase (at an increasing rate) as supplies increase toward values and will continue to increase (at a decreasing rate) as supplies exceed values.

The hypothesis for job search is similar to satisfaction; however it is the reverse in terms of direction. For example:

H2: For work environment, job search behavior will decrease (at an increasing rate) as supplies increase toward values and will continue to decrease (at a decreasing rate) as supplies exceed values.

3. METHODOLOGY

3.1 Sample

We were able to obtain a broad-based sample of IT employees through a national professional organization of IT employees, the AITP (Association of Information Technology Professionals). The entire membership was encouraged to participate in a web-based survey through a series of initial and follow-up email messages from the organization's Executive Director. Of the organization's 3,369 members, 262 voluntarily completed the on-line survey with the set of questions relevant for this research. The number of respondents used in the analysis mentioned below is less than 262 due to missing values on one or more variables.

3.2 Measures

Although the HRM practices measured in our study are similar in many respects to practices in Agarwal and Ferratt (2002, 1999) and Ferratt et al. (2005), the measurement limitations described in the latter suggest the need for new measures. Instrument development followed an iterative process similar to the procedure described by Churchill (1979). An initial instrument for measuring the research constructs – HRM practices, satisfaction, and job search behavior – was developed. This instrument was pilot tested with two organizations and further refinements of the instrument were then made.

Perceived HRM practices supplied and wanted. Based on our instrument development process above, we included items measuring these HRM practices previously studied in the IT HRM literature: opportunities for growth and development, participation/work flexibility, specificity of performance requirements, social interaction and support, compensation level, and employment security. Factor analysis led us to combine the first three into a factor which is similar to Ferratt et al.'s (2005) work environment and career development. The remaining factors are similar to their community building, incentives, and employment security factors. Thus, these four HRM practices are consistent with practices used in Ferratt et al. (2005) and studies in the broader HRM literature.

Outcome Variables. Job search behavior was measured using items based on 5-point scales, ranging from 1 (Strongly Disagree) to 5 (Strongly Agree). Finally, employment arrangement satisfaction was measured using three items based on 5-point scales, ranging from 1 (*Strongly Disagree*) to 5 (*Strongly Agree*).

3.3 Proposed Analysis, Results and Discussion

At present, we are considering the use of polynomial regression analysis (PRA) advocated by researchers in the "fit" area (e.g., Edwards & Parry, 1993). We intend to supplement PRA analysis with subgroup analysis for over fit and under fit groups. Guided by this proposed analysis, we will analyze the data and discuss the results within the limitations of our methodology.

4. REFERENCES

[1] Agarwal, R. and Ferratt, T. W. 2002. Enduring practices for managing information technology professionals. *Communications of the ACM*, 45(9): 73-79.

[2] Agarwal, R. and Ferratt, T. W. 1999. *Coping with labor scarcity in information technology: Strategies and practices for effective recruitment and retention.* Pinnaflex Press, Cincinnati, OH.

[3] Borgen, F. H., Weiss, D. J., Tinsley, H. E. A., Dawis, R. V., and Lofquist, L. H. 1968. The measurement of occupational reinforcer patterns. Minnesota Studies in Vocational Rehabilitation, 25.

---

[1] For simplicity, we refer to work environment and career development as "work environment."

[4] Churchill, G. A. Jr. 1979. A paradigm for developing better measures of marketing constructs. *Journal of Marketing Research*, 16(1): 64-73.

[5] Combs, J., Liu, Y., Hall, A., and Ketchen, D. 2006. How much do high-performance work practices matter? A meta-analysis of their effects on organizational performance. *Personnel Psychology*, 59(3): 501-528.

[6] Dawis, R. V., Lofquist, L. H., and Weiss, D. J. 1968. A theory of work adjustment: A revision. Minnesota Studies in Vocational Rehabilitation, 23.

[7] Dawis, R. V. and Lofquist, L. H. 1978. A note on the dynamics of work adjustment. *Journal of Vocational Behavior,* 12: 76-79.

[8] Dawis, R. V. and Lofquist, L. H. 1984. *A psychological theory of work adjustment.* University of Minnesota Press, Minneapolis, MN.

[9] Delery, J. E. and Doty, D. H. 1996. Modes of theorizing in strategic human resource management: Tests of universalistic, contingency, and configurational performance predictions. *Academy of Management Journal,* 39(4): 802-835.

[10] Edwards, J. R. 1991. Person-job fit: A conceptual integration, literature review and methodological critique. *International Review of Industrial/Organizational Psychology*, 6: 283-357.

[11] Edwards, J. R. 2008. Person– environment fit in organizations: An assessment of theoretical progress. *Academy of Management Annals*, 2: 167-230.

[12] Edwards, J. R. and Parry, M. E. 1993. On the use of polynomial regression equations as an alternative to difference scores in organizational research. *Academy of Management Journal*, 36: 1577-1613.

[13] Edwards, J. R. and Rothbard, N. P. 1999. Work and family stress and well-being: An examination of person–environment fit in the work and family domains. *Organizational Behavior and Human Decision Processes,* 77: 85-129.

[14] Felps, W., Mitchell, T. R., Hekman, D. R., Lee, T. W., Holtom, B. C., and Harman, W. S. 2009. Turnover contagion: How coworkers' job embeddedness and job search behaviors influence quitting. *Academy of Management Journal,* 52(3): 545-561.

[15] Ferratt, T. W., Agarwal, R., Brown, C. V., and Moore, J. E. 2005. IT human resource management configurations and IT turnover: Theoretical synthesis and empirical analysis. *Information Systems Research,* 16(3): 237-255.

[16] Ferratt, T. W, Prasad, J., and Enns, H. G., Synergy and its limits in managing information technology professionals. Forthcoming in *Information Systems Research.*

[17] Harrison, R. V. 1978. Person-environment fit and job stress. In, C. L. Cooper and R. Payne (eds.), *Stress at Work,* pages 175-205. Wiley, New York.

[18] Hunton, J. E., Hall, T. W., and Price, K. H. 1998. The value of voice in participative decision making. *Journal of Applied Psychology*, 83(5): 788-797.

[19] Huselid, M. A. 1995. The impact of human resource management practices on turnover, productivity, and corporate financial performance. *Academy of Management Journal*, 38(3): 635-672.

[20] Kahneman, D., and Tversky, A. 1979. Prospect theory: An analysis of decision under risk. *Econometrica,* 47: 263-291.

[21] Kristof, A. L. 1996. Person-organization fit: An integrative review of its conceptualizations, measurement, and implications. *Personnel Psychology,* 49(1): 1-49.

[22] Kristof-Brown, A. L., Zimmerman, R. D., and Johnson, E. C. 2005. Consequences of individuals' fit at work: A meta-analysis of person-job, person-organization, person-group, and person-supervisor fit. *Personnel Psychology*, 58: 281-342.

[23] Locke, E. A. 1969. What is job satisfaction? *Organizational Behavior and Human Performance*, 4: 309-336.

[24] Luftman, J., Kempaiah, R., and Rigoni, E. H. 2009. Key issues for IT executives 2008. *MIS Quarterly Executive*, 8(3): 151-159.

[25] Miner, J. B. 2005.*Organizational Behavior 1: Essential Theories of Motivation and Leadership*. M.E. Sharpe: Armonk New York.

[26] Pfeffer, J. 1998. Seven practices of successful organizations. *California Management Review*, 40(2): 96-124.

[27] Podsakoff, P. M., MacKenzie, S. B., Jeong-Yeon, L., and Podsakoff, N. P. 2003. Common method biases in behavioral research: A critical review of the literature and recommended remedies. *Journal of Applied Psychology,* 88(5): 879-903.

[28] Price, J. L. 2001. Reflections on the determinants of voluntary turnover. *International Journal of Manpower*, 22(7): 600-624.

[29] Price, K. H., Hall, T. W., van den Bos, K., Hunton, J. E., Lovett, S., and Tippett, M. J. 2001. Features of the value function for voice and their consistency across participants from four countries: Great Britain, Mexico, The Netherlands, and the United States. *Organizational Behavior and Human Decision Processes,* 84(1): 95-121.

[30] Williams, M. L., McDaniel, M. A., and Nguyen, T. 2006. A meta-analysis of the antecedents and consequences of pay level satisfaction, *Journal of Applied Psychology*, 91(2): 392-413.

Train and Retain– The Impact of Mentoring on the Retention of FLOSS Developers

Andreas Schilling
Centre of Human Resources Information Systems
University of Bamberg, Germany
+49 951 8632873
andreas.schilling@uni-bamberg.de

Sven Laumer
Centre of Human Resources Information Systems
University of Bamberg, Germany
+49 951 8632873
sven.laumer@uni-bamberg.de

Tim Weitzel
Centre of Human Resources Information Systems
University of Bamberg, Germany
+49 951 8632871
tim.weitzel@uni-bamberg.de

ABSTRACT

The acquisition of new knowledge is a critical task for software development. IT companies spend considerable resources in the training of their employees to succeed in a continuously changing industry. Depending on the voluntary commitment of their contributors, initiatives developing Free Libre Open Source Software (FLOSS) identified members' learning and their retention as vital. Although contributors' knowledge building has been repeatedly found to facilitate their project continuance, FLOSS projects are lacking operational advices on how to assist their members' learning. Drawing on previous literature which emphasizes project members' social interactions and their practical experiences to build new knowledge, we propose mentoring as a training method for FLOSS projects. Based on organizational experiences, we propose a measure to evaluate mentoring as an appropriate strategy for FLOSS initiatives to facilitate individuals' learning and to retain their contributors on longitudinal base.

Categories and Subject Descriptors

K.6.1 [**Management of Computing and Information Systems**]: Project and People Management - Training

General Terms

Management, Measurement, Human Factors,

Keywords

Open Source Software Development, Free Libre Open Source Software, Mentoring, Knowledge Building, Turnover Behavior, Retention

1. INTRODUCTION

The training and development of employees is a critical issue for organizations. According to a recent consulting study, a company loses up to 30% of its original knowledge per year [3]. Hence, to sustain in a continuously changing environment, the training and development of their employees is a top priority for organizations in order to foster building of new knowledge and retain their employees on a longitudinal base. As an industry which is characterized by substantial changes in short periods, software development requires the continuous adoption and processing of new knowledge. While IT companies spend considerable resources for the training and development of their employees, this is generally not possible for initiatives developing Free Libre Open Source Software (FLOSS) which have become a substantial part for IT work. Most websites worldwide are served using FLOSS [21] and most European and American companies are relying on FLOSS for their mission critical tasks [13]. Despite the relevance for the private and business sector most FLOSS projects are struggling with the severe consequences caused by the fluctuation of their contributor base. With every long-term contributor leaving, a FLOSS initiative may not only loose parts of its expertise but also the ability to understand and maintain parts of its codebase [16]. Hence, a lack of sustained developers not only affects the quality [25] of a FLOSS project but most commonly its continuance [5].

Although developers' knowledge building and their consideration by others have been identified as key drivers for their ongoing FLOSS commitment [12, 22], it has been neglected to analyze how existing members can assist this learning process and provide appropriate support. Missing insights on how knowledge sharing and social behavior of other members can facilitate individuals' learning and their retention, no practicable advice can be derived for managers of FLOSS initiatives on how to assist newcomers to their projects.

Drawing on organizational literature, this research seeks to develop an effective strategy for FLOSS initiatives to foster the ongoing commitment of project novices by assisting them in knowledge building and providing them with social support. In the organizational context mentoring has been found a very effective training and development method. It describes a dyadic training relationship between an experienced worker (mentor) and an inexperienced novice (protégé) [18]. Driven by the positive experiences of mentoring in the organizational domain, we will evaluate this training and development tool in the FLOSS context to facilitate newcomers' learning and provide them with social support in order to foster ongoing commitment. Hence, we address the research question:

Is mentoring an appropriate retention strategy for FLOSS projects by assisting newcomers in their learning and by providing them with social support?

Our research has theoretical and practical implications. We contribute to the FLOSS domain by evaluating mentoring as a viable training and development tool for fostering developer retention in this special context. Thus, our research provides managers of FLOSS initiatives with practicable advice of how to increase novices' retention behavior by facilitating their learning and providing them with social support. Furthermore, our research results contribute to the organizational context, which increasingly regards knowledge workers as volunteers [7]. Our evaluation of mentoring in a voluntarily driven context can, therefore, provide valuable measures and managerial implications for organizations, considering that most of them are lacking validation for their training efforts [11].

To evaluate mentoring in the FLOSS context, this research in progress paper provides an overview of the underlying hypotheses and the intended methodology. The remainder of this paper proceeds as follows: The next section introduces the theoretical background of our research by reviewing existing literature and detailing mentoring. Afterwards, we present our research model and formulate the corresponding research hypotheses. In section four, we detail our research methodology and give an outlook to our upcoming steps.

2. THEORETICAL BACKGROUND
After presenting existing research on knowledge building in FLOSS projects, the second subsection draws on organizational literature and details the types of knowledge which can be built though mentoring.

2.1 FLOSS Research
Existing FLOSS literature identifies project members' learning repeatedly as dominant driver for their sustained participation. Surveying 2600 FLOSS developers, Ghosh reveals that more than two thirds of them are driven to continue in their projects by the wish to acquire new knowledge [12]. Subsequent studies by David et al. support the importance of knowledge building for the retention of FLOSS contributors [6]. While previous study results underline the relevance of knowledge building for developers' ongoing commitment, FLOSS research on this topic is very scarce. Existing FLOSS literature examines the knowledge building process from the perspective of the individual developer, neglecting the organizational perspective of the FLOSS projects.

Using Legitimate Peripheral Participation theory to explain developers' sustained contribution behavior, Fang et al. suggest that FLOSS developers' learning behavior is situated in their everyday activities [10]. Rather than processing information in an isolated manner, situated learning occurs though social interactions with others, which encompass topic related discussions, giving and receiving feedback as well as making new proposals [9]. Beside the social context, situated learning puts a strong focus on practicing the acquired knowledge. Investigating developers' participation behavior in detail, Singh et al. propose a

Hidden Markov Model to capture the learning dynamics in FLOSS projects [24]. Their results support the assumption that FLOSS developers learn from their interactions with others while providing further insights. Developers with little knowledge depend strongly on the cooperation of existing project members. They learn most by interacting in problem related mailing list conversations which have been initiated by others. Starting conversations on the projects' mailing list, in turn, benefits most developers who already acquired a certain amount of knowledge. While developers who are highly skilled learn most when answering the questions posted by other project members. In addition, Singh et al. find positive learning effects resulting from code contributions [24]. However, these effects are much weaker than the learning effects resulting from mailing list interactions. These results indicate that project members not only experience knowledge gains from their interactions with others but also social support which in turn stimulates them in their doing. As examined by previous research, social support is in particular relevant for keeping novices' attached to the project [20, 22]. Qureshi et al. show that project members are stimulated to remain active in the project when they experience social support from other members [22]. Similarly, Li et al. highlight in their research the positive influence of project members' individualized consideration of novices [20].

Unfortunately, however, empirical research provides evidence that FLOSS projects have significant learning barriers for novices and do not provide them with enough individual consideration. According to Singh et al. it usually requires significant effort for FLOSS developers to transit into a higher learning state, which only few project members achieve [24]. The existence of high learning barriers for FLOSS developers is supported by research of Adams et al., who showed that it can take newcomers up to 60 weeks to become an effective contributor to a FLOSS project [1]. In addition to the high learning barriers, previous research suggests that FLOSS projects need to improve their considerations of newcomers. Qureshi et al. reveal that novices at FLOSS projects who have only few social ties to other project members in the beginning remain to be separated [22].

While existing FLOSS literature emphasizes on the one hand team members' knowledge building and social support for their project continuance, it finds on the other hand evidence that most projects have significant learning barriers and are neglecting to provide newcomers with individualized considerations. Moreover, there is to our knowledge no conceptual approach for FLOSS projects on how to facilitate project members in their learning and providing them with social support. In contrast to existing research, we will examine how contributors' knowledge building and their social support can be fostered from an organizational perspective. Drawing on prior research of Li et al. which identifies FLOSS developers' individualized consideration and intellectual stimulation to motivate their code contributions, we evaluate the use of mentoring in the FLOSS domain [20].

2.2 Mentoring
Originally introduced by Kram, mentoring describes an interpersonal relationship where an experienced employee (the mentor) provides functional advice and personal support to an inexperienced worker (the protégé) [18]. Providing both technical advice and interpersonal guidance, mentoring is considered an effective means for employees' training and development. In contrast to traditional training methods, mentoring relationships build a strong interpersonal bond between the two parties which

facilitates the transfer of various knowledge forms. By providing technical advice, mentors help their protégés building declarative knowledge. This form of knowledge describes employees' understanding of the required facts to accomplish their jobs successfully. In addition to this factual knowledge, mentors' technical guidance helps protégés to acquire job related skills, so that they become sooner familiar with job related practices. Besides assisting building declarative knowledge, mentoring helps protégés building procedural knowledge. With the transfer of this type of knowledge, protégés understand how to perform their work best. While traditional training methods are generally not capable of transferring this tacit form of knowledge, protégés develop this understanding very soon due to the strong social bond with their mentors. As a consequence to the effective transfer of both declarative and procedural knowledge, mentoring has been found superior to other training methods and repeatedly recommended for the training of employees [4, 8, 14].

Beyond protégés' training of job related knowledge mentoring programs are shown to be an important means for employees' future development. By assisting protégés in their career planning and helping them balancing their work with their private life, mentoring initiatives not only increase protégés' satisfaction with their self but also with their job. Empirical studies in the organizational context support this by showing that mentored employees experience higher levels of satisfaction for their job, which in turn stimulates their commitment to their organization [2]. Similarly, findings by Brashear et al. show that mentoring increases employees' performance and reduces their intention to leave [4].

3. RESEARCH MODEL
With respect to the positive effects mentors have in the organizational context, we evaluate in the following the use of mentoring as a strategy to train and sustain novices to FLOSS projects. Regarding individuals' retention behavior which we consider to be driven by their needs for competence and relatedness, we hypothesize that mentoring is a valuable training and development tool for FLOSS projects. On the one hand mentoring facilitates newcomers to experience knowledge gains and social support for their project work, which in turn make them persist longer in the project. On the other hand, FLOSS mentors foster individuals' persistence in the project by helping them in the long-term to develop greater satisfaction for their work. Figure 1 visualizes our research model.

Regarding the training of newcomers to FLOSS projects, mentoring is expected to facilitate the acquisition of declarative knowledge. Based on their practical experience, mentors are able to help newcomers in understanding the necessary facts and assist them in developing the necessary skillset for contributing to the project. Moreover, the interpersonal relationship between FLOSS mentors and their protégés is expected to transfer important procedural knowledge. As a result, protégés become sooner familiar with relevant practices on how to perform their code contributions best. Following previous research which repeatedly emphasizes FLOSS developers' learning for their project permanence, we suppose that these knowledge gains make protégés to stay in the project. Therefore, we hypothesize that FLOSS developers who progress in their declarative and procedural knowledge building show higher project retention. Consistent with empirical findings from the organizational domain, we hypothesize, therefore, that mentoring increases

protégés' project continuance through advancing their knowledge building:

Hypothesis 1a: Mentored project members experience higher levels of knowledge building than non-mentored members.

Hypothesis 1b: Project members' with higher levels of knowledge building retain longer in a FLOSS project.

In addition to the supportive effects for the transfer of various knowledge forms, protégés' strong relational bond with their mentors provides them with social support for their work. Empirical studies in the organizational context emphasize the importance of this social support for protégés. Allen et al. show that protégés who experience encouragement from their mentors show higher levels of well-being and commitment [2]. Research by Lankau et al. support these positive outcomes and show that protégés who perceive social support also show increased intentions to stay with their jobs [19]. Consistent with these findings from the organizational domain, we expect that protégés in the context of FLOSS experience similar feelings of social support with their mentors. In accordance with research findings by Qureshi et al. which show that these relatedness feelings influence contributors' continuance strongly [22], we expect them to be an important outcome of mentoring relationships in the FLOSS domain. Hence, based on prior research in the FLOSS and organizational domain we assume that mentoring in the FLOSS context produces feelings of social support amongst protégés, which in turn cause them to remain in the project and hypothesize:

Hypothesis 2a: Mentored project members experience higher levels of social support than non-mentored members.

Hypothesis 2b: Project members experiencing higher levels of social support retain longer in a FLOSS project.

Complementing the positive effects on protégés' everyday work, mentoring is considered a valuable tool for employees' long-term development within the organization. As a way to support employees' development mentors can help their protégés to balance their work with their private life or identify new paths for their future career within the organization [2]. Instead of the acquisition of new knowledge, this requires protégés to critically reflect their job with their desires and long-term goals. While the results of these reflections may not have immediate effects on protégés' behavior, they are an important determinant for employees' future within the organization. Individuals who perceive their work as satisfying show not only higher levels of commitment for their jobs but also fewer intentions to leave. In line with these findings, we expect that mentors similarly foster the positive development of novices to FLOSS projects. Similar to the organizational context protégés can learn from mentors in FLOSS projects how to combine their project work with their long-term goals and interests which in turn makes them perceive greater levels of satisfaction and enjoyment from their coding. As shown previously satisfying and enjoying feelings are important drivers for contributors' intention to remain in FLOSS projects [17, 23]. Consequently, we expect that mentoring in FLOSS projects has also a direct influence on protégés' retention behavior and hypothesize that:

Hypothesis 3: Mentored project members retain longer in a FLOSS project than non-mentored members.

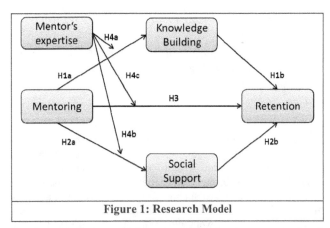

Figure 1: Research Model

Previous studies examining mentoring in the organizational context identify mentors' level of expertise as an important moderator for the positive outcomes of mentoring. In their exploratory research, Brashear et al. compared protégés who have been trained by mentors with high organizational knowledge to protégés who have been trained by mentors with no organizational experience [4]. Surprisingly, protégés of both groups showed higher performance, but only the protégés who had organizational experienced mentors had the wish to remain in their jobs. These findings are in support of prior research by Eby et al. who identified mentors who are lacking organizational competence as a main cause for dysfunctional mentoring relationships [8]. Examining empirically the ways how effective mentoring relationships are formed, Hamlin et al. analyzed the role of various personal characteristics of mentors and protégés in detail. Consistent with previous research, Hamlin et al. support that the effectiveness of mentoring relationships depends strongly on mentors' level of technical expertise and their level of interpersonal behavior [15]. In accordance with these findings from the organizational domain, we regard mentors' level of technical expertise and interpersonal competence most important in order to achieve positive mentoring outcomes in the context of FLOSS. We assume FLOSS developers build this kind of expertise by contributing to the FLOSS project. Consequently, FLOSS developers with a richer pool of project knowledge are supposed to mentor protégés better in terms of knowledge building and interpersonal support. Hence, we assume that higher experienced mentors are better in providing positive training and development effects to their protégés and hypothesize that:

Hypothesis 4a: Mentors' level of project knowledge positively moderates protégés' knowledge building.

Hypothesis 4b: Mentors' level of project knowledge positively moderates protégés' feelings of social support.

Hypothesis 4c: Mentor's level of project knowledge positively moderates protégés' retention behavior.

4. RESEARCH METHODOLOGY

To evaluate our research hypotheses, we will use a combination of archival records and survey data of mentored and non-mentored novices to FLOSS projects and compare them with each other. The combination of both actual and perceptual data offers important advantages for our evaluation compared to the use of only survey or archival records. On the one hand the extraction of objective figures enables us to evaluate mentors' expertise and the acquired knowledge gains and the invested time independently of protégés subjective perception, which has been identified as a

serious threat to validity for studies on mentoring [8]. On the other hand perceptual data helps us to adequately measure the satisfaction and social support which protégés are experiencing from their mentors. Considering that individuals differ in the ways they experience satisfaction from training initiatives and encouragement for their doing, we assume the use of perceptual data to be superior over archival records for measuring the social aspects of mentoring relationships.

An appropriate organizational setting to study the effects of mentoring in FLOSS projects is Google Summer of Code (GSoC). GSoC is an annual event in which experienced project members mentor the participating FLOSS developers for their code contributions. In line with mentoring practices in organizations, mentors offer technical advice and guidance to their protégés during GSoC and build an interpersonal relationship with them. In order to analyze the effects from this mentoring event, we will accompany participants of this year GSoC and put their learning progress and experienced social support in contrast to non-mentored FLOSS developers. To adequately distinguish the mentoring status of the analyzed developers in our evaluation, we will use a dichotomous variable called mentoring which is 1 for mentored and 0 for non-mentored FLOSS developers. Consistent with previous FLOSS research, we look at FLOSS developers' social and practical behavior for measuring the level of acquired knowledge [24, 25]. In particular, we measure FLOSS developers' knowledge gains by determining their amount of issued code commits and sent mailing list posts during the GSoC event. For this information, we will query the online service markmail.org which indexes the code repositories and mailing lists of most FLOSS projects that participate in GSoC. As for measuring protégés' knowledge gains, we assess mentors' level of expertise via their conversational and practical project behavior before the mentoring event. To do so, we determine their amount of mailing-list posts and submitted code commits as in the case of protégés. To evaluate the social support mentored FLOSS developers are experiencing, we will invite GSoC participants to participate in a survey. Thereby we will adopt survey items from research on Leader-Member-Exchange Theory (LMX) in order to evaluate the exchanged social support between protégés and their mentors.

Table 1: Measurement Model

Mentoring (dichotomous variable)	Indicating whether project member has been participated in GSoC (1) or not (0).
Protégés' knowledge building (objective measure)	Combined measure for protégés' amount of submitted mailing list posts and issued code contributions.
Mentors' level of expertise (objective measure)	Combined measure for mentors' amount of submitted mailing list posts and issued code contributions before the mentoring event.
Social Support (perceptual measure)	Survey items which have been used previously in LMX and mentoring research.
Project retention (objective measure)	Timespan in days between project members' first and most recent commit.

Finally, we rely on an objective measure for evaluating FLOSS developers' project permanence which has previously been used by Colazo et al. [5]. Developers' project retention is thereby determined by calculating the time difference between the timestamp of their most recent code commit and the timestamp of their very first commit. Table 1 provides an overview of the used measures.

5. REFERENCES

[1] Adams, P. J., Capiluppi, A., and Boldyreff, C. 2009. Coordination and productivity issues in free software: The role of brooks' law. In IEEE International Conference on Software Maintenance. IEEE, 319–328.

[2] Allen, T. D., Eby, L. T., Poteet, M. L., Lentz, E., and Lima, L. 2004. Career Benefits Associated With Mentoring for Proteges: A Meta-Analysis. Journal of Applied Psychology 89, 1, 127–136.

[3] Anderson, C. and Lee, S. 2007. IDC MarketScape: Worldwide IT Education and Training 2008 Vendor Analysis. http://www.idcresearch.com/research/view_lot.jsp?containerId=209799. Accessed October 31st.

[4] Brashear, T. G., Bellenger, D. N., Boles, J. S., and Barksdale ., H. C. 2006. An Exploratory Study of the Relative Effectiveness of Different Types of Sales Force Mentors. Journal of Personal Selling and Sales Management 26, 1, 7–18.

[5] Colazo, J. and Fang, Y. 2009. Impact of license choice on Open Source Software development activity. Journal of the American Society for Information Science & Technology 60, 5, 997–1011.

[6] David, P. A. and Shapiro, J. S. 2008. Community-based production of open-source software: What do we know about the developers who participate? Information Economics and Policy 20, 4, 364–398.

[7] Drucker, P. F. 2002. They're not Employees, They're People. Harvard Business Review 80, 2, 70–77.

[8] Eby, L., Butts, M., Lockwood, A., and Simon, S. A. 2004. Protégés Negative Mentoring Experiences: Construct Development and Nomological Validation. Personnel Psychology 57, 2, 411–447.

[9] Edmondson, A. 1999. Psychological Safety and Learning Behavior in Work Teams. Administrative Science Quarterly 44, 2, 350–383.

[10] Fang, Y. and Neufeld, D. 2009. Understanding Sustained Participation in Open Source Software Projects. Journal of Management Information Systems 25, 4, 9–50.

[11] Gartner Inc. 2007. Gartner EXP Says Organizations Must Evaluate Learning and Training Programs to Gauge Return on Investment. http://www.gartner.com/it/page.jsp?id=505592. Accessed October 31.

[12] Ghosh, R. 2005. Understanding Free Software Developers: Findings from the FLOSS Study. In Making Sense of the Bazaar: Perspectives on Open Source and Free Software, MIT Press, Ed., Cambridge, 1–23.

[13] Gold, A. 2007. Open Source Solutions: Seek Value Beyond Cost. Accessed 1 May 2011.

[14] Hale, R. 2000. To Match or Mis-Match? The Dynamics of Mentoring as a Route to Personal and Organisational Learning. Career Development International 5, 4/5, 223–234.

[15] Hamlin, R. G. and Sage, L. 2011. Behavioural criteria of perceived mentoring effectiveness: An empirical study of effective and ineffective mentor and mentee behaviour within formal mentoring relationships. Journal of European Industrial Training 35, 8, 752–778.

[16] Izquierdo-Cortazar, D., Robles, G., Ortega, F., and Gonzalez-Barahona, J. M. 2009. Using Software Archaeology to Measure Knowledge Loss in Software Projects Due to Developer Turnover. In 42nd Hawaii International Conference on System Sciences, 1–10.

[17] Ke, W. and Zhang, P. 2009. Motivations in Open Source Software Communities: The Mediating Role of Effort Intensity and Goal Commitment. International Journal of Electronic Commerce 13, 4, 39–66.

[18] Kram, K. E. 1988. Mentoring at work. Developmental relationships in organizational life. Univ. Pr. of America, Lanham, MD.

[19] Lankau, M. J. and Scandura, T. A. 2002. An investigation of personal learning in mentoring relationships: content, antecedents and consequences. Academy of Management Journal 45, 4, 779–790.

[20] Li, Y., Tan, C.-H., Teo, H.-H., and Mattar, A. T. 2006. Motivating Open Source Software Developers: Influence of Transformational and Transactional Leaderships. In Proceedings of the 2006 ACM SIGMIS CPR conference on computer personnel research Forty four years of computer personnel research: achievements, challenges & the future - SIGMIS CPR '06. ACM Press, 34.

[21] Netcraft. 2011. June 2011 Web Server Survey. http://news.netcraft.com/archives/category/web-server-survey/. Accessed 13 June 2011.

[22] Qureshi, I. and Fang, Y. 2010. Socialization in Open Source Software Projects: A Growth Mixture Modeling Approach. Organizational Research Methods 14, 1, 208–238.

[23] Shah, S. K. 2006. Motivation, Governance, and the Viability of Hybrid Forms in Open Source Software Development. Management Science 52, 7, 1000–1014.

[24] Singh, P. V., Tan, Y., and Youn, N. 2010. A Hidden Markov Model of Developer Learning Dynamics in Open Source Software Projects. Information Systems Research.

[25] van Liere, D. W. 2009. Title How Shallow is a Bug? Why Open Source Communities Shorten the Repair Time of Software Defects. In ICIS 2009 Proceedings.

Evaluation of E-Technology Acceptance:
An Empirical Analysis

Rahmath Safeena
College of Computers and Information Technology
Taif University, Saudi Arabia
e-mail: safi.abdu@gmail.com

Abdullah Kammani
College of Computers and Information Technology
Taif University, Saudi Arabia
e-mail: akamani@acm.org

ABSTRACT

Different types of technology are emerging in the new era of computing especially the E-Technology and its adoption is considered to be an important issue among the consumers. E-technology has developed into an unavoidable technology among the internet consumers. E-Technology considered in this study includes Technology used for E-Commerce, E-Services and E-Business application. This study investigates the influence of Perceived Benefit (PB), Perceived Impediment (PI), and Social Influence (SI) on E-Technology adoption. Questionnaire survey is used for getting the data and empirical analysis is done. The Statistical Package for Social Sciences (SPSS) version 12 was used for computation. As expected, the results have supported the hypothesis that perceived benefit and social influence have positive effect on the use of E-Technology and perceived impediments have negative effect on the use of E-Technology. The results of the regression analysis conducted on the factors indicate that PB, PI and SI on E-Technology were found to be the most influential factors explaining the use of E-Technology services. The result shows that perceived impediment is negatively related to the adoption of E-Technology use which supports the hypothesis and is in line with the previous studies. The finding refers to the fact that consumers use E-Technology for the benefits and also due to its easiness in use which provides in comparison to other service delivery channels. Social Influence has positive effect on the use of E-Technology as the individuals think that using the advanced technology will improve his image and status in the society. Customers are not ready to take any risk on using the new system and hence impediments show negative significance. Any organization which adopts E-Technology for their day-to-day activities can show their conveniences in their promotional and advertising activities. Organizations also need to engage in security enhancement activities such as encryption, firewall, and user protection and authenticity. Trust is one of the more influential factors, implying that controlling the risk of online data is more important than providing benefits. This finding is particularly important for managers as they decide how to allocate resources to retain and expand their current customer base. However, building a risk-free online environment is much more difficult than providing benefits to customers. Therefore, companies need to search for risk-reducing strategies that might assist in inspiring high confidence in potential customers. The proposed model makes an important contribution to the emerging literature on e-commerce, especially with regard to E-Technology adoption. This study was conducted in a particular region and generalization of the result will have some shortcomings as with any other research. Hence, the replication of this study on a wider scale with more customers across geographical and cultural boundaries is essential for the further generalization of the findings. By using a longitudinal study in the future, we could investigate our research model in different time periods and make comparisons, thus providing more insight into the phenomenon of online banking adoption.

Categories and Subject Descriptors
Information System Applications; Miscellaneous.

General Terms
Management

Keywords
E-Technology, Technology adoption, Perceived Benefit (PB), Perceived Impediment (PI), and Social Influence (SI)

SIGMIS-CPR'12, May 31–June 2, 2012, Milwaukee, Wisconsin, USA.
ACM 978-1-4503-1110-6/12/05.

Breakthrough Perpetual Organization with IT Governance

Sureerat Saetang
University of South Australia
School of Computer and Information Science
Mawson Lakes, Adelaide, Australia
saesy005@mymail.unisa.edu.au

Abrar Haider
University of South Australia
School of Computer and Information Science
Mawson Lakes, Adelaide, Australia
abrar.haider@unisa.edu.au

ABSTRACT

In corporate world with high competitive advantage, Information Technology (IT) performs as business foundation in organizations. IT Governance contains a variety of business tools and measures to operate IT structure and processes in supporting business strategy applicably. Taking a closer look in organizational IT structure and processes within organizations, workflow is essential to support automated business processes where documents, information, and tasks are progressed, together with, participants in different actions to accomplish business objectives by following business strategies and using IT systems. Moreover, workflow is considered as an integration of operational activity and active flow which drives as intra-organizational or private manoeuvre to achieve effective outcomes in complicated situations. Thus, workflow is one of the significant factors which support and accelerate business processes within organizations robustly and powerfully. Especially, an examination of workflow integrations can lead to a conceptual framework that will support researchers and executives to understand and realize the methods IT experts operate with other types of workflows in dissimilar development usage-contexts in workplaces. This study employs a qualitative approach in regarding to IT governance implementation by interviewing executives management in senior and middle level with open-ended and closed-ended questions. Semi-structured interviews and survey questionnaires were selected to collect data of this research from Australian and Thai organizations which have implemented IT governance. At this stage, data analysis has not completed yet. However, the findings from this research will be disclosed further in the following publications. Moreover, this research encourages Information Systems researchers to consider IT governance in their research by giving its importance to industry and its worldwide suggestions.

Categories and Subject Descriptor

H.0 Information Systems

General Terms: Management

Management

Keywords

Corporate governance, IT governance, Workflow

REFERENCES

[1] Hollingsworth, D. (1995). "Workflow Management Coalition The Workflow Reference Model." from http://www.wfmc.org/standards/docs/tc003v11.pdf.

Experiences in Service-Learning Pedagogy: Lessons for Recruitment and Retention of Under Represented Groups

Jeria Quesenberry
Carnegie Mellon University
224E PH, 5000 Forbes Avenue
Pittsburgh, PA USA 15213
+01 (412) 268-4573

jquesenberry@cmu.edu

Randy Weinberg
Carnegie Mellon University
224C PH, 5000 Forbes Avenue
Pittsburgh, PA USA 15213
+01 (412) 268-3228

rweinberg@cmu.edu

Larry Heimann
Carnegie Mellon University
224A PH, 5000 Forbes Avenue
Pittsburgh, PA USA 15213
+01 (412) 268-3211

profh@cmu.edu

ABSTRACT

In this poster, we summarize results from the Carnegie Mellon University *Information Systems in the Community Summer Institute*, which is an intensive service-learning experience in information systems (IS) for students from Historically Black Colleges and Universities (HBCUs).

Categories and Subject Descriptors

K.3.2 Computers and Information Science Education
K.6.1 Project and People Management

General Terms

Management, Human Factors, Theory

Keywords

IS Education, Service-Learning, African Americans, Race

1. BACKGROUND

Service-learning is a pedagogical approach where students apply course knowledge to solve a particular problem faced by a partner client in their local or global community. Service-learning initiatives have gained attention in the information systems (IS) curriculum over the last several years as a means to improve student learning in communication, teamwork and responsiveness to client need (e.g., [1] [2]). Further, research suggests that service-learning initiatives benefit all students, particularly women and racial minorities (e.g., [3]). Yet, many IS educational programs are unable to adopt such pedagogical approaches given the challenges of project constraints (time, quality, and cost), limited instructor experience, and lack of appropriate assessment tools.

2. RESEARCH OVERVIEW

This research seeks to better understand how service-learning initiatives can be used to prepare students for the IS workplace while addressing the under representation of African Americans in the field. Specifically, this poster summarizes research results from the Carnegie Mellon University *Information Systems in the Community Summer Institute*, which is an intensive, six-week, summer service-learning experience for students from Historically Black Colleges and Universities (HBCUs). In this program, students were exposed to contemporary practices in software development, project management, and teamwork through classroom lessons and a mentored, service-learning experience with nonprofit organizations in the Pittsburgh, Pennsylvania community.

The program was conducted over eight consecutive summers from 2004 to 2011, with 54 students from eleven HBCUs. A variety of interpretive research techniques were employed to assess student learning, curriculum effectiveness and contributions to research goals. These methodological activities included: entrance and exit questionnaires, face-to-face interviews, participant observations and feedback from community partner organizations.

We found that the service-learning projects enriched learning and helped students develop the skills necessary to be competitive in the IS field. For example, students' self-reported competency increased significantly over the course of the program in the areas of domain understanding, teamwork, project management, technical skills, and social impact. Students also expressed the expansion of their knowledge of career and graduate school opportunities. These results highlight several implications for the recruitment and retention of under represented groups in the IS field. We believe this program could be used as a model for others interested in effectively offering service-learning opportunities and reaching under represented populations in the IS discipline.

3. ACKNOWLEDGMENTS

This research is funded by the Andrew W. Mellon Foundation (Grant #30900675).

4. REFERENCES

[1] Olsen, A.L. (2008). "A Service Learning Project for a Software Engineering Course." Consortium for Computing Sciences and Colleges (CCSC) Conference, 130-136.

[2] Webster, L.D., and Mirielli, E.J. (2007). "Student Reflections on an Academic Service Learning Experience in a Computer Science Classroom." *Proceedings of the SIGITE Conference*, 207-211.

[3] Ferguson, R., Liu, C., Last, M. and Mertz, J. (2006). "Service-Learning Projects: Opportunities and Challenges." Proceedings of the ACM SIGCSE Conference, 127-128.

Leveraging the Crowd as a Source of Innovation: Does Crowdsourcing Represent a New Model for Product and Service Innovation?

Lee B. Erickson

College of Information Sciences and Technology
The Pennsylvania State University

lbe108@psu.edu

ABSTRACT

In today's fact-paced global marketplace, many organizations are turning to the "crowd" as a potential new source of innovation. However, little is known about the strategic use of crowd and how best to integrate them into internal processes. This paper presents preliminary findings from an ongoing grounded theory research study designed to identify trends and patterns associated with crowdsourcing by established organizations. Four common uses of the crowd are identified (i.e., productivity, innovation, knowledge capture, and marketing/branding). Further, key reoccurring themes related to task type, crowd knowledge, crowd location, and organizational goals, challenges, and value extraction are identified. Finally, a discussion of the emerging relationships between organizational goal, tasks to be completed, crowd characteristics, and the potential risks and benefits such initiatives create for organizations is provided.

Categories and Subject Descriptors

D.2.9 [**Management**]: Productivity.
K.6.1 [**People and People Management**]: Strategic information systems planning

General Terms

Management, Performance, Theory.

Keywords

crowdsourcing, productivity, innovation, knowledge capture, marketing/branding, grounded theory, framework, research in progress

1. INTRODUCTION

According to the U.S. Council on Competitiveness, U.S. companies face a competitive landscape that has "radically and irrevocably" changed [46]. In today's fast moving global economy, available natural resources and mass-produced commodity goods will no longer sustain economic growth. The economy will be powered instead by creativity and innovation [15]. However, with today's mobile workforce and the increasing need for diversity in the innovation process, many companies are finding that traditional internal teams are no longer sufficient [9, 31]. This gap – the gap between a firm's ability to generate

continuous innovation and the market's demand for innovation – is often referred to as an "innovation gap" [27] or an "innovation crisis" [35].

In an attempt to narrow their innovation gap and increase innovative potential, organizations are actively seeking alternative approaches to traditional processes. One growing alternative is "crowdsourcing." Crowdsouring is the process of reaching out to large groups of individuals to supplement or even replace current internal resources [21]. While researchers and organizations are beginning to experiment with crowdsourcing, currently little is known regarding the strategic uses of the crowd and the value of such initiatives. This understanding is critical to developing and extending theory related to the current state of the field [48], as well as developing guidelines for organizations planning to implement crowdsourcing initiatives.

This paper presents preliminary findings from research designed to identify themes and patterns associated with the use of crowdsourcing by established organizations. That is, the focus is on for-profit, established organizations attempting to leverage the crowd to replace or supplement current resources and processes and not on new organizations built on a crowdsourcing business model. The goal of this research is to begin to address the current lack of understanding surrounding this new practice.

2. LITERATURE REVIEW

In 2006, Jeff Howe, a writer for *Wired* magazine, noticed that more and more companies were taking advantage of online collaborative technologies to enlist the help of the "crowd" to complete a variety of tasks [21]. Howe coined the term "crowdsourcing" to represent this new business process. Many organizations are beginning to experiment with crowdsourcing initiatives. Across both academic and business literature, a wide variety of tasks are being performed by a wide variety of crowds. Further, organizations are realizing different value from these initiatives.

Organizations are leveraging the crowd as a new source of data [8, 51], to solve routine time-consuming tasks [2, 21], to develop advertising and market research [5, 51], and for ideas related to product innovation [11, 25]. Across this wide variety of tasks, organizations are turning to crowds outside their corporate boundaries as well as inside. Crowds include online product communities [5, 25, 39], online communities of interest [20], the general public [8, 19], and employees who typically would not participant in the task to be completed [41]. In fact, organizations are finding that employees may be the most significant source of ideas (42%), followed by business partners (36%), then customers (35%) [24].

When it comes to extracting value from the crowd there is limited evidence of the true value these initiatives bring. For example, when turning to the crowd for ideation related to product innovation, organizations may realize both tangible and intangible benefits [3, 23, 25, 30], but also experience unexpected increases in costs [26].

Finally, within the academic and business literature, there is little consensus on exactly which characteristics are most relevant to the understanding of crowdsourcing. Early frameworks include those that apply to any type of crowdsourcing activity [4, 50], as well as others that are targeted to a specific use of the crowd (e.g., product innovation) [7, 13, 38, 44]. These frameworks range from simple one-dimensional models [13, 22, 28] to complex multi-dimensional models with detailed descriptions of categories and sub-categories [35, 38].

While work is growing, crowdsourcing is a relatively new phenomenon and as such there has not been sufficient time to build a large body of research specifically related to this practice. Work to date has been helpful in describing the phenomenon of crowdsourcing at a broad level. However, a clear understanding of why and how companies are integrating the crowd into current internal practices, the characteristics that identify the best crowd for the job, and the risks and benefits associated with different uses of the crowd is lacking. Such an understanding would provide a roadmap from which researchers could anchor their research, as well as basic guidelines for practitioners.

3. RESEARCH QUESTION AND APPROACH

The goal of this research is to gain a clearer understanding of the uses of crowdsourcing by established organizations and to identify key characteristics related to risks, benefits, and value capture. Specifically, the essential research question to be addressed is: *How are organizations integrating the crowd (i.e., individuals not typically included) into their current product and service innovation processes?* Underlying this essential question are four supporting questions:

☐ Why do organizations turn to the crowd for product or service innovation?

☐ What tasks is the crowd being asked to perform?

☐ What are the facilitators of and barriers to implementing crowdsourcing initiatives?

☐ How do organizations determine the success of crowdsourced initiatives?

While there are many definitions of innovation [1, 49], as well as distinctions between types of innovation (e.g., radical vs. incremental) [36], for this study a broad view of innovation is used. Within this context, innovation refers to new ideas or solutions to problems that lead to improvements or advancements for the organization within their marketplace. Innovation may be incremental or breakthrough, result in reduced costs, improved productivity, or open new unexplored markets [1].

3.1 Methodology

The research methodology chosen to address the research question is grounded theory. Grounded theory was selected for four key reasons. First, grounded theory is particularly useful when studying emerging phenomenon with limited empirical work and existing theory [32, 37] as is the case with crowdsourcing. Second, as the objective of this research is to develop theory that identifies key uses of the crowd by established organizations, it is critical to uncover patterns of use within organizational contexts. Grounded theory is particularly useful in identifying patterns in

data and building theory that is empirically valid and grounded in context [17]. Third, as the research question focuses on changing processes within organizational contexts, it is imperative that the methodology selected be robust enough to allow for the inclusion of key organizational differences. Grounded theory allows for findings that take into account the complexities of organizational contexts and is well suited to studying process and change [37]. Finally, because the principal researcher has practical experience in business settings and with the technologies under study, grounded theory allows for the integration of this experience and knowledge into the analysis process, but also provides controls that reduce the risk of introducing bias into the results [14, 47].

As the goal of this research is to uncover patterns of use within organizational contexts to build theory and relevance to practice, a Glaserian approach to data analysis is preferred. This approach allows for a focus on abstract conceptualizations at an organizational level of enquiry versus a Straussian approach that is orientated more towards building full descriptions at an individual level of enquiry [32]. Additionally, the flexible coding used in the Glaserian approach is well suited to identifying broad reoccurring themes and most appropriate at an early stage of investigation [14, 45].

While grounded theory does not prescribe a specific ontology or epistemology [32], this study's research question seeks to understand *how* an observed phenomenon has come about and the processes at play. Therefore an interpretivist rather than positivist orientation is most appropriate [42]. An interpretivist epistemology reasons that understanding is the result of inductively exploring the social constructions of participants within context [43, 47]. Bringing a subjective interpretivist lens to the phenomenon of crowdsourcing generates understanding through the viewpoint of those who are experiencing it [33]. Further a focus on qualitative data combined with grounded theory, allows for the building of theory that is based on the perceptions of those engaged in the phenomenon and takes into account the specific contexts under study.

4. DATA COLLECTION AND ANALYSIS

In line with grounded theory techniques, patterns and trends are unfolding through an iterative process of data collection, coding, and categorization [6, 34]. While data collection and analysis is still underway, three primary sources of qualitative data have been collected to date: 1) a comprehensive and systematic review of scholarly crowdsourcing literature, 2) interviews with practitioners across a wide variety of organizations, and 3) exploratory case studies with organizations currently engaged in on-going crowdsourcing initiatives. The combination of qualitative data from these three sources was seen as a valuable way to gain deeper and more nuanced understanding of key themes and patterns via constant comparison [16]. Further, the inclusion of case studies was deemed especially useful in exploring new theory as part of the early stages of research and to build in-context understandings [18, 29, 34, 52]. As theory emerges and solidifies, additional theoretical sampling may be required to reach theoretical saturation and to facilitate the formation of substantive theory [40].

4.1 Crowdsouring Literature as a Source of Data

Prior crowdsourcing research was selected as a means of extracting relevant crowdsourcing uses, characteristics, and themes. A total of 71 peer-reviewed articles, conference papers, and books across a wide variety of disciplines were reviewed.

Because the great majority of crowdsourcing literature to date is descriptive case studies, literature is seen as a useful source of in-context use. It should be noted that in line with grounded theory methods, the focus here is on literature is as another source of data and not as a source of theoretical positioning [16].

4.2 Interviews and Case Studies as a Source of Data

Because examining crowdsourcing within the context of the organization is essential to answering the research question, interviews with practitioners were seen as critical to building useful theory. Additionally, interviews across multiple organizations allow for the emergence of within-case and cross-case patterns [12] also useful when building theory. Data collection from practitioners took place in two phases.

4.2.1 Phase One: Interviews with Practitioners

In phase one, CEOs, independent consultants, and directors/managers at governmental or public institutions tasked with facilitating regional innovation were interviewed. Interview questions focused on gaining an understanding of the current uses of crowdsourcing as well as building an understanding of the issues and challenges organizations may face. A total of 18 semi-structured interviews lasting between 30-60 minutes were conducted via phone. Based on analysis of interviews, it was determined that small to medium sized organizations were unlikely to be leveraging crowdsourcing practices due to perceived risks, costs, and lack of available resources. This finding informed the criteria used for phase two data collection.

4.2.2 Phase Two: Case Studies

For phase two, case study sites were selected based on the following criteria: mature companies (3+ year) with a minimum of 500 employees, who are currently reaching out to the crowd via online channels for input into on-going innovation/service initiatives. Six companies representing a broad range of industries were recruited for participation. A total of 28 individuals at multiple levels within these organizations were interviewed. Participants included CEO, Vice Presidents, Deputy Directors, Program Managers, Program Analysts, Research Scientists, interns, and entry-level employees. Interviews lasted between 60 to 90 minutes and open-ended questions built around a flexible interview protocol were used to focus discussions on the key questions under study [34]. Questions were designed to illicit information regarding the organization's motivation for engaging the crowd, the task(s) to be complete, the crowd being targeted, and the processes for integrating the crowd's input into current innovation processes. Additionally, participants were asked to describe both facilitators of and barriers to implementation, resources required, value realized, and unexpected outcomes/issues.

Because my purpose is to generate theory and not to test existing theory, no a priori categories were created. Instead, open coding was used to extract and collect themes until patterns began to emerge and higher-level categories could be created [43]. Throughout the data collection and analysis process extensive memoing was used to capture reoccurring themes as well as reflect on and conceptualize emerging theory [14, 16, 45]. Where possible, data from interviews is being triangulated with analysis of written documents such as product development plans, strategic plans, and interim or final reports. Member checking is also underway to establish the credibility of the interpretations and findings with select participants as well as experts in the field [43, 47].

While data analysis is still underway, the use of open coding techniques has revealed a number of initial descriptive themes and concepts [17]. A core category has been identified and selective coding is underway. The iterative process of data collection, conceptualizing the data, identifying themes and linkages continues with the objective of building theory in grounded fashion [43].

5. PRELIMINARY FINDINGS

Eight themes have been identified to date: common tasks, crowd knowledge/skills, crowd location, organizational motivations, goals, challenges, value capture, and ownership of work product. These eight themes have been collapsed into three broad categories: task characteristics, crowd characteristics, and organizational characteristics (see Table 1). Selective coding has begun around these broad categories.

5.1 Task Characteristics

Preliminary analysis reveals nine distinct tasks including ideation, filtration (e.g., voting or ranking), evaluation, design, development, complex problem solving (e.g., solutions to complex R&D pharmaceutical problems), completion of tasks difficult for computer but easy for humans (e.g., tagging of images), data collection (e.g., as training data for product algorithms), and knowledge sharing (e.g., for customer service). Depending on the specific organizational goal, crowds may be asked to complete one or more common tasks.

5.2 Crowd Characteristics

Two crowd characteristics have emerged: "knowledge/skills" and "location." Knowledge/skills consists of five different types: general, product, situational (e.g., event or location based), specialized (e.g., graphic design), and domain expertise (e.g., chemistry). Location is made up of two types: external (e.g., outside the boundaries of the firm) and internal (employees).

5.3 Organizational Characteristics

Finally, themes related to organizational characteristics include: motivations (both financial and non-financial), goals (i.e., to supplement, replace, or create), challenges (e.g., quality and accuracy), value capture (i.e., tangible/intangible and immediate/delayed), and ownership of work product (i.e., organizational, communal, or individual).

5.4 Emergence of Core Category and Preliminary Framework

As themes emerged, constant comparison between identified themes and data was instrumental in revealing the core category of "use" related to organization need. Specifically, the nine identified common tasks were collapsed into four key uses: 1) productivity, 2) innovation, 3) knowledge capture, and 4) marketing/branding. Further, the theme of organizational "motivation" was integrated into the theme for organizational "goals" to create a more nuanced description of why organizations turn to the crowd. A new category of "desired outcome" was also created to capture the desired results of each category of use (see Table 2).

While work is still in progress, emergent themes lay the foundation for a framework identifying key uses of the crowd by established organizations. Data collection and analysis continues to further conceptualize the data, identify patterns and linkages, and clarifying categories.

Task Characteristics	Common Tasks	- Ideation - Filtration - Evaluation - Design - Development - Complex problem solving - Completion of tasks difficult for computers but easy for humans - Data collection - Knowledge sharing
Crowd Characteristics	Knowledge/Skills	- General - Product/Service (i.e., specific to the sponsoring organization) - Situational (e.g., time, place, event) - Specialized (e.g., graphic design, programming) - Domain expertise (e.g., chemistry, medical) - Problem solving
	Location	- External (e.g., trusted partners, communities of interest, customers, general public) - Internal (i.e., employees)

Organizational Characteristics	Motivations	- Gaining/Retaining a competitive advantage
		   - Enhancing existing products
		   - Extending product line
		   - Developing new products
		   - Seeding new markets
		- Creating an innovative culture
		- Projecting an image of transparency and inclusion
		- Reducing costs/time

	Goals	- To supplement current processes/resources - To replace current processes/resources - To create new processes/resources
	Challenges	- Accuracy/Quality of work - Availability - IP leakage/Loss of competitive advantage - Clear articulation of the task - Internal acceptance/buy-in - Motivation of the crowd - Loss of control
	Value Capture	- Tangible (e.g., financial) - Intangible (e.g., awareness) - Immediate (e.g., cost savings) - Delayed (e.g., after commercialization of ideas)
	Ownership of Work Product	- Organizational - Communal - Individual

Table 2: Categories of Organizational Crowdsourcing Use

	Productivity	Innovation	Knowledge Capture	Marketing/Branding
Organizational Goal	To reduce time and/or costs by replacing current resources/ processes	To gain competitive advantage and increase innovative potential by supplementing current resources/ processes	To advance understanding or accuracy by capturing distributed knowledge to create new resources/ knowledge	To increase profits and brand affinity by engaging customers to supplement current resources/ processes
Desired Outcome	- Completion of routine, time-consuming tasks, or tasks difficult to automate	- Identification of evolutionary and/or revolutionary product/service opportunities	- Accumulation of knowledge in a central location - Additional source of training data to improve automated processes	- Creative outputs - Market insights - Increased market exposure

6. DISCUSSION

Data analysis to date has revealed four common uses of the crowd as well as eight characteristics. Moreover, and perhaps more promising, relationships between uses, common tasks, crowd and organizational characteristics are emerging. That is, different uses appear to link to specific tasks requiring different crowds with different knowledge/skills. Further, each use brings with it inherently different risks, challenges, and value.

For example, an organization attempting to increase *productivity* related to development of complex applications requires a crowd with specialized knowledge/skills related to programming. However, a task such as verifying the transfer of numbers from one document to another requires only general knowledge/skills. In these cases, organizations may realize immediate and tangible benefits (e.g., reduction in costs) from leveraging the crowd, but be challenged with ensuring quality and timely delivery.

Alternatively, organizations looking to enhance *innovation* related to current products/services, target crowds who have knowledge/skills of the current product/service offerings. When asking the crowd to weigh in on potential changes to design or development of products/services, specialized knowledge/skills of materials and manufacturing processes may be required. When it comes to value extraction related to *innovation*, because crowdsourcing is often used in the early stages of product innovation benefits may be delayed and therefore difficult to immediately quantify.

New potential theoretical implications are also emerging. Preliminary analysis reveals the crowd is often enlisted to "filter" or pair down ideas in the early stages of innovation. Such a finding may suggest a unique role of the crowd within the product development cycle and as such an extension to current models of innovation such as the "stage-gate" model [10]. While it is too soon to draw definitive conclusions about such potential theoretical implications, initial work indicates promising links between emerging theory and extent theory.

7. CONCLUSION

The Internet and collaborative social media tools are creating new opportunities for organizations to engage with and benefit from the crowd. The preliminary explanatory theoretical framework describe here identifies themes found in crowdsourced innovation related to organizational, task, and crowd characteristics. Further, relationships between specific uses and characteristics are emerging.

The anticipated theoretical contribution of this research is the development of a framework from which researchers can build understanding of the dynamics at play when integrating the crowd into current organizational processes. Its anticipated contribution to practice is the development of guidelines for matching the right crowd to the right job, as well as identifying potential risks, challenges, and value for organizations.

8. REFERENCES

[1] Baregheh, A., Rowley, J., & Sambrook, S. (2009). Towards a multidisciplinary definition of innovation. *Decision Management*, 47(8), 1323-1399.

[2] Barrington, L., Turnbull, D., O'Malley, & Lanckriet, G. (2009). User-centered design of a social game to tag music. *Proceedings of the ACM SIGKDD Workshop on Human Computation*, 7-10.

[3] Bishop, M. (2009, May) *The total economic impact of InnoCentive challenges. Single company case study.* Forrester Consulting.

[4] Bonabeau, E. (2009, Winter). Decision 2.0: The power of collective intelligence. *MIT Sloan Management Review*, 50(2), 45-52.

[5] Brabham, D. C. (2009). Crowdsourced advertising: how we outperform Madison Avenue. Retrieved June 30, 2010 from http://bit.ly/HtP2ci.

[6] Byrant, A. & Charmaz, K. (2007). *The SAGE Handbook of Grounded Theory.* London: SAGE Publications.

[7] Chanal, V. & Caron-Fasan, M. L. (2008, May). How to invent a new business model based on crowdsourcing: The Crowdspirit case. Paper presented at the *Conférence de l'Association Internationale de Management Stratégique*, Nice.

[8] Chilton, S. (2009). Crowdsourcing is radically changing the geodata landscape: Case study of OpenStreetMap. Paper presented at the *24th International Cartographic Conference*, Chile. Retrieved from http://bit.ly/H8PfTw.

[9] Christensen, J. F. (2006). Whither core competency for the large corporation in an open innovation world? In H. Chesbrough, W. Vanhaverbeke, & J. West (Eds.), *Open Innovation: Researching a New Paradigm*, (35-61). New York: Oxford University Press.

[10] Cooper, R. G. (1990). Stage-gate systems: A new tool for managing new products. *Business Horizons*, *33*(3), 44–54.

[11] Di Gangi, P. M., & Wasko, M. (2009). Steal my idea! Organizational adoption of user innovations from a user innovation community: A case study of Dell IdeaStorm. *Decision Support Systems*, 48(1), 303–312.

[12] Eisenhardt, K. M. (1989). Building Theories from Case Study Research. *The Academy of Management Review*, *14*(4), 532–550.

[13] Feller, J., Finnegan, P., Hayes, J., & O'Reilly, P. (2009). Institutionalizing information asymmetry: Governance structures for open innovation. *Information Technology & People*, 22(4), 297-316.

[14] Fernández, W. D. (2004). The grounded theory method and case study data in IS research: issues and design. *Information Systems Foundations Workshop: Constructing and Criticizing.*

[15] Florida, R. (2007). *The flight of the creative class. The new global competition for talent.* New York: HarperCollins.

[16] Glaser, B. G., & Holton, J. (2004). Remodeling Grounded Theory. *Forum: Qualitative Social Research*, *5*(2). Retrieved from http://www.qualitative-research.net/index.php/fqs/article/viewArticle/607/1315#g33

[17] Glaser, B. G., & Strauss, A. L. (1967). *The discovery of grounded theory.* New York: Aldine de Gruyter.

[18] Gregor, S. (2006). The nature of theory in information systems. *Management Information Systems Quarterly, 30*(3), 611.

[19] Haklay, M., & Weber, P. (2008). OpenStreetMap: User-Generated Street Maps. *IEEE Pervasive Computing*, *7*(4), 12–18.

[20] Hogue, C. (2011). Crowdsourcing for science. *Chemical & Engineering News, 89*(27), 22.

[21] Howe, J. (2006). The rise of crowdsourcing. *Wired, 14(6).*

[22] Howe, J. (2008). *Crowdsourcing: Why the power of the crowd is driving the future of business.* New York: Crown Business.

[23] Huston, L. & Sakkab, N. (2006, March). Connect and develop. Inside Procter & Gamble's new model for innovation. *Harvard Business Review.* 49(4), 58-66.

[24] IBM Global Business Services. (2006). *Expanding the Innovation Horizon. The Global CEO Study.*

[25] Jeppesen, L. B., & Frederiksen, L. (2006). Why do Users Contribute to Firm-hosted User Communities? The case of computer-controlled music instruments. *Organization Science, 17*(1), 45–63.

[26] Jouret, G. (2009). Inside Cisco's Search for the Next Big Idea. *Harvard Business Review, 87*(9), 43.

[27] Ketchen, D. J., Ireland, R. D., & Snow, C. C. (2007). Strategic entrepreneurship, collaborative innovation, and wealth creation. *Strategic Entrepreneurship Journal,* 1, 371-383.

[28] Kleemann, F., Voß, G. G., & Rieder, K. (2008, July). Un(der)paid innovators: The commercial utilization of consumer work through crowdsourcing. *Science, Technology & Innovation Studies,* 4(1) 5-26.

[29] Klein, H. K. & Meyers, M. D. (1999, March). A set of principles for conducting and evaluating interpretive field studies in information systems. *MIS Quarterly,* 23(1), 67-94.

[30] Lakhani, K. R., Jeppesen, L. B., Lohse, P. A., & Panetta, J. A. (2007, October). The value of openness in scientific problem solving. *Harvard Business School Working Paper 07-050.*

[31] Lakhani, K. R. & Panetta, J. A. (2007, Summer). The principles of distributed innovation. *Innovations,* 97-112.

[32] Lehmann, H. (2010). Grounded Theory and Information Systems: Are We Missing the Point? *2010 43rd Hawaii International Conference on System Sciences (HICSS)* (pp. 1–11). Presented at the 2010 43rd Hawaii International Conference on System Sciences (HICSS), IEEE.

[33] Meyers, M. D. (1997). Qualitative research in information systems. *MIS Quarterly,* 21(2), 241-242.

[34] Myers, M. D. (2009). *Qualitative research in business & management.* SAGE.

[35] Nambisan, S. & Sawhney, M. (2008). *The global brain. Your roadmap for innovating faster and smarter in a networked world.* New Jersey: Pearson Education.

[36] O'Connor, G. C. (2006). Open, radical innovation: Toward an integrated model in large established firms. In H. Chesbrough, W. Vanhaverbeke, & J. West (Eds.), *Open Innovation: Researching a New Paradigm,* (62-81). New York: Oxford University Press.

[37] Orlikowski, W. J. (1993). CASE Tools as Organizational Change: Investigating Incremental and Radical Changes in Systems Development. *MIS Quarterly, 17*(3), 309–340.

[38] Reichwald, R., Seifert, S., Walcher, D., & Piller F. (2004, January). Customers as part of value webs: Towards a framework for webbed customer innovation tools. Proceedings from *37th Hawaii International Conference on System Sciences.*

[39] Schau, H. J., Hemetsberger, A., & Kozinets, R. V. (2008). The Wisdom of Consumer Crowds. *Journal of Macromarketing, 28*(4), 339–354.

[40] Stern, P. N. (2007). On solid ground: Essential properties for growing grounded theory. In A. Byrant, & K. Charmaz (Eds.), *The SAGE Handbook of Grounded Theory,* (pp. 114-126). London: SAGE Publications.

[41] Stewart, O., Huerta, J., Sadder, M., Sakrajda, A., Marcotte. J., & Lubensky, D. (2009). Designing crowdsourcing community for the enterprise. *Proceedings of the ACM SIGKDD Workshop on Human Computation,* 50-53.

[42] Trauth, E. M., & Erickson, L. B. (2012). Philosophical framing and its impact on research. In M. Maro, G. Gelman, & A. Steenkamp (Eds.). *Research Methodologies, Innovations and Philosophies in Software Systems Engineering and Information Systems* (pp. 1–17). Hershey, PA: IGI Global.

[43] Trauth, E. M., & Jessup, L. M. (2000). Understanding Computer-Mediated Discussions: Positivist and Interpretive Analyses of Group Support System Use. *MIS Quarterly, 24*(1), 43–79.

[44] Trompette, P., Chanal, V., & Pelissier, C. (2008). Crowdsourcing as a way to access external knowledge for innovation: Control, incentive and coordination in hybrid forms of innovation. *24th EGOS Colloquium* (pp. 1–29).

[45] Urquhart, C., Lehmann, H., & Myers, M. D. (2009). Putting the "theory" back into grounded theory: guidelines for grounded theory studies in information systems. *Information Systems Journal, 20*(4), 357–381.

[46] U.S. Council on Competitiveness. (2008, October). *Compete: New challenges, new answers.* Washington, D.C.: Author.

[47] Walsham, G. (2003). *Interpretive case studies in IS research: Nature and method* (Vol. 4). Thousand Oaks, CA: SAGE.

[48] Wasko, M. M. & Teigland, R. (2004). Public goods or virtual commons? Applying theories of public goods, social dilemmas, and collective action to electronic networks of practice. *Journal of Information Technology Theory and Application,* 6(1), 25-41.

[49] West, J. & Gallagher, S. (2006). Patterns of open innovation in open source software. In H. Chesbrough, W. Vanhaverbeke, & J. West (Eds.), *Open Innovation: Researching a New-Paradigm,* (82-106). New York: Oxford University Press.

[50] Whitla, P. (2009, March). Crowdsourcing and its application in marketing activities. *Contemporary Management Research, 5(1),* 15-28.

[51] Wiggins, A. & Crowston, K. (2011). From conversation to crowdsourcing: A typology of citizen science. *Proceedings of the 44th Hawaii International Conference on System Science.* Kauai, Hawaii.

[52] Yin. R. K. (1989). *Case Study Research: Design and Methods.* London: Sage

Underrepresented Groups in Gender and STEM: The Case of Black Males in CISE

Curtis C. Cain
The Pennsylvania State University
307G IST Building
University Park, PA 16802
1.814.865.8952

caincc@psu.edu

ABSTRACT

The underrepresentation of Black males in the Information Technology and Computer, Information Science and Engineering (CISE) is a problem in academia and our society. Diversity and learning go hand in hand. People of different cultural, ethnic, religious, and societal backgrounds bring their various experiences with them when they come into a classroom. The more diverse the student, teacher and professor make-up, the more perspectives they can share about any given principle or concept. Therefore, heterogeneous classrooms contribute to diversity.

Having a more ethnically diverse IT field can help with the recruitment and retention of minority undergraduate students through role modeling and mentoring. The findings from this research will add to the growing body of knowledge about interventions to address underrepresentation of certain populations in the IT field. But the particular contribution is that the focus is on minority males. Researching this topic at the undergraduate level would be a starting point, but future research would allow me to study graduate students and faculty in academia to further understand underrepresentation throughout the entire academic pipeline in IT.

Categories and Subject Descriptors

K. Computing Milieu, K.3.2 Computer and Information Science Education, K.4 Computers and Society, K.4.2 Social Issues, K.6 Management of Computing and Information Systems, K.6.1 Project and People Management, K.7 The Computing Profession, K.7.1 Occupations.

General Terms

Theory, Management

Keywords

Diversity, Individual Differences, Theory, Men, Males, CISE, Gender, Race, Ethnicity, Masculinity, Digital Divide, Academic Pipeline, IT, Epistemology, IS

1. INTRODUCTION

The number of Black males who attend and graduate from the

nation's colleges and universities is steadily in decline and now at a critical and disturbing point. This trend has recently captured more focused attention from educational researchers, sociologists, economists, and administrators in higher education [1, 2]. Research indicates that this dilemma has roots that go back to elementary school and consequences that will influence future generations.

Post secondary participation and graduation rates of Black males within Science, Technology, Engineering and Mathematics (STEM) disciplines are declining rapidly. Black women, however, are realizing substantial growth in both of these areas and account for the majority of the increase in Black student college enrollment. The number of Black males who attend and graduate from the nation's colleges and universities is steadily in decline and now at a critical and disturbing point. Although this trend started in the decades ago, it has recently captured more focused attention from educational researchers, sociologists, economists, and administrators in higher education. Increased focus and attention can be attributed to increasing concern for the declining number of Black male teachers and professors in STEM. The decline of Black male teachers and professors has an impact on how Black students perceive their identity and select career paths. Research indicates that the dilemma of the dearth of Black males in higher education has roots that go back to elementary school and consequences that will influence future generations.

Diversity is greatly needed across all backgrounds as diverse culture need role models and mentors for its youth [3]. The concept of identity and seeing oneself in a role opens the door to the possibility of one assuming that role. There is no lack of data supporting these claims. However, what is lacking is sufficient research to analyze and understand the problem, and provide the basis for interventions that could lead to the reversal of the trend. Despite the dismal outlook for many Black males, there are those who successfully navigate through the higher education system to attain a baccalaureate degree. These are the men able to provide new insights about Black males who do participate in this higher education system and persist, and perhaps their experiences illustrate strategies that may assist those who do not.

The Individual Differences Theory of Gender and IT is the proposed theoretical approach to analyzing the issue of Black males in CISE. The Individual Differences Theory of Gender and IT was developed as a theoretical alternative to two opposing perspectives on the topic of underrepresentation of women in the technical workforce, essentialism and social construction.

Empowerment is defined as the next stage of the digital divide. Empowerment references a shift from access and use, to educational, workforce and societal gain. Just to be clear, empowerment within the digital divide is greater than having access to Facebook or sending personal text messages. It is being able to use the Internet and digital technology to communicate, access information, and create commerce. My goal is to determine what the societal, environmental and institutional influences on Black male students in CISE (Computer, Information Science and Engineering) disciplines.

2. LITERATURE REVIEW
2.1 Black Males in Higher Education
There has been a significant amount of research done on the adjustment, academic achievement, persistence, and rates of enrollment and graduation in postsecondary institutions. A large amount of the literature on Black males within educational environments, however, features quantitative studies comparing them with other subgroups.

The academic pipeline has been the topic of contentious debate in a variety of different contexts. The academic pipeline refers to how individual, environmental and institutional factors influence, hinder or divert one from reaching a goal [4]. There are numerous versions of the pipeline for various subsets of the population. Researchers have studied pipelines related to minorities and women for completion of secondary, post-secondary, graduate and professional education [5, 6, 7, 8].

Literature referring to leaks within the academic pipeline references the limited number of women and minorities in STEM disciplines [9, 10]. Margolis et al. [4] posit that America struggles with a stratified intellectual class system for which there are unintended consequences of well-intended policies at every level. They position the argument of inequality as the access and denial of access to Information Technology (IT), satisfactory educators and resources. They state the lack of the aforementioned resources, which are based on race, sex and socioeconomic status, becomes the accepted norm.

The academic pipeline is a concept that relates how individual, environmental and institutional factors influence, hinder or divert one from reaching a target goal [4]. There are numerous versions of the pipeline for various subsets of the population. For example, there are pipelines for minorities and gender within the academic ladder such as successful completion of high school, enrollment and completion of college, as well as professional and graduate school (5, 6, 7, 8]. Most of the literature referring to the faults within the academic pipeline references the limited number of women and minorities in STEM disciplines as students, scientists, teachers, professors and the information technology workforce [9, 10]. Margolis [4] posits that America struggles with a stratified intellectual class system for which there are unintended consequences of well-intended policies at every level.

Blacks are a heterogeneous population and traditional teaching methods have proven to exclude this group over time [13]. A 2003 study using national databases discovered that there are wide gaps between Black and White male educational attainment beginning with high school [11]. Jackson [11] found that 68 percent of Black males graduate high school compared to 79 percent of white males. The gap grows from 11 percent to 68 percent between Black male and white males when successful completion of the baccalaureate degree is considered [11]. The gap becomes even greater when looking at faculty positions of which there is an 81 percent gap between Black males and white males [11]. Jackson's study looked at the state of higher education across all major fields of study.

The underrepresentation of Black males in the Science, Technology, Engineering and Mathematics (STEM) is a problem in academia and our society. In 2003, 12.4 percent of the population was comprised of Blacks, of which only 16 percent had obtained a college degree [14]. In comparison, nearly one-third of Whites had obtained a college degree. The representation of Black males particularly in STEM fields is even sparser [9, 10, 15]. The issue of underrepresentation of Black males in higher education is intensified when the alternative is considered. Sixty percent of Black males who do not graduate from high school spend time in prison, and almost 30 percent of all Black men do [16].

2.2 Digital Divide
According to Mossberger et. al [17], the digital divide describes patterns of unequal access to Information Technology (IT). Unequal access to IT was based on varying socioeconomic factors, such as education, race, gender, age and income [17]. Latinos and African Americans were much less likely to have access to personal computers and thus felt the greatest impact of the digital divide (17, 4, 18]. Digital inequality on the other hand takes the digital divide a step further. It references not only differences in access, but also inequality between persons with formal access to the Internet [19]. DiMaggio [19] found that as Internet penetration increased and access to the Internet was becoming more widespread and that there was a new type of inequality that related to differentiation between groups of people. He suggested that the digital divide must be expanded beyond a binary view, those who have and those who do not, and include identifying critical dimensions of inequality and modeling the relationship between different forms of inequality. DiMaggio [19] continues by positing that society is the source of digital inequality and policies should be enacted to combat inequality.

Kvasny & Keil [20] conducted a case study in two Georgia cities; Atlanta and LaGrange in response to the cities attempts to readdress the digital divide. Their study was informed by Bourdieu's Theory of Social Reproduction, which describes a pattern of systemic and repeatable inequality that is capable of explaining persistent stratification despite efforts to reduce inequality [21]. Bourdieu's theory focused on the relationship between socioeconomic class, inclusive of education and social class. Bourdieu posits that education plays an important role in causing reproduction of social inequality and social exclusion. Kvasny's [20] study focused on evaluating Atlanta's initiative, which was to implement community-testing centers while LaGrange's initiative provided Internet via a set-top box, similar to a cable box. Their findings indicated that inequality was reproduced due to the lack of a mechanism that extended beyond access to actual empowered usage. Empowered usage is being able to use the Internet and digital technology to communicate, access information, and create commerce.

Scholars have replicated the results from studies like Kvasny's [20], which show the digital divide continues on today, but in different forms [13]. Today's digital divide is not one related to access, but rather related to empowered usage, which Kvasny's [20] findings indicated and that DiMaggio surmised in 2001 [19]. Kvasny's study was completed in the mid-2000s before the heavy uptick in mobile technology, which may have less of an impact in today's increasing mobile technology centric atmosphere. Kvasny's study is crucial as it indicated that the conceptualization of the digital divide should be expanded beyond the notion of "haves" and "have-nots". However, Kvasny's findings have shown that in the era of rapid computer expansion and Internet use that inequality remained a constant, which could be a precursor to today's mobile technology centric culture. The digital divide was once categorized as an access issue, between the "haves" and "have-nots", which was reproduced as a use issue in Kvasny's [20] IT study, indicating that with equal access a divide remains.

2.3 Black IT Usage and Identity

According to recent Pew Surveys, *Social Media & Mobile Internet Use Among Teens and Young Adults* [22] and *Mobile Access 2010* [23], mobile technology has changed the landscape of IT. Latinos and Blacks are more likely than the general population to access the Internet via cellular devices. According to Pew Research Center's *Mobile Access 2010* survey, 46 percent of Blacks use their phone to access the Internet compared with 33 percent of whites. More Blacks also use their phone to access their email; 41 percent compared to 30 percent for whites. Also, Blacks are more likely to use their cellular device for social media, such as Facebook and Twitter; 33 percent compared to 19 percent for whites. However, researchers have found that even with increased access to technology there is perpetuating segregation online that correlates to the physical world, which is inclusive of biological factors such as race and societal factors such as socioeconomic class and education. The finding that segregation online still exists could be a major hindrance to cross cultural learning. Researchers have also found that minority groups are also more likely to use their cellular devices for entertainment purposes rather than empowerment. Aaron Smith, a Pew senior research specialist, says there are obvious limitations on what you can do on a mobile device with updating a resume being the classic example. "Research has shown that people with an actual connection at home, the ability to go online on a computer at home, are more engaged in a lot of different things than people who rely on access from work, a friend's house, or a phone," Smith says [22, 23].

The findings from Pew are stated similarly in Jackson's 2008 study entitled *Race, Gender, and Information Technology Use: The New Digital Divide*. Jackson found that there are differences in how different ethnicities use the Internet and to what extent. According to Jackson [13], Black females were the most intense users of cell phones and use the Internet in more diverse ways than other groups. Furthermore, Jackson [13] found that Black males use the Internet less intensely than any other group, paving the way for presumptions that Black males may not view IT as a field that Blacks enter. Jackson's findings suggested that Black females embraced technology, leading all groups in text messaging, searching the Internet for information, as well as for health related information searching. Conversely, Black males lag behind other groups in IT usage with one exception: video gaming. Jackson echoed that research and interventions should bring together culturally relevant tools to increase representation of Black males in computing and increase their level of technical awareness. Scholars have contended that Black IT usage may relate to contemporary culture.

bell hooks [24] takes the reigns of critically discussing Black male identity due to the dearth of Black males who touch the subject. She is an Black theorist, author, intellect, scholar, and feminist. hooks [24] writes in *We Real Cool: Black Men and Masculinity* two sections in particular; about black men: don't believe the hype and the coolness of being real, where she discusses personal reflexivity. She bemoans the Black male identity for what she sees as being largely nonexistent and based on nothingness. Racial identity development as it relates to Black males is a concept that psychologist have studied intensely [25, 26, 27, 28]. hooks remains reflexive in her assessment of the Black male identity, by reflecting on her own interactions with Black males. Hooks draws

upon lived experiences, while taking a historical perspective of Black male identity. She then applies historical perspective to contemporary Black male constructs such as gangsta culture, education and Black male parenting. Presumably, hooks shaped the aforementioned contemporary constructs based on modern Black culture.

hooks is not alone in her critique of Black identity. Jackson [30, 31, 32] who is a Black male academic writing about identity joins hooks in a chorus that sings in perfect harmony of the Black identity that has been stripped of meaning and filled with the media's construction of what Black identity should be. Jackson and hooks both assert that Blacks should be the only group constructing their identity (i.e. not entertainment moguls). Jackson remains reflexive in his account of Black identity by reflecting what he calls self-reflection, by criticizing oneself and laying out in a transparent and honest fashion how his own lived experiences have shaped his conceptualization of identity and how it has changed. Particularly Black male identity has been challenged by academic systems that have long equated Black men to being intellectually inferior to white students and disinterested [25, 29]. Scholars have contended that Black students are intrinsically highly motivated; this motivation is not related to their academic self-efficacy [26, 27, 28, 29]. Reflexivity is part of this research.

2.4 Reflexivity

"Reflexivity requires an awareness of the researcher's contribution to the construction of meanings throughout the research process, and an acknowledgment of the impossibility of remaining 'outside of' one's subject matter while conducting research. Reflexivity then, urges us "to explore the ways in which a researcher's involvement with a particular study influences, acts upon and informs such research." [33, p. 228].

Bourdieu [34] recommends reflexivity to be used at all times throughout the research phases. He mentions that conscious attention to the influence of one's position is necessary to control bias. Bourdieu continues by stating that researchers must continuously reflect back on their own dispositions and remove prejudices that influence results. However, as Nightingale & Cromby [33] point out, it is impossible to remain outside of one's subject matter while conducting research. Reflexivity is viewed as the analytic attention to the role of the researcher in qualitative research [35].

Willig [36] contends that reflexivity does assist with controlling bias but that is not all reflexivity is about. She says that reflexivity allows us to reflect on our own reactions to the research that make understanding possible. Since there is no set format to address reflexivity, it can be difficult to ensure that reflexivity is being addressed. Instead, Willig [36] offers insight to how reflexivity can be addressed by including reflections of the role as the researcher and that those reflections be clear and honest. "A researcher's background and position will affect what they choose to investigate, the angle of investigation, the methods judged most adequate for this purpose, the findings considered most appropriate, and the framing and communication of conclusions" [37, p. 483-484]. As such some researchers say that reflexivity is necessary in qualitative research in establishing that the research is ethical and its findings are accountable, i.e. rigor, trustworthy [38, 39].

Dowling [40] positions the argument for reflexivity as one, which occurs on multiple levels. One level requires the researcher to be aware that he or she is unavoidably involved in the process and results of the research. Another level instructs that the researcher is aware of what is influencing the researcher's internal and external responses while also being aware of the researcher's relationship to both the research topic and research participants. When combined, these levels represent the two types of reflexivity: personal and epistemological. Similarities exist between reflection and reflexivity [41, 42]. Reflexivity is an awareness of the relationship between the researcher and participants. In order to be reflexive one must undergo self-reflection [43].

> 'Epistemological reflexivity' requires us to engage with questions such as: How has the research question defined and limited what can be 'found'? How has the design of the study and the method of analysis 'constructed' the data and the findings? How could the research question have been investigated differently? To what extent would this have given rise to a different understanding of the phenomenon under investigation? Thus, epistemological reflexivity encourages us to reflect upon the assumptions (about the world, about knowledge) that we have made in the course of the research, and it helps us to think about the implications of such assumptions for the research and its findings. [36, p.10]

Trauth [44] begins the discussion of gender and IT by addressing the need to change the thought process of women in IT from a homogenous group to heterogeneous. Howcroft and Trauth [45] add to the discussion of gender and IT as well as epistemological reflexivity. The researchers show how the methodological lens shifts from positivist, to interpretative to critical. They achieve reflexivity by including their own personal reflections throughout the paper. The researchers also display how gender research agendas within IT can change depending on the epistemology. While the study itself was interpretative, the researchers go on to show that if the study were done using a positivist or critical epistemology how the research question would differ. Trauth and Howcroft position the positivist researcher as a neutral and dispassionate scientist and the research question being whether there are any gender differences, which is largely a quantitative analysis. The goal, in particular, is to analyze gender differences, to see if they exist, not to explain why. As an interpretative researcher, the research question would be to understand how gender differences exist. The goal is to add additional understanding to growing body of knowledge about gender and IT. The criticism of interpretative work is that it does not go far enough. By that, the focus is on understanding society as a factor that influences inequality but does not question it. Critical researchers about gender and IT would seek to understand why gender inequality exists. Critical research seeks to challenge the powers that reproduce inequality [46].

> 'Personal reflexivity' involves reflecting upon the ways in which our own values, experiences, interests, beliefs, political commitments, wider aims in life and social identities have shaped the research. It also involves thinking about how the research may have affected and possibly changed us, as people and as researchers. [33, p.10]

Mruck & Breuer [47] discuss why it is difficult to achieve personal reflexivity and address our own biases, choices and experiences throughout the research process sufficiently. They say, due to our teaching that we are taught to exclude subjectivity. They continue by saying that we were taught to include only what may seem to be required by the epistemology and methodology as well as what we can control. By essentially being taught one process and ingraining it through repetition, it has become the culture of educators. With the culture of subjectivity ingrained in students, it is difficult for them to write about themselves as a part of the research. In essence, it is harder to achieve personal reflexivity than it should be. Personal reflexivity requires that researchers become aware of the multiple influences that they have on their research and how, in turn, the research affects them.

The culmination of these issues motivates a need for a better understanding of the ways in which academia is cultivating and nurturing the needs of Black male students pursuing degrees in IT. With this in mind, this paper focuses on the following research question: *What are the societal, environmental and institutional influences on Black male students in IT disciplines?*

3. METHODOLOGY

3.1 Individual Differences Theory of Gender and IT

The Individual Differences Theory of Gender and IT, consists of three major constructs to explain gender variation in participation in the IT field: individual identity, individual influences, and environmental influences [48]. The individual identity construct is one that consists of two sub-constructs: personal demographics and career items. This construct was applied in this study by analyzing ethnicity and family. The second construct, individual influences, consists of two sub-constructs: personal characteristics and personal influences. This construct was applied in this study by analyzing the presence, or lack thereof, of mentors and role models for Black males. Lastly, the environmental influences construct consists of four sub-constructs related to the geographic region; cultural influences, economic influences, policy influences, and infrastructure influences.

The Individual Differences Theory of Gender and IT was developed as a theoretical alternative to two opposing perspectives on the topic of underrepresentation of women in the technical workforce, essentialism and social construction. The essentialist perspective attributes women's underrepresentation in IT to biological factors [48, 44]. Trauth disagrees with the essentialist perspective arguing while some relevant differences in ability maybe biologically based they are not based on gender. Further, essentialism does not add contextual factors, which may affect an individual's perspective or interaction with technology. The other perspective used to understand gender and IT is social construction, which describes gender as "two separate groups of men and women who are affected by two different sets of sociological influences. Hence, men and women are viewed as having different or opposing socio-cultural characteristics, which subsequently affect their relationship to and adoption of technology." [49, p. 23]. Social construction identifies social forces, which may shape the male or female life, but does not consider individual agency or experiences that affect responses to those factors [48, 44]. Given the two differing theoretical perspectives of essentialism and social construction, they can be interpreted as describing partial elements of the situation experienced by women in the IT workforce. As Trauth [50] points out, "current theories about gender and IT do not fully account for the variation in men's and women's relationships to information technology and the IT field" (p. 1759). It is this variation that Trauth has argued is central to different people's experiences, decisions, and relation to technology.

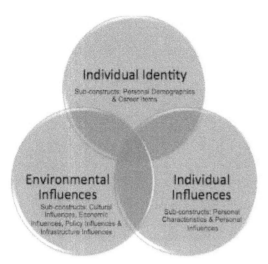

Figure 1. Individual Differences Theory of Gender and IT Venn Diagram

These constructs work together to give insight into women's decisions to enter and remain in the IT field. The individual identity construct encompasses personal demographics and career items, which consists of race, age, gender, job title and type of IT work. The individual influences construct encompasses factors such as personal influences, which include education level, personal abilities, experiences with computing as well as mentor and role models. The last construct, environment influences includes values that represent attitudes about culture and physical as well as organizational location such as attitudes about women and attitudes towards IT work. These constructs provide robust attributes by which to examine aspects of an individual's background, experiences and lifestyle. Trauth's theory represents an integral theoretical basis for research and opportunity for theory extension.

I would extend the Individual Differences Theory by expanding two constructs educational attainment and race and ethnicity. These constructs were in Trauth's original conceptual framework, however they were sub-constructs. Literature on Black males in the academic pipeline, the digital divide and higher education led to these constructs becoming integral main sub-constructs. As the theory is being applied to a new domain, Black males, how they differentiate between race, which is biological, and ethnicity, which is societally derived, and navigate between the two, is of interest. Being that Black males pursuing IT degrees is central to this investigation it is important to emphasize educational attainment in regards to career efficacy, self-efficacy, career goals, mentors, role models and institutional support. Adding these additional sub-constructs to the established theory would help to provide robust and comprehensive attributes by which to examine Black male in IT.

4. REFERENCES

[1] Akbar, N. i. 2002. The psychological dilemma of African American academicians. In L. Jones (Ed.), Making it on broken promises (pp. 31-42). Sterling VA: Stylus

[2] Trent, W. T. 1991. Focus on equity: Race and gender differences in degree attainment, 1975-76; 1980-81. In W. R. Allen, E. G. Epps & N. Z. Haniff (Eds.), College in black and white: African American students in predominantly white and in historically black public universities. Albany: State University of New York Press

[3] Blake, M.B., Gilbert, J.E. 2010. "Black Computer Scientists in Academe: an Endangered Species?", The Chronicle of Higher Education – Diversity in Academe September 19, 2010

[4] Margolis, J., Estrella, R., Goode, J., Holme, J.J., Nao, K. 2008. Stuck in the Shallow End: Education, Race, and Computing. The MIT Press.

[5] van Anders, S. M. 2004. Why the academic pipeline leaks: Fewer men than women perceive barriers to becoming professors. Sex Roles, 51(9/10), 511.

[6] Gallien, L. B., & Peterson, M. S. 2005. Instructing and mentoring the African American college student: Strategies for success in higher education. Boston: Pearson/Allen and Bacon.

[7] Evans, Z. 2001. Maintaining an open pipeline to higher education: Strategies that work. 18(8), 136.

[8] Hopkins, R. 1997. Educating black males: Critical lessons in schooling, community, and power. Albany: State University of New York Press.

[9] National Science Foundation, Division of Science Resources Statistics, Women, Minorities, and Persons with Disabilities in Science and Engineering: 2007, NSF 07-315 (Arlington, VA; February 2007). Available from http://www.nsf.gov/statistics/wmpd.

[10] National Science Foundation, Division of Science Resources Statistics, Women, Minorities, and Persons with Disabilities in Science and Engineering: 2009, NSF 09-305, (Arlington, VA; January 2009). Available from http://www.nsf.gov/statistics/wmpd/

[11] Jackson, J., F.L. 2003. Toward administrative diversity: An analysis of the African American male educational pipeline. Journal of Men's Studies, 12(1), 43.

[12] Peckham, J., Harlow, L.L., Stuart, D.A., Silver, B., Mederer, H. and Stephenson, P.D. 2007. Broadening participation in computing: issues and challenges, Proceedings of the 12th annual SIGCSE conference on Innovation and technology in computer science education, 9-13

[13] Jackson, L.A., Zhao ,Y., Kolenic, A., Fitzgerald, H.E., Harold, R. & Von Eye, A. 2008. Race, Gender, and Information Technology Use: The New Digital Divide. Cyber-Psychology & Behavior, 11, 4, pp. 437-442

[14] U.S. Census Bureau 2003: State and County Quick Facts. Data derived from Population Estimates, Census of Population and Housing, Small Area Income and Poverty Estimates, State and County Housing Unit Estimates, County Business Patterns, Nonemployer Statistics, Economic Census.

[15] Zweben, Stuart. 2009. "Upward Trend in Undergraduate CS Enrollment; Doctoral Production Continues at Peak Levels," Computing Research News, Volume 21, Number 3

[16] Monaghan, P. 2009. "Prison Studies", The Chronicle of Higher Education – Field Review November 4, 2009

[17] Mossberger, K., C. Tolbert, and M. Stansbury. 2003. Virtual inequality: Beyond the digital divide. Washington, D.C.: Georgetown University Press

[18] Watkins, S.C. 2011. The Young and the Digital: What the Migration to Social-Network Sites, Games, and Anytime, Anywhere Media Means for Our Future. Teaching theology & religion (1368-4868), 14 (1), p. 84.

[19] DiMaggio, P. and Hargittai, E. 2001. From the 'Digital Divide' to `Digital Inequality': Studying Internet Use As Penetration Increases. Working Paper #15, Summer 2001.

[20] Kvasny, L. and Keil, M. 2006. "The Challenges of Redressing the Digital Divide: A Tale of Two U.S. Cities", Information Systems Journal, Vol.16. No. 1, pp. 23-53.

[21] Bourdieu, P. and Passeron, J. C. 1977. Reproduction in Education, Society and Culture. Beverly Hills: Sage

[22] Pew Internet, a project of the Pew Research Center. Mobile Access 2010.
http://www.pewinternet.org/~/media//Files/Reports/2010/PIP_Mobile_Access_2010.pdf

[23] Pew Internet, a project of the Pew Research Center. Social media & Mobile Internet Use Among Teens and Young Adults. February 2010.
http://67.192.40.213/~/media/Files/Reports/2010/PIP_Social_Media_and_Young_Adults_Report_Final_with_toplines.pdf

[24] hooks, bell 2004. We Real Cool: Black Men and Masculinity, New York: Routledge.

[25] Franklin, A.J. 1999. Invisibility Syndrome and Racial Identity Development in Psychotherapy and Counseling African American Men. The Counseling Psychologist, Vol. 27, No. 6, pp. 761-793

[26] Cokley, K.O. 2003. What Do We Know about the Motivation of African American Students? Challenging the "Anti-Intellectual" Myth. Harvard Educational Review, Vol. 73, No. 4, Winter 2003.

[27] Cokley, K.O. 2002. Ethnicity, Gender and Academic Self-Concept: A Preliminary Examination of Academic Disidentification and Implications for Psychologists. Cultural Diversity and Ethnic Minority Psychology, Vol. 8, No. 4, 379-388

[28] Carter, R.T. and Goodwin, L. 1994. Racial Identity and Education. Review of Research in Education, Vol. 20, pp. 291-336

[29] Cokley, K.O. 2005. Racial(ized) Identity, Ethnic Identity, and Afrocentric Values: Conceptual and Methodological Challenges in Understanding African American Identity. Journal of Counseling Psychology, Vol. 52, No. 4, 517-526.

[30] Jackson, R. L. 1999. The Negotiation of Cultural Identity. Westport, CT: Praeger Press

[31] Jackson, R. L. (Ed.). 2004. African American Communication and Identities: Essential Readings. Thousand Oaks, CA: Sage.

[32] Jackson, R. L. 2006. Scripting the Black Masculine Body: Identity, Discourse and Racial Politics in Popular Media. Albany, NY: SUNY Press.

[33] Nightingale, D.J. Cromby, J., 1999, (Eds). Social Constructionist Psychology: A Critical Analysis of Theory and Practice, Buckingham: Open University Press

[34] Bourdieu, P. and Loïc J. D. Wacquant. 1992. An Invitation to Reflexive Sociology. Chicago and London: University of Chicago Press. p. 119

[35] Gouldner, A. 1971. The Coming Crisis in Western Sociology. New York, Basic Books.

[36] Willig, Carla, 2008. Introducing Qualitative Research in Psychology: Adventures in Theory and Method, Second Edition, Buckingham: Open University Press.

[37] Malterud, K. 2001. "Qualitative research: Standards, challenges and guidelines." The Lancet. 358: pp. 483-488.

[38] Jootun, D., McGhee, G., Marland, G.R. 2009. Reflexivity: promoting rigour in qualitative research. Nursing Standard. 23, 23, 42-46.

[39] Truex, D., Holmstrom, J., Keil, M. 2006. Theorizing in information systems research: A reflexive analysis of the adaptation of theory in information systems research. Journal of the Association for Information Systems Vol. 7 No. 12, pp. 797-821/December 2006

[40] Dowling, M. 2006. Approaches to reflexivity in qualitative research, Nurse Researcher, 13, 3, pp. 7-21.

[41] Giddens, A. 1976. New Rules of Sociological Method. London, Hutchinson.

[42] Carolan, M. 2003. Reflexivity: a personal journey during data collection. Nurse Researcher. 10. 3. 7-14

[43] Finlay, L. 2002. Negotiating the swamp: the opportunity and challenge of reflexivity in research practice, Qualitative Research, 2, 209-230.

[44] Trauth, E.M. 2002. "Odd Girl Out: An Individual Differences Perspective on Women in the IT Profession," Information Technology and People, Special Issue on Gender and Information Systems, Volume 15, Number 2: 98-118.

[45] Howcroft, D. and Trauth, E.M. (Eds.) 2005. Handbook of Critical Information Systems Research: Theory and Application. Cheltenham, UK: Edward Elgar Publishing.

[46] Kvasny L., Trauth, E.M. 2002. "The Digital Divide at Work and at Home: Discourses about Power and Underrepresented Groups in the Information Society." Global and Organizational Discourse About Information Technology. 273-294.

[47] Mruck, Katja & Breuer, Franz. 2003. Subjectivity and Reflexivity in Qualitative Research—The FQS Issues [17 paragraphs]. Forum: Qualitative Social Research, 4(2), Art. 23.

[48] Trauth, E.M., Quesenberry, J.L. and Huang, H. 2009. "Retaining Women in the U.S. IT Workforce: Theorizing the Influence of Organizational Factors," European Journal of Information Systems, Special Issue on Meeting the Renewed Demand for IT Workers, 18, 476-497.

[49] Trauth, E.M. and Quesenberry, J.L. 2007. "Gender and the Information Technology Workforce: Issues of Theory and Practice," in Managing IT Professionals in the Internet Age. P. Yoong and S. Huff (Eds.) Hershey, PA: Idea Group Publishing: 18-36.

[50] Trauth, E.M. 2006. Theorizing gender and information technology research using the individual differences theory of gender and IT. The Encyclopedia of Gender and Information Technology (pp. 1154-1159).

Links to the Source – A Multidimensional View of Social Ties for the Retention of FLOSS Developers

Andreas Schilling
Centre of Human Resources Information Systems
University of Bamberg, Germany
+49 951 8632873
andreas.schilling@uni-bamberg.de

ABSTRACT

Free Libre Open Source Software (FLOSS) is of vital importance for the daily life of many private and corporate users. However, the majority of all FLOSS initiatives fail, most commonly due to a lack of sustained developers. In contrast to previous research which used an individual centric or a structural perspective, this dissertation combines motivational and relational aspects to build a comprehensive understanding for FLOSS developers' ongoing project commitment. A unified research model is developed by drawing on established theories from organizational and sociological literature, in particular by combining Self-Determination-Theory (SDT) and Social-Identity-Theory (SIT). Both SDT and SIT have been found valuable concepts for staffing decisions in organizations. In addition to the development and evaluation of the research model, this dissertation derives operational strategies for project managers of FLOSS initiatives on how to enhance the retention behavior of their contributor base.

Categories and Subject Descriptors

K.6.1 [**Management of Computing and Information Systems**]: Project and People Management - Staffing

General Terms

Management, Measurement, Human Factors

Keywords

Open Source, Self-Determination-Theory, Social-Identity-Theory, IT Personnel, Job Satisfaction, Turnover Intention, Retention

1. INTRODUCTION

The infancy of software programming in the early 1960s was shaped by a strong sharing culture among developers. Contingent by the high hardware costs at that time, software development has nearly exclusively been done by academic researchers and engineers who perceived it as their duty to share their code with each other [32]. The early 1970s brought a radical change to this practice when commercial software development started to rise. In order to prevent their customers from studying and sharing their products' code, software companies employed special

licensing terms and technical limitations [9, 18]. Many programmers around the world who did not accept these restrictions formed communities developing Free Libre Open Source Software (FLOSS) whose code can be freely accessed, modified and shared with others. What started as a reaction to commercial software has become a pervasive element of modern IT. Not only do most mobiles worldwide run on FLOSS operating systems [14] but nearly half of American and European companies rely on software developed by FLOSS initiatives for their mission critical tasks [15]. Despite their relevance for corporate and private users, however, the majority of all FLOSS initiatives fail most commonly due to a lack of sustained developers [5]. Although previous research repeatedly identified developers' project retention as a top priority for FLOSS initiatives, there are no concepts or guidelines for project managers on how to address this critical issue.

This dissertation is intended to build a theoretical understanding why developers continue committing themselves to a FLOSS project and to provide managers of FLOSS initiatives with practicable advice on how to enhance the retention of their developer base. Regarding individuals' continuance behavior as a product of their motivation and stimuli from their social environment this research develops an integrated conceptual approach for FLOSS developers' permanence in contributing to the respective FLOSS project by considering both motivational and contextual factors. For the theoretic foundation, this model relies on Self-Determination-Theory (SDT) and Social-Identity-Theory (SIT). A literature review in the course of this dissertation reveals a good fit between the arguments of the two concepts and the various forms of motivation and social stimuli, which FLOSS developers are influenced by in their decision to continue their commitment and code development. In contrast to previous FLOSS literature which commonly analyzes the effects of developers' motivation and the influence of their social context as independent and unitary constructs [4, 19], this proposed research combines SDT and SIT to develop a differentiated understanding on how various forms of motivation and belongingness to social groups affect FLOSS developers' sustained project participation.

As a consequence this proposed dissertation provides relevant implications for literature and practice. First, it determines to which extend FLOSS developers' project retention is actually self-determined or rather a result of external stimuli. Second, this research answers the question to which amount FLOSS developers' belongingness to their social groups is relevant for their continuance behavior. Finally, the proposed dissertation gives insights into the various forms and dynamics of social relationships which are formed between developers of a FLOSS project. Based on this understanding, operational guidance is derived for managers of FLOSS projects on how to retain their developer base best and how to control relevant context factors influencing developers' ongoing commitment. Following Drucker to consider knowledge workers' commitment as voluntary this research contributes in addition to the organizational domain [10]. Therefore, the insights provided in this dissertation are also valuable for organizations in their staffing decisions.

The remainder of this proposal is structured as follows: First, the theoretical background of this research is detailed by presenting an overview of existing literature on FLOSS developers' continued project commitment and on the theoretical constructs which form the foundation of this dissertation. Then, in section three, the corresponding research model is developed and the corresponding hypotheses are formulated. Finally, section four contains a description of the used research methodology for evaluating the developed research model and describes the upcoming steps.

2. THEORETICAL BACKGROUND

This section starts with a review of previous FLOSS research on developer retention. Drawing on literature from the organizational domain, the second part of this section details the two theoretical concepts SDT and SIT on which this dissertation builds on.

2.1 FLOSS research

Although previous studies repeatedly identify developer retention as a key challenge for FLOSS projects to succeed, there has been only little research on this topic yet. The few studies which approach FLOSS developers' project retention do so by using primarily either an individual centric perspective or a social network perspective.

Examining the retention behavior of FLOSS developers using an individual centric perspective, previous research found various factors which drive ongoing contributions. Researchers previously reveal that members primarily remain active in a FLOSS project because it gives them a satisfying and enjoying feeling [20, 26]. However, as Fang et al. show members are not driven by enjoyment from the beginning on. They develop this feeling while contributing to the FLOSS project [13]. Instead, newcomers are generally driven by a particular need, so that they regard their contributions rather as instrumental. For example, project novices' motives for contributing can be focused towards gaining financial rewards or promoting one's personal career. Furthermore, Roberts et al. find that FLOSS developers are commonly driven to continue participation by status motivations [25]. Driven by this motive, team members primarily use their project contributions to showcase their coding abilities in order to enhance their perceived sought-after status within the community. Following von Hippel et al., another instrumental motive for contributors' continuance is their socialization progress with other project members [16]. As a result, members continue because they identify themselves with the project. This finding is supported by Qureshi and Fang [23]. Finally, Stewart et al. show that contributors' ideological convictions influence their continuance intentions [29]. Hence, sharing ideological views regarding the open-source movement with other project members stimulates not only individual's level of commitment intensity but also their continuance behavior.

FLOSS research analyzing FLOSS developers' social network suggests that their relationship with each other is relevant for their contribution behavior. Studying the historical contribution structure of 2378 FLOSS projects, Singh et al. show that it is the relationship between project developers with each other and with other related developers which has an important effect on the commitment spend on the project [28]. However, due to the structural lens which was used to examine contributors' relationships, it remains unclear why relational aspects between FLOSS developers are of relevance for their ongoing project commitment. Moreover, recent research findings suggest that FLOSS developers' relevant social context may vary and does not necessarily overlap with their current or previous collaboration partners. In particular, the empirical findings of Hu et al. suggest that FLOSS developers driven by status motives are rather influenced in their project participation by the valuation of their work from their local environment than by their previous collaboration relationships [17]. Similarly Ke et al. support that it depends on developers' driving motives whether their relatedness feelings towards other members within the FLOSS project positively affect the commitment they invest into the project [19].

Although previous FLOSS research supports the importance of developers' motivation and their social context in order to explain their project permanence, there is to our knowledge no integrated framework which combines these aspects adequately. Previous approaches which integrate motivational and situational factors consider developers' contribution motives either as bipolar or consider only FLOSS developers' social relationship with other project members as relevant. These research approaches, however, might be too limited for gaining a comprehensive understanding of FLOSS developers' project continuance given the research results of Ke et al. and Hu et al. which support the existence of different motivation forms and various social contexts which are relevant [17, 19]. In contrast to previous research, this dissertation seeks to build a comprehensive understanding for FLOSS developers' project continuance by differentiating not only their individual contribution motives but also the effects of their relevant social contexts. This multi-faceted research approach allows not only to adequately interpret how the various contribution motives affect FLOSS developers' project continuance differently but also what the relevant factors of their social contexts are and how they may amplify their intention to continue in the project. In addition to providing a broad understanding of FLOSS developers' continuance behavior, this twofold research approach helps project managers to derive practicable levers on how to increase the continuance of their developer base by changing relevant contextual factors. The next two sub-sections detail the theoretical foundation of this research.

2.2 Self-Determination-Theory (SDT)

Motivation, the driving force which energizes and sustains people to act in a particular way has previously been studied by various research methodologies [22]. In contrast to previous approaches which treat motivation as unitary and cumulative construct, SDT distinguishes between different motivation types which lead individuals to behave in certain ways [6]. SDT is based on the assumption that humans have three innate psychological needs which have to be satisfied in order to produce well-being. In particular, these needs are: the need for competence, relatedness and autonomy [6]. Behavior arising naturally through the satisfaction of these needs and which is entirely perceived self-determined by the individual is described as intrinsic motivation [7]. In contrast to this natural form of motivation, extrinsic motives describe human behavior that is caused by regulations outside of the individual. Based on the degree of perceived self-determination for these regulations and for one's doing, Deci et al. categorize four different forms of extrinsic motivated behavior

[6]. With the least amount of perceived self-determination, external regulation describes the most controlled form of motivation. Externally regulated behavior is performed in order to achieve an external reward or to avoid external punishment. A more self-determined form of motivation for which, however, people still perceive an external causality is introjected regulation [7]. Individuals driven by this motivation type perform a behavior to demonstrate their abilities to others in order to enhance their self-esteem and to maintain self-worth. The next motivation type along the self-determination continuum is identified motivation [6]. People driven by this motive consider their actions as necessary in order to accomplish a particular goal which they personally value. Finally, the most autonomous form of extrinsic motivated behavior is integrated regulation. Individuals with this motivation fully internalized the regulations so that they are congruent with their values and needs. Integrated motivation is considered in its effects very similar to intrinsic motivation, except that the behavior is accomplished for an instrumental purpose instead of fun [6].

Empirical findings from the organizational domain support the relevance of SDT for individuals' job retention. Driven by external or introjected motives, employees remain with their jobs only as long as they regard it necessary for achieving financial or status enhancements [6]. In contrast, employees perceiving their work as self-determined showed higher levels of commitment and job persistence. In addition, organizational studies find that employees who are experiencing satisfaction of their basic needs are approaching their work much more motivated and with higher continuance intentions [27].

2.3 Social-Identity-Theory (SIT)
SIT is a research approach originally proposed by Tajfel et al. to explain how individuals form feelings of belongingness towards social groups and how their membership makes them act in accordance with the group [30]. The basic assumption of SIT is that individuals have a need to maintain a positive feeling of their selves and that important parts of their selves are derived through their group membership. Tajfel et al. refer to these parts in SIT as individuals' social identity and define with their theory an understanding of the dynamics which underlie the identification process with social groups. Before the actual identification process, individuals categorize their relevant social groups. Because individuals vary in the ways in which they define social units, this categorization process can occur on different levels of abstraction [8]. For example, if individuals put a strong emphasis on themselves and their own career, their relevant social group may only involve themselves. Alternatively, people can abstract their relevant groups on the levels of working groups or based on nationality/ethnology aspects. After the categorization of the relevant social unit, individuals start to identify with it. According to Ellemers et al., this identification process can be structured into cognitive, affective and evaluative components [12]. The first stage in the identification process is described by the cognitive component. This component defines the process during which an individual matches his or her characteristics with potential fellow members and develops in turn feelings of belongingness with his or her social group. After individuals are consciously aware of their belongingness to a group, they begin to build an emotional attachment to their membership which marks the second step in the identification process. Finally, the evaluative component describes the process in which individuals attach a connotation to their group membership. This process involves that individuals

successfully view their group membership superior to other groups based on criteria which are meaningful to them, which in turn strengthens their belongingness to the group even further.

Studies evaluating SIT in the organizational context emphasize its relevance for understanding employees' feelings of relatedness towards their organization and their job permanence. Based on their research results, Dick et al. recommend managers to consider their employees' social identification level most important in order to employ appropriate means for facilitating their retention [8]. If an employee's social identity focuses on the personal or group level, managers have to use measures which make their organization salient to one's career or the relevant social group in order to facilitate retention. However, if employees' choose to identify with their organization, the authors recommend relying on measures which support the different aspects (cognitive, emotional, and evaluative) of individuals' identification process.

3. RESEARCH MODEL
This dissertation considers both FLOSS developers' participation motivation and the influence of their social context in order to develop an appropriate understanding of their continued project commitment. Therefore, SDT is used as theoretic foundation in order to model FLOSS developers' motivation to continue in their project. Complementing this perspective, SIT is employed as a research framework to model how different contextual factors can strengthen developers' individual types of motivation to remain in the project. Therefore, SIT is not only employed to categorize developers' relevant social group (external or internal of the FLOSS project) but also their identification progress with the project group (cognitive, affective or evaluative). The developed research model is visualized in Figure 1.

Existing research demonstrated that SDT is a universal concept, which can be successfully applied in various contexts including the FLOSS domain. While researchers repeatedly examined the effects of developers' contribution motives, most FLOSS research treats intrinsic and extrinsic motivation as unitary constructs. As one of the few studies which discusses extrinsic motivation as multidimensional, Ke et al. showed that FLOSS developers are driven by different motivational sub-forms in their efforts to contribute [19]. Although FLOSS literature on contributors' retention behavior does commonly not distinguish between the motivational sub-forms, previous research findings do support their existence due to different operationalizations of extrinsic and intrinsic motivations. Regarding paid contributors as externally motivated, Roberts et al. show that pecuniary rewards do stimulate FLOSS members' efforts for their project [25]. Although Roberts et al. focus their examination on FLOSS developers' contribution commitment, findings from the organizational domain suggest that there is also a positive relationship between externally regulated behavior and continuance intentions. According to Raymond, enhancing the sought-after status among peers is an important stimulus for developers to contribute to FLOSS projects [24]. Consistent with previous research findings [21, 25], introjected motivations are assumed to be an important facilitator for FLOSS contributors' intention to stay. Perceiving project permanence to be more self-determined, Fang et al. reveal that project members have to identify with the projects' goals and mission in order to sustain [13]. In line with their research, identified motivation is expected to stimulate contributors to continue in the FLOSS project. In addition, FLOSS developers intend to remain active in the project when they feel that the project group shares their ideological convictions [29]. Hence, integrated motivation is supposed to be a relevant driver for developer retention. Finally, existing literature emphasizes feelings of enjoyment and satisfaction for becoming sustained contributors in FLOSS projects [20, 26]. Therefore, intrinsic working motives are considered relevant for becoming long-term participants in a FLOSS project. Combining previous research and SDT, it is hypothesized that:

H1: External motivation is positively associated with FLOSS developers' continuance intention.

H2: Introjected motivation is positively associated with FLOSS developers' continuance intention.

H3: Identified motivation is positively associated with FLOSS developers' continuance intention.

H4: Integrated motivation is positively associated with FLOSS developers' continuance intention.

H5: Intrinsic motivation is positively associated with FLOSS developers' continuance intention.

According to SDT, the amount to which individuals perceive their actions as self-determined strongly affects the effort and time they invest into an activity [6]. Individuals who perceive their behavior as externally regulated are supposed to perform only temporarily so that they stop as soon as they do not get externally rewarded any more. In contrast, people perceiving their behavior as self-determined, are supposed to perform activities with much more effort and persistence. Based on findings from the organizational domain and recent research by Ke et al. [19], it is supposed that this applies also to FLOSS developers' project permanence. Consequently, it is assumed that FLOSS developers' intent to continue in the project is positively associated with the extent to which they perceive their behavior as self-determined:

H6: FLOSS developers' continuance intention is positively associated with the degree to which they perceive their behavior as self-determined.

As defined within SDT, individuals' motivations and their well-being are inherently intertwined with their needs for autonomy, competence and relatedness [6]. Acquiring an adequate understanding of FLOSS developers' sustained participation behavior, therefore, requires not only consideration of their driving motives but also of how these basic needs are satisfied by their work within the project. With their open participation practices and their public appreciation of members work via commit logs, FLOSS projects generally support individuals' needs for autonomy and competence. However, it is largely unexplored how FLOSS projects can satisfy the relatedness needs of their developers. This aspect, however, is a key for retaining FLOSS developers. On the one hand developers who perceive their behavior not as self-determined participate in FLOSS projects due to the rewards or valuation from others. On the other hand, people who perceive their behavior as self-determined are stimulated by the feeling of belongingness to the project group. To understand how feelings of relatedness develop between developers and how they affect their continuance, SIT is used in the following as a comprehensive framework for group behavior.

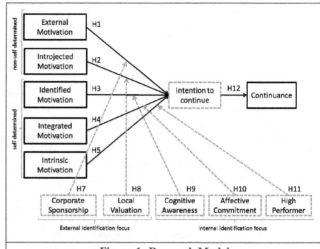

Figure 1: Research Model

During the last decade, IT-companies' commitment in FLOSS projects has steadily increased. However, the effects of corporate sponsorship on FLOSS developers' contribution behavior have shown to be rather complex. Instead of finding a monotonous relationship with developers' intention to stay, previous research rather suggests that sponsorship amplifies the continuance of developers who value financial rewards most important [1]. These findings are consistent with SIT, which suggests that individuals who identify with their career are most likely to be stimulated by the prestige of their doing amongst potential employers [8]. As a result, it is hypothesized that corporate sponsorship positively affects extrinsically motivated developers' continuance intention:

H7: Corporate sponsorship positively strengthens the continuation intention of externally motivated FLOSS developers.

Recent evaluations of SIT in various contexts show that geographic proximity is an important determinant for the social groups which individuals' choose to identify with. For example Zywica et al. show that the online behavior of college students with status driven motives is strongly depended on the valuation from their local peers [33]. Research by Hu et al. finds similar effects in the FLOSS domain. In particular, the researchers provide evidence that FLOSS developers who are looking to enhance their ego are strengthened in their contribution behavior by the local valuation for their work [17]. In line with these findings, we hypothesize that FLOSS developers with introjected motives who are looking to enhance their ego are stimulated in their continuance intention by the local valuation for their work:

H8: The valuation of their contributions by their offline environment strengthens the continuance intention of introjected motivated FLOSS developers.

Ellemers et al. consider individuals' cognitive awareness for their group membership as first step of their social identification process [12]. According to SIT, individuals need to successfully match the characteristics of the existing members with their own, so that they categorize themselves as belonging to the group. This awareness has substantial effects on individuals, as they want to perceive their membership as exclusive which in turn leads them to persist in the groups they feel belongingness to. Previous research supports this kind of awareness for FLOSS developers' identification with their project [2]. Given the need to perceive one's participation as self-determined and the conscious self-reflection of one's contribution behavior, cognitive awareness is supposed to stimulate FLOSS developers with an identified motivation in their continuance intention. Consequently, it is hypothesized that this cognitive awareness for belonging to the FLOSS project strengthens the continuance intention of developers with an identified motivation:

H9: The cognitive awareness of one's project membership strengthens the continuance intentions of identified motivated FLOSS developers.

Next to the cognitive awareness for belonging to the other members of the group, individuals build an affective commitment with the exiting team in order to identify with the group [12]. According to Bergami et al., affective ties are formed when individuals become emotionally attached to their job so that they feel enjoyment when working [3]. Integrated motivation is the most self-determined form of extrinsic regulation, matching best the enjoyment feelings of employed workers. Stewart et al. already show the positive results of FLOSS developers' affective feelings for their commitment [29]. In line with their findings, it is assumed that the affective attachment strengthens the continuance intention of FLOSS developers with an integrated motivation:

H9: Affective commitment for one's project strengthens the continuance intentions of integrated motivated FLOSS developers.

The evaluative component describes the last step for individuals' identification with their social group. This aspect involves individuals' value connotation for their membership [11]. For deriving a positive connotation for one's membership, individuals have to evaluate their group superior over other groups on the basis of intrinsic factors which are meaningful to them. After evaluating one's group superior over others, SIT suggests that individuals' feelings of joy and satisfaction are strengthened which in turn keeps them committed to their group. In the case of FLOSS, developers are supposed to evaluate whether their fellow members share their interests in coding and whether they are superior in their work. Consequently, developers who evaluate their project group over others are assumed to feel higher levels of fun when working for the project, which in turn strengthens their intention to remain in the project. Because this component requires one to perceive project work as enjoying, only intrinsic motivated developers are assumed to be strengthened by this component in their intention to continue:

H11: The presence of project members with a high community status strengthens the continuance intentions of intrinsic motivated FLOSS developers.

Energized by the different forms of motivation to contribute and the various forms and foci of social identification, FLOSS developers are supposed to show higher continuance intentions. Following organizational research, it is assumed that FLOSS contributors align their behavior based on their intentions [31]. As a result, team members' continuance intention is supposed to be the foundation for their actual project permanence. Assuming that the stronger FLOSS developers' intention to remain in the project the longer they will actually stay active, it is hypothesized that:

H11: FLOSS developers' continuance intention is positively associated with their actual project permanence.

4. RESEARCH METHODOLOGY

This dissertation is structured into three working packages in order to evaluate the developed research model and derive practicable guidance for managers of FLOSS initiatives on how to increase the retention of their developer base. The first package involves the longitudinal examination of FLOSS developers' motivation and identification. Taking into consideration that the probability of receiving pecuniary rewards increases for project developers based on companies' growing involvement in FLOSS projects, the proposed research model will be evaluated in a first step with three different reference groups: employed, temporarily paid and unpaid FLOSS developers. An arrangement with three big software companies, which are strongly involved in FLOSS development, makes it possible to survey new hires and experienced employees on their motivation and identification periodically for 6 months starting in January 2012 as part of this research. For studying the effects of temporarily remuneration on FLOSS developers, students of this years' Google Summer of Code (GSoC) have agreed to be surveyed on longitudinal base starting after the event in November. GSoC is an annual event in which the participating students receive a three-month stipend for their contributions to a FLOSS project. To examine the longitudinal motivation and identification behavior of unpaid FLOSS developers, invitations to a study will be posted in January on the mailing lists of various FLOSS projects. The survey items measuring the different constructs of the proposed research model use 5-point Likert scales and are primarily adopted from previous FLOSS research. Based on the perceptual data of the three study groups, the developed research model can be evaluated in a first step and preliminary insights can be provided at the doctorial consortium. Building upon the evaluation of the conducted studies, the second working package aims at the extraction and validation of objective metrics for the assessment of FLOSS developers' motivation and identification from an organizational perspective. To do so, participants' contribution and communication behavior will be studied in retrospect for patterns, which are indicative for their driving motivation and identification focus. Then, the extracted metrics will be assessed in a twofold approach. First, the derived measures will be used to explain the retention behavior of FLOSS developers in retrospect by mining the code repositories and mailing lists of several FLOSS projects. To complement this quantitative evaluation, the corresponding project members will be surveyed to validate the metrics' predictions in addition with their perceptual data. Finally, the last working package involves the practical application of the derived metrics in order to design concrete guidance for project managers of FLOSS initiatives. Therefore, a cooperation with popular FLOSS projects such as KDE, makes it possible to experiment with concrete actions (such as launching mentoring initiatives or conduct regional developer meetings) which can be applied based on the results of the derived key metrics in order to increase members' project permanence.

5. REFERENCES

[1] Alexy, O. and Leitner, M. 2007. A Fistful of Dollars: Financial Rewards, Payment Norms, and Motivation Crowding in Open Source Software Development. *SSRN Journal*.

[2] Bagozzi, R. P. and Dholakia, U. M. 2006. Open Source Software User Communities: A Study of Participation in Linux User Groups. *Management Science* 52, 7, 1099–1115.

[3] Bergami, M. and Bagozzi, R. P. 2000. Self-categorization, affective commitment and group self-esteem as distinct aspects of social identity in the organization. *British Journal of Social Psychology* 39, 4, 555–577.

[4] Christian, B., David, P., Raissa, D., Vladimir, F., and Premkumar, D. 2008. *Latent social structure in open source projects. Proceedings of the Sixteenth ACM SIGSOFT International Symposium on the Foundations of Software Engineering*. ACM Press, New York, N.Y.

[5] Colazo, J. and Fang, Y. 2009. Impact of license choice on Open Source Software development activity. *Journal of the American Society for Information Science & Technology* 60, 5, 997–1011.

[6] Deci, E. L. and Ryan, R. M. 2000. The 'What' and 'Why' of Goal Pursuits Human Needs and the Self-Determination of Behavior. *Psychological Inquiry* 11, 4, 227.

[7] Deci, E. L. and Ryan, R. M. 1995. Human Autonomy: The Basis for True Self-Esteem. In *Efficacy, Agency, and Self-Esteem*, M. Kernis, Ed. Plenum, New-York, 31–49.

[8] Dick, R., Wagner, U., Stellmacher, J., and Christ, O. 2004. The utility of a broader conceptualization of organizational identification: Which aspects really matter? *Journal of Occupational and Organizational Psychology* 77, 2, 171–191.

[9] Dixon, R. 2004. *Open Source Software Law.*

[10] Drucker, P. F. 2002. They're not Employees, They're People. *Harvard Business Review* 80, 2, 70–77.

[11] Edwards, M. R. 2005. Organizational identification: A conceptual and operational review. *International Journal of Management Reviews* 7, 4, 207–230.

[12] Ellemers, N., Kortekaas, P., and Ouwerkerk, J. W. 1999. Self-categorisation, commitment to the group and group self-esteem as related but distinct aspects of social identity. *European Journal of Social Psychology* 29, 2-3, 371–389.

[13] Fang, Y. and Neufeld, D. 2009. Understanding Sustained Participation in Open Source Software Projects. *Journal of Management Information Systems* 25, 4, 9–50.

[14] Gartner Inc. 2011. *Gartner Says Android to Command Nearly Half of Worldwide Smartphone Operating System Market by Year-End 2012*. http://www.gartner.com/it/page.jsp?id=1622 614. Accessed October 23rd.

[15] Ghosh, R. 2005. Understanding Free Software Developers: Findings from the FLOSS Study. In *Making Sense of the Bazaar: Perspectives on Open Source and Free Software*, MIT Press, Ed., Cambridge, 1–23.

[16] Hippel, E. von and Krogh, G. von. 2003. Open Source Software and the "Private-Collective" Innovation Model: Issues for Organization Science. *Organization Science* 14, 2, 209–223.

[17] Hu, D., Zhao, J. L., and Cheng, J. 2012. Reputation management in an open source developer social network: An empirical study on determinants of positive evaluations. *Decision Support Systems.*

[18] Kavanagh, P. 2004. *Open source software. Implementation and management.*

[19] Ke, W. and Zhang, P. 2010. The Effects of Extrinsic Motivations and Satisfaction in Open Source Software Development. *Journal of the Association for Information Systems* 11, 12, 785–808.

[20] Ke, W. and Zhang, P. 2009. Motivations in Open Source Software Communities: The Mediating Role of Effort Intensity and Goal Commitment. *International Journal of Electronic Commerce* 13, 4, 39–66.

[21] Lakhani, K. and Wolf, R. G. 2005. Why Hackers Do What They Do: Understanding Motivation and Effort in Free/Open Source Software Projects. In *Perspectives on Free and Open Source Software*, J. Feller, B. Fitzgerald, S. Hissam and K. R. Lakhani, Eds. MIT Press, Cambridge, MA.

[22] Locke, E. A. and Latham, G. P. 2004. What Should We Do about Motivation Theory? Six Recommendations for the Twenty-First Century. *The Academy of Management Review* 29, 3, 388–403.

[23] Qureshi, I. and Fang, Y. 2010. Socialization in Open Source Software Projects: A Growth Mixture Modeling Approach. *Organizational Research Methods* 14, 1, 208–238.

[24] Raymond, E. S. 1999. *The cathedral and the bazaar. Musings on Linux and open source by an accidental revolutionary.* O'Reilly, Sebastopol.

[25] Roberts, J. A., Hann, I.-H., and Slaughter, S. A. 2006. Understanding the Motivations, Participation, and Performance of Open Source Software Developers: A Longitudinal Study of the Apache Projects. *Management Science* 52, 7, 984–999.

[26] Shah, S. K. 2006. Motivation, Governance, and the Viability of Hybrid Forms in Open Source Software Development. *Management Science* 52, 7, 1000–1014.

[27] Sheldon, K. M. and Elliot, A. J. 1999. Goal Striving, Need Satisfaction, and Longitudinal Well-Being The Self-Concordance Model. *Journal of Personality & Social Psychology* 76, 3, 482–497.

[28] Singh, P., Tan, Y., and Mookerjee, V. Forthcoming. Network Effects: The Influence of Structural Social Capital on Open Source Project Success. *MIS Quarterly* (Forthcoming).

[29] Stewart, K. J. and Gosain, S. 2006. The Impact of Ideology on Effectiveness in Open Source Software Development Teams. *Management Information Systems Quarterly* 30, 2, 291–314.

[30] Tajfel, H. and Turner, J. 1986. The social identity theory of intergroup behaviour. In *Psychology of intergroup relations*. Nelson-Hall, Chicago, 7–24.

[31] Thatcher, J. B., Stepina, L. P., and Boyle, R. J. 2002. Turnover of Information Technology Workers Examining Empirically the Influence of Attitudes, Job Characteristics, and External Markets. *Journal of Management Information Systems* 19, 3, 231–261.

[32] von Krogh, G. and von Hippel, E. 2003. Special Issue on Open Source Software Development. *Research Policy* 32, 7, 1149–1157.

[33] Zywica, J. and Danowski, J. 2008. The Faces of Facebookers: Investigating Social Enhancement and Social Compensation Hypotheses; Predicting Facebook™ and Offline Popularity from Sociability and Self-Esteem, and Mapping the Meanings of Popularity with Semantic Networks. *Journal of Computer-Mediated Communication* 14, 1, 1–34.

How Employee Turnover Impacts Social Capital and Performance of Companies

Olav Spiegel
University of Cologne
Albertus-Magnus-Platz
50923 Cologne, Germany
+49 221 470-5319
spiegel@wim.uni-koeln.de

ABSTRACT

Recently, *The Wall Street Journal* proclaimed there is a "War for Internet Talent" among companies in the Information and Communication Technology (ICT) sector. At the same time, talented employees often become entrepreneurial and establish their own startups. Thus, my research is motivated by these guiding questions: Which turnover patterns/trends can be observed in the ICT industry from a macro perspective (i.e., where does social and human capital flow)? To what extent can startup performance in this industry be explained by the social capital aggregated from the turnover history of its founders—that is, from the ties to former employers? Which employees are key resources in terms of their individual contributions to the aggregate social capital of their current employers? Do brokerage opportunities create turnover incentives for employees?

As a first step to answering these questions, I aim to provide evidence that startup performance is not based exclusively on access to talent in the sense of individual human capital but is also determined by a social capital aspect resulting from their founder's career history. I apply social network analysis (SNA) combined with logistical regression on a large dataset of companies and people in the ICT sector to explore this topic.

Categories and Subject Descriptors

K.1 [**Computing Milieux**]: The Computer Industry – *statistics, suppliers;* K.7.0 [**The Computing Profession**]: General; K.6.1 [**Management of Computing and Information Systems**]: Project and People Management – *staffing.*

General Terms

Management, Performance, Economics, Human Factors.

Keywords

Turnover, Employee Mobility, Information and Communication Technology, ICT, Startups, Entrepreneurship, Social Capital, Social Network Analysis, SNA, Resource-Based View, Multilevel Networks, Human Capital, Venture Capital, Human Resource Management.

1. INTRODUCTION

Recent articles in online media suggest that competition for highly skilled knowledge workers in the Information and Communication Technology (ICT) sector has reached a new level. *The Wall Street Journal* even calls it the "War for Internet Talent" [25] building on and refining the general notion of war for talent [14, 41]. Web firms like Google, Facebook, Twitter, and others are adding large numbers of employees, increasingly at the expense of their competitors. For instance, more than 10 percent of Facebook's employees previously worked for Google [24]. At the same time, talented employees often become entrepreneurial and establish their own startups [37, 56]. Despite the considerable amount of entrepreneurial activity, little is known about the link between turnover and IT entrepreneurship [45].

Traditionally, the effect of human resources on company performance has been assessed from a human capital point of view with a focus on knowledge, skills, and experience (e.g., [32, 39]). Increasingly, organizational research has adopted a perspective of the firm as a social community or collective [38]. In particular, the construct of social capital has been applied to explain organizational advantage [40, 46]. The value of employees with a strong network of relationships goes far beyond their base of individual knowledge and skills, especially in complex and dynamic environments [22].

Employee turnover reduces human and social capital of the former employer, both of which negatively affect company performance [51]. Thus, attracting and retaining talented employees is an ongoing subject of interest for academic research [31, 35, 42]. Recent research on turnover provides a more differentiated perspective. Departing employees potentially create ties between former and new employers, increasing the social capital for the benefit of both sides [53]. For instance, turnover-induced ties are used for the bidirectional transfer of knowledge between companies [17].

My research is motivated by these guiding questions: Which turnover patterns/trends can be observed in the ICT industry from a macro perspective (i.e., where does social and human capital flow)? To what extent can startup performance in this industry be explained by the social capital aggregated from the turnover history of its founders—that is, from the ties to former employers? Which employees are key resources in terms of their individual contributions to the aggregate social capital of their current employers? Do brokerage opportunities create turnover incentives for employees?

This paper extends my earlier research paper presented at the International Conference on Information Systems (ICIS) 2011 [54].

The rest of this paper presents more theoretical foundations, a conceptual model and its application, research methods and data, potential contributions, and research outlook.

2. THEORETICAL FOUNDATION

This section introduces the concepts and theories on which the following conceptual model is based. Because of the space constraints for this paper, only a brief overview will be provided. For a more detailed background, please refer to my prior publication [54].

2.1 Company Performance

Starting with the resource-based view of the firm [50, 60], human resources have been considered a critical source of sustainable competitive advantage. Especially in knowledge-intensive firms [55] "human capital is the dominant factor" [3]. This atomistic view of actors has since been overcome by the recognition that all economic action is embedded in social structures [30].

More recent research conceptualizes the firm as a social community or collective that specializes in creating and transferring knowledge [38]. Consequently, the concept of social capital has been incorporated to explain differences in companies' performance [40, 46].

2.2 Social Capital

The concept of social capital has found broad acceptance and application far beyond its origins in the social sciences [2]. Social capital is "the sum of the actual and potential resources embedded within, available through, and derived from the network of relationships possessed by an individual or social unit" [46]. The main differentiator between social capital on the one hand and human and financial capital on the other is that social capital can only be accumulated with the help of other people [9].

There are different notions of social capital in the literature [6]. Structural social capital research, as the name suggests, focuses on explaining benefits for the actor as a function of the network structure within which she or he is embedded. Two major streams of research have developed here: the advantage of dense, cohesive networks between members of an organization that facilitate the pursuit of common goals [16] versus sparse, non-redundant networks that are rich in structural holes that create a competitive advantage [8]. The latter is also known as social capital of brokerage. The actor who bridges those structural holes—or, in other words, connects non-redundant sources of information—has an advantage derived from brokerage opportunities. These two perspectives on social capital integrate very well: the highest performance can be realized when individuals in a group or company span structural holes external to the group but retain cohesiveness within the group [10]. In my research, I focus on the effects of social capital of brokerage.

2.3 Employee Turnover

Employee turnover is typically associated with negative effects for the former employer. These effects can be differentiated into direct costs (e.g., for recruiting and training the successor) and indirect costs. The latter include loss of firm-specific human capital, demoralization of remaining employees, and loss of social capital embedded in the employees' relationships [57].

Not surprisingly, loss of social capital from employee turnover negatively impacts company performance [51]. However, the opposite can also be the case: employee turnover can potentially lead to the creation of a business tie between the former and new employer, resulting in increased social capital for both firms. In one study, the positive impact on performance even exceeded the loss in human capital incurred at the prior employer [53]. For instance, such turnover-induced ties can be used for the bidirectional transfer of knowledge between companies [17].

3. CONCEPTUAL MODEL

In the course of my extensive literature review, I have identified several research gaps I want to address with my studies. While the concept of social capital has been well integrated into the resource-based view of the firm, many problems remain in understanding the mechanisms underlying this phenomenon [15]. Also, research considering multiple levels of analysis—that is, the level of individuals within the organization and the level of relationships between those organizations—is just developing [44]. Recent research on employee turnover has revealed some considerable insights; however, more comprehensive studies are required to better comprehend the relationship between turnover, social capital, and company performance [17, 53]. This is where I am heading.

3.1 The Impact of Employee Turnover on Social Capital and Company Performance

Prior research has shown that social capital has an effect on organizational performance [40, 46], that social capital of individuals aggregates into the social capital of organizations [8, 40], and that employee turnover potentially induces business ties between former and new employer, increasing social capital and company performance [53].

Building on and expanding those research results, I hypothesize that any new employee creates social capital of brokerage for the new employer from the creation of informal inter-organizational ties to former employers, which consequently impacts company performance in a positive way. Those ties serve as complementary assets for the company as "Contacts can be leveraged to obtain knowledge, timely information, funding, credibility, and other desirable assets" [15].

The nature of those ties is informal in that they are not formalized in the sense of contracts or mutual agreements as opposed to formal company ties found in the context of joint ventures or industry corporations. These are inter-organizational ties because the level of investigation is the companies and their relationships, not the individuals. That is, ties that the individual employees possess are aggregated on the company level. This approach is theoretically grounded in the duality principle [7] and has been followed before—for example, in research on board interlocks [43].

The social capital of brokerage concept, as introduced above, can be applied to explain the competitive advantage a company gains from those turnover-induced ties. The structure and composition of those ties (e.g., exclusiveness or non-redundancy) can be analyzed to gain insights about the company under investigation. Furthermore, the structural comparison with other companies enables an analysis of the competitive landscape.

Here is an example to illustrate the conceptual model: Company B hires (poaches) a senior manager from Company A. The new employee provides Company B two things: knowledge and skills from prior work experience (i.e., human capital) and a tie to Company A and each other prior employer (i.e., social capital). Naturally, the value of this additional tie for Company B depends on two things. First, there are diminishing marginal benefits for new ties that are non-unique (i.e., ties to Company A existed before, so the value add of an additional tie is lower). Second, the value depends on Company A's position in the competitive landscape, meaning that if it is an innovation leader or laggard makes a difference.

One might argue that not all employees leave on good terms or that potential resources from distant contacts do not always lead to actual benefits. Regarding the first objection, leaving on bad terms means that the relationship to the former employer as an institution is broken. However, ties to former colleagues built over time, be it acquaintances or friends, will most likely remain intact. The strength of the tie will degrade over time, but since Granovetter, we know that weak ties are often a better source of information [29].

Regarding the second objection, it is true that some contacts will never be tapped or leveraged. However, a company will have a better chance of being able to reach out to the right contact for resources and/or information if the company is, through the ties of its employees, in a beneficial structural position: "Network brokerage is not a guarantee. It is a probability: Connecting across structural holes increases the risk of productive accident—the risk of encountering a new opinion or practice not yet familiar to colleagues, the risk of envisioning a new synthesis of existing opinion or practice, the risk of discovering a new source for needed resources" [11].

3.2 Research Hypotheses

These are the initial hypotheses that I intend to address with my research:

H1 Social capital of brokerage from informal inter-organizational ties as a result of employee turnover has a positive effect on company performance.

H2 The more knowledge-intensive a company/industry is, the stronger the impact of social capital of brokerage on company performance (knowledge-intensity moderates the effect of social capital of brokerage).

H3 The higher an employee's rank is, the stronger the contribution of his or her social capital of brokerage on company performance (the employees' management level in scope moderates the effect of social capital of brokerage).

The first hypothesis (H1) will be tested in the context of ICT startups, as described next.

3.3 Model Application on ICT Startups

For the aforementioned conceptual model, limiting boundary conditions, such as industry or organization type, should not apply. However, the intensity of anticipated effects will likely vary depending on the area of investigation.

For three reasons, I aim to empirically validate the model by analyzing the differences in startups' performance in the ICT sector. First, organizational social capital is particularly important in knowledge-based industries [22, 51]. As hypothesized in H2, the effects of social capital of brokerage will be stronger in industries like the vibrant and dynamic ICT sector.

Second, executives like startup founders provide the richest evidence regarding the effects of social capital [9, 61]. This is also hypothesized in H3. Entrepreneurship is inherently a network activity [23], and network-based research in the field of entrepreneurship has a long tradition [33]. As described further below, I will measure startup performance as a function of external funding. This allows me to properly reflect the probabilistic nature of social capital of brokerage [11]. Venture capitalists (VCs) assess a startup's potential success [21],

presumably taking into account the startup's social capital of brokerage. Also, as startups are typically small businesses, cohesiveness among the employees can be taken for granted, which allows for the effective use of the social capital of brokerage.

Third, social capital research in the context of entrepreneurship is still rare [49], and developing an understanding of entrepreneurship in the ICT sector has only just begun [45].

4. RESEARCH METHODS AND DATA

This section outlines the data source chosen and describes the data collection, cleansing, and normalization process. Next, there is a brief introduction into social network analysis (SNA), including the calculation of the social capital of brokerage. Finally, the variables and the regression model will be presented.

4.1 Data Source

My analysis is based on a free public database called CrunchBase [19], which is part of TechCrunch, a network of technology-oriented blogs and other web properties recently bought by the web company AOL [4]. On their website, CrunchBase provides structured profiles on technology companies, people, and funding activities. As of March 27, 2012, the database listed 85,821 companies and 113,875 people. The database is growing at a rapid pace: more than 5,000 new entries and more than 12,000 updates to existing entries are entered on average per month. CrunchBase includes companies in 18 categories, including consumer web, software, entertainment, eCommerce, and so on, with a focus on startups and entrepreneurial companies [28].

The CrunchBase data are collected using a Wikipedia-like crowdsourcing approach: everyone is invited to contribute knowledge. There is a vibrant community supported by a professional team from TechCrunch. For instance, I found that 50 percent of all company profiles have been updated at least once within the past 12-month period. Data quality is sufficiently high due to reciprocal user control and intensive use of external references to validate information [48]. With respect to data quality, Newman [47] notes that "Data on affiliation networks tend to be more reliable than those on other social networks, since membership of a group can often be determined with a precision not available when considering friendship or other types of acquaintance."

4.2 Data Collection

CrunchBase provides access to its database by means of an application programming interface (API). Data can be searched and downloaded by simple Hypertext Transfer Protocol (HTTP) requests [18] and is available in JavaScript Object Notation (JSON) format [36]. For example, Facebook's profile in JSON format is available at

http://api.crunchbase.com/v/1/company/facebook.js

I accessed the API by means of a Java-based parsing program and downloaded a complete set of the profiles to a local database for further processing. In the next step, I extracted the required attributes from the raw JSON data to build my network structures and the input variables for the regression model.

4.3 Data Cleansing and Normalization

While CrunchBase already provides rich and comprehensive data on companies in the ICT sector, there is still room for improvement. For instance, the database contains company profiles from all over the world, but there is a clear concentration on the United States. Also, there seems to be an emphasis on startups that have already received funding. These two examples highlight the need for some data cleansing and normalization. While I am quite confident that the CrunchBase data will serve my research needs, I will still maintain top-level scientific standards to avoid any kind of bias. More details on this matter will be provided after the data analysis is finalized.

4.4 Social Network Analysis

To calculate the social capital of brokerage inherent to each company, I apply SNA. SNA is a set of methods and tools initially developed for use in modern sociology [27], but over the years, researchers from across the social sciences have successfully applied this methodology. SNA models actors and their interrelationships in networks of nodes and ties (also referred to as edges). Actors can be individuals, groups, companies, or even more abstract items like patents. Ties represent a certain type of relationship: they can be directed (e.g., seeks advice from) or undirected (e.g., know each other). In addition, relationships may be modeled as binary (i.e., exists or not) as opposed to signed, ordinal, or valued (e.g., the amount of trade between two countries). A network can be fully connected or decomposed into components that are connected within, but not connected to, each other. Various measures and metrics have been proposed to describe network and actor properties [59]. Among them are density (i.e., proportion of existing vs. potential ties), in-degree and out-degree (i.e., number of incoming and outgoing ties), and metrics for centrality. Centrality measures are linked closely to the notion of power. One very prominent representative is betweenness centrality [26], which measures the extent to which an actor is on the shortest path between any other pair of actors. Thus, the more connections that depend on a given actor, the more power associated with that actor.

Based on the data collected from the CrunchBase website, I created a network of companies. Each company represents a single network node. Ties between any two companies (e.g., A and B) were created as follows: if a current employee of Company B has previously worked for Company A, there will be a directed tie from Company A to Company B. In other words, ties reflect a turnover relationship between companies. Due to the underlying nature of the ties, they are directed—that is, they point from one node to another. However, as prior research has shown [17, 53], the effects of social capital from turnover are bidirectional, so the originally directed ties are treated as undirected if not stated otherwise. For some of my other research questions (e.g., the analysis of turnover patterns and trends), I will utilize directed ties.

In some cases, there might not be a clear turnover situation, and one employee could belong to more than one company at the same time. For instance, this could occur if the same person founds two different startups or a person still works for her/his old employer while starting a new business. Those cases are treated like regular turnovers because the person still connects two or more companies.

Based on the network described above, I will use a standard SNA software tool like UCINET or Pajek to calculate each company's social capital of brokerage expressed by the betweenness centrality. As described next, this metric will be used in the regression model as the independent variable.

4.5 Variables and Regression Model

Moving from the network analysis to the regression model, I need to adjust my sample and filter only startup companies, because I want to measure the impact of social capital of brokerage on startup performance. The network used for the SNA included all companies for completeness of turnover histories and structural positions. I define companies in my dataset as startups if they are fewer than five years old and have fewer than 50 employees.

To test my hypothesis, I will use a logistic regression model with startup performance as the dependent (explained) variable and social capital of brokerage as the independent (explanatory) variable. The effect will be controlled further by variables on the company and individual levels.

4.5.1 Dependent Variable

Measuring startup companies' performance is not trivial. Unlike publicly traded companies, startups are not required to publish company data. Furthermore, actual revenues (if any at all) do not fully represent a startup company's real value. For technology startups, and even more for web startups, undergoing initial public offerings (IPOs) or being acquired by an established company are typical exit strategies. The success of VCs is often measured by the IPO rate or acquisition rate within their portfolios [1]. VCs are the primary source of selection for startups that have not yet exited [5]. Therefore, funding received through these investors "confirms the quality of the company and decreases the uncertainty about its potential success. […] The credibility associated with a funding event—emanating from the information available to the VC firm as well as its reputation—gives a strong signal about the quality of the startup" [21]. Other researchers follow the same argument for measuring a startup's potential success as a function of external funding [5, 13, 21]. Therefore, I incorporate whether a startup has received funding as a binary dependent variable in my model.

4.5.2 Independent Variable

Being able to identify opportunities that open up between otherwise unconnected fields and combining different views and unique information to form something new is essential for innovative startups [13]. Higher heterogeneity in the network surrounding an entrepreneur leads to higher diversity of information available to that entrepreneur [33]. In turn, diversity can lead to higher creativity and innovation [10] and grants access to unique information [13], all of which are particularly valuable for entrepreneurial companies. In a network, the degree of diversity is reflected by the amount of structural holes an actor bridges [8]. Such structurally advantaged positions are generally associated with social capital of brokerage and can be measured by the betweenness centrality value for that actor [10]. Hence, I use the startups' betweenness centrality values resulting from the analysis of my company network as an independent variable, which reflects the aggregated social capital of brokerage from their employees.

4.5.3 Control Variables

I incorporate control variables to account for other factors that could explain my dependent variable (i.e., startup performance). These factors can be situated at either the company or the individual level. Drawing on prior research [34, 58], I control for company age in years, number of founders, and company size as the total number of employees. At the individual level, I need to control for human capital-related factors. Because my unit of analysis is the company, I need to aggregate individual-level factors on that level as well. I deduce founding experience and managerial experience ([13, 34]) by counting such positions previously held by team members. In addition, I attribute for general work experience (total in years) and education level (number of degrees higher than bachelor's) [13, 20, 34].

4.6 Results

I presented some preliminary results at ICIS 2011 [54]. The final results from the regression analysis will be presented at the upcoming SIGMIS-CPR 2012 conference.

5. POTENTIAL CONTRIBUTIONS

My research contributes to different areas of ongoing academic interest. First, I add to a better understanding of turnover in the ICT sector in general and startups in particular. Second, by exploring turnover histories, I add a complementary social capital facet and new insights into sources of organizational advantage. Third, I add empirical evidence to the still small body of research on multilevel systems in the area of social network analysis.

In addition, my research will have direct practical applications. Recently, Burt and Ronchi [12] again confirmed the effect of social capital based on a field experiment to teach executives how to see social capital. I increase the awareness and effective use of social capital in two ways. First, I provide a way to differentiate startups in the ICT sector according to their social capital of brokerage. This can help explain and justify intuitive actions of companies and investors that otherwise seem to be irrational based on traditional views of human and social capital. Second, my results enhance the identification and understanding of strategic human resources—namely key employees rich in distinct social capital of brokerage. This is a prerequisite for effective retention management and an additional decision criterion for selecting and hiring (or even enticing) future employees based on their relationship context.

6. RESEARCH OUTLOOK

Based on my dataset, the initial findings on companies and people in the ICT sector are very promising, and I am confident in continuing and testing my hypotheses. At present, I am in the process of finalizing the data cleansing and normalization process.

My dataset yields comprehensive information on turnover patterns in general, which I will further explore by means of descriptive statistics. This will generate considerable insights regarding my other research questions: Which turnover patterns/trends can be observed in the ICT industry from a macro perspective (i.e., where does social and human capital flow)?

I conclude with a statement that calls for a more differentiated view regarding the proclaimed war for talent: "Instead of the old 'war' mentality, which frames turnover as a win-or-lose scenario, companies should adopt a more holistic perspective and consider the administrative, human-capital and social-capital implications of worker mobility" [52].

7. REFERENCES

[1] Abell, P. and Nisar, T. M. 2007. Performance Effects of Venture Capital Firm Networks. *Management Decision* 45, 5, 923–936.

[2] Adler, P. S. and Kwon, S.-W. 2002. Social Capital: Prospects for a New Concept. *The Academy of Management Review* 27, 1, 17–40.

[3] Alvesson, M. 1995. *Management of Knowledge Intensive Companies* 61. de Gruyter, Berlin.

[4] Arrington, M. 2010. *Why We Sold TechCrunch To AOL, And Where We Go From Here.* http://techcrunch.com/2010/09/28/why-we-sold-techcrunch-to-aol-and-where-we-go-from-here/. Accessed 3 May 2011.

[5] Baum, J. A. C. and Silverman, B. S. 2004. Picking Winners or Building them? Alliance, Intellectual, and Human Capital as Selection Criteria in Venture Financing and Performance of Biotechnology Startups. *Journal of Business Venturing* 19, 3, 411–436.

[6] Borgatti, S. P. and Foster, P. C. 2003. The Network Paradigm in Organizational Research: A Review and Typology. *Journal of Management* 29, 6, 991–1013.

[7] Breiger, R. L. 1974. The Duality of Persons and Groups. *Social Forces* 53, 2, 181–190.

[8] Burt, R. S. 1992. *Structural Holes: The Social Structure of Competition*. Harvard University Press, Cambridge, Massachusetts.

[9] Burt, R. S. 1997. The Contingent Value of Social Capital. *Administrative Science Quarterly* 42, 2, 339.

[10] Burt, R. S. 2001. Structural Holes versus Network Closure as Social Capital. In *Social Capital: Theory and Research*, N. Lin, K. S. Cook and R. S. Burt, Eds. Aldine Transaction, New Brunswick, 31–56.

[11] Burt, R. S. 2010. *Neighbor Networks - Competitive Advantage Local and Personal*. Oxford University Press, Oxford, New York.

[12] Burt, R. S. and Ronchi, D. 2007. Teaching Executives to See Social Capital: Results from a Field Experiment. *Social Science Research* 36, 3, 1156–1183.

[13] Burton, M., Sørensen, J. B., and Beckman, C. M. 2002. 7. Coming from Good Stock: Career Histories and New Venture Formation. In *Research in the Sociology of Organizations*. Emerald (MCB UP), Bingley, 229–262.

[14] Chambers, E. G., Foulon, M., Handfield-Jones, H., Hankin, S. M., and Michaels III, E. G. 1998. The War for Talent. *The McKinsey Quarterly*, 3, 44–57.

[15] Chisholm, A. M. and Nielsen, K. 2009. Social Capital and the Resource-Based View of the Firm. *International Studies of Management and Organization* 39, 2, 7–32.

[16] Coleman, J. S. 1988. Social Capital in the Creation of Human Capital. *The American Journal of Sociology* 94, 95–120.

[17] Corredoira, R. A. and Rosenkopf, L. 2010. Should Auld Acquaintance Be Forgot? The Reverse Transfer of Knowledge Through Mobility Ties. *Strategic Management Journal* 31, 2, 159–181.

[18] CrunchBase. 2011. *CrunchBase API*. http://www.crunchbase.com/help/api. Accessed 2 September 2011.

[19] CrunchBase. 2011. *CrunchBase Home*. http://www.crunchbase.com/. Accessed 20 April 2011.

[20] Davidsson, P. and Honig, B. 2003. The Role of Social and Human Capital Among Nascent Entrepreneurs. *Journal of Business Venturing* 18, 3, 301–331.

[21] Davila, A., Foster, G., and Gupta, M. 2003. Venture Capital Financing and the Growth of Startup Firms. *Journal of Business Venturing* 18, 6, 689–708.

[22] Dess, G. G. and Shaw, J. D. 2001. Voluntary Turnover, Social Capital, and Organizational Performance. *The Academy of Management Review* 26, 3, 446–456.

[23] Dubini, P. and Aldrich, H. 1991. Personal and Extended Networks Are Central to the Entrepreneurial Process. *Journal of Business Venturing* 6, 5, 305.

[24] Efrati, A. and Morrison, S. 2010. *Google to Give Staff 10% Raise*. http://online.wsj.com/article/SB10001424052748703523604575605273596157634.html. Accessed 3 May 2011.

[25] Efrati, A. and Tam, P.-W. 2010. *Google Battles to Keep Talent*. http://online.wsj.com/article/SB10001424052748704804504575606871487743724.html. Accessed 3 May 2011.

[26] Freeman, L. C. 1977. A Set of Measures of Centrality Based on Betweenness. *Sociometry* 40, 1, 35–41.

[27] Freeman, L. C. 2004. *The Development of Social Network Analysis: A Study in the Sociology of Science. A study in the sociology of science.* Empirical Press, Vancouver, BC.

[28] Goldenson, M. 2011. *The Math of TechCrunch, Part 1: Is TechCrunch Still About Startups?* http://techcrunch.com/2011/06/12/math-of-techcrunch-startups/. Accessed 2 September 2011.

[29] Granovetter, M. S. 1973. The Strength of Weak Ties. *The American Journal of Sociology* 78, 6, 1360–1380.

[30] Granovetter, M. S. 1985. Economic Action and Social Structure: The Problem of Embeddedness. *The American Journal of Sociology* 91, 3, 481–510.

[31] Hiltrop, J.-M. 1999. The Quest for the Best: Human Resource Practices to Attract and Retain Talent. *European Management Journal* 17, 4, 422–430.

[32] Hitt, M. A., Bierman, L., Shimizu, K., and Kochhar, R. 2001. Direct and Moderating Effects of Human Capital on Strategy and Performance in Professional Service Firms: A Resource-Based Perspective. *The Academy of Management Journal* 44, 1, 13–28.

[33] Hoang, H. and Antoncic, B. 2003. Network-Based Research in Entrepreneurship: A Critical Review. *Journal of Business Venturing* 18, 2, 165–187.

[34] Hsu, D. H. 2007. Experienced Entrepreneurial Founders, Organizational Capital, and Venture Capital Funding. *Research Policy* 36, 5, 722–741.

[35] Joseph, D., Ng, K.-Y., Koh, C., and Ang, S. 2007. Turnover of Information Technology Professionals: A Narrative Review, Meta-Analytic Structural Equation Modeling, and Model Development. *MIS Q* 31, 3, 547–577.

[36] JSON.org. 2011. *Introducing JSON.* http://www.json.org. Accessed 2 September 2011.

[37] Kessler, S. 2010. *Life After Google: 15 Startups Founded by Ex-Employees.* http://mashable.com/2010/08/26/ex-googler-startups/. Accessed 3 May 2011.

[38] Kogut, B. and Zander, U. 1996. What Firms Do? Coordination, Identity, and Learning. *Organization Science* 7, 5, 502–518.

[39] Kor, Y. Y. and Leblebici, H. 2005. How Do Interdependencies among Human-Capital Deployment, Development, and Diversification Strategies Affect Firms' Financial Performance? *Strategic Management Journal* 26, 10, 967–985.

[40] Leana, C. R. and Van Buren, H. J. 1999. Organizational Social Capital and Employment Practices. *The Academy of Management Review* 24, 3, 538–555.

[41] Michaels, E., Handfield-Jones, H., and Axelrod, B. 2001. *The War for Talent.* Harvard Business School Press, Boston, Massachusetts.

[42] Mitchell, T. R., Holtom, B. C., Lee, T. W., and Graske, T. 2001. How to Keep Your Best Employees: Developing an Effective Retention Policy. *The Academy of Management Executive (1993-2005)* 15, 4, 96–109.

[43] Mizruchi, M. S. 1996. What Do Interlocks Do? An Analysis, Critique, and Assessment of Research on Interlocking Directorates. *Annual Review of Sociology* 22, 271–298.

[44] Moliterno, T. P. and Mahony, D. M. 2011. Network Theory of Organization: A Multilevel Approach. *Journal of Management* 37, 2, 443–467.

[45] Mourmant, G., Gallivan, M. J., and Kalika, M. 2009. Another Road to IT Turnover: The Entrepreneurial Path. *European Journal of Information Systems* 18, 5, 498–521.

[46] Nahapiet, J. and Ghoshal, S. 1998. Social Capital, Intellectual Capital, and the Organizational Advantage. *The Academy of Management Review* 23, 2, 242–266.

[47] Newman, M. E. J. 2001. Scientific Collaboration Networks. I. Network Construction and Fundamental Results. *Physical Review E* 64, 1, 16131–16138.

[48] Olleros, X. F. 2008. Learning to Trust the Crowd: Some Lessons from Wikipedia. In *2008 International MCETECH Conference on e-Technologies (mcetech 2008).* IEEE Computer Society, Los Alamitos, California, 212–216.

[49] Payne, G. T., Moore, C. B., Griffis, S. E., and Autry, C. W. 2011. Multilevel Challenges and Opportunities in Social Capital Research. *Journal of Management* 37, 2, 491–520.

[50] Penrose, E. T. 1959. *The Theory of the Growth of the Firm.* Oxford University Press, Oxford.

[51] Shaw, J. D., Duffy, M. K., Johnson, J. L., and Lockhart, D. E. 2005. Turnover, Social Capital Losses, and Performance. *The Academy of Management Journal* 48, 4, 594–606.

[52] Somaya, D. and Williamson, I. O. 2008. Rethinking the 'War for Talent'. *MIT Sloan Management Review* 49, 4, 29–34.

[53] Somaya, D., Williamson, I. O., and Lorinkova, N. 2008. Gone But Not Lost: The Different Performance Impacts of Employee Mobility Between Cooperators Versus Competitors. *Academy of Management Journal* 51, 5, 936–953.

[54] Spiegel, O., Abbassi, P., Fischbach, K., Putzke, J., and Schoder, D. 2011. Social Capital in the ICT Sector - A Network Perspective on Executive Turnover and Startup Performance (Research-in-Progress). In *Proceedings of the International Conference on Information Systems (ICIS).*

[55] Starbuck, W. H. 1992. Learning by Knowledge-Intensive Firms. *Journal of Management Studies* 29, 6, 713–740.

[56] Taylor, C. 2011. *Skype's Real P2P Network.* http://gigaom.com/2011/04/25/skypes-real-p2p-network/. Accessed 3 May 2011.

[57] Ton, Z. and Huckman, R. S. 2008. Managing the Impact of Employee Turnover on Performance: The Role of Process Conformance. *Organization Science* 19, 1, 56–68.

[58] Vissa, B. and Chacar, A. S. 2009. Leveraging Ties: The Contingent Value of Entrepreneurial Teams' External Advice Networks on Indian Software Venture Performance. *Strategic Management Journal* 30, 11, 1179–1191.

[59] Wasserman, S. and Faust, K. 1994. *Social Network Analysis: Methods and Applications.* Cambridge University Press, Cambridge.

[60] Wernerfelt, B. 1984. A Resource-Based View of the Firm. *Strategic Management Journal* 5, 2, 171–180.

[61] Witt, P. 2004. Entrepreneurs' Networks and the Success of Start-Ups. *Entrepreneurship and Regional Development* 16, 5, 391–412.

Alternative Ways of Connecting IT Researchers with Target Public Audiences

Conrad Shayo
California State University
5500 University Pkwy
San Bernardino, CA 92407, USA
1.909.537.5798
cshayo@csusb.edu

Eileen M. Trauth
Pennsylvania State University
330C IST Building
University Park, PA 16802, USA
1.814.865.6457
etrauth@ist.psu.edu

Kate Kaiser
College of Business
Marquette University
Milwaukee, WI, 53201 USA
kate.kaiser@mu.edu

Frank Lin
California State University
5500 University Pkwy
San Bernardino, CA 92407, USA
1.909.537.5701
flin@csusb.edu

PANEL SUMMARY

There is a growing need for the CPR community to connect to a variety of public audiences in furtherance of communicating IT personnel research: students (K-12, undergraduate and graduate), parents, teachers, guidance counselors, practitioners, policy makers (others?). There are both practical and scholarly reasons why the CPR community would want to communicate its research results more broadly. The publication of our research in SIGMIS-CPR proceedings and the ACM digital library is not be the only effective way to reach our audience; many have no access to them. At the initial stages of planning any research study, we need to incorporate dissemination strategies. We need ask the following questions: Who are our target audiences and how are we going to reach them? Who will be responsible for the dissemination effort? What are our dissemination goals? What resources are available? Finally, did our dissemination effort produce the intended results?

There are many avenues for dissemination—some traditional, other non-traditional. For example, a summary of our research findings may be disseminated through traditional channels such as: press releases, media (TV, radio), newsletters, flyers or brochures, research briefs, and community meetings.

Other traditional channels could be: workplace seminars and K-12 class visitation opportunities. Non –traditional alternatives may include: theatre, YouTube presentations, and social media such as blogs, Facebook, Twitter and LinkedIn. The purpose of this panel is to discuss some of the alternative audiences and alternative means of communicating to them.

To do this the panelists will use examples of their own work to discuss issues with and rewards of using innovative means of reaching beyond the scholarly community to make CPR research accessible to a broader, public audience.

Communicating to Practitioners: [Kate Kaiser]. Relevance of research to practice is core to why researchers investigate phenomena. Practitioner organizations of both client and provider firms are wrestling with a shortage of IT skills, a change to less

technical skills, demand for more technology, and economic constraints. This maelstrom creates the incentive for research which can in turn help organizations solve these concerns. Individuals with IT career aspirations often lack realistic perspectives on career development while those with misperceptions of IT might be missing a fulfilling career option. CPR research can offer alternatives to these two potential entry-level candidates whose resources are in demand. Outreach of applied research is the essence of both academics and practitioners.

Communicating to Public Audiences: [Eileen Trauth]. The National Science Foundation recognizes the to communicate the results of scholarly work beyond the research community through the grant scheme in the Directorate for Education and Human Resources: *Connecting Researchers and Public Audiences* (NSF 11-546). The purpose of the CRPA grant is to develop creative ways to communicate the results of scientific research beyond the scholarly community. Scholars who have active NSF grants may apply to CRPA for funding to broaden the dissemination of their research findings beyond the scholarly audience. For the CPR community this would mean using CRPA funds to communicate to educators, counselors, parents and students about the IT field.

Research Dissemination—Best Practices Examples: [Frank Lin]. If some of our research outcomes identify areas where we can recruit young children to our field, then why don't we develop an effective dissemination plan to reach these children, their teachers or parents? What role should face-to-face meetings, peer influence or opinion leaders play? A quick search of the research dissemination strategies literature does provide us with some proven best practices, but how many researchers pay mere lip service to it? I will provide best practices and examples for setting a dissemination agenda for our SIGMIS-CPR community.

Alternative Forms of Research Dissemination: [Conrad Shayo]. The goal of any research dissemination effort is utilization. To promote utilization, we have to make sure our findings and recommendations reach our target audiences. How successful has the SIGMIS-CPR research community been in reaching our target audiences? How have we measured success? Are the current forms of research dissemination sufficient or should we pursue alternative forms? I will explore alternative forms of research

SIGMIS-CPR'12, May 31–June 2, 2012, Milwaukee, Wisconsin, USA.
ACM 978-1-4503-1110-6/12/05.

dissemination and suggest an agenda for action for the SIGMIS-CPR research community.

Categories & Subject Descriptors:
H.0, K.1, K.3, K.4, K.7

General Terms:
Computing Milieux, Information Systems

Keywords:
IT Research Dissemination, IT Personnel Research, Communicating IT Research

PANELISTS

Kate Kaiser studies IT skills and offshore outsourcing as IT faculty at Marquette University. She is investigating skills for healthcare IT and how curriculum can deliver focus for this growth area. She will discuss coordination of the IT Workforce Research Team efforts since 2005 and her participation in the IS 2010 Model Curriculum Task Force and the Society for Information Management (SIM).

Conrad Shayo studies and consults in the areas of IT assimilation, performance measurement and end-user computing. He participates as a California Awards for Excellence (CAPE) Examiner evaluating organizations that apply for the Malcolm Baldrige excellence award. He will discuss alternative forms of research dissemination and opportunities available for SIGMIS-CPR researchers.

Eileen M. Trauth is Professor of Information Sciences and Technology at The Pennsylvania State University where she studies gender, social inclusion and economic development in relation to the IT field. She is currently studying intersectionality of gender, ethnicity and socio-economic class, and developing creative ways to communicate about barriers in the technological professions. She will discuss her experience working on an NSF, CRPA grant to write and perform a play as a vehicle to communicate her research and theory development about barriers to under-represented groups in the IT field.

Frank Lin studies and consults in the areas of organizational assessment, business process improvement/redesign, organizational modeling, enterprise architecture, strategic use of information technology, diffusion of information technology in organizations, and global and cultural intelligence. He will discuss some of the proven best practices and provide examples we can use to set a research dissemination agenda for our SIGMIS-CPR community.

PANEL FORMAT
90 minute session. Panel moderator will give the background on the panel. Then each panelist will [say what each of us will do]. Then we will open it up to the audience to share their thoughts.

1. BIBLIOGRAPHY

Hawk, S., Kaiser, K.M., Goles, T., Simon, J., C.M. Beath, Bullen, C.V., Gallagher, K.P., Abraham, T., Frampton, K., The Information Technology Workforce: A Comparison of Critical Skills of Client and Service Providers, *Information Systems Management*, forthcoming.

Lawrence, R. (2006). Research dissemination: actively bringing the research and policy worlds together. *Evidence & Policy: A Journal of Research, Debate and Practice*, Volume 2(3), August, 373-384.

National Science Foundation. 2011. *Informal Science Education: Connecting Researchers and Public Audiences.* (Solicitation 11-546).

Topi, H., Valacich, J. S., Wright, R. T., Kaiser, K. ., Nunamaker, J. F., Sipior, J. C., and de Vreede, G. J. (2010) IS 2010: Curriculum Guidelines for Undergraduate Degree Programs in Information Systems, *Communications of the Association for Information Systems,* 26(18).

Trauth, E.M. 2011. *Addressing Gender Barriers in STEM through Theatre of Social Engagement.* www.eileentrauth.com/theatre-of-social-engagement.html.

Wilson, P.M., Petticrew, M., Calnan, M.W., Nazareth, I. (2010). Does dissemination extend beyond publication: a survey of a cross section of public funded research in the UK. *Implementation Science* 2010, **5**(61), 1 -8.

Zwieg, P., Kaiser, K. M. , Beath, C.M., Bullen, C. V., Gallagher, K.P., Goles, T., Howland, J., Simon, J. C., Abbott, P., Abraham. T., Carmel, E., Evaristo, R., Hawk, S., Lacity, M., Gallivan, M., Kelly, S., Mooney, J. G., Ranganathan, C., Rottman, J. W., Ryan, R., Wion, R. (2006) The Information Technology Workforce: Trends and Implications 2005-2008, *MIS Quarterly Executive*, 5(2), June, 47-55.

Mobile Recruiting: Insights from a Survey among German HR Managers

Stephan Böhm
RheinMain University of Applied Sciences
Department of Design | Computer Science
Wiesbaden, Germany
stephan.boehm@hs-rm.de

Susanne J. Niklas
RheinMain University of Applied Sciences/
Saarland University
Wiesbaden/Saarbrücken, Germany
susanne.niklas@hs-rm.de

ABSTRACT
Less than two decades ago the desktop-based Internet started to conquer the mass market. Today, Internet usage is ubiquitous and the primary source of information for many people. This might also be one reason why the Internet has also established as the media of choice for personnel marketing and recruiting. However, with the growing popularity and use of the mobile Internet HR managers are facing new challenges in their personnel recruitment activities. These challenges as well as opportunities associated with the deployment of innovative mobile technologies for personnel recruiting are often discussed in connection with the concept of "mobile recruiting" –but, what's behind it and does it really matter? To gain insights into the practitioners' awareness and assessment of mobile recruiting we conducted a survey among HR managers in Germany. The study was carried out first in 2009 and was repeated 2011. Key findings are presented in the paper at hand. The analysis shows that perceived relevance of mobile recruiting as well as its deployment increased at large.

Categories and Subject Descriptors
A.1. [**General Literature**]: Introductory and Survey. H.4.0. [**Information System Applications**]: General; H.4.3. [**Information System Applications**]: Communication Applications – *Internet.*

General Terms
Management, Measurement, Documentation, Human Factors

Keywords
Mobile Recruiting, E-Recruiting, Recruiting Strategy, Personnel Marketing, Status Quo Analysis

1. INTRODUCTION
The changes in the economic and demographic environment have intensified the scarcity of qualified personnel and talent shortages, leading to an increased "war for talents" [20]. According to a current study among German top 1.000 organizations seven out of ten organizations act on the assumption that difficulties in finding qualified personnel will further increase [22]. These developments put more pressure on HR mangers for identifying channels and instruments allowing efficient targeting of appropriate job candidates. At the same time, vast technical advances of mobile devices, networks and services have substantially changed media usage patterns and intensified mobile media usage.

However, despite the technical advances and the growing utilization, mobile media is still in an early stage. The current state can be compared to the status of the World Wide Web in the end of the 1990s. Today, nobody would doubt the necessity to deploy the Web for personnel marketing as well as recruiting activities. Anyhow, in the 1990s it was difficult to anticipate the further development of this new channel. Likewise, organizations currently face the question of integrating mobile recruiting into their HR management activities and, whether implementing functions supporting this new mobile channel into existing HR software and systems is necessary. Currently, this discussion manifests itself in special interest magazines, blogs and Web portals on mobile recruiting. But, apart from some contributions from UK [6, 10], comprehensive surveys and studies focusing on this topic are missing so far. Similarly, publications in scientific journals are not to find yet. Besides the novelty of the topic, this could be due to the fact that mobile recruiting is partly seen as a pure hype or buzzword [12], not sufficient to justify an own research topic (to date). However, a growing recognition and awareness of mobile recruiting as a term for the deployment of mobile technologies in personnel recruiting from the practitioner's side should be regarded as a stimulus for scientists to put some research efforts into this area and to support practice with science-based recommendations.

In order to understand to what extent the HR departments are already engaged in mobile recruiting and aware of its challenges and potential we conducted a survey among German HR managers in 2009. The study was repeated in 2011 to be able to identify trends in HR manager's assessment of mobile recruiting as well as shifts in the deployment of different mobile technologies. Accordingly, the remainder of this paper is organized as follows: section 2 describes the status of the mobile Internet as well as its upcoming relevance in the context of HRM. Section 3 will overview the methodology of the empirical investigation the results of which will be discussed in the thereafter section 4. Finally, section 5 contains the conclusions of this paper and an outlook on further research.

2. RESEARCH BACKGROUND
2.1 State of the Mobile Internet
The number of Internet users who use their mobile devices to access Internet and World Wide Web has strongly increased during the last two years. Likewise, 28 percent of all Internet users are currently accessing the Web via mobile phones in Germany –compared to only 18 percent in 2009 [1]. At the same time, usage intensity increased as well: the share of mobile Internet users who are using their phones daily for mobile Web access expanded from 33 to 58 percent. Mobile data volume per user has grown up to 166 MB per user/year in Germany and thus, rose by more than 300 percent between 2009 and 2011 [7]. It is obvious that this development is driven by the proliferation of

smartphones and flat-rate mobile data plans which enable a more simple and cost-effective mobile Web access. As well smartphones are starting to supersede other devices, being traditionally used for Web access while being on the move: in private contexts 47 percent of all users already abandon netbooks and laptops completely for mobile Web usage and 64 percent do not longer use these devices for mobile Web surfing in the office [1]. These trends may intensify in the course of technology, device advances and the forthcoming introduction of the 4G/LTE standard in Germany like in other countries as well.

Considering these developments, it appears quite possible that the PC era for surfing the Web changes to a mobile era as modern smartphones and tablets like iPad & Co will become preferred devices for accessing the Web. Those devices offer simple and intuitive user interfaces via multi-touch displays. They are handy and ready to use without lengthy boot-up times. WLAN or mobile broadband give the user freedom of using their devices anytime, anywhere. Innovation leaders like Google have already responded to the strategic importance of this development: at the 2010 Mobile World Congress in Barcelona Google's former CEO Eric Schmidt announced the "Mobile First" strategy which prioritizes mobiles devices for any future endeavors of the company [8].

2.2 E-HRM and the Mobile Internet

The evolution of an advanced electronic human resource management (e-HRM) has been widely analyzed. Especially the application of Internet-based technologies has been discussed as an important tool in gaining a competitive edge for employee attraction and recruiting on the labor market [2, 12, 13, 20]. By referring to the attraction of talents, recruiting can be classified into a company's staffing process. It is subsequent to an organizations personnel planning, followed by application management and candidate selection. Recruiting is also linked to employer branding and reputation [2, 5, 12]. Being a promising option for reaching a wide pool of applicants as well as being time and cost effective, "online" emerged as the most preferred recruiting channel [2, 13]. Corporate career websites as well as general-purpose and niche job boards have been identified as some of the most relevant e-recruiting sources [13]. According to the German speaking market in 2011, more than seven out of ten new hires trace back on online job postings [22]. Regarding preceding aspects of personnel marketing communication, Web 2.0 applications and social media achieve increasing influence as well. Social network sites like Facebook, LinkedIn or Twitter are gaining vast popularity and are permanently used. And, social network-usage not only acts a part within private communication with peers and friends but also within information screening and job search as well [14] and social networks are even considered in the context of job applications [18].

Taking account of the above described mobile Web developments it becomes obvious that any current online activity in the area of e-HRM can be extended towards a mobile usage scenario where mobile devices and services are used for access. In addition, the ongoing (mobile) Web usage behavior of being "always on" has been identified as an important trend and challenge HR departments are currently facing [12]. To explore these aspects as well as the basic application of mobile technologies within HR activities in terms of "mobile recruiting", the research project "ReMo-Media – Recruiting in the Mobile Media" was launched at Wiesbaden's RheinMain University, Germany, in 2008 funded by the Federal Ministry of Education and Research. At this, mobile recruiting refers to any organizational information provided for or

delivered to a mobile device in order to attract and hire potential applicants and employees [16]. But, what actually accounts for mobile recruiting? Due to the increasing diffusion of smartphones with high-resolution displays, powerful processors, large memory capacity, high-speed data rates and comfortable user-interfaces the differences between mobile and PC-based Internet access seem to dissolve. Against this background some may question the practical relevance to differentiate between PC-based and mobile Internet access in the context of e-HRM [15].

However, surfing common websites via mobile devices is just one part of the story –and, besides, not always the most preferable. Despite all technological developments, mobile devices still have resource-based limitations compared to desktop PCs or Laptops. Restrictions are e.g. characterized by eased computing power or memory size. Additionally, screens are still smaller as well as input options are harder to handle and performance is limited to battery power and networking connection [11]. This means, that accessing information designed for PCs via mobile devices is often possible but will not always provide an appropriate usage experience [11, 19]. Anyhow, besides those partially technological shortcomings, mobile devices are also characterized by some inherent advantages which common, conventional PCs do not, or not equally, hold. Here, functionalities like location based services should be named and native mobile applications which are specially designed for the devices' operating system thus, allowing making full use of the mobile devices' functionalities. Additionally to those functional and resource-based differences, contextual parameters like high levels of personalization, permanent availability, (online) accessibility and resulting use contexts when being "on the move" have to be considered.

In this connection, Kaasien [11] described two kinds of services for accessing the Internet via a mobile device: general services which are commonly used via a stationary PC and services especially designed for mobile devices. Regarding mobile accessible services, one can further distinguish between those services which are adapted from common stationary offerings (e.g. using content adaption or small screen rendering solutions) and those, which are specifically designed for mobile [17]. As a result, Internet services like the Web can be classified in a framework with three main categories as shown in Figure 1. Filling up this framework with the application area of (mobile) recruiting, the left category contains traditional e-HRM offerings like corporate career websites or job boards. Depending on the capabilities of the mobile device and/or the level of mobile-adaption provided by the server infrastructure, these offerings are additionally accessible via mobile devices to a greater or lesser extend (mid category). The right category applies for mobile-specific offerings especially designed to be accessed via a mobile device, like location based services or just simple SMS notifier. The latter kind of services can also be exemplified by job portal apps for the iPhone which are already numerously available in the German speaking market like in others as well. These apps are coming with features such as bookmarking favorite job postings, click-to-call (direct get through), location based services ("Where is the next job offering around me?") or the functionality to apply for a job by forwarding a link to a business network profile (e.g. LinkedIn, XING) or a job application uploaded to the job portal via PC before [3]. Beyond that, conventional print media can be linked towards the online world via mobile applications by e.g. enhancing paper-based advertisements with QR-Codes or just SMS short codes offering "text to apply" [21].

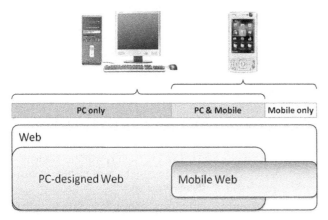

Figure 1. Mobile Internet/Web Access Types

Based on these considerations the research questions underlying this study were to what extend HR departments already take notice of these developments, how they value these as relevant according to their organizational recruiting activities as well as already implementing this to practice:

- Do HR executives already take note of mobile as an option for personnel recruiting?
- Do organizations already have experience with the implementation of mobile media into their recruiting activities?
- Are they satisfied with those mobile recruiting campaigns?
- Which application/technology is seen as most promising for mobile recruiting?
- Which are the intended goals and who is the targeted audience when applying mobile recruiting?

Answering these questions an empirical survey among German speaking HR managers was conducted. The methodology of this study is described in the next section.

3. METHODOLOGY

In order to analyze the awareness of mobile recruiting and the current state of deployment of mobile technologies for personnel recruiting in Germany a quantitative survey among HR managers was conducted in 2009 and 2011 [9]. The surveyed experts were contacted via various channels like email newsletters from co-operating industry associations, HR job portals, and other HR related websites. The questionnaire in 2011 covered the same measurement items as the one in 2009 [4]. Some additional items were included to account for the actual technological developments, applications and use cases (e.g. iPad related topics). Participants covered all sizes of companies. Most of the companies hired less than 500 new employees in the year prior to the studies. The participants have been mainly on the HR assistant and executive level but also covered the board level. In 2009 the survey was also announced on a sponsored HR email newsletter dedicated to the survey. Unfortunately this option was not available for the study in 2011 which explains the lower number of participants compared to 2009. The study was conducted in German language and due to privacy issues the respondents remained anonymous and therefore could not be linked cross-study. All the results presented in the next section are translated according to their meaning. Demographics of both surveys, 2009 and 2011, are depicted in Table 1.

Table 1. Demographic data of survey respondents

		2011		2009	
Total		159		367	
Company Size	≤ 100	48	30,2%	97	26,4%
	101 - 1.000	35	22,0%	86	23,4%
	1.001 - 10.000	25	15,7%	81	22,1%
	> 10.000	49	30,8%	72	19,6%
	n/a	2	1,3%	31	8,5%
New hires in the previous year	0	5	3,1%	21	7,4%
	1-10	42	26,4%	1	28,1%
	11-50	30	18,9%	65	23,7%
	51 - 100	16	10,1%	23	11,4%
	101 - 500	30	18,9%	31	17,2%
	> 500	28	17,6%	39	10,6%
	n/a	8	5,0%	187	1,6%
Position	Assistant	67	42,1%	108	29,4%
	Executive	60	37,7%	164	44,7%
	Mgmt. Board	20	12,6%	62	16,9%
	Others	8	5,0%	29	7,9%
	n/a	4	2,5%	4	1,1%

4. RESULTS

A first result of this study gives support that HR managers are currently looking for new recruiting channels to demonstrate innovation leadership in HRM. Here, the level of agreement of importance of new recruiting channels slightly increased between 2011 and 2009 as shown in Figure 2. As well, German HR managers have also a higher level of awareness regarding mobile recruiting and are more the opinion to be able to assess its opportunities than two years ago. The strongest increase was found regarding the statement that mobile recruiting and its deployment is currently discussed within the respondents' company. However, there is still no clear statement on the relevance of mobile accessibility on the selection of online job/HR portals. This could be an indicator that mobile recruiting is currently more important for personnel marketing and employer branding issues but not crucial for improving the efficiency or reach of online job offerings yet.

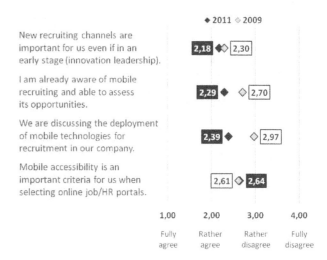

Figure 2. Results on the status of mobile recruiting

The majority of respondents have learned about mobile recruiting from HR magazines (64 percent) and colleagues within their own companies (62 percent). External consultants had only a low influence on bringing this topic into the HR departments (10 percent). There can also be noticed a high influence of the HR departments (45 percent) and its management (37 percent) as well as the executive board of the company (38 percent) to deploy mobile technologies for recruiting within the companies. IT (25 percent) and other departments (11 percent), agencies (6 percent) and external consultants (3 percent) are less involved in this decision.

A pre-condition for the deployment of mobile recruiting is the appropriate knowledge of the technological capabilities within the HR department. In the context of e-recruiting, the lack of knowledge on e-based recruiting systems has been noted as one of the "real" organizational challenges [2]. Almost 64 percent of the respondents in the recent study have already an idea on how to integrate mobile recruiting into the personnel marketing mix and 55 percent reported to know about the technological options applicable for mobile recruiting (2009: 38 percent).

As well, there is an increasing amount of organizations taking active part in mobile recruiting. 25 percent have used mobile technologies already for candidate interaction. This tripled the portion of organizations having experiences with mobile recruiting compared to 2009 (see Figure 3).

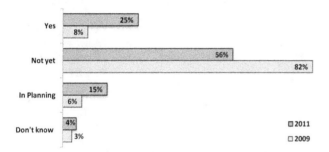

Figure 3. "Did your company already use mobile applications/technologies for candidate interaction?"

Many of the respondents indicated to use mobile technologies in recruiting as a singular activity. However, nearly half of the HR managers with mobile recruiting experiences stated to have implemented mobile technologies in the context of a long-term strategy. The survey also reveals a high degree of satisfaction of the HR managers on the results of their mobile recruiting activities in 2011: 13 percent stated to be very satisfied and 66 percent to be rather satisfied with the response and results achieved. Though, general satisfaction increased a restrained enthusiasm can be observed. Two years before 23 percent have been fully and 40 percent rather satisfied (compare Figure 4). The decrease of fully satisfied participants might be a result of the growing number of mobile recruiting campaigns in Germany. Thus, it is getting harder to draw the target group's attention and the pure fact of deploying innovative mobile technologies for recruitment is not any longer sufficient to impress potential job candidates.

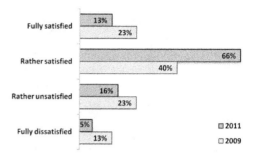

Figure 4. "How satisfied are you (so far) with the response from the target group according to the used mobile application/technology?"

Mobile social media (e.g. Twitter), mobile Web, SMS and iPhone Apps are the mobile media technologies that are most frequently used in the German HR departments with mobile recruiting experiences. These technologies are also the most popular and best known technologies in the context of recruitment among all respondents. However, some of the technologies like SMS, MMS, mobile video and Bluetooth show a strong decrease in popularity within the last two years. The reason could be that these technologies are going to be replaced by innovations (e.g. SMS vs. push notifications) or other developments in the mobile market (e.g. Bluetooth vs. dissemination of mobile broadband and flat-rates). Mobile recruiting applications attributed with a high level of importance by the 2011 respondents are mobile career websites (48 percent), social media on mobile devices (42 percent) and mobile job portals (44 percent). However, in the current survey, not more than 17 percent of the responding experts reported to have a mobile-optimized career website. Although this is still a small share, the number has more than doubled compared to 2009 (8 percent). Additionally, in 2011, nearly twice the number as in 2009 is actually planning the implementation of a mobile-optimized career website as shown in Figure 5.

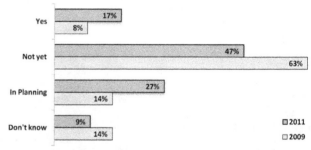

Figure 5. "Does your company have a mobile-optimized career website?"

When asked for the appropriate target group, respondents hold that mobile recruiting is most suitable for students/graduates or pupils/apprentices. Job offerings are the preferred content for mobile recruiting but only 47 percent of the respondents in the current survey can think of receiving job applications sent via mobile devices.

The ubiquity of mobile recruiting i.e. the independency from location and time of these offerings is valued as the greatest benefit from the user perspective and usability is seen as the most important success factor. From a company's perspective the respondents state a high or rather high potential benefit of mobile recruiting in the areas of increasing the reach of personnel marketing activities (90 percent), optimizing the personnel marketing portfolio (83 percent), increasing the popularity of the company

(83 percent) or support in building or maintaining an employer brand (78 percent). A significant lower proportion of respondents assumed these levels of benefit for improving applicant quantity (60 percent) or quality (24 percent) as well as cost reductions (47 percent).

A majority of the HR managers participating the study had no own experience with mobile recruiting so far, as shown in Figure 3. When asked for the reasons for not using mobile recruiting so far, most of the respondents answered that they had not adequately explored the possibilities of these new technologies yet (66 percent). Other most frequently stated barriers were unclear benefits (49 percent) and insufficient resources for implementation (43 Percent). However, asked on the perspective of mobile recruiting, the respondents strongly agreed to be very interested in this topic and that they want to know more about it. The level of agreement to this statement increased slightly within the last two years (as shown in Figure 6).

Figure 6. Results on the mobile recruiting perspective

As well, the questioned HR managers stated that mobile recruiting will gain more importance in the future and that companies have to build up appropriate skills and to implement respective organizational structures within the HR departments. The greatest shift between 2009 and 2011 could be observed regarding the readiness of the companies to deploy mobile technologies for recruiting within the next 24 month.

5. CONCLUSION

The results show that the awareness and application of mobile recruiting is still in an early stage but generally increased throughout the respondents in Germany. HR managers who deployed mobile technologies for personnel recruiting are mostly satisfied with the results of these activities and start to integrate mobile recruiting into their long-term HR strategy considerations.

Advantages are mainly attributed to communication aspects like an increased reach of the target group, the organizational awareness or in strengthening the employer brand. In this vein, extending the personnel marketing mix to mobile channels, explicitly allows for targeting young and mobile-savvy people like the Gen Y. Anyhow, professionals equipped with smartphones and being used to be online anytime and anywhere can be targeted as well. Besides, cross media mobile recruiting campaigns like the implementation of Mobile Tags to print ads can generally support an innovative employer brand –even if there is no direct job-related user interaction.

Commensurate to that, today's focus of mobile recruiting in Germany concerns more personnel marketing and communication aspects and just a small proportion of companies deploy mobile recruiting applications like mobile-optimized career websites already. But, expecting that the observed trends continue in the future, it can be assumed that mobile recruiting establishes itself as an integral part in the personnel marketing and recruiting portfolio. Further research is necessary to examine the specific requirements and characteristics of mobile recruiting, to establish some theoretical foundations within the e-HRM context and to derive scientifically founded recommendations for HR managers on how to adapt aspects of e-HRM to the challenges and opportunities of the new mobile channel. This study is work in progress and further effort is required to analyze statistical significance and causal relationships of the observations. Regarding the scope of the study its findings are limited to Germany. Anyhow, due to similar developments of mobile Web usage in other European countries as well as the United States it can be assumed that mobile recruiting is becoming equivalent relevant. Therefore it would be advisable to conduct a multi-country analysis on the international status and development of mobile recruiting.

6. REFERENCES

[1] accenture 2011. *Mobile Web Watch 2011: Die Chancen der mobile Evolution.* http://www.accenture.com/SiteCollectionDocuments/Local_ Germany/PDF/Accenture-Studie-Mobile-Web-Watch-2011.pdf. Accessed 11/07/2011.

[2] Barber, L. 2006. *e-Recruitment Developments*, Brighton, UK.

[3] Böhm, S., Jäger, W., and Niklas, S. J. 2011. Mobile Applikationen im Recruiting und Personalmarketing. *Wirtschaftsinformatik und Management*, 3/ 4, 14–22.

[4] Böhm, S. and Jäger, W. 2009. Mobile Recruiting 2009: Ergebnisse einer empirischen Studie zur Bewerberansprache über mobile Endgeräte. Hochschule RheinMain.

[5] Chapman, D. S. and Webster, J. 2003. The Use of Technologies in the Recruiting, Screening, and Selection Processes for Job Candidates. *International Journal of Selection and Assessment*, 11/2-3, 113–120.

[6] Davies, A. 2009. E.ON plugs into mobile recruitment communications to improve apprenticeship diversity. *Strategic HR Review*, 8/5, 40–41.

[7] Dialog Consult/VATM 2011. 13. Gemeinsame TK-Marktanalyse 2011: Ergebnisse einer Befragung der Mitgliedsunternehmen im Verband der Anbieter von Telekommunikations- und Mehrwertdiensten e. V. im dritten Quartal 2011. http://www.vatm.de/fileadmin/publikationen/studien/2011-10-27_TK-Marktstudie-2011.pdf. Accessed 11/07/2011.

[8] Hambeln, M. 2010. *Google CEO preaches 'mobile first'.* http://www.computerworld.com/s/article/9157778/Google_C EO_preaches_mobile_first_, Accessed 11/09/2011.

[9] Jäger, W. and Böhm, S. 2011. Mobile Recruiting 2011: Ergebnisse einer empirischen Studie zur Bewerberansprache über mobile Endgeräte. Hochschule RheinMain.

[10] 2010. The Future of Mobile Recruitment. Report of the "Mobile Recruiting Roundtable", London.

[11] Kaasinen, E. 2005. User acceptance of mobile services. Value, ease of use, trust and ease of adoption. VTT publications, Espoo.

[12] Laumer, S., Eckhardt, A., and Weitzel, T. 2010. Electronic Human Resources Management in an E-Business Environment. *Journal of Electronic Commerce Research*, 11/4, 240-250.

[13] Lee, I. 2007. An Architecture for a Next-Generation Holistic E-Recruiting System. *Communications of the Association for Information Systems*, 50/7, 81–85.

[14] NACE 2010. *Social Networking Accounts for Little Job-Search Activity*. http://www.naceweb.org/Publications/Spotlight_Online/2010/0609/Social_Networking_Accounts_for_Little_Job-Search_Activity.aspx. Accessed 11/02/2011.

[15] Niklas, S. J. Mobile is success in personnel marketing: a consumer-based analysis of quality and perceived value. In *SIGMIS-SPR'11 Proceedings of the 49th SIGMIS annual conference on Computer Personnel Research* (San Antonio, Texas, June 18-21, 2011), 91-95.

[16] Niklas, S. J. and Böhm, S. 2011. Applying Mobile Technologies for Personnel Recruiting. An Analysis of User-sided Acceptance Factors. *International Journal of eBusiness and eGovernment Studies*, 3,/1, 169–178.

[17] Niklas, S. J. and Strohmeier, S. 2011. Exploring the Impact of Usefulness and enjoyment on Mobile Service Acceptance. A Comparative Study. In *Proceedings of the 44th Hawaii International Conference on System Sciences* (Kauai, Hawaii, January 03-06, 2011).

[18] Plummer, M., Hiltz, S. R., and Plotnick, L. 2011. Predicting Intentions to Apply for Jobs Using Social Networking Sites: An Exploratory Study. In *Proceedings of the 44th Hawaii International Conference on System Sciences* (Kauai, Hawaii, January 03-06, 2011).

[19] Roto, V. and Kaasinen, E. 2008. The second international workshop on mobile internet user experience. In *Proceedings of the 10th International Conference on Human Computer Interaction with Mobile Devices*, (New York), 571–573.

[20] Thomas, S. L. and Ray, K. 2000. Recruiting and the Web: High-Tech Hiring. *Business Horizons*, 43/2, 43–52.

[21] Twiggs, C. 2011. *Marriage of mobile and recruitment eases job search*. http://www.lvrj.com/employment/by-candace-twiggs-130521473.html. Accessed 11/10/2011.

[22] Weitzel, T., Eckhardt, A., von Stetten, A., Laumer, S., Kaestner, T. A., and von Westrarp, F. 2011. *recruiting trends*. Otto Friedrich Universität Bamberg, Goethe Universität Frankfurt am Main, ISS Chris Universität Bamberg, monster.de, Bamberg & Frankfurt.

The Impact of Leadership on Participation and Trust in Virtual Teams

Kimberly Furumo
University of Hawaii at Hilo
200 W. Kawili Street
Hilo, HI 96720
808-874-7672
furumo@hawaii.edu

Emmeline de Pillis
University of Hawaii at Hilo
200 W. Kawili Street
Hilo, HI 96720
808-974-7469
depillis@hawaii.edu

Mark Buxton
University of Illinois Springfield
One University Plaza
Springfield, IL 62703
217-206-4847
mark_buxton@hotmail.com

ABSTRACT

As business continues to be conducted internationally, managers are expected to work in multinational environments and move from country to country (Early and Peterson 2004). Technology, globalization and travel costs have all caused organizations to rely more heavily on virtual teams (dePillis and Furumo 2007). The use of virtual teams has been used extensively for IT projects and particularly software development. In this research-in-progress study, three leadership conditions were analyzed. Preliminary results show that virtual teams led by Supportive leaders had higher levels of participation and trust among members than teams led by Commanding leaders.

Categories and Subject Descriptors

H.D.3 [**Group and Organization Interfaces**]: Collaborative Computing.

General Terms

Human Factors

Keywords

Virtual teams, leadership style, trust, team participation

1. INTRODUCTION

Virtual teams can be defined as geographically or organizationally dispersed groups of individuals that communicate via information communications technology in synchronous or asynchronous modes (Powell, Piccoli et al. 2004) Teams communicating asynchronously in an electronic environment face special challenges which threaten the performance of the virtual team. The flow of communication may be interrupted and confusion about the message cannot be clarified immediately. The lack of media richness (i.e., limited exposure to body language, gestures, and voice tone) also increases the likelihood of the communication being misunderstood.

These challenges increase the likelihood of conflict and poorly managed conflict can be detrimental to the performance of the team (McGrath 1991; Barki and Hartwick 2001; dePillis and Furumo 2007) Extant research of traditional teams shows that the

output of teams is often superior to that of an individual because of the synergy that comes from individuals sharing ideas and functional expertise. However, in virtual teams there is the chance that the technology will negatively impact performance.

2. LITERATURE REVIEW

2.1 Trust

Trust has been defined as "the willingness of a party to be vulnerable to the actions of another party based on the expectation that the other will perform a particular action important to the trustor, irrespective of the ability to monitor or control that other party" (Mayer, Davis et al. 1995). A lack of trust exists when one party does not have faith in the competencies of another or questions the motivation of the other to take the promised action as seriously (van der Smagt 2000). So, trust can be seen as a relationship between two or more individuals in which one perceives that the others are involved, are competent, will complete their fair share of the work, and will make an honest effort to meet commitments.

Trust is important in teams because it lowers transaction costs (Watson-Manheim and Belanger 2002). Individuals who do not trust fellow team members are more likely to monitor or double check each other's work to insure the quality of the team's output. This self-protective activity increases the amount of time and resources needed to complete a project. In virtual teams, trust becomes an important component in preventing psychological distance (Snow, Snell et al. 1996) and it increases confidence in relationships by promoting open information exchange (Hinds and Bailey 2000). Trust is often referred to as the glue that holds the virtual team together. Not surprisingly, trust has been identified as a determinant of effectiveness in virtual teams (Jarvenpaa and Leidner 1999; Walden and Turban 2000). Individuals who trust each other are likely to be more satisfied with the team experience since they perceive that their best interests are being served, while only having to complete their fair share of the team's task. Individuals who trust each other may be more likely to bring problems forth in an effort to resolve them effectively.

2.2 Leadership Style

University of Southern California professors Alan Rowe, Kathleen Reardon and Warren Bennis developed a typology of four leadership styles, which they called Commander, Logical, Inspirational, and Supportive. An individual will use only one or two of these styles most of the time (Reardon and de Pillis 1996). Rowe, Reardon and Bennis developed the Leadership Style Inventory to measure an individual's preference for a given leadership style.

Of the four styles of leadership, two stand out as somewhat opposite in approach. This first, the Commander style, describes a leader who is straightforward and sometimes authoritarian. Many entrepreneurs and executives incline toward a Commander style. A Commander makes decisions quickly and sticks to them, and is focused on results. The Supportive manager, on the other hand, strives to achieve consensus, and is concerned with the well –being and satisfaction of followers. This type of leader focuses on facilitating work.

Two other styles of leadership in the typology are the Logical style, in which the leader needs to collect and analyze information before coming to a decision and the Inspirational style which is associated with a visionary leader who sees the big picture. In this study, the focus was on the Commander and Supportive leadership types.

In this research-in-progress paper, the impact of a virtual team leader's leadership style on participation and trust levels in the virtual team is explored. Study participants, were surveyed to identify their predominant leadership style. Those scoring high in the Commander and Supportive styles were selected and assigned as leaders to virtual teams. As a control, a group of teams did not have a leader formally assigned.

3. METHODOLOGY

In this study, a quasi-experimental design approach was used. Participants in the study were upper- and graduate-level college students enrolled in business courses at two different universities, the University of Hawaii at Hilo and Niagara University. Students spent the semester working on three deliverables including an icebreaker activity and two cases in which students were asked to provide written recommendations of how they would handle a business problem.

At the onset of the project, students were asked to complete the Leadership Style Inventory, which measures individual leadership style. This twenty-item instrument was designed to analyze how managers in organizations prefer to lead. One's primary style can be Commander, Logical, Inspirational, or Supportive. The scale is designed so that a fixed number of points are divided among four leader styles, forcing the participant to indicate a preference. Students who rated extremely high on the Commander or Supportive leadership style, as opposed to having an evenly divided preference, were chosen as leaders of virtual teams. These leaders were initially assigned and then the remaining study participants were randomly assigned to teams. Approximately one-third of the teams were led by a Commander style leader, one-third led by a Supportive style leader and in one-third of teams no leader was assigned.

Students were asked to complete three deliverables throughout the semester. This first was an icebreaker activity intended to get team members acquainted and to be sure that they could use the technology. The second involved a case in which team members Of the four styles of leadership, two stand out as somewhat opposite in approach. This first, the Commander style, describes a leader who is straightforward and sometimes authoritarian. Many entrepreneurs and executives incline toward a Commander style. A Commander makes decisions quickly and sticks to them, and is focused on results. The Supportive manager, on the other hand, strives to achieve consensus, and is concerned with the well –being and satisfaction of followers. This type of leader focuses on facilitating work (Reardon and de Pillis 1996; de Pillis, Reardon

had to analyze costs and recommend an advertising strategy and the third deliverable required teams to recommend ways to implement technology in the grocery industry.

At the onset of the experiment, participants were asked to complete a survey which assessed various individual constructs including the Big Five Personality Dimensions and the LSI leadership instrument. The survey was completed at the same time that teams participated in the ice breaker activity. In this activity they were asked to name five things the team had in common and five things they differed on. The icebreaker activity allowed individual team members to introduce themselves and become familiar with the technology.

After completion of both the second and third deliverables, participants completed an additional survey designed to measure their level of trust in the team. They were also asked to provide open-ended feedback about what they liked and did not like about the team. In addition, the communication thread was collected and the number of posts made by each team member was recorded.

Students used the Google Wave product to communicate with team members. Prior to the start of the experiment all participating students were provided orientation about the Google Wave product. They were required to use a Gmail account sign-on to access the system. Students were free to use existing Gmail accounts or create new ones for the purposes of the virtual team. A dedicated technician was available to answer questions and walk participants through the registration steps. Once the students were registered, the icebreaker activity allowed them to familiarize themselves with the technology while getting to know fellow team members.

To assess perceived trust levels, a scale developed by Jarvenpaa, Knoll, and Leidner (Jarvenpaa, Knoll et al. 1998) was used. Their scale is based on previous instruments developed by Mayer, Davis, and Schoorman (Mayer, Davis et al. 1995) and Pearce, Sommer, Morris, and Frideger (Pearce, Sommer et al. 1992) to measure the level of trust in dyads. Jarvenpaa et al. (Jarvenpaa, Knoll et al. 1998) modified these instruments to reflect the team rather than a dyad by testing the two instruments at two different time points and across cultures. Both measures of trust were correlated but the instrument developed by Pearce and colleagues had higher reliability ($\alpha = .92$) and thus it was used as the basis of their modified survey. After testing, Jarvenpaa et. al.(Jarvenpaa, Knoll et al. 1998) reduced the 8-item scale to a 6-item instrument with a five-point Likert-type response scale anchored on one end with strongly agree and the other with strongly disagree. They reported Cronbach's alpha for the scale at .92.

While an abundance of data was collected, the focus of this initial study is on leader style, gender, trust, and participation. The independent variables were leadership condition and sex of the team members while the dependent variables were number of online posts (measure of participation), and individual member trust in the team which was measured at the conclusion of each of the two cases completed.

4. RESULTS AND DISCUSSION

Of the original 115 subjects assigned to teams, 5 were eliminated from the study because they dropped the course in which the virtual team activity was being completed. Table 1 provides a summary of the breakdown of males and females that were assigned to the different leadership conditions. Once leaders were identified and assigned to teams, the rest of the participants were randomly assigned to teams.

Table 1. Participant Counts

	Leadership Condition			
Sex	Commanding	Supportive	No Leader	Totals
Male	14	12	22	48
Female	21	23	18	62
Totals	35	35	40	110

To measure the significance of the relationships, ANOVA analyses were performed. In Table 2, participants were grouped according to the leadership condition of their team. Comparison of the groups showed that there is a significant relationship between the number of posts in each of the three different team leadership conditions. Members in teams in which a supportive leader was assigned, posted 31.47 messages on average, while members in teams with a commanding style leader posted an average 21.54 messages, and those in teams without an assigned leader posted 16.08 messages on average.

Table 2. ANOVA Results
Impact of Leader Style on Participation and Trust

Dependent Variable	Style of Leader	Mean	F	df	Sig.
Number of Posts	Commanding Supportive No Leader	21.54 31.47 16.08	3.852	$F_{2,110}$	.024
Trust (after 1st assignment)	Commanding Supportive No Leader	3.43 3.79 3.61	3.137	$F_{2,110}$	.047
Trust (after 2nd assignment)	Commanding Supportive No Leader	3.45 3.55 3.48	0.199	$F_{2,110}$	.820

Trust which could range from 1 (no trust) to 5 (complete trust) was also significantly different for the leadership conditions after completion of the first case activity but not after the second. Trust was highest for the members in teams with an assigned supportive leader (averaged 3.79) while it was lowest for members in teams with commanding leaders (3.43). Trust levels decreased after the second case was completed for members in the supportive leadership condition and the no leader condition but remained about the same for those in the commanding leadership teams.

These results provide some evidence that the style of the leader does impact initial trust and participation in virtual teams. Individuals in teams led by Supportive leaders were more likely to participate and reported higher levels of trust than members in teams led by Commander leaders. Commander leaders are straightforward and authoritarian, a quality that may impede trust development and participation in virtual teams. Since the benefit of teamwork is the synergy that comes from different points of view, leaders with a commanding style may be limiting the free exchange of ideas with their leadership style.

Supportive leaders strive to achieve consensus and are concerned with the well-being and satisfaction of team members. Members may feel more comfortable sharing ideas and seem to participate more possibly at the urging of the leader. These preliminary results need to be explored further by coding the communication transcripts to determine the patterns of interaction among team members.

While the supportive leaders seem to get members participating more quickly, there is no evidence that trust levels continue to remain high or that the output of the team is any better. Previous studies have identified composition of the team as another factor which may impact interaction in virtual teams. Age variability was limited in this study, since all participants were college students; however studying gender differences was possible Table 3 provides a summary of means for the dependent variables by leadership condition and gender. The number of posts represents the number of times a participant posted an online message for the virtual team. While some of the messages were longer than others, this indicator provides some measure of the participation of team members. Males, regardless of the team leadership condition they were assigned to, posted fewer messages than the females.

Table 3. Means for Dependent Variables
Groups Organized by Gender and Team Leadership Condition

		Leadership Condition (Leadership Style of the Assigned Leader)		
		Commanding	Supportive	No Leader
Males	# Posts	12.57	9.50	12.86
	Trust 1	3.63	3.88	3.47
	Trust 2	3.58	3.81	3.37
	n	14	12	22
Females	# Posts	27.52	43.45	20.00
	Trust 1	3.30	3.74	3.77
	Trust 2	3.37	3.41	3.61
	n	21	23	18

Specific gender group ANOVA tests results can be found in Tables 4 and 5. Leadership condition had an impact on number of posts and trust after the first case for females but not for males. Female members in teams that had supportive leaders were more likely to participate and reported higher levels of trust than those in commanding leader condition.

The next steps in this research study include grading the deliverables using a multi-rater method, coding the communication scripts and analyzing interaction patterns, studying whether members were satisfied with their leader, and whether an informal leader emerged for the teams in the experimental condition in which no leader was assigned.

Table 4. ANOVA Results
Impact of Leader Style on Participation and Trust
Females Only

Dependent Variable	Style of Leader	Mean	F	df	Sig.
Number of Posts	Commanding Supportive No Leader	27.52 43.45 20.00	3.787	$F_{2,62}$	.028
Trust (after 1st assignment)	Commanding Supportive No Leader	3.30 3.74 3.77	3.740	$F_{2,62}$	.030
Trust (after 2nd assignment)	Commanding Supportive No Leader	3.37 3.41 3.61	0.579	$F_{2,62}$	.564

Table 5. ANOVA Results
Impact of Leader Style on Participation and Trust
Males Only

Dependent Variable	Style of Leader	Mean	F	df	Sig.
Number of Posts	Commanding Supportive No Leader	12.57 9.50 12.86	.461	$F_{2,48}$	.634
Trust (after 1st assignment)	Commanding Supportive No Leader	3.63 3.88 3.47	2.146	$F_{2,48}$	.129
Trust (after 2nd assignment)	Commanding Supportive No Leader	3.58 3.81 3.37	2.547	$F_{2,48}$	.090

5. REFERENCES

[1] Barki, H. and Hartwick J. 2001. Interpersonal Conflict and its Management in Information System Development. *MIS Quarterly* 25(2), 195-228.

[2] de Pillis, E. G., Reardon, K.K. 1997. Leadership Styles in the MBA Pipleline: The Vanishing Supportive Woman. *Proceedings of the Western Academy of Management Annual Meeting, Squaw Valley, CA.*

[3] dePillis, E. and Furumo, K. 2007, Counting the Cost of Virtual Teams. *Communications of the ACM* 50, 93-95.

[4] Early, P. C. and Peterson R. S. 2004. The Elusive Cultural Chameleon: Cultural Intelligence as a New Approach to Intercultural Training for the Global Manager. *Academy of Management Learning & Education* 3(1), 100-115.

[5] Hinds, P. J. and Bailey D. E. 2000. Virtual Teams: Anticipating the Impact of Viruality on Team Process and Performance. *Academy of Management Proceedings.*

[6] Jarvenpaa, S. L., Knoll, K. and Leidner, D.E. 1998. Is Anybody Out There? Antecedents of Trust in Global Virtual Teams. *Journal of Management Information Systems*14(4), 29-64.

[7] Jarvenpaa, S. L. and Leidner, D.E. 1999. Communication and Trust in Global Virtual Teams. *Organization Science* 10(6), 791-734.

[8] Mayer, R. C., Davis, J. H., and Schoorman, F.D. 1995. An Integrative Model of Organizational Trust. *Academy of Management Review* 20(3), 709-734.

[9] McGrath, J. 1991. Time, Interaction, and performance (TIP): A Theory of Groups. *Small Group Research* 22, 147-174.

[10] Pearce, J. L., Sommer S. M., Moris, A. and Frideger, M. 1992. *A Configurational Approach to Interpersonal Relations: Profiles of Work Place Social Relations and Task Interdependence.* Graduate School of Management, Irvine, CA.

[11] Powell, A., Piccoli, G. and Ives, B. 2004. Virtual Teams: A Review of Current Literature and Direction for Future Research. *DATA BASE for Advances in Information Systems* 35(1), 6-36.

[12] Reardon, K. K. and de Pillis, E. 1996. Multichannel leadership: Revisiting the false dichotomy. *Integrating Theory and Research in Communication*, 399-407.

[13] Snow, C. C.,Snell, S.A. , and Davison, S.C. 1996. Use Transnational Teams to Globalize Your Company. *Organizational Dynamics* 24(4), 50-67.

[14] van der Smagt, T. 2000. Enhancing Virtual Teams: Social Relations vs. Communication Technology. *Industrial Management & Data Systems* (3/4), 57-80.

[15] Walden, P. and Turban, E. 2000. Working Anywhere, Anytime and with Anyone. *Human Systems Management* 19, 213-222.

[16] Watson-Manheim, M. B. and Belanger, F. 2002. Support for Communication-Based Work Processes in Virtual Work. *e-Service Journal*, 61-82.

A Mixed Bag: How Work and Retirement Influence Older Adults' ICT Use

Johanna L.H. Birkland

School of Information Studies
Syracuse University
Syracuse, NY USA
jlbirkla@syr.edu

ABSTRACT

Many societies are aging, while Information and Communication Technologies (ICTs) use is increasingly being required by governments and workplaces. However, little is known about ICT use by older adults. This research-in-progress paper outlines a case study methodology which seeks to examine the domestication of ICTs by older adults in their everyday lives. Preliminary results suggest that work is an important context that influences ICT introduction, use, and meanings.

Categories and Subject Descriptors
K.7.1 **The Computing Profession**: Occupations

General Terms: Human Factors

Keywords: Older Adults, Careers, Work Trajectories, Retirement, ICT Use, Domestication Theory, Adoption

INTRODUCTION

The population in the United States is aging, with a predicted 147% increase in the number of older adults (those over age 65) from 2000-2050 (U.S. Census Bureau, 2008). At the same time, Information and Communication Technologies (ICTs) are increasingly being used in work, leisure, and government. Despite these two trends towards an aging population and greater ICT use, very little is known about if and how older adults are using ICTs in their everyday lives (Birkland & Kaarst-Brown, 2010).

Several calls have been made for researchers to take a wider perspective on older adults' ICT usage (Bouwhuis, 2006; van Bronswijk et al., 2009), however; most studies have concentrated on assistive devices. The study described in this research in progress paper seeks to generate theory on how and why ICTs are used in older adults' daily lives. One understudied area is the role of work and retirement in impacting ICT use by older adults (Birkland & Kaarst-Brown, 2010).

This study asks how ICTs are domesticated by older adults in their everyday lives. This includes how ICTs are introduced to,

displayed, and the meaning they develop to older adults. Usage of ICTs by older adults is examined in several contexts, including work, leisure, family, and their citizen/community involvement. The preliminary findings of this paper concentrate on the how work and retirement shape ICT use.

PREVIOUS WORK

This study uses domestication theory as a theoretical framework to understand aspects of ICT use and to inform the interview guide. Domestication theory proposes that ICTs are introduced into individual's lives (adopted), used in different ways (creating routines), displayed (placed in the home or elsewhere), and then develop meaning to individuals (Silverstone & Haddon, 1996; Silverstone & Hirsch, 1992). Most research covering older adults' ICT use has focused on examining older adults' ICT adoption, rather than understanding the rich context of use and meaning of use (Paul & Stegbauer, 2005; Selwyn & Gorard, 2008). Using domestication theory as a foundation, this study seeks to understand adoption as one in series of steps of integrating an ICT into a person's life (Lie & Sørensen, 1996; Silverstone, Hirsch, & Morley, 1994).

Most domestication studies have focused on the home/family environment (Silverstone & Hirsch, 1992). Both of the two existing studies of ICT domestication by older adults have focused on English retirees home use (Buse, 2009; Haddon, 2000). Haddon (2000) explored older adults' home use of the television and telephone. Older adults felt that their usage of the telephone and television had increased after they retired. However, retirees were not compared to workers. As more individuals continue to work beyond the traditional age of retirement (Burtless & Quinn, 2001; Young, 2002), it is important to consider working older adults. Workers may have differing exposures to ICTs, technical support, and training than retirees. One of the goals of this work is to understand how different work trajectories influence older adult ICT use.

METHODS

The case methodology was chosen for this study, as it enables the researcher to understand "nuanced reality," or how previously unexamined variables may impact the phenomenon being studied (Flyvberg, 2006). Fifteen case studies of older adult ICT use are planned. Each case study is composed of an older adult and several members of the older adult's social network (friends, family members, or coworkers).

Table 1. Description of Participants, Number of Interviews, and Total Interviews for the Study

Participants and Method	Description	# Interviews / Case	Totals
Primary Participants: Interviews with Older Adults	One-on-one semi-structured interviews with older adults	3 interviews per older adult	15 Cases (45 Total Interviews with Older Adults)
Secondary Participants: Interviews with members of the Older Adult's network	One-on-one semi-structured interviews with 2-3 members of network; Snowball sampling with referral provided by the primary participant	2-3 interviews per case	15 Cases (30-45 Total Interviews with Secondary Participants)

Each older adult, or primary participant, is interviewed three times for approximately 2 hours. Two or three members of the older adult's social network (secondary participants) are also interviewed to understand how relationships impact older adults' ICT domestication (Table 1).

This study focuses on older adults born from 1936-1946, comprising the younger members of the Lucky Few birth-cohort (Carlson, 2008, 2009). Previous studies of older adults have ignored how birth-cohort's (generations) can influence ICT exposure (Birkland & Kaarst-Brown, 2010). The lucky few birth cohort was chosen as these individuals are "young" older adults, and more likely to have a diversity of work statuses (retired and working). Participants will be recruited across a diversity of current work statuses, including full-time and part-time workers, retirees, and house-spouses. Attention will be paid to recruit both knowledge workers and labor workers. Work statuses and histories will be matched as closely as possible across both male and female participants. Participants are recruited using a snowball strategy starting from referrals (Goodman, 1961). This sampling strategy was chosen to avoid issues in previous studies of older adults, which tend to concentrate on "captive" populations, such as institutionalized older adults (Birkland & Kaarst-Brown, 2010).

PRELIMINARY RESULTS

Two of the planned 15 cases have been completed. Both were white women who lived near a medium sized city in the northeastern area of the U.S.:

"Natalie" is a retired upper middle class retired woman who previously worked as a biologist. She has a bachelor's degree and is an avid horse rider, gardener, and crafter. Natalie and her ex-husband started a biological testing company. She retired when the business was sold as a result of their divorce.

"Jackie" is a lower middle class woman who works part-time. She worked in the insurance industry and was forced to retire because of health reasons from a top management position. She attended 3 years of college. She was recently widowed, which has further threatened her financial stability.

Additional findings from further cases will be presented at the conference. Preliminary findings indicate that:

- *Work is an important context that introduces ICTs. Both Natalie and Jackie were first exposed to computers in their work.*

Natalie did not directly use a computer in her work as she "had my secretary do it." During her divorce she became concerned about her company's financial state. With the help of her cousin she installed a key stroke recorder on one of the work computers. She got "confidence" which later led to her exploring the internet for her hobbies in retirement.

Jackie used both a mainframe and later a personal desktop computer in her career in the insurance industry. After she left her job, she began using eBay to raise money. Her first exposure to digital photography (her main hobby) came from her purchase of a digital camera to post pictures on eBay.

- *Work exposes older adults to ICTs, but income impacts what the older adult purchases in retirement:*

Natalie has a high retirement income and she purchases any ICT she believes will be useful (currently she plans to buy an iPad). She missed access to the copy machine when she retired, so she purchased a printer/copier. When it broke, she replaced it.

Since Jackie retired "it's been struggles– now I've got peanuts." When her husband died as she could no longer afford a landline- it "never rang" so she replaced it with a magicJack (VOIP) phone. With new technologies she says: "I don't investigate it any further if it doesn't meet my needs or is too expensive!"

- *"Retirement" is not necessarily just a time for leisure as many older adults continue to work beyond age 65. Some older adults hold multiple jobs and work in several different industries in retirement, however, not all these jobs involve the use of ICTs:*

When Jackie first left work she used eBay to raise extra money. She stopped because of frequent interface updates: "And every summer they change everything… And I'd be lost. And I'd have to start learning all over again." Jackie now uses garage sales and Craigslist.

Since leaving her full-time job due to health reasons, Jackie has worked as a seasonal retail worker, a museum guide, an administrative assistant, and a server. Currently, Jackie works part-time as a server. She relies heavily on her magicJack phone as the restaurant calls her on an as-needed basis for work. She has found it increasingly hard to find part-time work "because a lot of people won't hire people my age."

- *ICTs associated with work were often viewed negatively by individuals once they leave their careers:*

  Jackie, who used the telephone substantially in her insurance work, strongly dislikes speaking on the phone. She only uses her magicJack phone when necessary. She often leaves her cell phone at home to avoid taking calls.

CONCLUSION

The two cases discussed in this paper are examples of the diverse life and work trajectories of older adults. Natalie and Jackie both had well-paying jobs previous to retirement as "knowledge workers." However, due to health concerns, Jackie had to leave her career early. She now works in the service industry for minimum wage. These work histories- not only the status of the jobs worked (owner of a company versus management), but also the types of jobs (laboratory versus desk jobs), influenced these women's experience with ICTs during their working careers. During retirement, these women were affected by their differing incomes in their opportunities and ability to purchase new and replace broken ICTs.

These cases bring up important questions: Are there differences between women and men and the meaning of ICTs they use(d) in their work? Are there differences in ICT exposure between laborers and knowledge workers? Does this difference continue into retirement? How do different work trajectories (types of jobs worked and current work statuses) impact ICT use? Is there an interaction between type of work (knowledge versus labor) and current income that impacts use?

Further cases will address these questions. The findings from these additional cases will be presented at the conference.

REFERENCES

[1] Birkland, J. L. H., & Kaarst-Brown, M. L. (2010). 'What's so special about studying old people?': The ethical, methodological, and sampling issues surrounding the study of older adults and ICTs. In F. Sudweeks, H. Hrachovec & C. Ess (Eds.), *Proceedings of the seventh international conference on Cultural Attitudes Towards Technology and Communication* (pp. 341-356). Vancouver, B.C., Canada.

[2] Bouwhuis, D. G. (2006). Not care but leisure. *Gerontechnology, 5*(2), 63-67.

[3] Burtless, G., & Quinn, J. F. (2001). Retirement trends and policies to encourage work among older Americans. In P. P. Budetti, R. V. Burkhauser, J. M. Gregory & H. A. Hunt (Eds.), *Ensuring health and income security for an aging workforce* (pp. 375-415). Kalamazoo, MI: W.E. Upjohn Institute for Employment Research.

[4] Buse, C. E. (2009). When you retire, does everything become leisure? Information and communication technology use and the work/ leisure boundary in retirement. *New Media & Society, 11*, 1143-1161.

[5] Carlson, E. (2008). *The Lucky Few: Between the Greatest Generation and the Baby Boom* New York: Springer.

[6] Carlson, E. (2009). 20th-Century: U.S. Generations. *Population Reference Bureau, 64*(1).

[7] Flyvberg, B. (2006). Five misunderstandings about case-study research. *Qualitative Inquiry, 12*(2), 219-245.

[8] Goodman, L. A. (1961). Snowball sampling. *Annals of Mathematical Statistics, 32*, 148–170.

[9] Haddon, L. (2000). Social exclusion and information and communication technologies. *New Media & Society, 2*(4), 387-406.

[10] Lie, M., & Sørensen, K. H. (1996). Making technology our own?: Domesticating technology in everyday life. In M. Lie & K. H. Sørensen (Eds.), *Making technology our own?: Domesticating technology in everyday life* (pp. 1-30). Boston: Scandinavian University Press.

[11] Paul, G., & Stegbauer, C. (2005). Is the digital divide between young and elderly people increasing? [Electronic Version]. *First Monday*, 10. Retrieved June 16, 2007 from http://www.firstmonday.org/issues/issue10_10/paul/index.html.

[12] Selwyn, N., & Gorard, S. (2008). What computers can't do for you. *Adults Learning, 19*(6), 26-27.

[13] Silverstone, R., & Haddon, L. (1996). Design and the domestication of information and communciation technologies: technical change and everyday life. In R. Mansell & R. Silverstone (Eds.), *Communication by design: the politics of information and communication technologies* (pp. 44-74). New York: Oxford University Press.

[14] Silverstone, R., & Hirsch, E. (1992). *Consuming technologies: Media and information in domestic spaces*. New York: Routledge.

[15] Silverstone, R., Hirsch, E., & Morley, D. (1994). Information and communication technologies and the moral economy of the household. In R. Silverstone & E. Hirsch (Eds.), *Consuming technologies: Media and information in domestic spaces* (pp. 15-31). New York: Routledge.

[16] U.S. Census Bureau. (2008). *Table 3. Percent Distribution of the Projected Population by Selected Age Groups and Sex for the United States: 2010 to 2050 (NP2008-T3)*. Retrieved. from http://www.census.gov/population/www/projections/summarytables.html.

[17] van Bronswijk, J. E. M. H., Bouma, H., Fozard, J. L., Kearnes, W., Davison, G. C., & Tuan, P.-C. (2009). Defining gerontechnology for R&D purposes. *Gerontechnology, 8*(1), 3-10.

[18] Young, M. B. (2002). *Holding on: How the mass exodus of retiring Baby Boomers could deplete the workforce how employers can stem the tide*. Retrieved September 2, 2008. from http://www.hr.state.tx.us/linkage.pdf.

Examining the Influence of Cultural Values on the Post-Adoptive Use of Knowledge Management Systems

Stefan Tams
HEC Montréal
Montréal (Québec), Canada
stefan.tams@hec.ca

Jason Thatcher
Clemson University
Clemson, USA
jason.b.thatcher@hotmail.com

Mark Srite
University of Wisconsin-Milwaukee
Milwaukee, USA
msrite@uwm.edu

ABSTRACT

This research-in-progress examines culture's consequences on routine knowledge sharing behavior. It employs two complementary cross-cultural theories to develop an integrative model of culture and habitual system use in the context of knowledge management. More specifically, using the Theory of Basic Human Values and the Theory of IT-Culture Conflict, we posit that such cultural values as an emphasis on active mastery and change of the environment may, under certain conditions, lead to habitual knowledge management system use for knowledge sharing. In carefully selecting and integrating these two theories, this study overcomes major methodological problems inherent in much prior cross-cultural IS scholarship. We propose a quantitative methodology to test the model and discuss why structural equation modeling is the best-fitting data-analytic technique for quantitative cross-cultural IS research.

Categories and Subject Descriptors

H.4 [Information Systems Applications]: Miscellaneous

General Terms

Management

Keywords

Knowledge Management, Culture, Habit, Post-adoption, Theory of IT-Culture Conflict, Theory of Basic Human Values.

1. INTRODUCTION

Knowledge sharing among organizational members has become increasingly important for firm success (Sambamurthy and Sumramani, 2005). Yet, despite the wide diffusion of knowledge management systems (KMS) as a means to facilitate this sharing, organizations are still struggling in their attempts to generate such contributions as their members often refrain from contributing routinely to such systems (Bock, Zmud, Young-Gul and Jae-Nam, 2005). Instead, employees often evaluate the anticipated costs and rewards of distinct contributions on a case-by-case basis (e.g., Bock et al., 2005; Kankanhalli, Tan and Kwok-Kee, 2005), implying that each knowledge contribution is evaluated individually. Such individual evaluations of knowledge

contributions are associated with significant mental effort (Wood and Neal, 2007) and may often result in the decision not to contribute (Bock et al. 2005; Kankanhalli et al. 2005). Hence, enterprises may benefit substantially from an understanding of how routine contributions can be generated.

Routine contributions to knowledge management systems represent a form of post-adoptive use, meaning that these occur after knowledge contributors have initially accepted the KMS (Cooper and Zmud, 1990). Central to this routine system use is the concept of habit (Jasperson, Carter and Zmud, 2005). Habitual KMS use by knowledge contributors signifies that individuals contribute unconsciously and automatically whenever the contextual stimuli associated with the contribution behavior are present (Limayem, Hirt and Cheung, 2007). As such, habitual use may be a richer form of the use concept than, for example, simple usage intentions (Burton-Jones and Straub, 2006). However, research on habitual KMS use as well as on the role of habit as a primary outcome variable in the post-adoption context is limited. Prior KM research has focused on intentional contributions associated with initial rather than habitual KMS use (Bock et al. 2005; Kankanhalli et al. 2005; Kim, Malhotra and Narasimhan, 2005; Wasko and Faraj, 2005). Past habit research has focused on the limits the habit construct can impose on the predictive power of intentions (Kim et al., 2005; Limayem et al., 2007), rather than on the role of habitual system usage as a primary outcome variable in the post-adoption context. Hence, more work is needed in these areas.

One influence on the formation of habitual KMS use by knowledge contributors may be such cultural values as helpfulness and social power (Alavi and Leidner, 2001; Davenport and Prusak, 2000; Garud and Kumaraswamy, 2005). Such values may impact an individual's interest in knowledge sharing as well as the person's willingness to use a KMS. The resulting goal-directed and intentional KMS use may eventually become unintentional and triggered by associated contextual stimuli once the behavior has become a habit through its repetition in a stable context (Oulette and Wood, 1998; Wood, Tam and Witt, 2005; Wood and Neal, 2007). Similar to the concept of habit, culture may be more relevant in the post-adoption context than in the more rational context of initial-acceptance (Cooper and Zmud, 1990), since cultural influence on system use does not involve the formation of rational beliefs about such consequences as system usefulness or ease of use (Leidner and Kayworth, 2006; Myers and Tan, 2002). However, while knowledge management (KM) research recognizes the importance of culture in determining KMS use by knowledge contributors (Alavi and Leidner, 2001; Davenport and Prusak, 2000; Garud and Kumaraswamy, 2005), it has yet to fully explain this cultural impact. Further, much prior cross-cultural IS research focuses on culture's influence on initial acceptance behavior in the context of the technology acceptance model (TAM) rather than on post-adoptive behavior.

In light of the criticality of knowledge contributions for organizational success in tandem with the struggle associated with generating such contributions, especially since the globalization of business requires individuals from diverse cultural backgrounds to work together, we examine the following research question: *How does culture shape habitual knowledge management system use by an individual for making a knowledge contribution?*

By investigating culture's influence on habitual KMS use for knowledge sharing, this study integrates knowledge sharing behavior with the concepts of habit as a form of post-adoptive use and culture as a factor impacting the post-adoptive use of IT. In contrast to much prior cross-cultural IS-scholarship, this research goes beyond TAM and uses a broad theoretical base consisting of two cross-cultural theories. This paper further contributes to the literature on habit by examining this concept as a primary outcome variable associated with system use. Additionally, while prior KM scholarship has focused on intentional, and hence initial and irregular, contributions, this research examines habitual, post-adoptive KMS use by knowledge contributors. This issue of post-adoptive use and its relationship to the central themes of the study are explored in the paragraphs that follow.

The paper is structured as follows. The next section introduces the Theory of Basic Human Values (Schwartz, 1992; 1994), The Theory of IT Culture Conflict (Leidner and Kayworth, 2006), and the concept of habit (Wood and Neal, 2007) as a means to frame a model of culturally-determined habitual knowledge sharing in organizations. The third section develops a series of research hypotheses suggesting that certain cultural values impact the frequency of KMS use for contributing knowledge, which in turn leads to habitual KMS use for contributing knowledge under the condition of contextual stability. The fourth section discusses why a quantitative methodology is appropriate to test the model, the measures used, and why structural equation modeling is the best-fitting analytic technique. The paper concludes with an overview of its contributions.

2. THEORETICAL BACKGROUND

The literature on habit and a complementary set of two cross-cultural theories will guide model development in the knowledge management context. The two cross-cultural theoretical lenses are the Theory of Basic Human Values and the Theory of IT Culture Conflict.

Schwartz's (1992; 1994) Theory of Basic Human Values proposes several specific cultural values that concern the relationship between an individual and a group. Similar to Hofstede's (1980) work, which indicates that such values as power distance, individualism/collectivism, masculinity/femininity, and uncertainty avoidance differ across cultures on the country level, the Theory of Basic Human Values can, thus, serve to identify specific cultural values that have the potential of influencing knowledge sharing. However, Schwartz's framework may be superior to Hofstede's work since it combines a stronger theoretical foundation with more recent data (Okazaki and Mueller, 2007). Schwartz' theory posits two bipolar value dimensions (Self-Transcendence – Self-Enhancement and Openness to Change – Conservation) that comprise ten higher order value types (Self-Transcendence: Universalism,

Benevolence; Self-Enhancement: Achievement, Power; Openness to Change: Self-Direction, Stimulation, Hedonism; Conservation: Tradition, Conformity, Security), which can constitute exogenous variables in explanatory research models (see Table 1). While these variables may explain the extent to which individuals tend to share their knowledge, they are not directly related to the use of technology. Hence, the Theory of IT Culture Conflict is needed to predict whether this tendency results in actual technology use for knowledge contributions.

Table 1. Bipolar Value Dimensions and Value Types

Value Dimension	Explanation	Value Type
Self-Transcendence	Voluntary commitment to the welfare of others	Universalism
		Benevolence
Self-Enhancement	Enhancement of own personal interests even at the expense of other individuals	Power
		Achievement
Openness to Change	Following own intellectual interests to actively adapt to and change one's environment	Self-Direction
		Stimulation
		Hedonism
Conservation	Preservation of status quo	Tradition
		Conformity
		Security

The Theory of IT Culture Conflict (TITCC) (Leidner and Kayworth, 2006) explicitly theorizes about the IT artifact. It posits that individuals are more likely to use an IT when its inherent values are in agreement with the cultural values held by the individuals. In doing so, the Theory of IT Culture Conflict complements the generic concepts advanced by the Theory of Basic Human Values. More specifically, if certain values are associated with a general tendency to share knowledge, TITCC can predict whether this tendency will crystallize through the use of technology. For example, peoples' value-based tendency to share knowledge may result in a greater likelihood to use KMS systems because the values inherent in these systems (e.g., knowledge sharing is valued by KMS) are in agreement with the values held by the individual. By contrast, peoples' value-based tendency to hoard knowledge may result in a smaller likelihood to use KMS systems because the values inherent in these systems are in conflict with the values held by the individual.

The two theories are complementary and of substantial value if integrated to form a model of culture and KMS use. The Theory of Basic Human Values contributes ten exogenous variables that may be associated with the tendency to share knowledge. On the basis of this tendency, the Theory of IT Culture Conflict explicitly indicates the extent to which individuals might use a KMS to make a knowledge contribution. Accordingly, these two theories together allow us to examine the relationship between cultural values and the frequency of KMS use by knowledge contributors. Finally, the literature on habit informs the examination of how the ten cultural values might influence the formation of unconscious and automatic KMS use by individuals for contributing knowledge.

3. HYPOTHESES

Based on our theoretical framing for this study, the following paragraphs develop hypotheses that probe our research topic. The research model is shown in Figure 1, with construct definitions presented in Table 2.

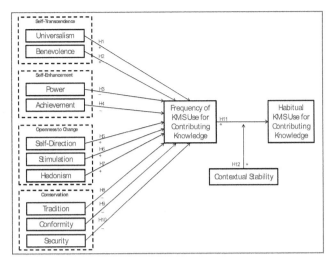

Figure 1. Research Model

Table 2. Construct definitions

Construct	Definition	Reference
Universalism	Extent to which a culture emphasizes understanding, appreciation, tolerance, and protection of the welfare of all people and nature	Schwartz, 1992; 1994
Benevolence	Extent to which a culture emphasizes preservation and enhancement of the welfare of close others in daily interaction	Schwartz, 1992; 1994
Power	Extent to which a culture emphasizes social status, prestige, and control or dominance over people and resources	Schwartz, 1992; 1994
Achievement	Extent to which a culture emphasizes personal success through the demonstration of competence	Schwartz, 1992; 1994
Self-Direction	Extent to which a culture emphasizes independent thought and action for choosing, creating, and exploring	Schwartz, 1992; 1994
Stimulation	Extent to which a culture emphasizes variety and excitement in life to maintain an optimal level of activation	Schwartz, 1992; 1994
Hedonism	Extent to which a culture emphasizes pleasure or sensuous gratification for oneself	Schwartz, 1992; 1994
Tradition	Extent to which a culture emphasizes respect of, commitment to, and acceptance of its customs and ideas	Schwartz, 1992; 1994
Conformity	Extent to which a culture emphasizes restraint of actions, inclinations, and impulses likely to violate social expectations	Schwartz, 1992; 1994
Security	Extent to which a culture emphasizes safety, harmony, and stability of society, relationships, and the self	Schwartz, 1992; 1994
Frequency of KMS Use for Contributing Knowledge	Extent to which an individual uses a KMS for contributing knowledge	Limayem et al., 2007; Wood et al., 2005
Contextual Stability	Extent to which KMS Use for contributing knowledge occurs under a stable physical and temporal context	Limayem et al., 2007; Wood et al., 2005
Habitual KMS Use for Contributing Knowledge	Extent to which an individual's KMS use for contributing knowledge is automatic because of learning	Limayem et al., 2007; Wood et al., 2005

Self-Transcendence includes the value types Universalism and Benevolence and refers to the extent to which a culture emphasizes voluntary commitment to the welfare of others (Schwartz, 1992). As such, Self-Transcendence may be positively associated with the tendency to share knowledge since contributions to any kind of knowledge repository tend to be voluntary, altruistic, and directed towards the welfare of others (Wasko and Faraj, 2005). In other words, to the extent to which people identify with a culture that emphasizes voluntary commitment to the welfare of others, they may be more likely to share their knowledge. According to TITCC, these individuals may be more likely to use a KMS for contributing their knowledge since such use would conform to their value of self-transcendence (Leidner and Kayworth, 2006). It should be noted that we are referring to the volitional use of KMS and that Self-Transcendence does not take into account mandatory factors such as required use of a KMS and incentives for contributions. Thus:

H1: Universalism is positively associated with the frequency of KMS use for contributing knowledge.

H2: Benevolence is positively associated with the frequency of KMS use for contributing knowledge.

By contrast, Self-Enhancement, which includes the value types Power and Achievement, refers to the extent to which a culture motivates people to seek and enhance their own personal interests even at the expense of other individuals (Schwartz, 1992). As such, a culture valuing Self-Enhancement may be negatively associated with the tendency to share knowledge since protecting one's own interests entails knowledge hoarding, for example, because "knowledge is power" (Bock et al., 2005; Wasko and Faraj, 2005). In other words, to the extent to which individuals identify with a culture that values commitment to selfish interests, they might be more inclined to hoard their knowledge. According to TITCC, persons may be less likely to use a KMS for contributing knowledge in this case since such use would violate their shared value of serving selfish interests first (Leidner and Kayworth, 2006). Formally:

H3: Power is negatively associated with the frequency of KMS use for contributing knowledge.

H3: Achievement is negatively associated with the frequency of KMS use for contributing knowledge.

Openness to Change includes the value types Self-Direction, Stimulation, and Hedonism, and it refers to the extent to which a culture motivates people to follow their own intellectual interests in unpredictable and uncertain directions (Schwartz, 1992) to actively adapt to and change their environment. The general tendency to value environmental change may be positively associated with the general tendency to share knowledge. Specifically, the more an individual values change in general, the more change initiatives the person will support. Such support involves collaboration, which in turn involves knowledge sharing. More specifically, changing an environment towards some desired end may involve active collaboration because combined efforts tend to produce greater changes than individual efforts, particularly in human enterprises, whose members often work together towards common goals (Schein 1996). Collaboration involves knowledge sharing so that knowledge of the desired end state and the process involved in achieving it can spread across individuals; thus facilitating a combined effort (Alavi and Leidner, 2001; Davenport and Prusak, 2000). Hence, to the extent to which individuals identify with a culture that emphasizes environmental change, they might be more prone to work towards disseminating knowledge. According to TITCC, such people may be more likely to use a KMS for contributing knowledge since such use would conform to their value of change (Leidner and Kayworth, 2006). For example, to the extent to which individuals identify with a firm's goal of leaving its traditional market and entering a new one, they may be more likely to disseminate their knowledge regarding major players in the new market. The more an individual values change in general, the more such initiatives the individual will support. Formally:

H5: Self-Direction is positively associated with the frequency of KMS use for contributing knowledge.

H6: Stimulation is positively associated with the frequency of KMS use for contributing knowledge.

H7: Hedonism is positively associated with the frequency of KMS use for contributing knowledge.

By contrast, Conservation, which includes the value types Tradition, Conformity, and Security, refers to the extent to which a culture motivates people to preserve the status quo (Schwartz, 1992). The general tendency to preserve the status quo along with the certainty it provides may be negatively associated with the general tendency to share knowledge. More specifically, using the logic outlined above, the more an individual values the status quo, the more change initiatives the person will hinder. Such hindrance involves dissociation, which in turn involves knowledge hoarding. Hence, to the extent to which people identify with a culture that emphasizes the status quo, they might be less prone to work towards disseminating knowledge. According to TITCC, such individuals may be less likely to use a KMS for contributing knowledge since such use would violate their shared value of conservation (Leidner and Kayworth, 2006). Formally:

H8: Tradition is negatively associated with the frequency of KMS use for contributing knowledge.

H9: Conformity is negatively associated with the frequency of KMS use for contributing knowledge.

H10: Security is negatively associated with the frequency of KMS use for contributing knowledge.

Research on habit indicates that the frequency of past behavior performance is an important prerequisite to habit formation. Only when the focal behavior is performed repetitively will the cognitive processes involved in initiating the behavior become automatic and unconscious; strong habits develop over time. Monthly performance of a focal behavior will generally promote weaker habit formation than daily performance of the same behavior (Limayem et al., 2007; Oullette and Wood, 1998). Thus:

H11: The frequency of KMS use for contributing knowledge is positively associated with habitual KMS use for contributing knowledge.

Since habits are initiated by specific contextual stimuli such as physical location or time, the physical and temporal context have to be stable. Only then can strong associations between contextual stimuli and behavior performance form. In contrast, frequent repetitions of the focal behavior under contextual instability may only result in weak habit formation since no association can develop between the behavior and a specific contextual stimulus (Wood et al., 2005; Wood and Neal, 2007). Thus, we propose contextual stability to be an important component in the explanation of the habit construct:

H12: This relationship is moderated by contextual stability so that it is stronger for higher levels of contextual stability.

4. PROPOSED RESEARCH METHOD

The relatively strong theory-base for our research model renders a quantitative approach more than adequate by reducing many of the methodological and definitional problems inherent in much prior quantitative cross-cultural IS scholarship (Karahanna, Evaristo and Srite, 2002). Consistent with prior quantitative research (e.g., Chattopadhyay and George, 2001), this study will employ a large-scale survey to increase research relevance. A random sample of individuals with KMS access will be queried. To ensure that KMS use is important to these individuals, we will survey knowledge workers from a large multinational consulting

firm. Consultants heavily rely on knowledge to perform their jobs and often receive outcome-based compensation, implying that knowledge transfer is important to them.

This research will measure culture by querying individuals regarding their cultural values (see Table 3). Respondents will be asked to rate the extent to which each basic value represents a guiding principle in their lives (Schwartz, 1992). The instrument will employ a 9-point scale: Opposed to my values (-1), not important (0), unlabeled (1, 2), important (3), unlabeled (4, 5), very important (6), and of supreme importance (7). By keeping the analysis at the level of the individual it is not necessary to segment the sample into subgroups with certain characteristics. The people in the sample will vary according to their preference for the ten value types. Our approach will ensure high internal validity compared to past studies that most often have not employed actual measurements of relevant cultural values (Straub, Loch, Evaristo, Karahanna and Srite, 2002), but rather drawn conclusions on the basis of potentially outdated country scores (i.e., operationalizing a cultural value as, say, U.S. citizens). To further increase the internal validity of this study, we will control for individual differences.

Table 3. Measurement of Cultural Values

Bipolar Value Dimension	Value Type	Value	Explanatory phrase
Self-Transcendence	Universalism	A World at Peace	free of war and conflict
		Social Justice	correcting injustice, care for the weak
		Equality	equal opportunity for all
		Inner Harmony	at peace with myself
		Protecting the Environment	preserving nature
		Broad-Minded	tolerant of different ideas and beliefs
		Wisdom	a mature understanding of life
		A World of Beauty	beauty of nature and the arts
		Unity with Nature	fitting into nature
	Benevolence	A Spiritual Life	emphasis on spiritual not material matters
		Forgiving	willing to pardon others
		Honest	genuine, sincere
		Loyal	faithful to my friends, group
		Helpful	working for the welfare of others
		Responsible	dependable, reliable
		True Friendship	close, supportive friends
		Meaning in Life	a purpose in life
		Mature Love	deep emotional and spiritual intimacy
Conservation	Tradition	Humble	modest, self-effacing
		Detachment	from worldly concerns
		Devout	holding to religious faith and belief
		Moderate	avoiding extremes of feeling and action
		Respect for Tradition	preservation of time-honored customs
		Accepting My Portion in Life	submitting to life's circumstances
	Conformity	Self-Discipline	self-restraint, resistance to temptation
		Honoring of Parents and Elders	showing respect
		Obedient	dutiful, meeting obligations
		Politeness	courtesy, good manners
	Security	National Security	protection of my nation from enemies
		Family Security	safety for loved ones
		Social Order	stability of society
		Clean	neat, tidy
		Reciprocation of Favors	avoidance of indebtedness
		Sense of Belonging	feeling that others care about me
Self-Enhancement	Power	Social Recognition	respect, approval by others
		Preserving My Public Image	protecting my "face"
		Healthy	not being sick physically or mentally
		Authority	the right to lead or command
		Wealth	material possessions, money
		Social Power	control over others, dominance
	Achievement	Self-Respect	belief in one's own worth
		Intelligent	logical, thinking
		Successful	achieving goals
		Capable	competent, effective, efficient
		Ambitious	hardworking, aspiring
		Influential	having an impact on people and events
Openness to Change	Self-Direction	Freedom	freedom of action and thought
		Creativity	uniqueness, imagination
		Independent	self-reliant, self-sufficient
		Choosing Own Goals	selecting own purposes
		Curious	interested in everything, exploring
	Stimulation	A Varied Life	filled with challenge, novelty, and change
		An Exciting Life	stimulating experiences
		Daring	seeking adventure, risk
	Hedonism	Enjoying Life	enjoying food, sex, leisure, etc.
		Pleasure	gratification of desires

Other measures will be adapted from existing literature where available. For example, habit-related constructs have regularly been evaluated through explanatory questionnaires (e.g., Kim et al., 2005; Limayem et al., 2007). To ensure adequate adaptation of measures to the cross-cultural context, this study will follow the guidelines advanced by Karahanna et al. (2002). These guidelines aim at enhancing multi-group equivalence, a key methodological concern in cross-cultural IS research. Enhanced multi-group equivalence will result in reduced measurement error.

Covariance-based structural equation modeling (SEM) will be used for analyzing both the measurement and structural models since SEM accounts for the latent nature of the culture construct. Indeed, culture is not directly observable, and in contrast to more traditional techniques such as multiple regression analysis, constructs that are not directly observable can be explicitly included in structural equation models. Culture, however, might be even more complex. Some scholars indicate that culture should be modeled as a second-order factor, further supporting the superior adequacy of SEM over more traditional tools (Kline, 1998).

The data that will be collected for this study will be examined for the extent of between-culture variance using the intra-class correlation (Cohen, Cohen, West and Aiken, 2003). In case that substantial between-group variance will be present, the data will be analyzed through multilevel SEM (MLSEM) (Cheung, Leung and Au, 2006). This technique combines the strengths of hierarchical linear modeling and SEM. Thus, MLSEM accounts for the multilevel nature of much cross-cultural data without sacrificing the researcher's ability to address the special analytical concerns inherent in cross-cultural IS research. More specifically, the tool enables the researcher to examine factor structures and structural relationships at the levels of the individual and the culture (see Cheung et al., 2006, for a detailed discussion)..

5. Conclusion

Results from the proposed study will impact our understanding of the interdependencies among culture and habit in the KM context. By explaining culture's influence on habitual KMS use for knowledge sharing, we integrate knowledge sharing behavior with the concepts of habit as a form of post-adoptive use and culture as a factor impacting the post-adoptive use of IT. In combining these concepts, we also contribute to the three literature streams individually by overcoming some of their major limitations. In contrast to much prior cross-cultural IS scholarship, we go beyond TAM and Hofstede's (1980) criticized work (see, e.g., Myers and Tan, 2002, for a comprehensive review) and use a stronger theoretical base consisting of two cross-cultural theories. In so doing, we reflected on past cross-cultural IS research to open the gateway for strong cross-cultural scholarship in the future of IT adoption research. Furthermore, to the best of our knowledge, this study is among the first to examine culture's consequences in the post-adoption context rather than the domain of initial acceptance of IT.

This research further contributes to the literature on habit by examining the concept as a primary outcome variable and incorporating contextual stability as a crucial component of the concept's nomological network into the model. In so doing, this study is among the first to incorporate the environmental context into a variance model concerned with habit formation. Finally, while prior KM scholarship has focused on intentional and hence initial and irregular contributions (e.g., Bock et al. 2005;

Kankanhalli et al. 2005; Wasko and Faraj, 2005), we seek to explain how organizations can encourage habitual, post-adoptive KMS use by knowledge contributors. This may help managers in charge of cross-cultural (e.g., cross-regional, cross-national, or cross-religious) teams or divisions enhance the knowledge flow throughout their units. Our results will provide managers with a better understanding of what cultural values foster KMS use for knowledge sharing, and it will allow them to better evaluate the payoffs resulting from cultural change management in terms of the individual impacts of IT.

6. REFERENCES

[1] Alavi, M., and Leidner, D. E. (2001) Review: Knowledge management and knowledge management systems: Conceptual foundations and research issues, *MIS Quarterly*, 25, 1, 107-136.

[2] Bock, G-W., Zmud, R. W., Young-Gul K. and Jae-Nam L. (2005) Behavioral intention formation in knowledge sharing: Examining the roles of extrinsic motivators, social-psychological forces, and organizational climate, *MIS Quarterly*, 29, 1, 87-111.

[3] Byrne, B. M. (2006) Structural equation modeling with EQS: Basic concepts, applications, and programming (2nd ed.), Mahwah, NJ US: Lawrence Erlbaum Associates Publishers.

[4] Chattopadhyay, P., and George, E. (2001) Examining the effects of work externalization through the lens of social identity theory, *The Journal of Applied Psychology*, 86, 4, 781-788.

[5] Cheung, M. W., Leung, K., and Au, K. (2006) Evaluating multilevel models in cross-cultural research: An illustration with social axioms, *Journal of Cross-Cultural Psychology*, 37, 5, 522-541.

[6] Cohen, J., Cohen, P., West, S. G., and Aiken, L. S. (2003) *Applied multiple regression/correlation analysis for the behavioral sciences (3rd ed.)*. Mahwah, NJ US: Lawrence Erlbaum Associates Publishers.

[7] Conner, K. R., and Prahalad, C. K. (1996) A resource-based theory of the firm: Knowledge versus opportunism, *Organization Science*, 7, 5, 477-501.

[8] Cooper, R. B., and Zmud, R. W. (1990) Information technology implementation research: A technological diffusion approach, *Management Science*, 36, 2,123-139.

[9] Davenport, T. H., and Prusak, L. (2000) Working knowledge: How organizations manage what they know (paperback). *Harvard Business School Press Books*.

[10] Gallivan, M., and Srite, M. (2005) Information technology and culture: Identifying fragmentary and holistic perspectives of culture, *Information and Organization*, 15, 4, 295-338.

[11] Garud, R., and Kumaraswamy, A. (2005) Vicious and virtuous circles in the management of knowledge: The case of infosys technologies, *MIS Quarterly*, 29, 1, 9-33.

[12] Hofstede, G. (1980) Culture's consequences international differences in work-related values. Beverly Hills, CA: Sage Publications.

[13] Jasperson, J., Carter, P. E., and Zmud, R. W. (2005) A comprehensive conceptualization of post-adoptive behaviors

associated with information technology enabled work systems, *MIS Quarterly,* 29, 3, 525-557.

[14] Kankanhalli, A., Tan, B. C. Y. and Kwok-Kee W. (2005) Contributing knowledge to electronic knowledge repositories: An empirical investigation, *MIS Quarterly,* 29, 1, 113-143.

[15] Karahanna, E., Evaristo, R., and Srite, M. (2002) Methodological issues in MIS cross-cultural research, *Journal of Global Information Management,* 10, 1, 48.

[16] Kim, S. S., Malhotra, N. K., and Narasimhan, S. (2005) Two competing perspectives on automatic use: A theoretical and empirical comparison, *Information Systems Research,* 16, 4, 418-432.

[17] Kline, P. (1998) The new psychometrics: Science, psychology, and measurement. London: Routledge.

[18] Leidner, D. E., and Kayworth, T. (2006) Review: A review of culture in information systems research: Toward a theory of information technology culture conflict, *MIS Quarterly,* 30, 2, 357-399.

[19] Limayem, M., Hirt, S. G., and Cheung, C. M. K. (2007) How habit limits the predictive power of intention: The case of information systems continuance, *MIS Quarterly,* 31, 4, 705-737.

[20] Malhotra, N. K., Kim, S. S., and Patil, A. (2006) Common method variance in IS research: A comparison of alternative approaches and a reanalysis of past research, *Management Science,* 52, 12, 1865-1883.

[21] Myers, M.B., Calantone, R.J., Page Jr. T.J., and Taylor, C.R. (2000) An application of multiple-group causal models in assessing cross-cultural measurement equivalence, *Journal of International Marketing,* 8, 4, 108-121.

[22] Myers, M. D., and Tan, F. B. (2002) Beyond models of national culture in information systems research, *Journal of Global Information Management,* 10, 1, 24.

[23] Okazaki, S., and Mueller, B. (2007) Cross-cultural advertising research: Where we have been and where we need to go, *International Marketing Review,* 24, 5, 499-518.

[24] Ouellette, J. A., and Wood, W. (1998) Habit and intention in everyday life: The multiple processes by which past behavior predicts future behavior, *Psychological Bulletin,* 124, 1, 54-74.

[25] Sambamurthy, V., and Subramani, M. (2005) Special issue on information technologies and knowledge management, *MIS Quarterly,* 29, 1, 1-7.

[26] Schein, E. H. (1996) Culture: The missing concept in organization studies, *Administrative Science Quarterly,* 41, 2, 229-240.

[27] Schwartz, S.H. (1992) *Universals in the content and structure of values: theoretical advances and empirical tests in 20 countries,* in Zanna, M. (Ed.), Advances in Experimental Social Psychology, Vol. 25, New York, NY: Academic Press, pp. 1-65.

[28] Schwartz, S. H. (1994) Are there universal aspects in the structure and contents of human values?, *Journal of Social Issues,* 50, 4, 19-45.

[29] Straub, D. W. (1989) Validating instruments in MIS research, *MIS Quarterly,* 13, 2, 147-169.

[30] Straub, D., Boudreau, M., and Gefen, D. (2004) Validation guidelines for is positivist research, *Communications of AIS Article* 13, 380-427.

[31] Straub, D., Loch, K., Ev Aristo, R., Karahanna, E., and Srite, M. (2002) Toward a theory-based measurement of culture, *Journal of Global Information Management,* 10, 1, 13.

[32] Vandenberg, R. J., and Lance, C. E. (2000) A review and synthesis of the measurement invariance literature: Suggestions, practices, and recommendations for organizational research, *Organizational Research Methods,* 3, 1, 4-69.

[33] Wasko, M. and Faraj, S. (2005) Why should I share? Examining social capital and knowledge contribution in electronic networks of practice, *MIS Quarterly,* 29, 1, 35-57.

[34] Wood, W., and Neal, D. T. (2007) A new look at habits and the habit-goal interface," *Psychological Review,* 114, 4, 843-863.

[35] Wood, W., Tam, L., and Witt, M. G. (2005) Changing circumstances, disrupting habits, *Journal of Personality and Social Psychology,* 88, 6, 918-933.

Research in Progress: Fun versus Productivity and Intentions to Use ICT's in Bolivia

Indira R. Guzman
Trident University International
5757 Plaza Dr.
Cypress, CA 90630, USA
1-714-816-0366

indira.guzman@trident.edu

Michelle L. Kaarst-Brown
Syracuse University
218 Hinds Hall
Syracuse, NY 13244, USA

1-315-559-2451

mlbrow03@syr.edu

ABSTRACT

Despite decades of studies on the use of information and communication technologies (ICT's) and almost as many decades of research on national cultural variables around the world, the people of Bolivia may be among the least studied on both counts. This research in progress provides a brief overview of our research that seeks to begin closing this gap. This study applies the technology acceptance model and individual espoused cultural values using a societal sample of 1129 Bolivian respondents seeking to understand how computers and Internet are being accepted by users in a country where many conditions of ICT development such as infrastructure, electronic commerce or electronic government have been only moderately established.

Categories and Subject Descriptors

K.4 COMPUTERS AND SOCIETY

General Terms

Performance, Human Factors.

Keywords

TAM, Technology Acceptance Model, Hofstede, Technology Use, Internet Use, Intention to Use, Culture, Bolivia.

1. INTRODUCTION

"Bolivia has faced a challenge: the challenge of elaborating and developing a national strategy that could create social inclusion through the use of ICT's, therefore, reduces the country's Digital Divide. Besides the divide between Bolivia and other Latin American countries, Bolivia has faced a major problem: the divide between its own borders (urban and rural)" (Aramayo-Careaga, 2006:4).

Despite decades of studies on the use of information and communication technologies (ICT's) and almost as many decades of research on national cultural variables around the world, the people of Bolivia may be among the least studied on both counts. A review of the countries included at Hofstede's web site shows inclusion of 13 countries in South and Central America, with the somewhat glaring exclusion of Bolivia. (See http://www.geert-hofstede.com/) Similarly, a search of studies involving computer adoption, information systems, and other ICT studies reveals a

lack of research on technology adoption and use in this unique South American country.

This research in progress paper provides a brief overview of our research that seeks to begin closing this gap. Our survey results from 1129 community respondents contribute to understanding two broad questions:

(1)   How does a diverse group of citizens of La Paz, Bolivia (the administrative capital) accept "computers" and "internet applications"?

(2)   How espoused cultural values impact acceptance of computers and the internet when the general ICT conditions are in development or under developed?

To answer these questions, our study applies Hofstede's (1980) definitions of cultural values to over 1100 people in La Paz, Bolivia. Despite the criticisms of Hofstede's widely used model, we believe that Hofstede's approach will provide a comparable set of cultural variables and, to our knowledge, is the first study of its kind to do so in Bolivia.

Second, we apply the technology acceptance model or TAM (Davis, 1989, Srite and Karahanna, 2006; Shih, 2004) using a societal sample, rather than an organizational sample, seeking to understand how computers and technology are being accepted but users in a country where many conditions of ICT development such as infrastructure, electronic commerce or electronic government have been minimally established in comparison to countries of developed economies..

A third distinguishing feature of this research and potential contribution is the distribution method used to extend the sampling framework outside the organizational or university setting and into a community of Internet and ICT users.

Given the increased attention to the role of social media and social networking as entrées for younger and older people, we feel this study has a wide range of potential implications for research into ICT use by people in developing economies or non-organizational settings. This research-in-progress paper provides an overview of the motivation and methods for this research. If accepted, our presentation will provide data analysis and results to generate conference discussion about the acceptance of computers and Internet in developing countries like Bolivia.

2. BOLIVIA – DEMOGRAPHICS AND DIFFERENCES

Bolivia has been struggling with how to exploit ICT's for broader benefit to the country's population for over a decade now. This goal has been pursued through strategic plans, inclusion of stakeholders from private and public sectors, and engagement within educational institutions. For various economic and infrastructure reasons, mobile telephone technologies have deployed rapidly, however, the use of computers lags behind many developed countries and several South American countries as it does in Bolivia.

Bolivia is a country of over 10.1 million people (WDI - 2009), split more or less equally between males and females. In terms of literacy, men have a reported high literacy rate of 93.1%, with women averaging much lower at only 80.7%. Table 1 provides an overview of some key demographic statistics related to population. According to the national statistics institute (Instituto Nacional de Estadisticas) the major departments in Bolivia are La Paz with 2.349 million people and Santa Cruz with 2.029.471.

Table 1: Selected Bolivian Population Demographics

Country Demographics for Bolivia (source: CIA World Factbook at October 2011)			
		Male	Female
Population (at July 2011 est.)	10,118,683		
Age Structure (at July 2011 est.)			
0-14 years	34.60%	17.65%	16.99%
15-64 years	60.70%	29.79%	30.93%
65 years and over	4.60%	2.05%	2.59%
Median Age	22.5 years	21.8 years	23.2 years
Literacy (2001 Census) Definition: age 15 and over can read and write.			
Total population	86.70%	93.10%	80.70%
Ethnic Groups			
Quechua	30%		
Mestizo (mixed white & Amerindian ancestry)	30%		
Aymara	25%		
White	15%		
Languages (2001 census)			
Spanish (official)	60.70%		
Quechua (official)	21.20%		
Aymara (official)	14.60%		
Foreign Languages	2.40%		
Other	1.20%		
Urbanization (2010)			
Urban Population	67.00%		
Annual Rate of Change (2010-15 Est)	2.20%		
Major Cities and Population (2009)			
La Paz (capital)	1.642 Million people		
Santa Cruz	1.584 Million people		

Table 2 provides an overview of technology statistics for Bolivia including telephone and internet figures that we could gather so far. It is interesting to note in Table 2 below that cell phone outnumber land lines by almost ten to one (10:1). In addition, growth of land lines has increased from only 3 per 100 people to 7 per 100 people since 1995 – a fifteen year time span in which growth of cell phones increased from zero in 1997 to 73 per

hundred by 2009. The year 2009 saw a 146% increase in cell phone subscriptions over the previous year. Internet use figures are almost two years old and are likely much higher now, but reflect even more rapid diffusion, likely among the urbanized centers such as La Paz, Santa Cruz, and Cochabamba. In terms of other indicators of ICT development, electronic commerce in B2C is used only by few banks for personal banking but it is not customary to make transactions over the Internet. In terms of government initiatives, only about 15% of government services provide this capability. Most of the government websites are static and do not offer interaction. In developed countries, on the other hand, citizens use the technology to perform several transactions to businesses as well as government. In this study we want to see how individuals accept the technology under those conditions of ICT development.

2.1 Migration and ICT's

Bolivia experiences a net migration of slightly less than 1%, supporting that there are fewer immigrants, and a larger number of Bolivian's leaving the country. In a 2008 newspaper article the Bolivian Institute of Foreign Trade (Instituto Boliviano de Comercio Exterior) reported that migration is an important issue facing Bolivia, with one in four Bolivian citizens residing outside the country (Antelo-Lopez, 2008). This supports opportunities for ICT's to serve an important role in helping Bolivian expatriates stay in touch with family and friends who remain in the country. This fact may also speak to a drain of technical knowledge and skills.

Table 2: Selected Development Statistics for Bolivia

Selected Development Statistics for Bolivia (Source: World Development Indicators (WDI) and Global Development) Finance (GDF)			
	2000	2005	2009
Labor Force (millions)	3.54	4.03	4.46
# Internet Users (,000)	120	480	1,102.5
% Change since 1995	2400 %	9600 %	220,500 %
# Internet Users per 100	1	5	11
# Land Lines (,000)	510.8%	646.3%	810.1%
# Land Lines per 100	6	7	8
% Change since 1995			
# Cellular subscriptions per 100	7	26	73
% Change since 1995	700%	2600%	7300%
# New Businesses Reg.	--	1,515	2,504

2.2 Bolivia, Technology and Computerization

Like many technologically evolving countries, Bolivia has become a member of the new telecommunications era, with wide diffusion of cellular phones. Infrastructure development in many countries has evolved unequally, however. Whereas most countries have shifted from cybercafés to personal computer use, Bolivia seems content to rely on the social and community environment provided by local cyber cafes. Rather than seek personal ownership, even the large cities such as Las Paz are rife with small, high-tech cafes that cater to locals even more than to the tourists. The explanation for this is largely economic as, Internet access from home is very expensive with prices starting at $35 monthly for a very low speed of 384Kbps . Considering that the minimum wage in Bolivia is about $100 a month , this cost is beyond what the majority of citizens can afford. As a result, cyber café's have become a staple in the technology infrastructure of even major cities such as La Paz.

The Technology Acceptance Model has been modified and replicated for more than two decades in IS research and has proven to be a very robust model in understanding user's intention to use an information system (Jackson et al., 1997; Legris et al., 2003; Vankatesh & Davis, 2000). This model is based on two main concepts of perceived ease of use and perceived usefulness. Some studies suggest, however, that the model accounts for only 40% of intentions to use (IU) an information system (Legris et al., 2003). Other factors such as trust and natural cultural values have also been cited as critical in determining a user's intentions to use ICT's (Srite and Karahanna, 2006). In this study we use TAM to examine the acceptance of computers and internet but citizens of Bolivia.

2.3 Bolivia and Espoused National Cultural Values

Several authors have argued for a multi-level view of cultural factors that influence individual use of the Internet (Kaarst-Brown and Evaristo, 2002; Gallivan and Srite, 2005; Srite and Karahanna, 2006) Hofstede's studies about culture became the most popular comparison factors for national cultures, however, Hofstede's instrument (1980) was not designed to measure culture at the individual level. Therefore, we look into individual-level manifestations of culture as presented by Srite and Karahanna (2006) and also discussed by Gallivan and Srite (2005) and Karahanna et al. (2005).

In their study, Srite and Karahanna incorporated espoused national cultural values as moderators to the Technology Acceptance Model (TAM), drawing from Hofstede (1990) to include: masculinity/femininity, individualism/collectivism, power distance, and uncertainty avoidance. They found that espoused masculinity/femininity values moderated the relationship between perceived ease of use and behavioral intention. It could be argued that Bolivia likely shares similar cultural variables as other South American countries, however, this argument would be as false as suggesting that Italy and Germany share the same cultural values. Research also supports that individuals espouse national cultural values to differing degrees, however, we hope this study of over 1000 people living in La Paz will extend our understanding and provide comparable data on how these variables might relate to technology acceptance and use by the peoples of Bolivia. This will allow us to address whether the cultural variables of other South American countries are similar or different from those in Bolivia, and if lessons learned from ICT studies conducted in neighboring South American countries are applicable to Bolivia and its population.

3. METHODOLOGY

Initiated by the first author, this study pursued a traditional survey design, drawing from two validated survey instruments, and then adding additional open-ended questions to elicit additional explanations and comments about the way people use computers and the Internet. Survey responses include 914 electronic responses and 215 paper responses for a total of 1,129 surveys available for analysis. Interesting elements of the survey development and execution include the following:

- Survey developed to separate TAM items related to the IT artifact (computer) from those related to browser application (Internet)

- Translation and reverse translation by multiple parties

- Electronic or paper survey completion options

- Elicitation of responses using a social network approach to reach the broader community

The survey has three sections. The first section uses validated items related to the Technology Acceptance Model for computer use, followed by section two on espoused national cultural values. This is followed by validated items related to TAM and Internet use. The questions for the first sections were adapted from Srite and Karahanna (2006) for use with a general audience rather than the college students used by those authors referring to primary activities, rather than college work. The second section about espoused national cultural values also comes from Srite and Karahanna (2006). The third set of questions comes from Shih (2004).

3.1 TAM Exploration of both Artifact and Application

Drawing from survey instruments used in prior studies, our survey focused on both the "computer" as an artifact and on the "Internet" as an application or capability of the computer. We also included open questions about "access" to computers, so that we can triangulate and develop more nuanced meaning about intentions, availability, and the difference between artifact and application. For example, we asked people to distinguish location of use of the computer or use of the internet.

3.2 Translation and Reverse Translation

The validated survey items were translated from English to Spanish by the first author (a native Spanish speaker) and then reverse translated to English by another native Spanish speaker. Demographic and open ended questions were initially written in Spanish, and were translated into English by an independent Spanish speaker.

3.3 Electronic and Paper Options

In order to minimize bias due to potential discomfort with computers, we offered all respondents the option to complete the survey either on paper or online. As noted above, we received 914 online responses and 215 paper responses, for a total of 1129 responses. We intend to analyze both groups separately and apply appropriate statistical methods to see if the format of the survey relates to the findings. We initiated the analysis of the data collected only which provided initial results for this research in progress.

3.4 Use of Social Network Elicitation

The term "snowball sampling" is often used to refer to identifying a sample of respondents based on a strategy of following a story line or chain of evidence. Given our goal to reach a diverse sample of Bolivians, we used a method more closely related to social network analysis – what we are referring to as a social network distribution approach. Students from the business administration major of a private university in La Paz, were asked to request responses from 10 to 15 people they knew. Students were offered extra points in three different classes, as part of helping distribute the surveys. The goal was to obtain a diverse group of respondents, beyond simply their friends and family members to fill out the survey.

A total of 140 students participated in distributing surveys, suggesting that we should have received back between 1400 and 2100 surveys. We received a total of 1129, supporting a response rate calculation of between 54% and 81%. This is a very good response rate that can be attributed to the social component of the distribution strategy with personalized requests from known persons. It is still too early in the data analysis to speculate on the generalizability or randomness of the sample, however, we intend to do multiple tests across ages, work status, and paper versus online survey results to see what patterns emerge related to the research questions and sample.

4. EARLY FINDINGS

Our early analysis of the online surveys has yielded some interesting findings related to both the survey distribution methods and the survey data. Table 1 below presents the demographics for the online survey respondents. After cleaning the digital data, 896 online surveys were usable for analysis. We were able to capture a diverse slice of the general population, addressing variables such as Gender, Education, Years of Work Experience, and membership in the IT profession.

Table 3: Online Respondent Demographics

Online Respondents N=896	Number	Percentage
Gender (missing = 6, 0.7%)		
Male	509	56.8 %
Female	381	42.5 %
Education		
High School	562	62.7 %
Bachelor	216	24.1 %
Graduate Certificate	60	6.7 %
Masters	38	4.24 %
Doctorate	7	0.78 %
Work Experience (missing=3, 0.3%)		
None	321	35.83 %
Less than a year	232	25.89 %
Between 1 to 3 years	162	18.08 %
Between 4 to 10 years	89	9.93 %
Between 11 to 20 years	42	4.69 %
More than 20 years	47	5.25 %
IT Professionals (missing=12, 1.3%)		
IT Professionals	187	20.9%
Non IT Professionals	697	77.8%

Our online survey responses show good range and distribution by gender, work experience, and association with the IT profession. As noted in the Table 1 above, almost 35% of the population is younger than 15 years of age. As we continue with the data analysis, it will be interesting to see if the age distribution is older for those who preferred to complete the paper survey.

Our early analysis also indicates that the factor loadings on items and reliability are high – ranging from .77 to .94 with Cronbach alpha's of .794 to .897. These factor loadings compare well with those in the source papers. (See Table 4.)

Our analysis of cultural factors suggest that we have captured some dominant espoused cultural characteristics, which will be further analyzed by age, work experience, gender, and survey format, as well as compared to other findings.

5. SUMMARY: UNIQUELY BOLIVIA?

The research questions motivating this study are based on developing new insights into factors that influence intentions to use computers or internet applications in a developing country like Bolivia. This has practical as well as theoretical implications. From a practical view, our findings may help assess the readiness of urban Bolivian's to accept new online government services and electronic business initiatives. From a research view, since the scales used to measure variables worked out so well in Spanish, this study will provide other researchers with scales in Spanish that can measure both TAM and Espoused National Cultural Values. In addition, the survey distribution using a "social network distribution" approach combined with choice of paper or online survey may also yield valuable nuance about ICT use in Bolivia based on generational differences, actual use of the computer or internet applications, and other demographics.

Table 4: Sample of Translation with Factor Loadings and Cronbach Alpha (CA)

Ease of Use Codes	English	Spanish	Reverse Translation	Factor Loads	CA PEU .865
PE0U1	It is easy for me to become skillful in using computers	Es fácil para mi llegar mostrar habilidad en el uso de computadoras	It is easy for me to become skillful in using computers	0.820	
PE0U2	I find computers easy to use.	Para mi utilizar computadoras es fácil.	Using computers is easy to me	0.868	

6. ACKNOWLEDGMENTS

We are indebted to the many participants of this study and to the reviewers for their comments.

7. REFERENCES

[1] Antelo-Lopez, E. (2008). Migrantes bolivianos: "2,5 millones de héroes y heroínas". Comercio Exterior, (159).

[2] Aramayo-Careaga, Gonzalo and UNDP Bolivia (2006) The elaboration and development of the Bolivian Information and

Communication Technologies for Development Strategy – ETIC.

[3] Davis, F. D. (1989). Perceived Usefulness, Perceived Ease Of Use, And User Acceptance. MIS Quarterly, 13(3), 319-339.

[4] Gallivan, M., & Srite, M. (2005). Information Technology and Culture: Identifying Fragmentary and Holistic Perspective of Culture. Information & Organization, 15(4), 295-338.

[5] Jackson, C. M., Chow, S., & Leitch, R. A. (1997). Toward an understanding of the behavioral intention to use an information systems. Decision Sciences, 28(2), 357-389.

[6] Legris, P., Ingham, J., & Collerette, P. (2003). Why do people use information technology? A critical review of the technology acceptance model. Information & Management, 40, 191-204.

[7] Kaarst-Brown, M.L. & Evaristo, J.R.E. (2002) "International Cultures and Insights into Global Electronic Commerce".

Global Information Technology and Electronic Commerce, 4th Edition, Edited by Palvia P., Palvia S. and Roche, E. 255-274.

[8] Karahanna, E., Evaristo, R., & Srite, M. (2005). Levels of Culture and Individual Behavior: An Integrated Perspective. Journal of Global Information Management, 13(2), 1-20.

[9] Shih, H.-P. (2004). Extended technology acceptance model of Internet utilization. Information Management, 41, 719-729

[10] Srite, M., & Karahanna, E. (2006). The Role of Espoused National Cultural Values in Technology Acceptance. [Article]. MIS Quarterly, 30(3), 679-704.

[11] Venkatesh, V. and Davis, F. D. (2000) "A Theoretical Extension of the Technology Acceptance Model: Four Longitudinal Field Studies," Management Science (46:2), 186-204.

Exploring the Role of Mentoring in the IS Profession: A Cross-National Comparison

Monica Adya
Department of Management
Marquette University
Milwaukee, WI 53201
+1 414-288-7526

monica.adya@marquette.edu

John Cotton
Department of Management
Marquette University
Milwaukee, WI 53201
+1 414-288-7558

john.cotton@marquette.edu

ABSTRACT

Workplace mentoring is beneficial to protégés, most often, in the form of career related and psychosocial support. Mentoring is found to positively impact career progression and satisfaction, is positively correlated with affective commitment, and negatively related to turnover behavior. For academics and practitioners concerned about more effective integration and participation of IS professionals in the IT workforce, mentoring may provide a solution for mitigating the effects of a high-pressure, masculine work environment. While mentoring has been examined to some extent in the general management literature, it has received only passing attention in information systems (IS) research, particularly in a global context. The unique characteristics and demands of the IS profession and increasing trends toward offshoring warrant an IS-specific examination of mentoring behaviors, preferences, and influences. In this study, we propose to conduct a cross-cultural study of mentoring among Indian and American IS professionals. Our study hopes to yield beneficial insights for mentoring practice and research in the IS profession.

Categories and Subject Descriptors

H.1.2 [**User/Machine Systems**]: Information Systems – *human factors*.

General Terms

Human Factors.

Keywords

Formal and informal mentoring, career anchors, offshoring, organizational commitment, self-efficacy, career commitment, and turnover.

1. INTRODUCTION AND MOTIVATION

Workplace mentoring benefits protégés, most often, in two ways – through career-related development and psychosocial support [11]. Career development relates directly to improving career prospects for the protégé, for instance by providing greater visibility, coaching, and challenging assignments. Psychosocial support, in contrast, focuses on supporting the self-image and

increasing the competence of the protégé, through counseling, friendship, and role modeling [4]. Empirical research finds that career progress, career satisfaction, and turnover are related to whether an individual has a mentor [4]. Mentoring is positively correlated with affective commitment and negatively related to turnover behavior [19]. It is also found to positively influence personal learning and job satisfaction [12].

Although workplace mentoring has been examined at length in the general management literature, its role in the IS profession has not received the same level of attention. At most, discussions of mentoring in the IS workplace are prescriptive. Mentoring is recommended as a way to better integrate women in IS careers [6], for developing leadership capabilities among IS professionals [9], and for enhancing perceptions of organizational support among IS professionals [2]. In a cross-cultural context, exploratory results indicate differential mentor and mentoring preferences across cultures [1]. However, this research generally focuses on Europe versus the U.S., is prescriptive and provides little insight into how mentoring initiatives should be designed to accommodate the IS professional.

It can be argued that outcomes of mentoring for IS professionals may not be different from any other profession. However, IS presents certain unique characteristics and challenges that warrant a specific examination. First, IS is perceived to be more stressful because of the evolutionary nature of technology and processes and related pressures of career development [21] and deadline-driven work often leading to role overload [14, 21]. Working professionals engaged in such stressful conditions may find the psychosocial aspects of mentoring to be beneficial in managing work pressures. Second, IS professionals have a choice of engaging in managerial or technical roles as they move up the career ladder [7]. Transition between these career paths is challenging because of different skill set preferences for these roles but may be facilitated by career-related mentoring. Third, globalization of IT work creates additional complexities in understanding the IS workforce and its needs. Offshoring has resulted in greater diversity than ever before in the form of contractual employees from offshore as well as client locations [1]. Furthermore, in light of continuing shortage of IT skills, greater numbers of foreign-born professionals are present in the workforce. Offshore providers struggle with turnover and retention issues among their staff [13] while client sites wrestle with uncertainty and changing skill needs imposed on their staff [3]. The very nature of these issues warrants a closer cross-cultural examination of mentoring. Finally, both academics and practitioners concerned with integration and participation of women and minorities in the IS workforce may look to mentoring to potentially mitigate the negative effects of a masculine, high pressure work environment [1, 23].

As an exploration of the needs addressed above, our study seeks to examine the prevalence and impact of mentoring on the IT profession in a cross-cultural context. Specifically, we propose to examine the following questions in the context of U.S.-based client and Indian provider corporations:

a. What mentoring practices and behaviors are prevalent in US client and Indian provider firms?

b. To what extent do these mentoring practices impact career attitudes, career progression, organizational commitment, and turnover intentions?

c. How do career anchors influence mentoring behaviors and preferences?

d. What cross-cultural factors influence mentoring practices, behaviors, and preferences between Indian and American IS professionals?

2. CONSTRUCT DEVELOPMENT AND METHODOLOGY

2.1 Participant Sample

To meet the above objectives, we plan data collection of three samples – (a) Indian IS professionals working in India, (b) American IS professionals working in the US, and (c) Indian IS professionals working in the US. Companies and professional institutions in both India and US will be approached to solicit participation of their employees and members respectively. NASSCOM maintains a database of over 1300 Indian IT firms that can be approached for participation. We consider samples of 150 Indian and American professionals each to be sufficient for this early exploratory study. There is relatively low repatriation of American professionals to India and when this does occur, these individuals are often in leadership positions that are better suited to mentor roles. While the influence of foreign-born mentors on native mentees is, in itself, interesting, its examination is beyond scope of this study. Further, our study is designed to examine the protégé perspective and examining paired mentor-protégé roles, again while interesting, is beyond scope of this study. Although no specific cultural measures will be included in the survey, the analysis will be conducted across these national samples to elicit differences that might exist.

2.2 Mentoring Measures

Mentoring literature has examined two primary aspects of mentoring: (a) the nature of its formalization i.e. formal or informal mentor-protégé relationships and (b) functions served by the mentors for the protégés, specifically career development and psychosocial. In this preliminary study, we examine these two dimensions of mentoring relationships and discuss their implementation in greater detail:

Formalization of Mentoring Relationship: Mentoring relationships can be developed informally through a one-on-one interactions or the relationship can stem from a formal program designed to bring together protégés and mentors. Protégés involved in informal mentoring relationships view their mentors as more effective and typically receive greater compensation than those engaged in formal mentoring relationships [20]. Furthermore, formal mentoring relationships are found to be less

effective for women as compared to men [20]. This is of particular relevance for IS where formal mentoring programs are being developed and promoted for improved integration of women in a masculine field. The impact of formal versus informal mentoring relationships has not been examined across cultures. Nor has the impact of mentoring with women been studied across cultures. Measures for formal-informal construct used in this study are obtained from [20].

Mentoring Functions: As indicated earlier, mentors provide career development and psychosocial support to protégés. Preliminary studies suggest that men and women benefit differentially from career development and psychosocial support. Further, early findings indicate differences in mentoring expectations at a cross-cultural level. Adya [1], for instance found that South Asian women IS professionals expected more career development out of their mentoring relationships as opposed to their American peers who seemed to rely on mentoring for greater psychosocial support. To this end, a further examination of mentoring expectations is proposed in our study. Specific measures for examining mentoring roles are obtained from [20].

2.3 Outcome Measures

An extensive body of empirical research suggests that mentoring has a positive influence on career satisfaction and turnover intentions [4]. Mentoring is also found to be positively correlated with affective commitment and negatively related to turnover behavior [19] and positively influences job satisfaction [12]. Many of these outcome variables have been of significant concern in the IS literature as well. We extrapolate these findings to the IS domain to propose an examination of the following outcome measures:

a. *Satisfaction with Mentoring*: A protégé's satisfaction with a relationship was measured by a four item scale originally developed by [20]. The scale uses a seven-point Likert response format where higher values represent greater satisfaction with the mentoring relationship.

b. *Job Satisfaction* using the single item measures of JDI facets proposed by [17]. This scale consisting of five items was found to be highly correlated (rs from 0.6 to 0.73) with the full JDI and in some cases accounted for incremental variance in outcome measures [17].

c. *Career Satisfaction* using a five item measure proposed in [5]. This measure captures satisfaction with accomplishment of career goals, compensation, and skill development among others.

d. *Self efficacy* – Considering the psychosocial benefits of mentoring, we examine perceived self-efficacy in the existing role as an outcome of mentoring engagements. Specifically, we examine general self-efficacy using a 3-item measure proposed in [18] but also include a measure of social self-efficacy [22].

e. *Organizational Commitment* – While affective commitment and mentoring have been examined in the IS literature, albeit to a limited extent, because of both the career development and psychosocial effects of mentoring, in this study we propose to examine affective, normative, and continuance commitment at the organizational level, specifically using the mentoring scale developed in [16]. This scale proposes 6 items each for affective, normative, and continuance commitment, yielding a total of 18 items.

f. *Turnover Intentions* – Finally, considering the significant concern in the IS academic and practitioner regarding retention of skilled IS professionals, turnover intentions will be examined using a three-item scale utilized in [8].

2.4 Career Anchors
Finally, we propose that an individual's career orientation can have a strong influence on the success of mentoring relationships. In effect, a misalignment between career orientation and nature of mentoring relationships can diffuse the benefits on outcome measures such as career and organizational commitment, job satisfaction, and turnover intentions. In contrast, when the mentor's role is aligned with career orientation of the protégé, greater synergies can result in more positive outcome. To this end, we examine two well-examined career anchors in IT – managerial competence and technical competence – with the supposition that (a) greater technical-orientation among South-Asian professionals [1] and (b) greater managerial orientation among American IT professionals will define their approach to and expectations from mentoring relationships. Additionally, we propose to examine other anchors such as identity, variety, geographic security, autonomy, and organizational stability which are found to have strong influence in a cross-cultural context, specifically in the case of Indian IS professionals [15]. For instance, Indian IS professionals demonstrate a greater tendency for geographic security considering the strong family oriented culture which drives them to stay closer to parents and extended families [15]. Similarly, influences of national culture on career anchors are expected to emerge.

Considering the newness of this research in the IS domain, we propose to conduct path analysis on the above variable to draw out preliminary causal relationships between the above constructs. Figure 1 below provides a preliminary conceptual model which will evolve to a more specific path model:

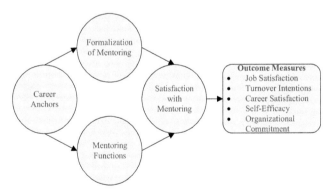

Figure 1: Preliminary IS Mentoring Model

3. CONCLUSION
The distinctive nature of the IS profession raises questions about the need for a modified approach to mentoring among its professionals. In this study, we propose to address this need along with examining the issues in a cross-cultural context. Our proposed research presents numerous opportunities:

a. It potentially raises a new research stream to address improved integration and retention in the IS workplace.

b. Our findings can provide prescriptive recommendations to organizations in how to expend resources and effort towards more effective mentoring for IS professionals.

c. It can potentially raise interesting recommendations and research effort towards cross-cultural transfer of mentoring practices. This has strong implications for client organizations that, for instance, have co-located provider teams.

4. REFERENCES
[1] Adya, M.P. 2008. Women at work: Differences in IT career experiences and perceptions between South Asian and American women. *Human Resource Management*, 47, 3, 601-635.

[2] Allen, M. Armstrong, D., Reid, M.F., and Reimenschneider, C.K. 2008. Factors impacting the perceived organizational support of IT employees. *Information & Management*, 45, 8, 556-563.

[3] Bullen, C.V., Abraham, T., Gallagher, K., Kaiser, K.M., and Simon, J. 2007. Changing IT skills: The impact of outsourcing strategies on in-house capability requirements. *Journal of Electronic Commerce in Organizations*, 5, 2, 24-25.

[4] Chao, G.T., Walz, P. & Gardner, P.D. 1992. Formal and informal mentorships: A comparison on mentoring functions and contrasts with nonmentored counterparts. *Personnel Psychology*, 45, 3, 619-636.

[5] Greenhaus, J.H, Parasuraman, S. & Wormley, W.M. 1990. Effects of race on organizational experiences, job performance, evaluations, and career outcomes. *Academy of Management Journal*, 33, 1, 64-86.

[6] Igbaria, M. & Chidambaram, L. 1997. The impact of gender on career success of information systems professionals: A human capital perspective. *Information Technology & People*, 10, 1, 63-86.

[7] Igbaria, M., Greenhaus, J.H., & Parasuraman, S. 1991. Career orientations of MIS employees: An empirical analysis, *MIS Quarterly*, 15, 2, 151-169.

[8] Irving, G.P., Coleman, D.F., & Cooper, C.L. 1997. Further assessments of the three-component model of occupational commitment: Generalizability and differences across occupations. *Journal of Applied Psychology*, 82, 3, 444-452.

[9] Kakabadse, A.& Korac-Kakabadse, N. 2000. Leading the pack: Future role of IS/IT professionals. *Journal of Management Development*, 19, 2, 97-155.

[10] Kram, K.E. 1985. *Mentoring at Work*, Scott Foresman, Glenview, IL.

[11] Kram, K.E. 1983. Phases of the mentor relationship. *Academy of Management Journal*, 26, 4, 608-625.

[12] Lankau, M.J. and Scandura, T.A. 2002. An investigation of personal learning in mentoring relationships: Content,

antecedents, and consequences. *Academy of Management Journal*, 45, 4, 779-790.

[13] Levina, N. and Vaast, E. 2008. Innovating or doing as told? Status differences and overlapping boundaries in offshore collaboration. *MIS Quarterly*, 32, 2, 307-332.

[14] Moore, J.E. 2000. One road to turnover: An examination of work exhaustion in technology professionals. *MIS Quarterly*, 24, 1, 141-168.

[15] Lacity, M.C., Iyer, V.V., and Rudramuniyaiah, P.S. 2008. Turnover intentions of Indian IS professionals. *Information Systems Frontiers*, 10, 2, 225-241.

[16] Mayer, J.P., Allen, N.J, & Smith, C.A. (1993). Commitment to organizations and occupations: Extension and test of a three-component conceptualization. *Journal of Applied Psychology*, 78, 4, 538-551.

[17] Nagy, M.S. 2002. Using a single item approach to measure facet job satisfaction. *Journal of Occupational and Organizational Psychology*, 75, 77-86.

[18] Pan, W., Sun, L.Y., & Chow, I.H.S. 2011. The impact of supervisory mentoring on personal learning and career outcomes: The dual moderating effect of self-efficacy. *Journal of Vocational Behavior, 78,* 264-273.

[19] Payne S.C. and Huffman A.H. 2005. A longitudinal examination of the influence of mentoring on organizational commitment and turnover. *Academy of Management Journal,* 48, 158–168.

[20] Ragins, B.R. & Cotton, J.L. 1999. Mentor functions and outcomes: A comparison of men and women in formal and informal mentoring relationships. *Journal of Applied Psychology*, 84, 4, 529-550.

[21] Sethi, V., King, R.C., and Quick, J.C., 2004. What causes stress in information systems professionals? *Communications of the ACM*, 47, 3 (March), 99-102.

[22] Shearer, M., Maddux, J.E., Mercandante, B., Prentice-Dunn, S., Jacobs, B., and Rogers, R.W. 1982. The self-efficacy scale: Construction and validation. *Psychological Reports*, 51, 663-671.

[23] Trauth, E.M. 2004. Odd girl out: An individual differences perspective on women in the IT profession. *Information Technology & People*, 15, 2, 98-118.

Measuring Alignment within Relationships among Socio-Technical System Components: A Study of Wiki Technology Use

Andrea Hester
Southern Illinois University Edwardsville
Department of Computer Management and Information Systems
School of Business
Edwardsville, IL 62026-1106

1-618-650-3715

anheste@siue.edu

ABSTRACT

Wiki technology provides capabilities for collaborative knowledge management. Web 2.0 technologies such as wikis eliminate the boundaries of time and space, and support higher levels of social interaction. In order to achieve the highest return from information systems, organizations must match the capabilities of technology with their complex social environments. This research proposes examination of organizational information systems as socio-technical systems that involve interacting relationships among the main components of actors, structure, tasks and technology. Alignment within the relationships will facilitate increased system use; however, gaps in alignment may impede system use and result in poor performance or system failure. The pilot study presented here gives insight into how alignment can be measured by evaluating underlying factors affecting the relationships and subsequent system use.

Categories and Subject Descriptors

H.1.2 [**Models and Principles**]: User/Machine Systems – *human factors*.

H.5.3 [**Information Interfaces and Presentation**]: Group and Organization Interfaces – *collaborative computing*.

General Terms

Management, Human Factors.

Keywords

Socio-technical system, System use, Wiki technology.

1. INTRODUCTION

Fifty years ago, the role of information systems was that of automating manual systems, primarily accounting systems. The chief concern of management at the time was how to get employees to use technology to improve the efficiency and effectiveness of work processes. Training employees to use computers allowed organizations to make the transition to information system utilization. As computer-based systems continued to evolve, implementation issues involved a new set of problems. Information systems users were accustomed to certain systems and were reluctant to change. As the 20th century came to an end, a significant amount of IS research was devoted to change management.

At the turn of the century, networked computer and communication systems were recognized as the new era bringing about change in organizations (Kling, 2000). Today those technologies have matured from Web 1.0 to Web 2.0. Web 2.0 systems and applications advance previous one-way, read-only interaction with the Internet into increased social interaction and connection among users. Web 2.0 technologies facilitate an environment of social computing that promotes user participation and collaboration. These new technologies stimulate a resurgence in IS research that involves focus on social aspects of computing.

Despite the maturation of information systems over the past fifty years, understanding of user acceptance continues to be a difficult and complex process. Innovative technologies, such as Web 2.0, involve layers of complexity rooted in social dynamics. A balance between technological capabilities and the social structures of organizations is needed for successful system outcomes. This paper suggests consideration of socio-technical systems theory as a tool to examine the relationships among the social and technical sub-system components of a work system. We suggest that having even just one of the potential relationships out of alignment can impede utilization and overall performance.

More work on drilling down to the source of potential gaps in alignment within socio-technical systems is needed. This research seeks to answer the question of what are underlying factors related to situations of misalignment. More specifically, we seek to identify dimensions that capture the essence of relationships involving aligning pairs of the socio-technical system components: actors, structure, task and technology. This paper presents a pilot study involving CMIS undergraduate students enrolled in a senior-level project management course. The pilot study aims to provide a detailed delineation of the socio-technical system that is exemplified by the course. In addition to describing and exploring each element of the socio-technical system, this paper provides results of a survey completed by the students at the end of the semester. The survey results are used to formulate constructs of alignment and their influence on system use.

1. RELEVANT THEORY

In seminal work in socio-technical systems theory, Bostrom and Heinen describe the organizational work system as being composed of a social sub-system and a technical sub-system (Bostrom & Heinen, 1977). The social sub-system is comprised of structure and people, and the technical sub-system is comprised of technology and tasks (See Figure 1). Bostrom and Heinen note that management information systems (MIS) have a direct effect on the technical sub-system components. Nonetheless, MIS problems and failures often stem from organizational behavior issues which involve the social sub-system components. In their work, the authors propose that a socio-technical systems approach will provide a realistic view of organizations. Bostrom and Heinen recommend that when designing MIS a deeper understanding of and focused attention on the independent yet interacting components of the socio-technical system is neededThe text should be in two 8.45 cm (3.33") columns with a .83 cm (.33") gutter.

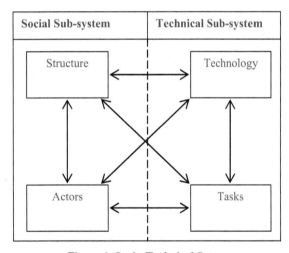

Figure 1. Socio-Technical System.

Maintaining viability and competitive advantage often involves adopting technological advancement (Appelbaum, 1997). More often than not, adopting such technological innovations involves significant change within organizations. Considering the organization as a socio-technical system will provide a basis for applying change methods and techniques to assist in technology adoption. In more recent work, Lyytinen and Newman draw on socio-technical systems theory to develop a model describing information system change as socio-technical events that occur at multiple levels (Lyytinen & Newman, 2008). Table 1 summarizes definitions of each socio-technical system component and adapted descriptions of the nature of the relationships among the components. Lyytinen and Newman describe a "gap" as a misalignment in a given relationship that may cause instability in the system and ultimately reduce system performance.

Table 1. Socio-technical System Components and Relationships

Socio-Technical Components	Definition
Actor	Actors include an organization's members and its main stakeholders who carry out or influence the work.
Structure	The structure covers systems of communication, systems of authority, and systems of workflow. It includes both the normative dimension, that is, values, norms, and general role expectations, and the behavioral dimension, that is the patterns of behavior as actors communicate, exercise authority, or work.
Task	Task describes the work systems goals and purpose and the way in which the work gets done within the organization.
Technology	Technology tools used in the work system.

Component Relationships	Description
Actor-Structure	Following operating procedures, alignment with structure, structures provide support to actors in their tasks
Actor-Task	Actors understand and carry out tasks, actors are trained to perform tasks
Actor-Technology	Actors understand and accept technology, actors adapt technology to environment
Task-Technology	Technology is adequate to support tasks
Task-Structure	Structure is aligned with task, adequate structure defined for tasks
Technology-Structure	Technology is adapted and modified for given structure, structure takes advantage of capabilities of technology

Research addressing issues of change management involving MIS continues to fall short of providing a generalizable approach that focuses too much on technical aspects and not enough on social aspects (Bostrom, Gupta, & Thomas, 2009). The extensive research examining the "fit" between an organization and an information system is often too narrow in scope and neglects to provide an encompassing view of symbiotic entities functioning at multiple levels of analysis (Strong & Volkoff, 2010). More work is needed to examine the interaction between technical and social aspects and the extent to which a gap in a given relationship can be detrimental in successful system use.

2. RESEARCH FRAMEWORK

2.1 Research Site and Environment

The research environment for this study provides a mock organization environment for analysis. The subjects of the study are CMIS undergraduate students enrolled in a senior-level project management course. The course is designed to implement an actual project where students play the part of members of project sub-teams. The socio-technical system demonstrated by the course involves using information systems to plan and develop an application following tenets of project management. The main goal of the project is to design and produce a "University Student Housing Wiki". In addition to the wiki website, other required outputs include various project management deliverables.

2.2 Socio-Technical System Components

The first step in analyzing the research environment is to translate the project management course into a socio-technical work system. The technical sub-system components are technologies and tasks. Two main technologies were used heavily in the course. Microsoft Project was used as the primary project management software. Charting a project from start to finish is one of the goals of the course. The course also used web-based wiki software. The wiki was used by students for task and project management. Also, creating an actual wiki was the end product of the project.

The focus of this pilot study is on the use of wiki technology. Wiki technology can serve as an effective knowledge management system by connecting users and capturing dispersed knowledge. However, learning to share and contribute knowledge remains an unconventional process that requires users to adapt to a new routine of collaboration. For the course, the project tasks were defined by a conjointly created work breakdown structure. In addition to the basic collaboration and project management tasks, the main tasks are to acquire, store and present knowledge of the options for housing for university students.

The social sub-system components are people and structures. The 19 students in the course play the role of the social actors and users of the information systems. The structure is defined by the project sub-teams: design (5 members); implement (7 members); market and evaluate (5 members); and project management (2 members). The design, implement and marketing sub-teams each have a team leader. The project management team is comprised of the project manager and project analyst.

2.3 Model Development

The social and technical sub-systems are each composed of two components, and then each component has an interacting relationship with each other component both inside and outside of their corresponding sub-systems. This gives six relationships: Actor-Structure, Actor-Task, Actor-Technology, Task-Technology, Task-Structure, and Technology-Structure. For this pilot study, the Actor-Task and Actor-Structure relationships were not operationalized. Given the confined and finite nature of the course, tasks and structure were fairly strictly defined and the actors chose their sub-team membership which also determined their set of tasks. The dynamics of these relationships certainly had an influence as discussed later. However, constructs and items for survey testing were not formulated due to the smaller scope of this study.

Performance of the socio-technical system is assessed based on use of the system. As the path to achieving the project goal is to engage in knowledge processes, use of the system should denote that the users are participating in creating a source of knowledge. Other performance outcomes will be discussed; however, for the purposes of measurement, an extensive usage log was maintained to monitor tasks performed in the wiki. Depicted in Figure 2, the research model depicts the socio-technical component relationships and their influence on system use.

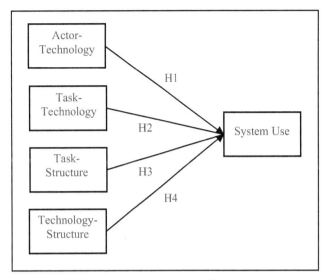

Figure 2. Socio-Technical Alignment.

2.4 Hypotheses

Increased understanding and acceptance of technology by users will strengthen the actor-technology relationship and increase use of the technology.

H1: Alignment among actors and technology will have a positive influence on system use.

Increased user perceptions of alignment among tasks and technology will strengthen the task-technology relationship and increase use of the technology.

H2: Alignment among tasks and technology will have a positive influence on system use.

Increased user perceptions of alignment among tasks and structure will strengthen the task-structure relationship and increase use of the technology.

H3: Alignment among tasks and structure will have a positive influence on system use.

Increased perceptions of alignment among technology and structure will increase use of the technology.

H4: Alignment among technology and structure will have a positive influence on system use.

2.5 Measures

2.5.1 Socio-Technical System Relationships

Four of the six potential relationships among components of the socio-technical system are analyzed in this study. Hierarchical Latent Variable modeling is used to operationalize the four main constructs. Each construct denoting alignment among two components is a second-order latent variable measured by a broad spectrum of dimensions captured by first-order latent variables (see Table 2). Questionnaire items measuring the variables are given in Appendix A. All items were measured on a 7-point Likert scale.

The Actor-Technology relationship is characterized by the actors understanding and accepting the technology. Dimensions that may capture this relationship include perceived ease of use, perceived external control and habit. Perceived ease of use is the degree to which a person believes that using a particular system would be free of effort (Davis, 1989). Perceived external control relates to an individual's perception of the availability of knowledge, resources, and opportunities required to perform the specific behavior (Venkatesh, 2000). When actors are able to easily use the technology or at least perceive that they have the means available to use the technology, we can say that the actor and technology are aligned. Perceived ease of use and perceived external control address the understanding portion of the relationship between actor and technology. The notion of habit addresses the accepting portion of the relationship. Habit refers to the non-deliberate, automatically inculcated response that individuals may bring to IS usage (Limayem & Hirt, 2003). Habit represents full acceptance of technology.

Table 2. Relationship Constructs and Measures

Construct	First-order Latent Variables
Actor-Technology Alignment	• Perceived Ease of Use • Perceived External Control • Habit
Task-Technology Alignment	• Perceived Usefulness • Flexibility • Task-Technology Fit
Task-Structure Alignment	• Enjoyment in Helping Others • Reciprocity Expectation • Social Loafing
Technology-Structure Alignment	• Social Presence • Group Well-Being • Member Support

System users need to perceive that the technology is adequate to support the tasks. Dimensions that may capture the relationship between task and technology include flexibility, perceived usefulness, and task-technology fit. As users proceed through their work processes, they need the technology to adapt to their tasks. Flexibility refers to the way the system adapts to changing demands of the user (Wixom & Todd, 2005). While flexibility gives an indicator of capability to perform tasks, users also want the technology to have an impact when it comes to their performance. Perceived usefulness is the degree to which a person believes that using a particular system would enhance his or her job performance (Davis, 1989). Finally, a straight-forward approach to measuring the task-technology relationship is to incorporate the established dimensions of Task-Technology Fit Theory. Task-technology fit refers to the congruence among the perceived capabilities of technology, task requirements, and the competence of users with the task and the systems (Goodhue, 1998).

The task-structure relationship is described as having adequate structure defined for tasks. Structure involves the norms and behaviors associated with the systems of authority and workflow. The approach taken here is to use dimensions that capture the perceptions that engaging in the required tasks will be valued by peers and superiors within the structure. The proposed dimensions include enjoyment in helping others, reciprocity expectation, and social loafing. Enjoyment in helping others refers to the perception of pleasure obtained from helping others through knowledge contributed to a knowledge system (Kankanhalli, Tan, & Wei, 2005). Enjoyment in helping others focuses on contributing freely, while reciprocity expectation emphasizes contributing with the presumption that the relationship will be give and take. Reciprocity expectation is the belief that current contribution to a knowledge system would lead to future request for knowledge being met (Kankanhalli, et al., 2005). On the other hand, users may also have negative feelings regarding contribution. Social loafing refers to the behavior in

which an individual tends to exert less effort when working with others than when working alone (Lin & Huang, 2009).

The relationship between technology and structure can be described as the technology being adapted and modified for a given structure, and the structure takes advantage of capabilities of technology. When using a technology as a collaborative knowledge management tool, the capabilities of the technology should foster a cooperative and supportive environment. Awareness of this kind of accommodating environment may be measured as perceptions of group well-being and perceptions of member support. Also, collaborative technologies have the capability of ubiquitous computing that allows users to participate and contribute any time and any place. While these capabilities provide many advantages, users still have a need for human contact. Social presence is a technology's ability to convey the psychological impression of the physical presence of its users (Brown, Dennis, & Venkatesh, 2010). The proposed dimensions of group well-being, member support and social presence are indicative of perceptions of technology-facilitated cohesiveness and connectivity. These perceptions may in turn strengthen the task-structure relationship.

2.5.2 Dependent Variable

Measures for the dependent variable of system use include both self-reported and actual measures of usage. This study attempts to capture a more rich assessment of self-reported usage by measuring usage according to three dimensions: frequency, duration and choice (Burton-Jones & Straub, 2006). The scale to measure frequency is less than once a month, once or twice per month, several times per month, several times per week, once or twice per day, or several times per day. The scale to measure duration is almost never, less than 1/2 hour, 1/2 - 1 hour, 1 - 2 hours, 2 - 3 hours, or more than 3 hours. The scale for choice indicates percentage of time the technology was used, measured as 0 - 19%, 20 - 39%, 40 - 59%, 60 - 79%, or 80 - 100%. The validity of self-reported usage is a highly debated topic. Therefore, this study also includes actual usage. One of the advantages of wiki technology is the ability to track history, and if necessary roll-back to previous versions. As each transaction occurs in the wiki, it is recorded in the history and users have the option of receiving email notification of transactions. The transaction log was recorded and analyzed to provide a measure of actual usage. For the analysis, transactions were classified into nine categories: Communicate, Add Page Content, Edit/Modify Page Content, Delete Page Content, Roll Back, Organize Page Content, Organize Wiki, Link/Tag, and File Management. The Add, Edit/Modify, and Delete categories were further delineated according to number and size of elements, with elements pertaining to the actual text in terms of letters, words, sentences, and paragraphs. Using this taxonomy, each transaction was documented according to user. The usage was then summarized and categorized in terms of very low (less than 6 transactions), low (6-22 transactions), moderate (23-42 transactions) and high usage (more than 42 transactions), denoted by a scale from 1 to 4.

3. RESEARCH ANALYSIS

3.1 Method

The partial least squares (PLS) method was used to examine the hypotheses. PLS is recommended as an analysis method for complex models focusing on prediction, and allows for minimal demands on measurement scales, sample size, and residual distribution (Chin, Marcolin, & Newsted, 2003). PLS also allows for hierarchical latent variable models, necessary for this research model (Wetzels, Odekerken-Schröder, & van Oppen, 2009). A two-stage analysis was performed using confirmatory factor analysis to assess the measurement model followed by examination of the structural relationships. Path modeling and analysis was performed using Smart-PLS (Ringle, Wende, & Will, 2005).

3.2 Empirical Findings

In the first stage of analysis, the measurement model was assessed for reliability and validity (see Appendix B). Reliability was assessed by composite reliability and the average variance extracted (AVE). The composite reliability scores exceed the recommended threshold of 0.70 (Chin, 2010). The AVE scores exceed the recommended threshold of 0.50. Appendix B also presents the squared correlations among constructs. Discriminant validity is assessed as follows. If we see that the AVE for a given construct is higher than the squared correlation with any other variable, then this indicates that the construct is more highly related to its own measures than to other constructs. As opposed to previous methods of displaying the correlations and square root of AVE, this updated method allows for discerning of the differences more easily (Chin, 2010). Convergent and discriminant validity are also evident when each indicator loads higher on the corresponding construct than on the other constructs. The item indicator cross-loadings indicated sufficient convergent and discriminant validity.

The second stage of analysis assessed the structural model, including examination of path coefficients and the R^2 value. The path between Actor-Technology Alignment and System Use resulted in a significant positive path. The paths between the other three relationships and System Use were not significant. Figure 3 presents the resulting path values and R^2 value.

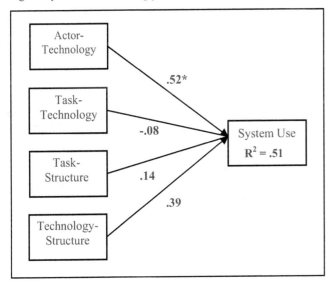

Figure 2. Socio-Technical Alignment.

Hypotheses 1 through 4 examine the relationship between the independent variables representing alignment among socio-technical system components and the dependent variable of system use. Results are based on the t-test with the corresponding t-values and p-values given in Table 3. Supported hypotheses are indicated with an x and corresponding p-value highlighted with bold text. H1 was supported; however, H2, H3, and H4 were not supported.

Table 3. Relationship Constructs and Measures

Hypothesis		t-value	p-value
H1:	Alignment among actor and technology will have a positive influence on system use. **X**	1.58	**.05**
H2:	Alignment among task and technology will have a positive influence on system use.	0.18	.43
H3:	Alignment among task and structure will have a positive influence on system use.	0.43	.33
H4:	Alignment among technology and structure will have a positive influence on system use.	0.90	.18

4. DISCUSSION AND CLOSING REMARKS

The research presented in this paper is a pilot study and is subject to limitations. The sample size is rather small; however, the results may still give an indication as to the appropriateness of the dimensions chosen to represent the alignment relationships. Conclusions can be drawn from the analysis results. Hypothesis H1 was supported by the data. This may be interpreted to mean that an alignment among actor and technology was present and had a positive influence on system use. Hypotheses H2, H3, and H4 were not supported, indicating a possible misalignment among the corresponding components.

Further insight may be provided by the observations of the students over the duration of the course. At the beginning of the course, students were able to make a choice as to which sub-team to participate in. Many students chose the implement sub-team which may be an indication of their desire to be more hands-on with the project and eager to use the technology. The implement sub-team did appear to be heavier users of the wiki. Each of the teams had strong team leaders; however, the project manager did not perform as well as expected. The project manager was more of a reporter than a leader. He tended to collect information and give status reports, yet he did not serve as a strong leader of the whole group. The implement team kept the wiki updated with their progress, but the project manager wanted separate update reports as opposed to just monitoring the wiki. These observations may be indicators of misalignment in several areas, including the relationship that was not measured, actor-structure. Furthermore, although many students did participate in the wiki with moderate to heavy levels of usage, there were also situations of very low to low levels of usage. The reluctant users may have had issues with any of the three relationships that were not shown to have a significant influence on usage. In particular, the market and evaluate sub-team may not have had a strong sense of task-technology alignment. Although they were encouraged to use the wiki for basic collaboration and communication tasks, the market and evaluate members did not need to use the wiki for their main project tasks. The design sub-team also presented an interesting observation. As the members worked on designing the various pages of the end-product wiki, they used Microsoft Word to provide the layout for each page. Thus, despite the significant positive impact of actor-technology alignment on system use, the design members may have been exhibiting habitual use of Microsoft Office as opposed to taking full advantage of the capabilities of wiki technology. Overall, the performance of the project team as a whole was viewed favorably by both the instructor, and the customer (in this case the University Housing department).

Despite the limitations, the research presented here provides a first step in a rigorous effort to develop a model that captures the essence of alignment of relationships among socio-technical system components. User acceptance and change management continue to be important topics for both researchers and practitioners. The model proposed here provides measures that may reveal predictive indicators for increased information system use. Further research should involve a larger data sample as well as multiple environments exhibiting a variety of actors, structures, tasks and technologies.

5. REFERENCES

[1] Appelbaum, S. H. 1997. Socio-Technical Systems Theory: an Intervention Strategy for Organizational Development. *Management Decision, 35*(6), 452-463.

[2] Bostrom, R. P., Gupta, S., & Thomas, D. 2009. A Meta-Theory for Understanding Information Systems Within Sociotechnical Systems. *Journal of Management Information Systems, 26*(1), 17-47.

[3] Bostrom, R. P., & Heinen, J. S. 1977. MIS Problems and Failures: A Socio-Technical Perspective; Part I: The Causes. *MIS Quarterly, 1*(3), 17-32.

[4] Brown, S. A., Dennis, A., & Venkatesh, V. 2010. Predicting Collaboration Technology Use: Integrating Technology Adoption and Collaboration Research. *Journal of Management Information Systems, 27*(2), 9-53.

[5] Burton-Jones, A., & Straub Jr., D. W. 2006. Reconceptualizing System Usage: An Approach and Empirical Test. *Information Systems Research, 17*(3), 228-246.

[6] Chin, W. W. 2010. How to Write Up and Report PLS Analyses. In V. Esposito Vinzi, W. W. Chin, J. Henseler & H. Wang (Eds.), *Handbook of Partial Least Squares* (1st ed., pp. 655-690). Verlag Berlin Heidelberg: Springer.

[7] Chin, W. W., Marcolin, B. L., & Newsted, P. R. 2003. A Partial Least Squares Latent Variable Modeling Approach for Measuring Interaction Effects: Results from a Monte Carlo Simulation, Study and an Electronic-Mail Emotion/Adoption Study. *Information Systems Research, 14*(2), 189-217.

[8] Davis, F. 1989. Perceived Usefulness, Perceived Ease of Use, and User Acceptance of Information Technology. *MIS Quarterly, 13*(3), 319-339.

[9] Dennis, A. R., & Reinicke, B. A. 2004. Beta Versus VHS and the Acceptance of Electronic Brainstorming Technology. *MIS Quarterly, 28*(1), 1-20.

[10] Goodhue, D. L. 1998. Development and Measurement Validity of a Task-Technology Fit Instrument for User Evaluations of Information Systems. *Decision Sciences, 29*(1), 105-131.

[11] Kankanhalli, A., Tan, B. C. Y., & Wei, K.-K. 2005. Contributing Knowledge to Electronic Knowledge Repositories: An Empirical Investigation. *Management Information Systems Quarterly, 29*(1), 113-143.

[12] Kling, R. 2000. Learning About Information Technologies and Social Change: The Contribution of Social Informatics. *The Information Society, 16*(3), 217-232.

[13] Limayem, M., & Hirt, S. G. 2003. Force of Habit and Information Systems Usage: Theory and Initial Validation. *Journal of the Association for Information Systems, 4*, 65-97.

[14] Lin, T.-C., & Huang, C.-C. 2009. Understanding social loafing in knowledge contribution from the perspectives of justice and trust. *Expert Systems with Applications, 36*(3, Part 2), 6156-6163.

[15] Lyytinen, K., & Newman, M. 2008. Explaining Information Systems Change: A Punctuated Socio-Technical Change Model. *European Journal of Information Systems, 17*, 589-613.

[16] Ringle, C. M., Wende, S., & Will, A. (2005). SmartPLS (Version 2.0 beta). Hamburg, Germany: University of Hamburg.

[17] Strong, D. M., & Volkoff, O. 2010. Understanding Organization-Enterprise System Fit: A Path to Theorizing the Information Technology Artifact. *MIS Quarterly, 34*(4), 731-756.

[18] Venkatesh, V. 2000. Determinants of Perceived Ease of Use: Integrating Control, Intrinsic Motivation, and Emotion into the Technology Acceptance Model. *Information Systems Research, 11*(4), 342.

[19] Wetzels, M., Odekerken-Schröder, G., & van Oppen, C. 2009. Using PLS Path Modeling for Assessing Hierarchical Construct Models: Guidelines and Empirical Illustration. *Management Information Systems Quarterly, 33*(1), 177-195.

[20] Wixom, B. H., & Todd, P. A. 2005. A Theoretical Integration of User Satisfaction and Technology Acceptance. *Information Systems Research, 16*(1), 85-102.

6. APPENDIX A

Survey Items for First-Order Constructs

First-Order Construct	Items	Source
Perceived Ease of Use	• Learning to operate PBWorks is easy for me. • I find it easy to get PBWorks to do what I want it to do. • It is easy for me to become skillful at using PBWorks.	(Davis, 1989)
Perceived External Control	• I have control over using PBWorks. • I have the knowledge necessary to use PBWorks. • Given the resources, opportunities and knowledge it takes to use PBWorks, it would be easy for me to use PBWorks.	(Venkatesh, 2000)
Habit	• The use of PBWorks has become a habit for me. • I don't even think twice before using PBWorks. • Using PBWorks has become natural to me.	(Limayem & Hirt, 2003)
Perceived Usefulness	• Using PBWorks enhances my productivity in the CMIS 470 project. • I find PBWorks useful in my activities for the CMIS 470 project. • Using PBWorks improves my performance in the CMIS 470 project.	(Davis, 1989)
Flexibility	• PBWorks can be adapted to meet a variety of needs. • PBWorks can flexibly adjust to new demands or conditions. • PBWorks is versatile in addressing needs as they arise.	(Wixom & Todd, 2005)
Task-Technology Fit	• The functionalities of PBWorks were very adequate. • The functionalities of PBWorks were very appropriate. • The functionalities of PBWorks were very useful.	(Goodhue, 1998)
Enjoyment in Helping Others	• I like helping other people by sharing my knowledge, ideas or work. • I enjoy sharing my knowledge, ideas or work with my team mates. • It feels good to help someone else by sharing my knowledge, ideas or work.	(Kankanhalli, Tan, & Wei, 2005)
Reciprocity Expectation	• When I share my knowledge, ideas or work with team mates, I believe that I will get an answer for giving an answer. • When I share my knowledge, ideas or work with team mates, I expect somebody to respond when I'm in need. • When I contribute knowledge to my team, I expect to get back knowledge when I need it.	(Kankanhalli, et al., 2005)
Social Loafing	• During meeting times devoted to group work for the CMIS 470 project . . . • I contribute less knowledge, ideas or work than I know I can. • I give less effort on group work than other members. • I take it easy if others are around contributing to the group work.	(Lin & Huang, 2009)
Social Presence	• Using PBWorks to interact with others creates a warm environment for communication and/or collaboration. • Using PBWorks to interact with others creates a sociable environment for communication and/or collaboration. • Using PBWorks to interact with others creates a personal environment for communication and/or collaboration.	(Brown, Dennis, & Venkatesh, 2010)
Perceived Group Well-Being	• PBWorks contributes to my team's cohesiveness. • PBWorks helps my team to socialize and develop relationships. • PBWorks helps me to build and maintain my team as an intact and continuing social group.	(Dennis & Reinicke, 2004)
Perceived Member Support	• PBWorks contributes to the individual growth and development of team members. • PBWorks is a good way to interact with my teammates. • PBWorks is a good way to find out what people know and to build networks.	(Dennis & Reinicke, 2004)

7. APPENDIX B

	CRE	AVE	PEOU	PExCont	Habit	Actor-Tech	PUsf	Flex	TTF	Task-Tech	EnjHelp	RecEx	SocLoaf	Task-Struct	SocPres	GrpWell	MemSupp	Tech-Struct	SysUse
Ease of Use	0.89	0.73	1.00																
External Control	0.88	0.70	0.68	1.00															
Habit	0.90	0.75	0.49	0.64	1.00														
Actor-Technology Alignment	0.93	0.62	0.81	0.90	0.83	1.00													
Usefulness	0.95	0.85	0.24	0.29	0.40	0.37	1.00												
Flexibility	0.90	0.74	0.24	0.40	0.33	0.37	0.30	1.00											
Task-Tech Fit	0.92	0.79	0.34	0.45	0.36	0.44	0.51	0.70	1.00										
Task-Technology Alignment	0.94	0.63	0.35	0.48	0.46	0.50	0.74	0.76	0.90	1.00									
Enjoyment in Helping	0.93	0.82	0.02	0.00	0.00	0.00	0.01	0.12	0.16	0.10	1.00								
Reciprocity	0.91	0.77	0.17	0.09	0.12	0.14	0.08	0.33	0.39	0.30	0.63	1.00							
Social Loafing	0.90	0.75	0.04	0.05	0.05	0.06	0.01	0.14	0.10	0.08	0.21	0.36	1.00						
Task-Structure Alignment	0.69	0.58	0.09	0.04	0.06	0.06	0.04	0.26	0.28	0.20	0.78	0.88	0.58	1.00					
Social Presence	0.93	0.82	0.33	0.30	0.30	0.37	0.35	0.51	0.68	0.64	0.12	0.33	0.05	0.21	1.00				
Group Well-being	0.88	0.71	0.19	0.15	0.18	0.20	0.38	0.24	0.47	0.46	0.05	0.22	0.03	0.12	0.74	1.00			
Member Support	0.74	0.48	0.26	0.32	0.30	0.35	0.25	0.51	0.65	0.57	0.13	0.32	0.10	0.23	0.89	0.73	1.00		
Technology-Structure Alignment	0.93	0.62	0.29	0.27	0.28	0.33	0.37	0.45	0.65	0.61	0.10	0.31	0.06	0.20	0.95	0.89	0.93	1.00	
System Use	0.70	0.50	0.25	0.41	0.39	0.43	0.31	0.16	0.19	0.29	0.01	0.10	0.01	0.02	0.33	0.27	0.26	0.32	1.00

Organizational Uses of the Crowd: Developing a Framework for the Study of Crowdsourcing

Lee B. Erickson
The Pennsylvania State University
College of Information Sciences
and Technology
703-625-7966

lbe108@psu.edu

Irene Petrick
The Pennsylvania State University
College of Information Sciences
and Technology
814-867-1336

lpetrick@ist.psu.edu

Eileen M. Trauth
The Pennsylvania State University
College of Information Sciences
and Technology
814-865-6457

etrauth@ist.psu.edu

ABSTRACT

"Crowdsourcing" is commonly defined as the use of large groups of individuals by organizations to perform tasks traditionally performed by employees or designated agents. Currently, organizations are turning to the crowd to complete a wide variety of organization tasks. However, we know little about the types of tasks completed, the different crowds that participate, and the characteristics that manifest themselves in these initiatives. Preliminary findings from a grounded theory study designed to identify patterns and themes found in crowdsourced initiatives have revealed four common uses of the crowd (i.e., productivity, innovation, knowledge capture, and marketing/branding). Additionally, reoccurring themes related to the knowledge the crowd brings to the task, the location of the crowd, as well as organizational challenges and value capture have been identified. Emerging patterns and relationships among the four identified uses and these reoccurring themes are discussed.

Categories and Subject Descriptors

D.2.9 [**Management**]: Productivity.
K.6.1 [**People and People Management**]: Strategic information systems planning

General Terms

Management, Performance, Theory.

Keywords

crowdsourcing, productivity, innovation, knowledge capture, marketing/branding, grounded theory, framework, research in progress

1. INTRODUCTION

P&G, a multi-national manufacturer, is struggling to find a way to inject fluoride powder into toothpaste tubes without releasing it into the air. Pepsi is looking for the next great flavor for the Mountain Dew line along with the name, logo, label design, and advertising pitch. NetFlix needs a more accurate way to predict movie preferences for its rental customers. And, The Guardian

newspaper needs to search through 500,000 expense claims documents to identify potential erroneous claims. While these organizations face radically different challenges, each is leveraging online technologies to reach out to the "crowd" for help. The act of a company or institution turning to the crowd to complete tasks once performed by employees or designated agents is commonly referred to as "crowdsourcing" [11]. Social media tools now allow companies to more easily connect with the crowd. As such, IT executives and professionals are faced with deciding whether, and how, the crowd can be leveraged as a new source of productivity, innovation, knowledge, and creativity. Currently, we know little about which crowd best supports different organizational needs or what challenges and value such initiatives bring. Do different crowds bring different skills? Do different tasks require different crowds? What are the benefits and potential risks of turning to the crowd?

This paper presents preliminary results from an ongoing research study designed to identify trends and patterns associated with the use of the crowd by established organizations. As the focus of the research is on established businesses, we do not address new businesses built on a crowdsourcing model. Additionally, because crowdsourcing is a relatively new and emergent phenomenon with limited empirical research and theory, a grounded approach to building theory is taken [19]. In line with grounded theory methods, an initial literature review was conducted for the purposes of identifying the problem to be addressed [8]. A more thorough literature review that is grounded in the emergent theory has yet to be conducted as analysis and theory building is still ongoing [6].

2. LITERATURE REVIEW

Within both academic and business literature, crowdsourcing is commonly used to refer to any type of online activity that includes a large group of people [1, 4, 5, 10, 12]. Studies vary greatly in terms of the definition of crowdsourcing, the tasks completed by the crowd, as well as the risks and benefits to organizations. Frameworks describing and identifying relevant characteristics of crowdsourcing vary with respect to the characteristics deemed most relevant [2, 4, 7, 14, 16, 20, 21, 22, 24, 26]. Further, organizations report both tangible and intangible benefits [13], while others experience less positive outcomes [15].

Early work has been instrumental in helping to understand the phenomenon of crowdsourcing at a broad level. However, we are only just beginning to understand who the "crowd" is and what characteristics are most desirable to organizations. Such understanding is critical in extending theory related to this new phenomenon [25], as well as providing guidance to corporations who wish to implement such initiatives.

3. RESEARCH STUDY

The goal of this research is to identify key characteristics of crowdsourcing with the purpose of building explanatory theory to provide greater understanding of the relationships at play [9]. Further, as the goal of this research is to uncover patterns of use within organizational contexts, an interpretivist qualitative approach is taken [17].

3.1 Data Collection and Analysis

The first round of data collection consisted of two primary data sources. First, a preliminary review of academic crowdsourcing literature was conducted. In total, 71 publications (i.e., peer-reviewed journal articles, conference papers, and books) across a wide variety of disciplines were reviewed. Additionally, to uncover patterns of use within contextual setting, a series of semi-structured interviews were conducted with practitioners currently leveraging the crowd to complete one or more organizational tasks. Interviews lasted between 60-90 minutes each and a flexible interview protocol with open-ended questions focused discussions on organizational motivations for leveraging the crowd, the specific tasks to be completed, and perceived impacts on the organization. A total of 29 interviews were conducted with individuals holding managerial and lower-lever positions within six large organizations representing a variety of industries. Data were analyzed using grounded theory techniques to elicit emergent themes.

4. PRELIMINARY FINDINGS

In line with grounded theory techniques, patterns and trends are unfolding through an iterative process of data collection, coding, and categorization [3, 18]. While data collection and analysis is still in progress, initial categories are emerging. Next, an overview of identified categories is presented. This is followed by a discussion of a preliminary framework outlining characteristics and patterns across categories.

4.1 Emergent Framework

Through identification, constant comparison, and grouping of characteristics commonly associated with crowdsourcing, five reoccurring themes have emerged, specifically: 1) common tasks performed by the crowd, 2) crowd knowledge, 3) crowd location, 4) organizational challenges, and 5) the value to organizations (see Table 1).

4.1.1 Common Tasks

While organizations leverage the crowd for a variety of different reasons, six common tasks emerged from the data: 1) completion of routine time-consuming activities (e.g., tagging images), 2) collection of distributed data (e.g., as training data for product algorithms), 3) sharing of knowledge (e.g., for customer service), 4) marketing (e.g., creation of advertising), 5) product innovation (e.g., ideation for new or improved products), and 6) complex problem solving (e.g., difficult R&D issues).

4.1.2 Crowd Knowledge

Across this variety of tasks, five different types of crowd knowledge have been identified: 1) general, 2) situational (e.g., event or location based), 3) product/service, 4) specialized (e.g., graphic design) and 5) domain expertise (e.g., chemistry). For example, when leveraging the crowd for translation of documents from English to Spanish, individuals must have specialized knowledge in English, Spanish, and typing. However, when verifying the transfer of numbers from one document to another only general knowledge is needed.

Table 1. Emergent Themes Related to Crowdsourcing

Emergent Themes	Characteristics
Common Tasks	-Routine time-consuming activities -Data collection -Knowledge sharing -Marketing -Ideation -Design -Development -Filtration -Evaluation -Complex problem solving
Crowd Knowledge	-General -Situational (e.g., time, place, event) -Product/Service (i.e., specific to the sponsoring organization) -Specialized (e.g., graphic design, programming) -Domain expertise (e.g., chemistry, medical)
Crowd Location	-Internal (i.e., employees) -External (e.g., trusted partners, communities of practice/science, customers, general public)
Organizational Challenges	-Accuracy/Quality of work -Availability -IP leakage/Loss of competitive advantage -Clear articulation of the task -Internal acceptance/buy-in -Motivation of the crowd -Loss of control
Value Capture	-Tangible (e.g., financial) -Intangible (e.g., awareness) -Immediate (e.g., cost savings) -Delayed (e.g., after commercialization of ideas)

4.1.3 Crowd Location

The targeted crowd is often influenced by factors such as the organization's access to the crowd, the experimental nature of the initiative, and the organization's need for secrecy or transparency. As such, crowds can be broken into two broad categories, internal and external. "Internal" crowds consist of employees whose jobs do not generally include participation in the task to be completed. "External" crowds include individuals outside the organization such as communities of practice, customers, and the general public.

4.1.4 Organizational Challenges

Crowdsourcing also brings unique challenges and issues for organizations. Common issues include how best to ensure accuracy and quality of work, how to ensure the crowd will be available when needed, and how to reduce risks related to IP leakage or loss of competitive advantage. Additionally, common organizational concerns include difficulties related to clearly articulating the task to be completed, gaining internal acceptance/buy-in, motivating the crowd, and losing control over the process and outputs.

4.1.5 Value Capture

The value organizations realize from turning to the crowd also varies. Benefits can be both tangible, such as reduction in costs, as well as intangible, such as fostering brand affinity or creating a more innovative culture. Additionally, benefits may be immediate or delayed.

While work is still in progress, patterns are beginning to emerge across identified themes. Continued data collection and analysis is in progress to further conceptualize the data, identify patterns and linkages, and clarifying categories. As theory solidifies, additional theoretical sampling may be required to reach theoretical saturation and to facilitate the formation of substantive theory [23].

5. DISCUSSION

The five emergent themes described above lay the foundation for a framework identifying key uses of the crowd. As data analysis continues, patterns and relationships between these themes continue to emerge. Specifically, the seven common tasks that have been identified to date have been further collapsed into a core category of "use" that includes: 1) productivity, 2) innovation, 3) knowledge capture, and 4) marketing/branding. Data also suggests that each use may map to specific crowd characteristics as well as specific organizational challenges and value (see Table 2).

For example, when leveraging the crowd for *productivity*, organizations are attempting to reduce costs associated with routine,

time-consuming tasks that are difficult to automate. Tasks may require general knowledge, such as matching numbers across documents, or specialized knowledge as when translating documents from one language to another. Because organizations are attempting to reduce costs, external crowds are most desirable as costs are typically lower and limited overhead is incurred. Organizational challenges include ensuring the crowd completes the task when needed and at the quality required. This may be particularly problematic when outputs and deadlines are associated with product/service offerings to customers. Finally, if successful, value is typically tangible and immediate (e.g., immediate reduction in costs).

On the other hand, when the crowd is used for innovation such as to generate ideas for new product innovation, organizations are looking to retain or gain competitive advantage by supplementing current resources (most typically internal R&D groups). Organizations are looking for diverse crowds to increase the likelihood of generating unique or novel ideas. Because a common concern with these types of initiatives is leakage of new ideas or loss of competitive advantage organizations often look to internal crowds to help with ideation. Further, issues related to buy-in or acceptance of the crowd as an appropriate and useful source of innovation are common especially in contexts where innovation has previously been the responsibility of in-house R&D teams. Because ideas must be vetted and commercialized before value can be captured, tangible benefits in terms of profits are often delayed.

Table 2: Preliminary Framework for Crowdsourcing Uses and Key Characteristics

	Productivity	Innovation	Knowledge Capture	Marketing/Branding
Organizational Motivation	- Reduction in costs - **Replacing** current resources	- Retaining/Gaining competitive advantage, increasing innovative potential - **Supplementing** current resources	- Advancing understanding or accuracy - **Creating** new knowledge resource	- Increasing profits and brand affinity - **Supplementing** current resources
Common Tasks	- Routine, time-consuming tasks difficult to automate	- Ideation - Evaluation - Filtration - Design - Development - Problem solving	- Data collection - Knowledge sharing	- Creative - Market insights
Crowd Knowledge	- General - Specialized	- Product/Service - Specialized - Domain expertise	- Product/Service - Situational - Domain expertise	- Product/Service - Specialized
Crowd Location	- External	- Internal - External	- Internal - External	- External
Organizational Challenges	- Accuracy/Quality of work - Availability	- IP leakage/loss of competitive advantage - Clear articulation of the task - Internal acceptance/buy-in	- Motivating the crowd to share	- Control of the crowd
Value Capture	- Tangible - Immediate	- Tangible - Delayed	- Tangible - Immediate and delayed	- Tangible - Immediate and delayed

6. CONCLUSION AND FUTURE WORK

Based on a review of literature and interviews with practitioners, a preliminary framework matching organizational need to key characteristics of the crowd has been presented. Data analysis to date suggests four common organizational uses of the crowd as well as specific patterns related to each use. The theoretical contribution of this study is the development of a framework from which researchers may begin to further define key uses and characteristics of crowdsourcing. Additionally, its contribution to practice is the development of preliminary guidelines for matching the right crowd to the right job.

7. REFERENCES

[1] Archak, N. (2010). Money, glory and entry deterrence: Analyzing strategic behavior of contestants in simultaneous crowdsourcing contests on TopCoder.com. Proceedings of *The 19th International Conference on World Wide Web*, 21-30.

[2] Bonabeau, E. (2009, Winter). Decision 2.0: The power of collective intelligence. *MIT Sloan Management Review*, 50(2), 45-52.

[3] Bryant, A. & Charmaz, K. (2007). *The SAGE Handbook of Grounded Theory*. London: SAGE Publications.

[4] Chanal, V., & Caron-Fasan, M. L. (2008, May). How to invent a new business model based on crowdsourcing: The Crowdspirit case. Paper presented at the *Conférence de l'Association Internationale de Management Stratégique*, Nice.

[5] Chilton, S. (2009). Crowdsourcing is radically changing the geodata landscape: Case study of OpenStreetMap. Paper presented at the *24th International Cartographic Conference*, Chile.

[6] Dey, I. (2007). Grounding categories. In A. Bryant & K. Charmaz (Eds.), *The SAGE Handbook of Grounded Theory*, (pp. 167-190). London: SAGE Publications.

[7] Feller, J., Finnegan, P., Hayes, J., & O'Reilly, P. (2009). Institutionalizing information asymmetry: Governance structures for open innovation. *Information Technology & People*, 22(4),

[8] Glaser, B. G. & Strauss, A. L., (1967). *The Discovery of Grounded Theory: Strategies for Qualitative Research*. Chicago: Aldine Publishing Company.

[9] Gregor, S. (2006, September). The nature of theory in information systems. *MIS Quarterly*, 30(3), 611-642.

[10] Halavais, A. (2009, April). Do dugg diggers Digg diligently? Feedback as motivation in collaborative moderation systems. *Information, Communications & Society*, 12(3), 444-459.

[11] Howe, J. (2006). *Crowdsourcing: A definition*. Retrieved November 30, 2009 from http://www.crowdsourcing.typepad.com/cs/2006/06/crowdsourcing_a.html.

[12] Howe, J. (2008). *Crowdsourcing: Why the power of the crowd is driving the future of business*. New York: Crown Business.

[13] Jouret, G. (2009). Inside Cisco's Search for the Next Big Idea. *Harvard Business Review*, 87(9), 43.

[14] Kleemann, F., Voß, G. G., & Rieder, K. (2008, July). Un(der)paid innovators: The commercial utilization of consumer work through crowdsourcing. *Science, Technology & Innovation Studies*, 4(1) 5-26.

[15] Knudsen, M. P., & Mortensen, T. B. (2011). Some immediate – but negative – effects of openness on product development performance. *Technovation*, 31(1), 54-64.

[16] Malone, Laubacher, R., & Dellarocas, C. (2010). The Collective Intelligence Genome. *MIT Sloan Management Review*, 51(3), 21-31.

[17] Meyers, M. D. (1997). Qualitative research in information systems. *MIS Quarterly,* 21(2), 241-42.

[18] Meyers, M.D. (2009). *Qualitative Research in Business Management*. London: SAGE Publications Ltd.

[19] Orlikowski, W. (1993). CASE Tools as organizational change: Investigating incremental and radical changes in systems development. *MIS Quarterly*, 7(3), 309-340.

[20] Reichwald, R., Seifert, S., Walcher, D., & Piller F. (2004, January). Customers as part of value webs: Towards a framework for webbed customer innovation tools. Proceedings from *37th Hawaii International Conference on System Sciences*.

[21] Sawhney, M., Verona, G., & Prandelli, W. (2005, Autumn). Collaborating to create: The Internet as a platform for customer engagement in product innovation. *Journal of Interactive Marketing*, 19(4), 1-14.

[22] Schenk, E. & Guittard, C. (2009). Crowdsourcing: What can be outsourced to the crowd and why? Manuscript. Retrieved from L'archive ouverte pluridiciplinaire database.

[23] Stern, P. N. (2007). On solid ground: Essential properties for growing grounded theory. In A. Bryant & K. Charmaz (Eds.), *The SAGE Handbook of Grounded Theory*, (pp. 114-126). London: SAGE Publications.

[24] Trompette, P., Chanal, V., & Pelissier, C. (2008). Crowdsourcing as a way to access external knowledge for innovation: Control, incentive and coordination in hybrid forms of innovation. Proceedings of *the 24th EGOS Colloquium*.

[25] Wasko, M. M. & Teigland, R. (2004). Public goods or virtual commons? Applying theories of public goods, social dilemmas, and collective action to electronic networks of practice. *Journal of Information Technology Theory and Application*, 6(1), 25-41.

[26] Whitla, P. (2009, March). Crowdsourcing and its application in marketing activities. *Contemporary Management Research*, 5(1), 15-28.

Creativity in Dyads: The Role of Closeness and Media Multiplexity

Xiqing Sha
National University of Singapore
13 Computing Drive
65-65162767

xiqing@nus.edu.sg

Yi Wu
National University of Singapore
13 Computing Drive
65-65162767

wuyi@nus.edu.sg

Klarissa Chang
National University of Singapore
13 Computing Drive
65-65162791

changtt@comp.nus.edu.sg

ABSTRACT
Identifying the features of social ties that facilitate the generation of creative ideas deepens the understanding of relational factors in dyadic communication that trigger creative thinking. Tie strength, which is the key factor that shape creativity, has ambiguous effects on shaping creativity. Specifically, strong ties have both positive and negative effects on creativity when it is examined from a structural perspective and social perspective. It is also unclear that through what kind of mechanisms behind that trigger strong ties have an opposite association with creativity. Therefore this study distinguishes different tie types of tie strength and investigates how they have opposite effects on creativity. Furthermore, this study also examines whether the usage of multiple media in dyadic communication would influence the interaction. Our finding shows that dyads that are strongly connected by multiple ties (i.e., professional ties, personal ties) are less likely to share diverse expertise but more likely to obtain thoughtful responses from each other. Compared to dyads using a single communication media, dyads that use multiple communication media are less likely to share diverse expertise due to communication cost and redundant information exchanged. However the dyads are more likely to respond to each other with thoughtful answers when they use multiple communication media. These findings provide both theoretical contribution to extant literature and practical implications.

Categories and Subject Descriptors
A.1: Introductory and survey

Keywords
Professional closeness; personal closeness; media multiplexity; dyadic analysis; creativity.

1. INTRODUCTION
The importance of creativity has been highlighted as a crucial factor that effectively manages the innovation process in organizations and gain competitive advantage. The generation of creative ideas is the result of social interaction through which different perspectives and approaches are assembled in a novel combination [1]. Recently, scholars have begun to identify the features of social network ties that shape creativity at work [2-7].

According to Granovetter's [19] strength-of-weak-tie theory, the concept of tie strength has been considered as a basic characterization of social relationship. It is well documented in the previous literature that weak ties, not the strong ties, favor individual creativity because they have structural properties that facilitate access to diverse knowledge (e.g., [29]). Previous research have identified that strong ties hinder creativity for they constrain different perspective, have a high risk of sharing redundant information, and create pressure toward conformity [29]. However, from a social perspective, scholars also witness a positive effect of strong ties on creativity for they represent intrinsic motivation and social support in communication process [8].

Although both of the insights obtained from previous work are invaluable, they suffer from a number of ambiguities. First, the concept of strong ties confounds different tie types: advice ties and friendship ties. Thus, when one examines the effects of tie strength of relationships on creativity by measuring the communication frequency and closeness, it is not clear whether creativity benefits from advice ties, or from friendship ties, or from both. Second, given that strong ties have a contradict effects on the generation of creative ideas; it is not clear that through what mechanism the strong ties positively or negatively associate with creativity. To address these ambiguities, this study theoretically and empirically distinguishes between the effects of advice ties and friendship ties on creativity and investigates the mechanisms that mediate the effects of tie strength and creativity.

Specifically we distinguish two types of ties from advice network and friendship network, i.e., professional tie and personal tie, and investigate how they shape creativity. As one of the indicators of tie strength, closeness describes the strength of a tie that has an impact on communication and knowledge transfer process [9-11]. We define *professional closeness* as the frequency of two persons in a dyad exchange information on work-related issues [12]. And *personal closeness* is defined as the extent to which the dyad shares activities about non-work related issues.

In addition, scholars have paid attention to how communication media affect creative process recently [13]. In their seminal work, Haythornthwaite and Wellman [14] suggest that intensive work relationships and close friendship tend to use multiple media to meet their communication needs, namely *media multiplexity*. Multiple media complements with each other to provide individuals better access to rich format of information, ease the transfer of tacit knowledge, and facilitate flexibility in fulfilling communication needs [14, 15]. Therefore this study also investigates the potential effects of multiple media in the communication process that facilitate the generation of creative ideas.

2. THEORETICAL BACKGROUND

2.1 Network Perspective of Creativity

The network perspective of investigating creativity sources from the attributes of dyadic ties [16]. Among the different types of dyadic ties, ties that are connected to friends play an essential role in problem solving in organizational context [17]. Ties that are connected to people with similar working roles are helpful in building up social identity and facilitate knowledge sharing. Thus dyadic ties reflect social resources and contribute to knowledge creation [18].

Tie strength describes an interpersonal tie as "the combination of the amount of time, the emotional intensity, the intimacy and the reciprocal services which characterize the tie" [19, p1371]. Previous studies have suggested that strong ties hinder individual creativity for the reason that frequent interactions indicate high level of knowledge redundancy, thus hinder the access to diverse knowledge and less likely to stimulate autonomous thinking [20]. On the other hand, strong ties may also facilitate creative performance that individuals in dyads intrinsically enjoy working together, and are more likely to be conducive to foster the generation of creative ideas [21, 22].

The contradict effects of strong ties on individual creativity are due to different underlying mechanism that intriguer the creativity based on attributes of dyadic ties. To be specific, there are two potential mechanisms that mediate the relationships between network ties and creativity, namely *expertise diversity* and *expertise responsiveness*. *Expertise diversity* indicates non-redundant knowledge between dyads and plays as a key factor that facilitates the generation of creative ideas [23]. *Expertise responsiveness* refers to the extent that the source in the dyads provides timely and thoughtful feedbacks to the recipient. Therefore expertise diversity controls the amount of knowledge overlapping between the source and the recipient [11], while expertise responsiveness makes sure the quality and depth of interactions.

2.2 Media Multiplexity Theory

Media multiplexity theory suggested that frequent communication between dyads seldom rely on one single media to satisfy their communication needs. Instead, the dyads who are engaged in the intensive work relationships and close friendships intend to use several kinds of media to communicate. Previous studies have investigated that how multiple media can be used in combination to support communication, and how social relationships correlated with media usage. For example, Haythornthwaite [24] observed a non-linear relationship between tie strength and the choice of communication media in organizations. Specifically, weakly-tied communicators with low motivation to communicate and low influence on each other's behaviours are more likely to rely on organizational and single communication media. In contrast, strongly-tied communicators use the organizationally established media as a base and build their multi-media communications.

Multiple media complements with each other to provide rich cues to ease the sharing of tacit knowledge especially when the expertise providers encounter the difficulties of knowledge codification and verbalization [9, 15]. Thus the usage of multiple media improve both accuracy and efficiency in expertise sharing, deepens the understanding of problems for generating thought-through interactions and solutions. Furthermore, multiple media offers people with benefits of each communication media in an integrated way to obtain different types of expertise from different experts to accomplish a task [15]. To access diverse knowledge, multiple media provides rich choices for individuals to select the media to access the specific expert they need to interact with and the specific type of expertise they want to obtain. To sum up, media multiplexity expands the communication channels for individuals to access diverse knowledge and improve the responsiveness of interactions.

3. RESEARCH MODEL AND HYPOTHESES

Professional closeness has been identified to inhibit the generation of creative ideas. Low level of professional closeness reduce the chance of sharing similar knowledge and enables creative thinking [20]. The dyads that communicate frequently on work-related issues are less likely to produce creative outcomes for the high knowledge overlapping [11, 25]. Thus we predict:

H1: Professional closeness is negatively associated with expertise diversity.

Personal closeness is associated with the individuals' intrinsic motivation to engage in a relationship [26]. Homphily theory posits that people intend to develop close relationships with people who share similar attitudes, beliefs and personal characteristics [27]. It creates a common ground and a shared mental model between the dyads. Thus we propose:

H2: Personal closeness is negatively associated with expertise diversity.

On the other hand, strong professional ties and personal ties link dyads that are intrinsically willing to work together. The dyads with high level of closeness communicate and understand each other easily and their behaviours are predictable [28]. High frequency of communication is likely to enhance the mutual understanding about each other's expertise and thinking. The quick flow of information through strong ties may further encourage the responsiveness of each other [29]. Thus we propose:

H3: Professional closeness is positively associated with expertise responsiveness.

H4: Personal closeness is positively associated with expertise responsiveness.

Media multiplexity provides multiple ways to the dyads to meet different communication needs. For the dyads that are connected by close professional ties, they conform to rely on group-wide single communication media to satisfy formal communications [14]. Thus multiple media are effective to enrich the content of professional communication, improve the accuracy and effectiveness of interaction especially when knowledge is complex and technologically know-how. It provides rich cues to represent more diverse information in terms of various formats via different communication channel. Thus we predict:

H5a: The negative relationship between professional closeness and expertise diversity will be weakened by media multiplexity.

Sociologists have documented that dyads that are connected by strong personal ties interact more frequently using various communication media. It means that the dyads who share a good friendship with each other are more likely to communicate frequently using other multiple media but with similar information. Therefore they experience high risks to communicate overlapped information with one media, and across different media. In addition, the dyads need to spend much time in managing communications across each media, thus it is likely to reduce the efficiency of information exchange. Thus we predict:

H5b: The negative relationship between personal closeness and expertise diversity will be strengthened by media multiplexity.

In organizations, strongly-tied dyads use the group-wide communication media and continue to add other media according to their needs [14, 24]. In addition to the base media, the great variety and frequency of information exchanges between strongly tied dyads lead them to seek out other means of communication to use. Multiple media has different ability of providing rich cues that enables the dyads develop good understanding of problems. Therefore it is more beneficial for the dyads to respond to each other with desirable answers. Thus we predict:

H6a: The positive relationship between professional closeness and expertise responsiveness will be strengthened by media multiplexity.

H6b: The positive relationship between personal closeness and expertise responsiveness will be strengthened by media multiplexity.

Expertise diversity has been identified as a crucial factor that helps generate creative outcomes [25, 29, 30]. The dyads with diverse knowledge are able to greatly reduce the redundant information exchange and refresh their mind by coming-in new ideas. Thus we propose:

H7: Expertise diversity is positively associated with creativity.

Exchange of complex knowledge requires intensive and immediate feedbacks [18]. Previous studies found that the partner's level of responsiveness determines the outcome of creative ideas [23]. First, generation of creative ideas depends on how available and accessible the source is to the recipient. Second, generating creative ideas is time-consuming and requires much efforts and motivation. A high level of mutual responsiveness within the dyads would maintain the motivation of interacting for creative ideas and reduce the waiting time during interactions [10]. Therefore we predict:

H8: Expertise responsiveness is positively associated with creativity..

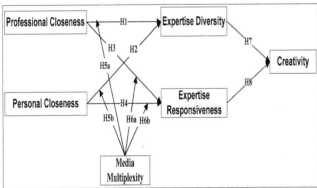

Figure 1. Research Model

4. METHEDOLOGY

4.1 Sample

The setting for our empirical analysis is academic teams from graduate courses in a major university in Asia. Participants were employees in knowledge-intensive organizations that were pursuing their master's degree at the same time. Participants were asked to form teams at the beginning of this course, and finish several projects before the course was ended. Finishing the projects requires the ability of developing shared understanding of each other's expertise and generating creative ideas collaboratively. Team members were able to access various communication media, including emails, telephone, instant messaging, collaborative tools and other social media tools (e.g., Facebook, Wikis) based on their communication needs. Following the convention of social network studies [31, 32], we collected data for most of the variables using onsite survey with a method of name generation. All respondents were asked to evaluate each team member, and encouraged to list people they know from outside of their teams. Finally we got 72 responses out of 79 invited participations, resulting in a 91% response rate. Demographic data were obtained from the employees' resumes.

4.2 Measurements

The primary dependent variable, *creativity*, was measured by single item, adapting from previous studies [33]. On a four-point scale ranging from 1 (strongly disagree) to 4 (strongly agree), respondents were required to rate the extent to which they agree or disagree with the statement "I often develop new ideas with this person when providing solutions to customers". A one-mode matrix was constructed to map the mutual evaluation of creative performance.

For *professional closeness*, respondents were asked to indicate their average communication frequency (i.e., knowledge seeking and knowledge sharing) on work-related issues with the identified person during the past three months (never, sometimes, often, and very often). For *personal closeness*, they were asked to rate the extent to which they agree or disagree with the statement: "I often go out with this person for non-work related issues", scaling from "strongly disagree" to "strongly agree".

Expertise diversity was measured by a self-report item asking respondent whether they feel overlapping with the person in terms of professional views and beliefs. *Expertise responsiveness* measures the degree of reciprocal and desirable response happened between the dyads, by using single item "when asking work-related questions, to what extent do this person respond fast and try to provide thought-through answer and not just a formal reply"[23].

Media multiplexity was derived from media-usage matrices. It was measured by asking respondents to indicate the frequency (1=never, 2=monthly, 3=weekly, 4=several times a week) of each media they use to communicate with each of the identified person. The listed communication media included instant messaging, e-mail, one-to-one telephone call, social media and collaborative tools. Following previous studies [34], media multiplexity captured these tools used at least once a week in the dyads. The responses were put into matrices such that a cell value of 1 in each matrix indicated that a member (in the row) had used that media to communicate with a specific member (in the column) at least weekly, otherwise 0. Following Haythornthwaite and Wellman [14]'s study, media multiplexity was measured by summing these matrices to create a single matrix with cell values ranging from 0 (no media used per week) to 4 (all medium used per week).

In addition to the primary variables, several control variables were included in the analysis, including background similarity, shared experience and culture similarity. Background similarity measured whether the dyads had similar education. Shared experience measures the common projects the dyads have worked on in the past, using one question "How many common projects have you worked with this person previously". Culture similarity measures whether the two persons in the dyads have the same attitude toward creativity, by coding from their nationality.

4.3 Preliminary Analysis

To test the model statistically, network correlations and regressions were performed. Network data do not satisfy assumptions of statistical inference in classical regressions because the observations are not independent. Consequently, special procedures known as quadratic assignment procedure (QAP) and multiple regression quadratic assignment procedure (MRQAP) [35, 36] was used to run the correlations and multiple regressions, respectively. QAP and MRQAP are identical to their non-network counterparts with respect to parameter estimates, but use a randomization permutation technique [37, 38] to construct significance tests. Significance levels for correlations and regressions are based on distributions generated from 2,500 random permutations. In the first step of MRQAP, Pearson correlations between the dependent and the independent network matrices are calculated. In the second step, the significances of the association between the matrices are determined by using a random permutation method. To test our hypotheses, we used MRQAP that is implemented in the software package UCINET [35]. Table 1 shows the correlations among variables. Table 2 shows the results of hypotheses testing.

Table 1. Correlations

Var	Mean	SD	1	2	3	4	5	6	7	8	9
1.BS	0.63	0.48									
2.CS	1.73	1.05	0.05								
3. SE	0.71	0.05	0.05	0.34							
4.PR	2.21	1.03	0.09	0.45	0.35	-					
5. PE	1.44	0.78	0.13	0.36	0.36	0.35	-				
6. MM	1.50	1.55	0.07	0.38	0.29	0.33	0.23	-			
7. ED	2.19	0.66	-0.07	-0.05	-0.24	-0.49	-0.31*	-0.39	-		
8.ER	3.05	0.81	0.02	0.17	0.18	0.28*	0.17*	0.15	-0.19	-	
9. DC	2.73	0.75	-0.02	0.22	0.36	-0.41*	0.23*	0.41	-0.43*	0.24*	-

*$p<.05$, ** $p<.01$
(BS=Background similarity; CS= Culture similarity; SE=Shared experience; PR=Professional closeness; PE=Personal closeness; MM= Media multiplexity; ED= Expertise diversity; ER= Expertise responsiveness; DC=Dyadic creativity)

Table 2. Hypotheses Testing

Control variables	Beta
Background similarity	0.002
Culture similarity	0.068*
Shared experience	-0.465**
Direct effects	
Professional closeness on creativity	-0.508*
Personal closeness on creativity	0.334*
Professional closeness on expertise diversity	-0.498**
Professional closeness on expertise responsiveness	0.247*
Personal closeness on expertise diversity	-0.111*
Personal closeness on expertise diversity	0.059*
Expertise diversity on creativity	0.521**
Expertise responsiveness on creativity	0.132*
Moderating effects	
Professional closeness * Media multiplexity on expertise diversity	-0.204**
Personal closeness * Media multiplexity on expertise diversity	-0.316**
Professional closeness * Media multiplexity on expertise responsiveness	0.037*
Personal closeness * Media multiplexity on expertise responsiveness	0.217*
Adjusted R-squared	31.3%

* $p<.05$, ** $p<.01$

5. CONCLUSION REMARKS

This study differentiates two types of tie strength (i.e., professional closeness, personal closeness) to explain the ambiguous effects (i.e., positive or negative) of tie strength on creativity in previous studies. The findings confirm that that closeness in professional ties and advice ties has an opposite effect on creativity. Consistent with previous studies on creativity, the findings show that expertise diversity helps generate creative ideas at the dyadic level. Furthermore, not only the diversity of expertise is contributable of creative ideas, the thought-through responses from the other person in the dyadic communication are also likely to facilitate generation of new ideas by easing the exchange of tacit and complex knowledge. In addition, it is believed that the use of multiple media could facilitate the generation of creative ideas within dyads due to the benefits of easing the accessing to each other in the communication and exchanging of thought-through responses. However, the usage of multiple media may harm the exchange of diverse knowledge due to the communication cost to maintain the multiple communication channels and the overlapped knowledge exchange within multiple media.

6. REFERECENS

[1] T. Allen, Managing the Flow of Technology, Cambridge,MA: MIT Press, 1977.

[2] D. Obstfeld, "Social networks, the tertius iungens orientation, and involvement in innovation," Administrative Science Quarterly, vol. 50, no. 1, pp. 100-130, 2005.

[3] R. S. Burt, "Structural holes and good ideas," The American Journal of Sociology, vol. 110, no. 2, pp. 349-399, 2004.

[4] R. Cross, and J. Cummings, "Tie and network correlates of individual performance in knowledge-intensive work,"

Academy of Management Journal, vol. 47, no. 6, pp. 928-937, 2004.

[5] S. Rodan, and c. Galunic, "More than network structure: How knowledge heterogeneity influences managerial performance and innovativeness," Strategic Management Journal, vol. 25, pp. 541-562, 2004.

[6] B. Uzzi, and J. Spiro, "Collaboration and creativity: The small world problem," American Journal of Sociology, vol. 111, no. 2, pp. 447-504, Sep, 2005.

[7] L. Fleming, S. Mingo, and D. Chen, "Brokerage and collaborative creativity," Administrative Science Quarterly, vol. 52, no. 3, pp. 443-475, 2007.

[8] A. M. Isen, K. A. Daubman, and G. P. Nowicki, "Positive affect facilitates creative problem solving," Journal of personality and social psychology, vol. 52, no. 6, pp. 1122, 1987.

[9] M. Hansen, "The search-transfer problem: The role of weak ties in sharing knowledge across organization subunits," Administrative Science Quarterly, vol. 44, no. 1, pp. 82-111, 1999.

[10] R. Reagans, and B. McEvily, "Network Structure and Knowledge Transfer: The Effects of Cohesion and Range," Administrative Science Quarterly, vol. 48, pp. 240-267, 2003.

[11] R. Reagans, "Preferences, identity, and competition: Predicting tie strength from demographic data," Management Science, vol. 51, no. 9, pp. 1374-1383, Sep, 2005.

[12] A. Wu, J. M. DiMicco, and D. R. Millen, "Detecting professional versus personal closeness using an enterprise social network site." pp. 1955-1964.

[13] J. M. Burkhardt, and T. Lubart, "Creativity in the Age of Emerging Technology: Some Issues and Perspectives in 2010," Creativity and Innovation Management, vol. 19, no. 2, pp. 160-166, 2010.

[14] C. Haythornthwaite, and B. Wellman, "Work, friendship, and media use for information exchange in a networked organization," Journal of the American Society for Information Science, vol. 49, no. 12, pp. 1101-1114, 1998.

[15] Y. C. Yuan, I. Carboni, and K. Ehrlich, "The impact of awareness and accessibility on expertise retrieval: A multilevel network perspective," Journal of the American Society for Information Science and Technology, vol. 61, no. 4, pp. 700-714, 2010.

[16] M. Csikszentmihalyi, " Implications of a Systems Perspective for the Study of Creativity," Handbook of creativity, R. J. Sternberg, ed., p. 313, Cambridge, UK: Cambridge University Press, 1999.

[17] K. Jehn, and P. Shah, "Interpersonal Relationships and Task Performance: An Examination of Mediating Processes in Friendship and Acquaintance Groups," Journal of Personality and Social Psychology, vol. 72, no. 4, pp. 775-790, 1997.

[18] R. Cross, and L. Sproull, "More than an answer: Information relationships for actionable knowledge," Organization Science, vol. 15, no. 4, pp. 446-462, 2004.

[19] M. S. Granovetter, "The strength of weak ties," The American Journal of Sociology, vol. 78, no. 6, pp. 1360-1380, 1973.

[20] J. E. Perry-Smith, and C. E. Shalley, "The social side of creativity: A static and dynamic social network perspective," Academy of Management Review, vol. 28, no. 1, pp. 89-106, Jan, 2003.

[21] T. Amabile, Creativity in context: Westview Pr, 1996.

[22] T. M. Amabile, S. G. Barsade, J. S. Mueller et al., "Affect and creativity at work," Administrative Science Quarterly, vol. 50, no. 3, pp. 367-403, 2005.

[23] A. Fliaster, and F. Schloderer, "Dyadic ties among employees: Empirical analysis of creative performance and efficiency," Human Relations, vol. 63, no. 10, pp. 1513-1540, Oct, 2010.

[24] C. Haythornthwaite, "The strength and the impact of new media." p. 10.

[25] M. E. Sosa, "Where Do Creative Interactions Come From? The Role of Tie Content and Social Networks," Organization Science, vol. Articles in Advance, pp. 1-21, March 11, 2010, 2010.

[26] P. V. Marsden, and K. E. Campbell, "Measuring tie strength," Social Forces, vol. 63, no. 2, pp. 482-501, 1984.

[27] C. A. O'Reilly, K. Y. Williams, and S. Barsade, "Group demography and innovation: Does diversity help? In (Ed.), (Vol. 1, pp. 183-207)," Composition, Research on managing groups and teams, D. H. Gruenfeld, ed., pp. 183-207, 1998.

[28] D. E. Byrne, The attraction paradigm: Academic Pr, 1971.

[29] J. E. Perry-Smith, "Social yet creative: The role of social relationships in facilitating individual creativity," Academy of Management Journal, vol. 49, no. 1, pp. 85-101, Feb, 2006.

[30] G. Cattani, and S. Ferriani, "A core/periphery perspective on individual creative performance: Social networks and cinematic achievements in the Hollywood film industry," Organization Science, vol. 19, no. 6, pp. 824-844, 2008.

[31] J. Scott, Social network analysis: a handbook, London: Sage Publications, 2000.

[32] S. Wasserman, and K. Faust, Social network analysis: Methods and applications: Cambridge Univ Pr, 1994.

[33] J. M. George, and J. Zhou, "When openness to experience and conscientiousness are related to creative behavior: An interactional approach," Journal of Applied Psychology, vol. 86, no. 3, pp. 513, 2001.

[34] T. Sykes, V. Venkatesh, and S. Gosain, "Model of acceptance with peer support: A social network perspective to understand individual-level system use," MIS Quarterly, vol. 33, no. 2, pp. 371-393, 2009.

[35] S. P. Borgatti, M. G. Everett, and L. C. Freeman, "UCINET 5.0 Version 1.00," Natick: Analytic Technologies, 1999.

[36] D. Krackhardt, "Predicting with networks: Nonparametric multiple regression analysis of dyadic data," Social Networks, vol. 10, no. 4, pp. 359-381, 1988.

[37] E. S. Edgington, "Approximate Randomization Tests " Journal of Psychology vol. 72, no. 2, pp. 143-149, 1969.

[38] E. Noreen, Computer Intensive Methods for Testing Hypotheses: An Introduction. , New York: John Wiley & Sons 1989.

Schema Accuracy and Career Challenges for Men in the Information Technology Workplace

Deborah J. Armstrong
Florida State University
College of Business
Tallahassee, FL 32306
01-850-644-8228

djarmstrong@cob.fsu.edu

Cynthia K. Riemenschneider
Baylor University
Hankamer School of Business
Waco, TX 76798
01-254-710-4061

cindy_riemenschneider@baylor.
edu

Margaret F. Reid
University of Arkansas
Fulbright College of Arts and Sciences
Fayetteville, AR 72701
01-479-575-3356

mreid@uark.edu

ABSTRACT

Much of the diversity literature in the IT field has focused on the perspectives of women and racioethnic minorities. We expand this exploration by looking at perceptions of the unique challenges and barriers to advancement facing men in the IT workplace utilizing a cognitive lens and schema accuracy theory. In addition to evoking the unique challenges men perceive they face different from women, we also collected data from women regarding their perceptions of men's unique challenges. We found a minimal level of shared understanding occurring around interactions between the sexes (i.e., cross-gender interaction). These findings advance our understanding of the cognitive overlap (and lack thereof) regarding the perceptions of the unique challenges and barriers facing men in the IT field, and provide an initial step toward developing a shared understanding of the IT work environment.

Categories and Subject Descriptors

K.7.1 [**The Computing Profession**]: Occupations

General Terms

Management

Keywords

IT personnel, IT workforce, schema accuracy, gender

1. INTRODUCTION

Diversity can be conceptualized as the distribution of differences among the members of a group with respect to a common attribute [23]. Much of the diversity literature has focused on diversity by exploring the outcomes of group diversity (or lack thereof), and utilizing the perspectives of women and racioethnic minorities.

For example, gender diversity has been found to positively influence teamwork [19] and team cohesion [24]. Interestingly, Chatman and Flynn [9] demonstrate that demographic differences are initially more powerful than cognitive differences, but over time, the impact of demographic differences dissipates.

Collison and Hearn [11] suggest that men's universal status and their occupancy of the normative standard state have rendered them invisible as objects of analysis. Consistent with this perspective, we find the preponderance of gender diversity research is focused on utilizing men as a comparative baseline. For example, group diversity research has found that: Caucasian women and racial/ethnic minorities saw more value in, and felt more comfortable with, diversity than Caucasian men [44]; men responded to increased group heterogeneity with more negative work attitudes than women [64]; and men responded more negatively than women to being in the minority in their work groups [62]. From our review of the literature, what appears to be lacking is an analysis of gender diversity issues utilizing both men's and women's perspectives of the same focal group.

High schema accuracy allows group members to understand how other members of their group think about an issue. With increased understanding, group members will have more accurate explanations for group members' behavior and may be able to predict reactions [51]. High schema accuracy may also reduce bias toward group members and any associated problems [51] as well as foster the development of shared understanding between group members. A pre-cursor to the development of shared understanding (and ultimately a shared schema) of the challenges and barriers faced by men and women in the IT field is an understanding of the different schema that individuals bring to the workplace regarding these issues.

Over 20 years ago, Thomas [59] asserted that if two candidates met the qualifications of a position, often, in order to meet equal opportunity objectives, firms would give preference in hiring and promotion to white women and racioethnic minorities over white men. He goes on to state that these staffing efforts were often interpreted by white men as a compromise of organizational standards and unfair favoritism. Are these sentiments still prevalent? How do men view their career prospects in today's IT workplace? What are women's perceptions of men's opportunities and challenges in the IT workplace? This line of inquiry prompted our overarching research question: Do men and women perceive that men face unique challenges in the IT workplace?

This study seeks to understand the concepts that participants associate with the challenges men in the IT field face that women do not in order to explore the overlaps and gaps in their schemas (i.e., assess the level of schema accuracy). An understanding of the gaps may aid the process of increasing schema accuracy so as to develop shared understanding and ultimately shared schema of a more diverse and accepting IT work environment.

2. BACKGROUND

A schema is an organized cognitive structure of a domain in which the concepts and relationships between the concepts comprise the schema [26]. Other names for the concept include semantic nets [35], frames of reference [17], and mental model [3]. Schemas guide action and interpretation of the world around us and allow individuals to explain behavior in their environment. Schemas tend to change slowly even when events and environments change rapidly [25].

Generally speaking, the idea of shared schemas (also referred to as a team or group mental model [42]) refers to the representation of the knowledge of team or group tasks, equipments, roles, goals, and attitudes that is shared by members [7, 12, 36, 53]. This enables group members or teammates to interpret cues in a similar manner, make compatible decisions, and take appropriate action [29, 31]. While there are varying terminologies utilized in the literature, for simplicity we use the term *group* to represent a social system that produces an outcome for which members have collective responsibility [22], and *schema* because of the developed conceptual basis, increasing empirical support, and implications for group development [42].

There are several typologies of shared schemas. One typology groups schemas into task-related and team-related [31, 32, 40]. Task-related schemas involve an understanding of technology, equipment and tasks; and team-related schemas are member and interaction-oriented and involve an understanding of team member characteristics, patterns of interaction among members, and the location of sources of information [8].

Another typology further delineates shared schemas into four types: task-specific knowledge, task-related knowledge, knowledge of teammates, and knowledge of attitudes or beliefs [6]. According to Chou, Wang, Wang, Huang and Cheng [10, p. 1716],

> "Task-specific knowledge refers to knowledge about the specific procedures, sequences, actions, and strategies that are necessary to perform a task. Task-related knowledge refers to knowledge of information about team roles/ responsibilities and interaction patterns. Knowledge of teammates involves team members' knowledge of each other – teammates' preferences, strengths, weaknesses, and tendencies to maximize team performance. Finally, knowledge of attitudes or beliefs refers to knowledge of teammates' general attitudes, values, or beliefs toward work tasks, working environments, or the work itself."

Previous research has established that a shared schema can contribute to effective group performance via a common understanding of task requirements, procedures and/or group processes [6, 8, 39]. Thus, we focus on the development of shared schemas with regard to group members' knowledge of the attitudes, beliefs and values of other members.

Researchers have found evidence of a relationship between group effectiveness and the similarity of members' cognitions [38, 50], and that divergent schemas may cause problems because of miscommunication and disorganization [28]. Group member schema similarity is the degree to which group members have similar schemas regarding a specific domain [49]. Schema similarity consists of two components: congruence (i.e., agreement) and accuracy [49]. Congruence indicates the amount of similarity between two schemas. Accuracy refers to the extent to which individuals can report another's schema of a specific domain accurately; or the similarity of one person's perception of another person's actual schema [41, 51].

As stated previously, high schema accuracy indicates that group members understand how other members think about a focal domain or issue. With regard to schema accuracy, Huber and Lewis [27, p. 12] assert that "… members may depend on demographic cues (such as gender) to make assumptions about others' knowledge and perspectives … and, consequently, may make erroneous assumptions about others' mental models." Edwards, Day, Arthur and Bell [15] found schema accuracy to be a much stronger predictor of team performance than schema similarity. Within the IS literature the research on schema accuracy, similarity and group level shared schemas is noticeably absent. In one of the only relevant studies identified, Tegarden, Tegarden and Sheetz [58] studied cognitive diversity in top management teams at an IT services organization and identified cognitive factions (sub-groups of individuals with diverse views and beliefs within a team).

Thus as a first step toward the goal of understanding and developing shared schemas with regard to group members' knowledge of the attitudes, beliefs and values of other members about gender diversity and the IT work environment, it is necessary to understand the schemas that individuals bring to the table regarding the challenges and barriers faced by men and women. This study seeks to understand the concepts that participants associate with the unique challenges men in the IT field face in order to explore the overlaps and gaps in their schemas. An understanding of the gaps can aid the process of increasing schema accuracy so as to develop shared understanding and ultimately shared schemas of a more diverse and accepting IT work environment.

3. METHOD

Believing that much of our social reality is both constructed and perpetuated through discourse [5], we used an interpretive perspective and explicate common and unique themes evoked from gendered group interaction. From these cognitions we identify the salient challenges and barriers (concepts) within the participants' schema to address the research question.

3.1 Data Source and Procedure

Focus groups have high face validity, can capture real-life data, are flexible, can provide speedy results, are inexpensive [4], and provide a more relaxed context for participants, thereby increasing the chance of spontaneous responses from members

[37]. This method is particularly appropriate for this research because we are using a social constructivist approach and thus take the view that a schema can be elicited through group discourse [13]. The use of group interviews provides a glimpse into how individuals jointly construct and give meaning to the challenges faced by men in the IT workplace. In addition, interviews help the researchers acquire a richer understanding of the phenomenon under study at early stages of an investigation and can thus inform subsequent stages of the research [57].

One of the sources of knowledge about the IT workplace are IT managers - those who supervise IT personnel, interact with technology, and frequently mediate the interface between IT and other functional areas [21, 45]. The role of managers is especially germane to this research because managers are the gatekeepers who reflect explicit and/or implicit values of the profession both to their subordinates, and others. We used IT managers as participants exclusively so we could control for job tasks (e.g., managing the portfolio of IT applications; technology; application development; the IT function; and IT-organizational relationships [21]) since they are so varied in the IT field.

We conducted six focus groups with managers working in the IT department at the headquarters of three companies. Consistent with the theoretical sampling process [16, 20], the companies selected were chosen for their similarities and differences. The companies are similar in that all three have in-house IT departments that are housed at the corporate headquarters, and differ on several organizational dimensions such as industry, geographic location, size and culture. TransCo is one of the largest publicly held transportation logistics companies in North America, with annual revenues of more than $2 billion. FoodCo, founded in 1935, is one of the world's largest processors and marketers of protein, the second-largest food production company in the Fortune 500. BevCo was founded in 1933 and is one of the world's largest family-owned winery. It produces and distributes wine under 16 different labels to over 90 countries. Admittedly, the context of these three firms (very large, in-house IT organizations) might have an influence on how these IT managers in the sample experience the IT profession. While these three organizations constitute a convenience sample, as this exploratory research is focused on generating insights for theory development, we believe this sampling approach is acceptable. Convenience samples are appropriate when the goal is depth of understanding around a specific phenomenon rather than generalizability [2].

The primary contact with each organization was the CIO who identified the focus group participants. Participants were recruited via email invitation and the contact person within the organization handled the room scheduling and invitation process. Our participants were 45 IT managers, which is consistent with sample sizes in other top-tier qualitative studies [18]. Eight male managers and 9 female managers participated from TransCo; 8 men and 5 women participated from FoodCo; and 8 men and 7 women participated from BevCo. The managers had been with the company an average of 9.9 years (female - 10.5 yrs; male - 9.4 yrs) and had worked in IT for 15.7 years (female - 14.9 yrs; male - 16.5 yrs). In addition, 61% of the managers had more years in the IT field than years in the company indicating that the majority of them had worked in IT for more than one organization. Due to the potentially sensitive nature of the topics discussed, and to increase interviewee trust in the researchers, a decision was made not to gather additional demographic information from the participants.

The focus group interviews, which ranged from 45 to 65 minutes, were tape recorded and then transcribed verbatim. Each session began with the researchers introducing themselves, welcoming participants to the session and thanking them for attending, and stating that the researchers were studying issues facing IT professionals. The facilitators reiterated that participation was strictly voluntary, the participants could leave the session at any time, and that anything said was being recorded – but strictly confidential. To ensure confidentiality each participant was given a number, and asked to use those numbers instead of each other's names in the conversation.

Two same sex researchers were present for each focus group (i.e., male researcher-males respondents; female researcher-female respondents) so as to reduce any gender-based hesitancy on the part of the participants that might occur if the opposite gender was present. The researchers were trained in group interview techniques to promote consistency and reduce interviewer variance. While differences in the evoked schemas could be attributed to the different researchers, we do not believe this to be the case. The interview guide was strictly adhered to by the researchers (confirmed in the verbatim transcriptions), and all questions were answered. The complete interview guide is available from the first author. After removing the researchers' questions from the transcriptions, the aggregate transcript length for each gender was exactly the same (26 pages), with the focus group transcript page length ranging from a minimum of 7 to a maximum of 11 pages (men 10, 7, 9 pages; women 7, 8, 11 pages), indicating a similar level of questioning and probing.

This study is part of a larger project that looks at manager's perceptions in the IT workplace. What is presented here is a portion of the interviews focused on the question posed to the participants "Do you think men in the IT workplace face different challenges than women?" The social constructivism perspective views the researchers as participants in the process [60]. While steps were taken to mitigate researcher bias in the data collection and analysis processes (e.g., tape recording interviews as opposed to relying on researcher notes), the researchers acknowledge that they are representing the identity of the IT managers as experienced through their own subjectivity.

3.2 Data Analysis

In recent years, content analysis has emerged as a common methodology for aggregating and drawing inferences from textual material in organizational research [14, 47]. Content analysis is also becoming more prevalent in the IT literature [30, 48, 61] and is regarded as an appropriate approach to examine whether patterns in the content support research questions. This methodology can be used to code responses to open-ended questions [63] from a variety of sources (e.g., surveys, interviews, and focus groups). In this study content analysis was used to make inferences from text (in this instance collected via focus group interviews).

Since schemas are held within the mind, to understand schemas we explicate and study the cognitive concepts that appear in the statements made by the participants. Our task was to elicit the relevant concepts from what participants said regarding the unique challenges and barriers facing men in the IT workplace and place these concepts into coherent representation scheme. The research team (from three different disciplines) systematically examined the interview transcriptions to identify the challenges and barriers.

During the data analysis process the researchers developed a coding scheme consisting of concepts and themes. Similar to Joshi and Kuhn [30] and Todd, McKeen, and Gallupe [61] a phrase was used as the base unit of analysis to develop the coding scheme. While there is a growing body of literature regarding the IT workplace, the absence of an established framework for the unique challenges facing men in the IT workplace presented an opportunity. The researchers chose not to develop a coding scheme a priori, but inductively as the concepts emerged from the interview transcripts. As the researchers have collectively been studying IT workforce issues for over 32 years we would argue that the emergent coding scheme is not a-theoretical, but grounded in theory and organic in nature [55]. Each of the researchers provided independent coding of the texts using their research perspective, literature base, and own best judgment. In the coding process, words that are frequently mentioned in the statements are grouped together, and a word or word group is created to summarize the meaning of the phrase. The researchers developed the 'labels'; however the challenges (i.e., concepts) emerged from the participants through the phrases captured in the language of the participants. The researchers were neither expected nor required to give identical coding to the phrases. The individually coded phrases were discussed and all discrepancies were resolved through discussion in order to reach 100% agreement.

4. RESULTS

Our overarching research question is: Do men and women perceive that the challenges and barriers that males face in the IT workplace are different than those faced by females? We begin by discussing the concepts and themes identified by the men and then address the concepts and themes identified by the women.

4.1 Men's Perspective

The men see that they face 10 challenges. Descriptions of the key challenges that emerged from the participants are included in Table 1. According to Strauss and Corbin [56, p. 13], "Analysis is the interplay between research and data. It is both science and art....Creativity manifests itself in the ability of researchers to aptly name categories...and extract an innovative, integrated, realistic scheme from masses of unorganized raw data." The themes (also shown in Table 1) are unifying categories for a set of related concepts. Thus, the themes were arrived at inductively after the researchers studied the transcripts, the challenges, and reflected on the existing literature, and attempted to create a logical representation for the discussion of the findings.

As indicated in Table 1, the men in our study discussed concepts included in two themes - Gender and Work Climate and Interaction themes. The women discussed concepts included in four themes - Gender and Work Climate, Interaction, Stress &

Burnout and Work-family Conflict. The first theme is labeled Gender & Work Climate and contains concepts focused on the challenges men face in the workplace as a result of gender issues. This theme contains six concepts: Actions Company Can Take, Gender, Gender Composition: Company, Gender Equity, Work-Related Gender Expectations and Reverse Discrimination. Illustrating the perceived relationship between Gender and Work-Related Gender Expectations FoodCo male manager 2 stated,

I do think the men have the most challenging opportunities thrown at them. I think we're asked to deliver a whole lot more than the women... That's just the way it's always been and the way it's always gonna be.

Another challenge perceived by the men that they face is dealing with the reverse discrimination that results from organizations trying to achieve gender equity. In essence the men feel they are facing a glass ceiling of their own. Discussing reverse discrimination, FoodCo male manager 8 stated,

That organizations are trying to recreate themselves to mirror the population as a whole and what they're trying to do is offset the current inequity that tends to favor the white male as being in those senior positions so they're focusing on bringing in females and minorities to fill positions which means that for white males the tap has essentially been cut off.

Within the Interaction theme, men identified four concepts: Behavior Modification, Cross-Gender Interaction, Message Design and Politically Correct. The Cross Gender Interaction and Behavior Modification concepts are focused on questions like how do I talk to this person, how do I treat this person, how do I understand this person's perspective because I am a (man/woman) and she/he is a (woman/man)? This theme is exemplified by the quote from BevCo male manager 1,

I think there are gender issues that happen and you have to be cognizant of them. You can't talk to your employees the way you used to not if there's gender involved and they're going to bring that up. So you can't ride, you know, people like you used to be able to get productivity out of them, because now you're being mean. So you have to be a lot more politically correct.

Discussing cross gender interaction and the need to be politically correct, BevCo male manager 5 stated,

Some of the challenge is sometimes is being, feeling like you have to be more politically correct or more sensitive because you're dealing with a woman as opposed to dealing with another guy where you can just blast out what's on your mind.

Table 1. Challenge Descriptions

Theme	Challenge	Identified By*	Sample Phrases From Interview Transcripts
Gender & Work Climate	Gender	B	If you were a man; if I was a woman
	Actions Company Can Take	M	We're all challenged to try to reach that [male/female] equilibrium
	Gender Composition: Company	M	You have very few women on the software side of it.
	Gender Equity	M	It doesn't matter what gender you are.
	Gender Expectations: Work	M	I'm the only female and if you're looking at me differently than you're looking at everybody else in this room.
	Reverse Discrimination	M	More often than not, the female candidate would get that position.
Interaction	Behavior Modification	B	I talked like one of the guys and not like one of the girls.
	Cross-Gender Interaction	B	Because he's looking at it as a man and I see it differently and those kinds of things.
	Message Design	B	There was a little bit of a challenge in adjusting my communication method.
	Politically Correct	M	Feeling like you have to be more politically correct or more sensitive.
	Feedback	W	I can tell through the interview process that they [women] are getting this perception that they're not as good as the men.
	Threats	W	She was accused of being too aggressive.
Stress & Burnout	Performance Challenges	W	I think the pressure to perform; one challenge is to be productive.
	Time Relative to Men	W	If I had the time to spend extra, after 5; If I had the time to spend that a lot of men have.
Work-family Balance	Gender Expectations, Family	W	It seems to always fall on the responsibility of the mom.
	Work-family Balance	W	When the child is sick… you feel like you want to be there and you want to focus, but yet you also … you feel your responsibility to work as well.

* Legend:

B = both men and women identified this concept as a challenge for men

M = only men identified this concept as a challenge for men

W = only women identified this concept as a challenge for men

4.2 Women's Perspective

The women also identified 10 concepts as those related to the unique challenges men in the IT field face that women do not (see Table 1). The only concept that the women identified as a challenge for men with regard to gender and the workplace was Gender. As BevCo female manager 2 stated regarding gender, "If it is perceived that you are an equally qualified candidate and are getting a promotion over another equally qualified candidate who happens to be male, you just have to watch your performance."

For the Interaction theme, the women identified five challenges focused on the impact of gender in workplace interactions: Behavior Modification, Cross-Gender Interaction, Feedback, Message Design, and Threats. As BevCo female manager 6 stated, "I think as far as challenges that men face is maybe having to be constantly aware of like that sensitivity, especially in a meeting where like participant 4 said where you may only have one female." While discussing Cross-Gender Interaction, BevCo female manager 1 stated,

At my previous employer one of the male managers I had there had admitted that he didn't know how to deal with female emotions or female situations where they needed to take off time to go spend with their family, the necessities of a female's responsibilities and their emotional makeup.

The smallest themes which contain concepts only identified by women as challenges for men are Stress & Burnout and Work Family Balance. The Stress & Burnout theme is exemplified by the quote by FoodCo female manager 9, "If I had the time to spend that a lot of men have to spend, extra, after 5 o'clock, to do that extra little bit of extra effort, it probably couldn't have hurt." The Work-Family Balance theme exemplified by the quote from FoodCo female manager 2, "When a man stays home, it's like 'Wow, what a great father!' When a woman does it, it's like 'Oh, she has to stay home again with the kids.' It's normal, expected."

5. DISCUSSION

Looking at Table 1 we see that there are four concepts that both men and women identified as challenges for men that women do not face. The common concepts are Gender, Behavior Modification, Cross-Gender Interaction, and Message Design, with three of these concepts focused on interaction (Gender is included in the Gender and Work Climate theme).

From the participant quotes, we see that the unique challenges men perceive they face seem to revolve around having to modify their communication when interacting with women, being less harsh/direct and more sensitive to women's communication style as captured in the *Behavior Modification, Message Design* and *Cross Gender Interaction*. For example, BevCo male participant 4 stated, "I would venture to say that there are more men in here who feel like if this [department] were all men they would handle some situations differently, they would speak to each other differently." The women seem also identified interaction issues as exemplified by the quotes:

You know, there's things that you have to try to learn to live with like language and well, you know, and rude comments and things like that. So I think that men have to be aware of those things and sensitive to it and have to try to watch those things. [BevCo female manager 6]

I will not be caught anywhere with a man one on one, ever, ever. Not behind an office door, you know, not even when there's a window because nobody can tell what we're talking about. I would never take a vendor to lunch by myself and I have a vendor who comes in quarterly, I will not do it. Because there are too many situations, innuendos ... [BevCo female manager 4]

There are six unique challenges identified by each gender. In describing the unique challenges men face in the IT workplace, the men focused on structural and organizational level concepts (e.g., Reverse Discrimination, Actions the Company Can Take), whereas the women were more focused on more individual level concepts (e.g., Work-family Balance and Performance Challenges).

It is interesting to note that in addition to a different level of analysis in the concepts identified as challenges for men (organizational versus individual) several of the concepts identified by the women as challenges for men seem to be more focused on the women and their own challenges. For example, in the women's statements the Work-Family Balance concepts (Feedback, Gender, Gender Expectations, Family and Work-Family Balance) seem to be addressing a double standard (e.g. when a man spends time away from work with children it is positive, but when a woman spends time away from work with children it is a negative).

Many of the concepts emerging from the women are not direct "challenges" for the men (e.g., Work-Family Balance, Threats). The women seemed focused on their own challenges, and comparing their situation to men's so that they could not articulate challenges in the IT workplace unique to men. One explanation for this finding may be that anxious individuals tend to be more self-focused than less anxious individuals, and when people are overly self-focused they exert most of their cognitive efforts on managing their own behavior at the expense of being attentive to perceiving others [46].

Team member 'sharedness' should be understood as 'similar' not 'identical', that is, team members possess some overlap in their schemas rather than an identical mapping. When group members share schemas, they are more likely to draw common interpretations of an event or problem, come up with similar solutions, or respond to the situation in a like manner. Studies have shown that shared schemas and more specifically shared understanding is an important factor linked to group performance [8, 33, 54].

For the participants in this study there seems to be a minimal amount of shared understanding. Recall that schema accuracy is the similarity of one person's perception of another person's schema to the other person's actual schema [41]. With regard to the challenges facing the men in this study, it appears that there is minimal overall accuracy (only four concepts in common) on the part of the women. Three of the 4 commonly identified concepts can be found in the Interaction theme. From this data, we could say that the women in these organizations may have a base level of understanding regarding the unique challenges facing men in IT with regard to interaction. Both the men and the women appear to see that men must consider and sometimes modify their communication style and message when interacting with women. Thus, schema accuracy is relatively high for this theme.

In contrast, with the Gender & Work Climate theme only one of the 6 concepts (Gender) was identified by both men and women. The women did not seem to have an accurate picture of the challenges and barriers men face (that they did not) within the IT work environment. The men articulated several issues regarding the changes within the organization that promote gender equity and increased gender diversity within the managerial ranks, up to and including reverse discrimination. The women did not articulate these concerns and thus may have a blind spot regarding the perceived impact of affirmative action and equal employment initiatives on men.

In addition, only women identified challenges related to Stress & Burnout, and Work-family Balance. As stated previously, the fact that these concepts were more focused on the challenges the women themselves are facing or comparing their experience with that of men (e.g., if I had the extra time men do), was an interesting and unexpected development.

Taking the findings together, we see that the collective level of schema accuracy is quite low. Of the 10 concepts identified by the men as challenges they face, the women only accurately identified four. The women displayed a high level of schema accuracy (identified three of the four challenges men identified), and modicum of shared understanding (reflected in the evoked statements) regarding men's challenges interacting with women. On the other hand, the women displayed a low level of schema accuracy (identified one of the six challenges men identified) and negligible shared understanding with regard to the influence of gender within the IT work environment.

5.1 Limitations and Future Research

A familiar criticism of qualitative methods is that the dependence on convenience samples and small sample sizes may limit generalizability. While the findings may not be generalizable in the traditional (i.e., statistical) sense, interpretive (i.e., analytic) generalizability seeks to formulate theory so that it not only explains the current observations, but also helps researchers understand, anticipate, and navigate similar settings [1, 34, 52, 65].

Another limitation concerns the specific qualitative method employed. As with any qualitative study, a large number of coding choices were made and these could alter the analysis and results. We used multiple raters (across three disciplines) at every stage of the process and discussed all coding decisions to reach 100% agreement. Future research may extend the ideas presented here to develop measures and perhaps quantitatively confirm (or refute) our findings.

One might say that the sample is a limitation. Our sample included men and women from multiple organizations, and all of the participants were managers from in-house IT departments. We believe that managers were appropriate because they have both the experience of the IT professional as well as the more holistic perspective afforded to management. Future research could expand the sample size, and perhaps utilize different samples of IT professionals (e.g., database administrators) to find the extent to which other IT personnel agree with the elements that emerged from this study.

Although these are acknowledged limitations, we believe the importance of the subject and lack of research in this case outweighs these potential concerns. The results presented here should be viewed not as creating the ultimate framework that is demonstrable in all settings, but as providing a foundation worthy of further exploration. Empirical validation and elaboration of these findings with other samples and in other settings is needed as it will sharpen and enrich the challenges developed and yield a more complete understanding of the phenomenon.

5.2 Implications

Our first implication for theory is via the exploration of the male perspective with regard to the challenges faced within the IT field. Traditional IT diversity research has taken up the perspective of the minority group (e.g., women) and looked for explanations about the lack of diversity in the field. To truly understand a phenomenon, we assert that a 360 degree view is necessary. To add richness to the discussion of diversity in IT, we look at the unique challenges men face in the IT field from the perspective of both men and women. We believe our findings provide the impetus for further work in the area of cross-group diversity. Understanding the perspectives of various subgroups may allow researchers and practitioners to see these issues differently and afford new insights from a mix of views.

To date there has been limited work on the concept of schema accuracy as a mechanism for enhancing the development of shared schemas. This work addresses that gap by providing insights into the utilization of this mechanism by studying the accuracy of two groups regarding the career challenges and barriers unique to men in the IT field. Researchers may use the concept of schema accuracy to explore a wide variety of cognitively based phenomenon both within the IT field and beyond.

One of the first steps in the development of shared schemas is the recognition that differences exist among group members, not just with regard to the issues/content of the schema, but also with regard to assumptions and interpretations underlying the issues [43]. Low schema accuracy between subgroups can reduce information flow between members of different subgroups and can cause subgroup members to be dismissive of the validity or usefulness of information from members of the other subgroup [27]. By listening to other group members clarify ideas and provide rationales for their interpretations, members may proceed from acknowledging there are different perspectives, to understanding the different perspectives, to developing a truly shared schema that incorporates the diverse perspectives.

The appreciation of diversity and the incorporation of different perspectives may enhance group performance [6]. The predictive ability of shared schemas may enable managers to identify groups with potential issues and develop ideas regarding how these issues can be addressed [6]. For example, a lack of shared schema regarding cross-gender interaction could be the root problem of ineffective communication. Unsure of how to communicate with members of the opposite gender, individuals may avoid communication whenever possible. Training interventions targeted at surfacing underlying issues such as these may help increase a sense of shared schema and ultimately improve group effectiveness.

6. CONCLUSION

Much of the diversity literature in the IT field has focused on diversity by exploring the perspectives of women and racioethnic minorities. We expand our exploration of diversity by looking at the challenges and barriers to advancement that are unique to men in the IT workplace. We found a minimal level over schema accuracy – with the primary area of shared understanding occurring around the Interaction theme. These findings advance our understanding of the cognitive overlap (and lack thereof) regarding the challenges and barriers facing men in the IT field, and provide an initial step toward developing shared schemas of the IT workplace.

7. REFERENCES

[1] Altheide, D. L. and Johnson, J. M. 1994. Criteria for assessing interpretive validity in qualitative research. In *Handbook of Qualitative Research*, N.K. Denzin and Y.S. Lincoln, Eds. Sage Publications, London, UK, 1994, 485-499.

[2] Armstrong, D. J. 2005. Causal mapping: a discussion and demonstration. In *Causal Mapping For Research in Information Technology*, V.K. Narayanan, and D.J. Armstrong, Eds. Idea Group Publishing, Hershey, PA, 20-45.

[3] Axelrod, R. 1976. *The Structure of Decisions*, Princeton University Press, Princeton, NJ.

[4] Babbie, E. 1995. *The Practice of Social Research*, 7th Edition, Wadsworth, New York, NY.

[5] Berger, P.L. and Luckmann, T. 1966. *The Social Construction of Reality: A Treatise in the Sociology of Knowledge*, Doubleday, New York, NY.

[6] Cannon-Bowers, J.A. and Salas, E. 2001. Reflections on shared cognition. *Journal of Organizational Behavior*, 22, 195–202.

[7] Cannon-Bowers, J.A., Salas, E., and Converse, S.A. 1990. Cognitive psychology and team training: training shared mental models and complex systems. *Human Factors Society Bulletin*, 33, 1–4.

[8] Cannon-Bowers, J.A., Salas, E., and Converse, S.A. 1993. Shared Mental Models in Expert Team Decision Making. In *Current Issues in Individual and Group Decision Making*, N.J. Castellan, Jr., Ed. Erlbaum, Hillsdale, NJ, 221–246.

[9] Chatman, J. and Flynn, R. 2001. The influence of demographic heterogeneity on the emergence and consequences of cooperative norms in work teams. *Academy of Management Journal*, 44, 956-974.

[10] Chou, L.F., Wang, A.C., Wang, T.Y., Huang, M.P., and Cheng, B.S. 2008. Shared work values and team member effectiveness: the mediation of trustfulness and trustworthiness. *Human Relations* 61(12), 1713-1742.

[11] Collison, D., and Hearn, J. 1994. Naming men as men: implications for work, organization and management. *Gender, Work and Organization*, 1, 2-22.

[12] Cooke, N.J., Kiekel, P.A., Salas, E., Stout, R., Bowers, C.A., and Cannon-Bowers, J.A. 2003. Measuring team knowledge. *Group Dynamics: Theory, Research, and Practice*, 7(3), 179-199.

[13] Denzin, N. and Lincoln, Y. 2000. *Handbook of Qualitative Research*, Sage Publications, Thousand Oaks, CA.

[14] Duriau, V.J., Reger, R.K., and Pfarrer, M.D. 2007. A content analysis of the content analysis literature in organization studies: research themes, data sources, and methodological refinements. *Organizational Research Methods*, 10, 5-34.

[15] Edwards, B. D., Day, E. A., Arthur, W., Jr., and Bell, S. T. 2006. Relationships among team ability composition, team mental models, and team performance. *Journal of Applied Psychology*, 91(3), 727-736.

[16] Eisenhardt, K. M. 1989. Building theories from case study research. *Academy of Management Review*, 14(4), 532-550.

[17] Fiol, C.M. 1994. Consensus, diversity, and learning in organizations. *Organization Science*, 5(3), 403-420.

[18] Gershon, A., Gowen, L.K., Compian, L., and Hayward, C. 2004. Gender-stereotyped imagined dates and weight concerns in sixth-grade girls. *Sex Roles: A Journal of Research* 50(7-8), 515-523.

[19] Gibson, C.B. and Zellmer-Bruhn, M.E. 2001. Metaphors and meaning: an intercultural analysis of the concept of teamwork. *Administrative Science Quarterly*, 46, 274-303.

[20] Glaser, B., and Strauss, A. 1967. *The Discovery of Grounded Theory: Strategies of Qualitative Research*, Wiedenfeld and Nicholson, London, UK.

[21] Gray, P., King, W.R., McLean, E.R., and Watson, H.J. 1994. *Management of Information Systems*, 2nd Edition, Dryden Press, Fort Worth, TX.

[22] Hackman, J.R. 1990. *Groups That Work (and Those That Don't): Creating Conditions for Effective Teamwork.* Jossey-Bass, San Francisco, CA.

[23] Harrison, D.A., and Klein, K.J. 2007. What's the difference? diversity constructs as separation, variety, or disparity in organizations. *Academy of Management Review*, 32, 1199-1228.

[24] Harrison, D.A., Price, K.H., and Bell, M.P. 1998. Beyond relational demography: time and the effects of surface - and deep - level diversity on work group cohesion. *Academy of Management Journal*, 41(1), 96-107.

[25] Hodgkinson, G.P. 1997. Cognitive inertia in a turbulent market: the case of UK residential estate agents. *Journal of Management Studies*, 34(6), 921-945.

[26] Howell, W.C., and Cooke, N.J. 1989. Training the human information processor: a review of cognitive models. In *Training and Development in Organizations*, I. L. Goldstein, Ed. Jossey-Bass, San Francisco, CA, 121–182.

[27] Huber, G.P., and Lewis, K. 2010. Cross-understanding: implications for group cognition and performance, *Academy of Management Review*, 35(1), 6-26.

[28] Jackson, S.E., May, K.E., and Whitney, K. 1995. Understanding the dynamics of diversity in decision making teams. In *Team Effectiveness and Decision Making in Organizations*, R. Guzzo and E. Salas, Eds. Jossey-Bass, San Francisco, CA, 204-261.

[29] Johnson, T.E., and O'Connor, D.L. 2008. Measuring team shared understanding using the analysis-constructed shared mental model methodology. *Performance Improvement Quarterly*, 21(3), 113-134.

[30] Joshi, K D., and Kuhn, K.M. 2007. What it takes to succeed in information technology consulting: exploring the gender typing of critical attributes. *Information Technology & People*, 20(4), 400-424.

[31] Klimoski, R., and Mohammed, S. 1994. Team mental model; construct or metaphor. *Journal of Management*, 20(2), 403-437.

[32] Kozlowski, S.W.J., and Bell, B.S. 2003. Work groups and teams in organizations. In *Handbook of Psychology: Industrial and Organizational Psychology, Volume 12*, W.C. Borman, D.R. Ilgen, and R.J. Klimoski , Eds. John Wiley and Sons, New York, NY, 333-375.

[33] Kraiger, K.S., and Wenzel, L.H. 1997. Conceptual development and empirical evaluation of measures of shared mental models indicators of team effectiveness. In *Team Performance*

Assessment and Measurement: Theory, Methods, and Applications, M.K. Brannick, E. Salas and C. Prince, Eds. Lawrence Erlbaum, Hillsdale, NJ, 63-84.

[34] Lee, A.S., and Baskerville, R.L. 2003. Generalizing generalizability in information systems research. *Information Systems Research*, 14(3), 221-243.

[35] Leinhardt, G., and Smith, D.A. 1985. Expertise in mathematics instruction: subject matter knowledge. *Journal of Educational Psychology*, 77, 247–271.

[36] Lim, B.C. and Klein, K.J. 2006. Team mental models and team performance: a field study of the effects of team mental model similarity and accuracy. *Journal of Organizational Behavior*, 27, 403–418.

[37] Madriz, E. 2000. Focus groups in feminist research. In *Handbook of Qualitative Research*, N. Denzin and Y. Lincoln , Eds. Sage Publications, Thousand Oaks, CA, 835-850.

[38] Marks, M.A., Sabella, M.J., Burke, C.S., and Zaccaro, S.J. 2002. The impact of cross-training on team effectiveness, *Journal of Applied Psychology*, 87, 3-13.

[39] Mathieu, J.E., Heffner, T.S., Goodwin, G.F., Salas, E., and Cannon-Bowers, J.A. 2000. The influence of shared mental models on team process and performance. *Journal of Applied Psychology*, 85, 273–83.

[40] Mathieu, J.E., Heffner, T.S., Goodwin, G.F., and Cannon-Bowers, J.A. 2005. Sealing the quality of teammates mental modes: equifinality and normative comparisons. *Journal of Organizational Behavior*, 26, 37-56.

[41] McNeese, M.D., Rentsch, J.R., and Perusich, K. 2000. Modeling, measuring, and mediating teamwork: the use of fuzzy cognitive maps and team member schema similarity to enhance decision making. *IEEE International Conference on Systems, Man, and Cybernetics*, 2, 1081-1086.

[42] Mohammed, S., and Dumville, B.C. 2001. Team mental models in a team knowledge framework: expanding theory and measurement across disciplinary boundaries. *Journal of Organizational Behavior*, 22(2), 89-106.

[43] Mohammed, S., and Ringseis, E. 2001. Cognitive diversity and consensus in group decision making: the role of inputs, processes, and outcomes. *Organizational Behavior and Human Decision Processes*, 78(1), 25-62.

[44] Mor Barak, M.E., Cherin, D.A., and Berkman, S. 1998. Organizational and personal dimensions in diversity climate: ethnic and gender differences in employee perceptions. *Journal of Applied Behavioral Science*, 34(1), 82-104.

[45] Osterman, P. 2008. *The Truth About Middle Managers: Who They Are, How They Work, and Why They Matter*. Harvard University Press, Boston, MA.

[46] Patterson, M.L. 1996. Social behavior and social cognition. In *What's Social about Social Cognition? Social Cognition Research in Small Groups*, J.L. Nye and A.M. Brower , Eds. Sage Publications, London, UK, 87-105.

[47] Patton, E., and Johns, G. 2007. Women's absenteeism in the popular press: evidence for a gender-specific absence culture. *Human Relations*, 60, 1579-1612.

[48] Pavlou, P.A., and Dimoka, A. 2006. The nature and role of feedback text comments in online marketplaces: implications for trust building, price premiums, and seller differentiation. *Information Systems Research*, 17(4), 391–412.

[49] Rentsch, J.R., and Hall, R.J.1994. Members of great teams think alike: a model of team effectiveness and schema similarity among team members. In *Advances in Interdisciplinary Studies of Work Teams, Series on Self Managed Work Teams*, M.M. Beyerlein and D.A. Johnson , Eds. JAI Press, Greenwich, CT, 223-262.

[50] Rentsch, J.R., and Klimoski, R. 2001. Why do great minds think alike? antecedents of team member schema agreement. *Journal of Organizational Behavior*, 22, 107-120.

[51] Rentsch, J.R., and Zelno, J.A. 2003. The role of cognition in managing conflict to maximize team effectiveness. In In*ternational Handbook of Organizational Teamwork and Cooperative Working*, M.A. West, D. Tjosvold, and K.G. Smith, Eds. John Wiley and Sons, Ltd., Hoboken, NJ, 131-150.

[52] Sanday, P.R. 1979. The ethnographic paradigm(s). *Administrative Science Quarterly*, 24(4), 527-538.

[53] Smith-Jentsch, K.A., Mathieu, J.E., and Kraiger, K. 2005. Investigating linear and interactive effects of shared mental models on safety and efficiency in a field setting. *Journal of Applied Psychology*, 90, 523–535.

[54] Stout, R.J., Cannon-Bowers, J.A., and Salas, E. 1996. The role of shared mental models in developing team situational awareness: implications for training. *Training Research Journal*, 2, 86-116.

[55] Strauss, A., and Corbin, J. 1968. *Basics of Qualitative Research: Grounded Theory, Procedures, and Techniques*. Sage Publications, Newbury Park, CA.

[56] Strauss, A., and Corbin, J. 1998. *Basics of Qualitative Research Techniques and Procedures for Developing Grounded Theory, 2nd Edition*. Sage Publications, Thousand Oaks, CA, 1998.

[57] Tashakkori, A., and Teddlie, C.1998. *Mixed Methodology: Combining Qualitative and Quantitative Approaches*. Sage Publications, Thousand Oaks, CA.

[58] Tegarden, D.P., Tegarden, L.F., and Sheetz, S.D. 2009. Cognitive factions in a top management team: surfacing and analyzing cognitive diversity using causal maps. *Group Decision and Negotiation*, 18(6), 537-566.

[59] Thomas, R.R. 1990. From affirmative action to affirming diversity. *Harvard Business Review*, (March-April), 107-117.

[60] Thomas, R.R., and Davies, A. 2005. Theorizing the micro-politics of resistance: new public management and managerial identities in the UK public services. *Organization Studies*, 26(5), 683-706.

[61] Todd, P., Mckeen, J., and Gallupe, B. 1995. The evolution of IS job skills: a content analysis of IS job advertisements from 1970 to 1990. *MIS Quarterly*, 19(1), 1-26.

[62] Tsui, A., Egan, T., and O'Reilly, C. 1992. Being different: relational demography and organizational attachment. *Administrative Science Quarterly*, 37, 549 579.

[63] Weber, R. 1990. *Basic Content Analysis, Second Edition*. Sage Publications, Newbury Park, CA.

[64] Wharton, A., and Baron, J. 1987. So happy together? the impact of gender segregation on men at work. *American Sociological Review*, 52, 574-587.

[65] Yin, R.K. 1984. *Case Study Research: Design and Methods*, Sage Publications, Beverly Hills, CA.

Analyzing Citation Impact of IS Research by Women and Men: Do Women Have Higher Levels of Research Impact?

Mike Gallivan
Georgia State University
CIS Department
Robinson College of Business
Atlanta, Georgia, USA
001 (404) 413-7363

mgallivan@gsu.edu

ABSTRACT

Over the past decade, the SIG MIS conference has become a leading venue for research on gender issues in the IT workforce. The question of women's research impact relative to men is important for several reasons. First, if research by women is not cited as often as that of men, it would be necessary to ask why. In that case, the explanation may be due to the fact that women publish their work in venues that are less visible relative to men; because women publish on topics that draw less interest from a broad audience (resulting in fewer subsequent studies that cite their work); or that women's research, as a whole, is of lower quality than that of men. Conversely, if research by women IS scholars is cited more often than research by men, it is again worth asking why: is it because women (as a whole) publish in more visible, higher-quality venues than men, because women publish on topics that interest a broader audience, because their research addresses more timely or controversial topics, or their research is of higher quality, relative to men? We test various hypotheses to show that papers published by women in five leading IS journals are cited more frequently than papers by men, after controlling for the journal and the subject matter of the papers. The effect is small, but significant. We conclude that this is because (a) women publish in MIS Quarterly at a higher rate relative to men – which happens to be the IS journal that receives the most citations; (b) women are under-represented among authors in three journals that receive fewer citations; and (c) women generally publish few papers on topics that receive the lowest rates of citations.

Categories and Subject Descriptors

H.m Miscellaneous

General Terms

Measurement.

Keywords

Citations, Gender, Gender Discrimination, Research Impact

1. INTRODUCTION

Over the past decade, the SIG MIS conference has become a leading venue for research on gender issues in the IT workforce. Relevant topics have included potential barriers and stereotypes that may dissuade girls and young women from pursuing computer interests in secondary school – or choosing college majors or careers in IT-related areas. During these years, a host of studies have focused on career experiences of women in IT consulting [14, 15], or other jobs [25], as well as the effect of national culture [31], regional culture within a given country [30] or other factors shaping girls' and women's choice of IT careers [33]. Although holding a faculty position in information systems (IS) or computer science is just one end of the continuum of educational pursuits in this area, few studies have tackled issues facing women in academic careers in IS or computer science – including even the SIG MIS conference.

Among the few exceptions we found was an interpretive study examining the experiences of minority women (and men) in IS PhD programs [23], and an empirical study examining differences in the research productivity of men and women IS scholars [10]. Since we regard women's experiences in IS and computer science academic careers as relevant to understanding their experiences as IT employees and managers, we consider whether gender is associated with the impact of scholarly work published in academic IS journals. The question of whether women are fairly represented among the authors of IS academic research has been raised previously – at least within the context of authors in two leading IS journals – *MIS Quarterly* and *Journal of MIS* [17] – or among the list of most productive IS researchers [10]. To our knowledge, however, no empirical study has examined whether research published by women in scholarly IS journals or computer science journals achieves the same level of citation "impact" as comparable research by men.

The question of women's research impact relative to men is important for several reasons. First, if research by women is not cited as often as that of men, it would be necessary to ask why. In that case, the explanation may be due to the fact that women publish their work in venues that are less visible relative to men; because women publish on topics that draw less interest from a broad audience (resulting in fewer subsequent studies that cite their work); or that women's research, as a whole, is of lower quality than that of men. Conversely, if research published by women is cited as frequently as that of men (i.e., no significant difference in either direction), it is worth knowing whether this has always been the case in the IS field – or whether this is a relatively recent phenomenon as more women have joined the ranks of associate editors, senior editors, and editors-in-chief of leading journals. Finally (and here, we foreshadow our results), if scholarly research by women IS scholars is cited more often than similar research by men, it is worth celebrating this fact – but also asking why: is it because women (as a whole) publish in more visible, higher-quality venues than men, because women publish on topics that interest a broader audience, because women's research addresses more timely or controversial topics, or because women's research is of higher quality, on average? The latter explanation (i.e., higher quality) may, in turn, suggest the existence of discriminatory bias against women in the review process, as they seek to publish their work in leading journals.

If indeed women must meet higher thresholds of quality in order to publish their work (or higher levels of other attributes, such as timeliness of the topic, rigor, or relevance), and this, in turn manifests in a higher level of citations, this means that only high-quality research by women is being published – while just "average" quality research by women faces barriers to publication that average quality work from men does not [3]. If there is a consistently higher level of citation impact for women's research that cannot be explained by their choice of topics, then this may suggest bias in the review process. While this question of the relative impact of women's research has not been a topic of interest to the IS or computer science communities, it has been considered in several other fields – such as accounting [8], physical and biological sciences [34], information science [24], and even in legal services research [3].

The paper is structured as follows. The next section reviews prior studies of gender and research impact, formulating hypotheses for IS scholars, based on what we know from other fields. We also hypothesize about factors that may trigger higher or lower levels of citation impact that women's publications accrue, relative to similar publications by men. These triggers include (a) the selectivity and visibility of journals in which men and women publish; (b) the choice of topics or type of research methods employed by women; (c) time effects (i.e., women publishing a higher fraction of papers in recent years when most IS journals exhibit higher levels of citation impact. We then describe the methods we used to collect and analyze citation data for five leading journals and our results. We explain the value of our results for understanding the history of the IS field, as well as the "social life of IS research" [7]. We conclude with limitations and areas for future research.

2. LITERATURE REVIEW

In the physical and biomedical sciences, it has long been known that women publish fewer papers than men – a phenomenon that has been labeled a "productivity paradox" [6, 32]. It is not our purpose to review this very large body of work on gender and research productivity – which usually focuses on the relative number of journal papers published by men and women in a given field.[1] This work has been reviewed many times already – including in the "hard" sciences [34], in the humanities [12], economics [13], and for many social sciences – including various business disciplines [11]. While most of these studies conclude that women publish fewer papers than men on a per capita basis, some empirical studies argue that this can be explained by women working in institutions with fewer resources – including less time for research. On a positive note, many of these studies observe that women generally accrue equivalent numbers of citations to

their work (across all their publications) as men. This latter finding is the true paradox, since – if women publish 15%-35% fewer papers than men (which is a typical finding) but women accrue the same total number of total citations over their careers, this implies that women's research is more heavily cited on a per paper basis [32].

Although surprising, this is exactly the conclusion reached by several authors [5, 32]. One explanation proposed is that women focus more on the *quality* of their publications, rather than on the *quantity*. By focusing more on quality, this implies that, on average, women submit fewer papers to journals than men. It also means that women are more likely to self-censor by delaying or refraining from submitting papers for journal review until their work reaches a high level of quality. We emphasize that the latter explanation is speculative [32], but it may account for the observed results of women having equivalent numbers of citations to men, on average, despite having fewer publications: quality rather than quantity matters. Regardless of the fact that such an explanation is favorable to women, the actual mechanism underlying why women's research is cited more often (per paper) than that of men has not been empirically demonstrated. Several rival explanations exist for the "quality rather than quantity" thesis. In fact, although many writers conclude that papers by women are cited more often than comparable papers by men, the outcome variable being analyzed is variers across these studies.

Most studies have considered the *lifetime total citation counts* of men and women in a given field and – like most other citation-related data – there is enormous variance within a given field for the set of women examined (as well as for the set of men examined). Thus, the enormous variances encountered in analyzing citation data (which are usually much larger than the mean values) may dwarf any true but small differences in citation impact that may exist between men and women.[2] In addition to studies that focus on the total lifetime citation counts for men and women, some studies have analyzed the *average number of citations per published paper* for men and women [8], finding higher average citations for women's papers than for ones by men. But again, the devil is in the details. Since citation counts and averages are not normally distributed, then it is prudent for scholars analyzing such citation data to avoid typical statistical comparisons that assume normal data (e.g., T-tests, ANOVA), unless they are careful to remove outlier values. It is even better to use approaches that are suited to analyzing non-normal data – including reporting *median* values to compare women's and men's citations (rather than means, which can be biased by outliers), and also non-parametric tests (such as Mann-Whitney U-test for comparing non-normal data for two groups).

As with any paradoxical result, unraveling the mystery of whether and why women's research may be cited more per paper requires attention to details – in terms of the data included in such analyses (which types of articles, from which journals, and for what years are citations counted) and details of the statistical tests (what other factors are controlled for – such as publication year, publication outlet, handling of outliers, etc.). In addition to the

---

[1] Some studies also count books and articles in edited books; however, most studies focus just on journal papers.

[2] For example, some studies that report no difference between the total lifetime citations for men and women in a given field neglect to specify how they arrived at this result. Since citation data are not normally distributed (but very skewed – with a few extremely highly-cited scholars), then *median* values are better measures than *means*.

fact that citation data can be tracked using several sources – Google Scholar vs. Web of Science – the actual *metric* being compared for men and women is also critical. Since women, as a whole, gained entry to most disciplines more recently than most men, on average, then the effect of women's delayed entry into a given academic field will have different effects on different metrics. The unit of analysis will also vary for different metrics:

- Total lifetime numbers of citations to scholar's body of published work (unit = the individual author)
- Average (mean/median) citations per published paper (unit = the individual journal paper)
- Average (mean/median) citation *rate* per year since year of publication (unit = the individual journal paper)

The first two metrics are strongly biased in favor of scholars who began their careers earlier; in contrast, the last metric is biased toward a time period when studies published in a given field are cited more heavily (i.e., typically more recently). In fields where women (as a whole) began their academic careers later than men, achieving equivalent numbers total lifetime citations (the first metric) is a near-impossible challenge. If the data support such a result, as some have claimed [2, 32], this implies that each paper by a woman scholar is cited *much* more frequently than a comparable paper by a man. For example, if women, on average, have only had 80% as much time to accrue citations to their research as men (because the average career tenure for women in a field is only 80% as long) but women accrue equivalent total lifetime numbers of citations, this implies that women's research must be cited 25% more often. If true, this represents an incredible accomplishment! Such evidence of equivalent or higher lifetime total citations for women scholars in a given field has often been reached indirectly,[3] rather than via direct empirical analysis. Two exceptions to the indirect path to showing women's greater impact per paper are studies that have directly shown that women's research is cited more often than papers by men [3, 5]. One such study was based on an analysis of citations to articles in elite law review journals [3]; another studied examined citations to papers published by Spanish post-doctoral researchers across a range of science disciplines [5].

As we stated above, the first two metrics in the bulleted list are biased toward authors who started their publishing careers earlier. Thus, it is inadequate to simply compute the average numbers of citations (i.e., averaging across papers by the same authors), and then compare these averages for men and women. The problem is that it is unfair to compare citation *counts* for papers published years or even decades apart. What is more useful is to compare citation counts to papers published during the same era (i.e., within two-to-five years of each other), or to analyze citations to papers using the third metric in the bulleted list (above): *citation rate* (i.e., number of citations per year), where citations are divided by the number of years that a paper has been in the public domain to be cited.[4] In this paper, we focus on this

metric – citation rate – where the average reflects the total number of citations to a single paper divided by elapsed time since its date of publication. In this study, we do not sum or average citation data across multiple papers by a given author.

In reviewing the literature, we found few studies that considered gender effects using this method – using citation *rate* as the outcome variable. Most studies counted the total number of citations that each paper received, regardless of the actual year of publication. For instance, in a study by Borrego et al., the authors conclude: "articles by female [Spanish] Ph.D. holders are cited significantly more often than articles by male Ph.D. holders, even when self-citations … were excluded" [5, p. 98].

In a study that *did* analyze citation rates (i.e., citations per year), Ayres and Vars [3] analyzed papers in three elite law reviews, searching for evidence of reviewer or editor bias in accepting papers for publication by certain categories of authors. For example, they reasoned that if papers published in *Harvard Law Review* by Harvard faculty consistently received fewer citations than ones published by non-Harvard faculty authors, this could indicate that the quality threshold necessary for "local" Harvard professors to have their papers accepted in the *Harvard Law Review* was lower than for "non-local" authors – who must achieve a higher quality threshold to be published. Consistent with their hypothesis, Ayres and Vars found lower citation rates for papers by "local" faculty who published in three elite law reviews (Harvard, Yale, Stanford), in turn, triggering their claim that such authors have an easier path to publication (i.e., a lower quality threshold is required). More germane to our study, Ayres and Vars also analyzed each author's gender and ethnic minority status – although they included these attributes as covariates, rather than to test specific hypotheses or theories related to race or gender discrimination. Nevertheless, their results are useful.

Based on Ayres and Vars' analysis of the effect of gender and race (after controlling for other factors, such as the paper topic and the authors' status as a "local" or "non-local" author), they found that papers published by women in these law reviews accrued 47% higher citation rates than papers by men. The effect was even more dramatic for minority female authors – who averaged 160% higher citation rates than non-minority men (more than least 2½ times the number of citations per year than papers by non-minority men!). These results led them to speculate that papers submitted by women (and especially, minority women) experienced bias during the reviewing process – and thus had to achieve a higher quality threshold to be accepted. To supplement their analysis, the authors calculated the probability that papers by women would be among the "20% of least-cited papers." They concluded "articles by women were significantly less likely to be among the least-cited [papers than ones by men] (p = 0.03)" [3, p 443]. Most importantly, they interpreted both sets of results showing higher citation rates to women's work in elite law reviews as having three possible explanations:

> First, editors may be biased against articles by women – setting a higher quality threshold for their acceptance. Second, editors may set the same quality threshold for both male- and female-authored articles but, conditional on

---

[3] For instance, we characterize as "indirect" the logic that says that if women and men have equivalent citations but men publish significantly more papers, then citations to women's research must be higher per paper [8].

[4] Some publishers have begun to post papers on their websites prior to publication (e.g., INFORMS' *Articles in Advance*), which may hugely increase the number of citations to a paper

---

prior to publication and during the paper's first one or two years after publication. Since the "impact factor" is computed just on the first two years, this availability of papers to cite before the actual publication date will have a huge impact on journals' impact factors.

[submissions] being above this threshold, the articles by women were of higher average quality. Third, readers might cite female-authored articles more *not* because of their higher quality but for some other reason…[which] encompasses a wide variety of criteria that differ from an article's quality. To provide [an] … illustration, international law articles may be cited [much] less frequently than other articles because there are fewer opportunities each year for these articles to be cited (at least, in Social Sciences Citation Index).

Although the exact mechanism underlying the fact that papers by women are cited more often than those of men is not known, the last explanation offered by Ayres and Vars includes the possibility that a paper's subject matter has an impact (since future papers on international law are the ones most likely to cite previous papers on the same topic; however if these law reviews publish few articles on international law, then prior, high-quality articles on the topic will be under-cited). Ayres and Vars also raise the possibility of deliberate bias in authors' citation practices when they posit: "citing authors might, as a theoretical matter [of principle], discriminate against [citing previous] articles by men" [3, p. 444]. We believe that their study provides evidence that is quite fascinating – suggesting a puzzle that has yet to be unraveled.

3. CONCEPTUAL DEVELOPMENT AND HYPOTHESES

We start our theory building by positing that the IS field will be similar to various other disciplines where higher citations to women's research have been demonstrated – accounting, chemistry, information science, etc. For us to posit otherwise (i.e., to expect that gender will be *unrelated* to citation impact in IS), would require that we justify why the IS field is different from these other fields where higher citations to research by women is known to occur. With women representing 25% of IS faculty members [21], although the ratio of women among IS faculty with PhD degrees is lower, we have no reason that expect that IS will differ from other fields where this phenomenon has been shown to occur. Thus, we posit:

H1: Journal papers published by women authors will be more frequently cited than those of men.

If indeed journal papers by women are *more* frequently cited, as a whole, compared to those by men, there are several possible explanations that either individually, collectively, or via interactive effects (i.e., multiplicative effects) may explain the result. Some of these explanatory effects suggest the possible existence of gender bias, while other factors suggest that men or women selectively make choices that subsequently but indirectly, cause their papers to be cited more or less often. We review evidence for two such choices – research topic and journal outlet – and measurement artifacts.

3.1 Citations differ based on research topic

It is possible that some topics within a given discipline generate more citations – whether this is due to certain topics being "hot" (i.e., highly citable) at a given time, more interesting, or simply having a larger number of scholars working in that area. Consider the latter effect associated with the relative size of the research communities working on a specific topic. If the number

of scholars who study IT adoption and usage is six times larger than the number of IS researchers who conduct "design science" research, then prior studies on IT adoption and usage will be cited six times as often as design science papers (on average), assuming that all else is equal. "All else" includes the assumption that scholars in different sub-communities have similar submission rates, acceptance rates, and citation norms. This explanation is based solely on the relative size of the communities, rather than any implicit suggestion that the average quality of research differs by topic.

While the above explanation assumes that an equivalent fraction of papers are accepted for publication on each research topic (i.e., IT adoption and use, design science, etc.), this fraction of accepted papers may also be subject to deliberate intervention by journal editors – for example, in editorial policies that call for publishing more "design science" or scientometrics work [27]. A journal editor's decision to publish more papers on a given topic – whether design science, scientometrics, action research or any topic – will necessarily ensure that previous papers published on the same topics will be cited more often. For instance, in the late 1990s, *MIS Quarterly*, proposed a Call for Papers on "intensive research methods" – and accepted papers were published across a series of issues in 1999 [20]. Likewise, *Information Systems Research* published two special issues on the topic of measuring the value of Ecommerce in 2002 [28]. In both cases, the editorial goal of publishing special issues on a given topic in high visibility outlets (*MIS Quarterly* and *ISR*, respectively), virtually ensured that previous studies on the given topic will be cited *much* more often than they would have been in the absence of the special issues. This represents one possible explanation for why some topics may be cited more frequently than others: editors' deliberate policies to publish more studies on a given topic.

While it appears sensible that papers belonging to different topics will yield higher or lower numbers of subsequent citations to them, this effect may be difficult to demonstrate empirically, unless a given discipline has a standard set of subject area codes, which are consistently listed in the paper (i.e., subject codes or keyword codes). Such standardization of research topic classifications facilitates comparative analyses of citations by topic, with the possibility of showing which topics are consistently cited more often than others. In economics, a set of 24 standard JEL codes (*Journal of Economics Literature*) are consistently used, which can be included as covariates in scientometric studies. In one analysis of citations to economics papers published in eight leading journals, Medoff [22] reported that papers on one topic were consistently cited more often than average ("economic development, technological change and growth"), and no other topics were cited significantly *less* often than average. Likewise, a standard set of topic categories exists in legal research, so that it is possible to show that papers on two topics ("constitutional law" and "jurisprudence") are consistently cited at higher-than-average rates in law reviews whereas papers on "international law" are consistently cited less frequently than average [3].

The IS field has not identified a standard typology of topics which are consistently shown on published papers; however, Sidorova et al [26] identified an emergent typology consisting of 13 topics, as well as five levels of analysis categories. They generated their subject area (and level of analysis) categories based on latent semantic analysis of words appearing in all abstracts of papers published in three leading North American IS journals since each journal's initial year of publication. Since it is possible to use the set of 13 subject categories that Sidorova et al [26] derived to classify papers into topic areas, it is feasible to analyze the effect of topic on papers' citation rate – analogous to prior empirical work in economics [22] and legal research [3].

While it is indeed possible to analyze the effect of topic on citation rates, at a conceptual level, we have no *a priori* reason to expect that men or women will be more likely to publish papers on topics that are more or less "citable." In short, we lack an *a priori* expectation that women will be more likely to publish papers on certain topics, relative to men. While scholars in some fields have argued that women are more likely to use qualitative, interpretive research methods than men – presumably, because women seek to understand their informants' point of view – we are not aware of this argument having been offered in the IS field. Moreover, the set of subject codes that Sidorova et al. [26] identified do not lend themselves to dichotomizing into distinct research methods (qualitative vs. quantitative) or epistemologies (positivist vs. interpretive).[5] All (or nearly all) the topics they identified can be investigated using a range of research methods and epistemological positions – including survey research, qualitative field research, conceptual papers, or review papers. We thus posit a null hypothesis regarding the effect of gender on choice of topics:

H2: There is no difference in the likelihood of women publishing on a given topic, relative to men

The above null hypothesis means, in effect, that, if women account for 20% of published papers across a set of journals, then we expect that women will account for 20% of papers on each topic area. Any contrary results – whereby women publish significantly *more* or *less* than 20% of the papers on a given topic – will lead to rejection of the null hypothesis.

3.2 Journal Quality Influences Citations

We intuitively know that more citations generally accrue to papers in a high-quality or high-visibility journals (which is the notion of "journal impact factor"). Some journals have distinct patterns of higher or lower average rates of citations, which are believed to be relatively constant over time. Thus, one factor that indirectly triggers the rate of citations a paper receives is the journal where it is published. In addition to requiring that we control for the journal in any empirical study that aggregates citation data across several journals, there is also a possible gender "angle" to the question of journal venue. If women's publications are distributed unequally (non-randomly) across a set of journals, and if the different journals have varying "impact factors" (average citation rates), then this may cause research by women to be cited more or less than that of men. For example, if women authors publish 20% of all papers across a set (or "Basket") of journals, but they publish 25% of papers in the higher-quality (or higher-visibility) journals in the set – but just 15% of papers in lower-quality (or lower-visibility) journals in the

set, then women's research will have greater citation impact, compared to men. In this example, the result of women's work accruing higher citations is due to their work being over-represented in the highest-quality journals and under-represented in lower-quality journals, relative to women's overall 20% representation among IS authors.

We created the above example to illustrate that the publication venue can directly influence the rate of citations that papers published in them receive – which may be one explanation why papers by women are cited more frequently than those of men. In the IS field, we have no reason to expect that women or men are more likely to publish in the higher-quality (i.e., higher-visibility) or in the lower-quality journals, relative to their representation across a larger set of journals. Of course, the study of three law reviews by Ayres and Vars [3] indeed suggests a bias in the reviewing process in favor of men (as well as "local" faculty authors) and against women and minority authors (as well as "non-local" authors), but another study of acceptance rates of papers by different groups of authors – based on gender, race, and faculty rank – in an elite management journal found no evidence of editorial bias toward or against women, or toward authors of any race, faculty rank (assistant, associate, or full professor) or other personal attributes. In that study, a former Editor-in-Chief of *Academy of Management Journal* (Jan Beyer) and colleagues examined but found no evidence for gender bias on the acceptance of papers submitted to *AMJ* [4]. In view of this lack of gender-bias in *AMJ*'s review process,[6] we do not expect to find gender bias in the review process for a set of IS journals. Instead, we assume a constant ratio of papers by women in the highest-quality journals that is equivalent to women's fraction of published papers across the set of journals analyzed.

H3: There is no difference in the fraction of papers published in the highest-quality IS journals by men and women (compared to the ratio of papers by men and women in a larger set of journals).

3.3 Other Artifacts (including introduction of new journals that cite previous studies)

It has been shown that, for the most part, academic journals' *impact factors* tend to increase over time. This means that the mean number of citations to a paper published in year $x+1$ will be higher than the mean number of citations to a paper published in year x. Although not a universal law (since specific journals may decline in quality or visibility – or journals may deliberately change their editorial mission over time[7]), the general trend is one

---

[5] There are a few possible exceptions, involving topics related to IS economics. One of the topics identified by Sidorova et al is "IT and markets" which consists of quantitative, positivst studies, and few or no qualitative and/or interpretive ones. Thus, a methodological bias will be present for this topic, such that if we believe the claim that women are more likely to conduct qualitative studies, then women will be underrepresented as authors of this topic. A second category that Sidorova et al identified is related to economics: "the value of IT."

[6] Beyer and her colleagues [6] found no "main effect" of gender on acceptance rate, and thus they concluded that gender bias did not exist. They also analyzed two-way interactions between gender and faculty rank, but found no effect for such combinations of gender or rank. They did find support for a three-way interaction between gender x rank x receipt of major funding. This 3-way interaction revealed that male tenured faculty who had major grant funding s were more likely to have a paper accepted than tenured women with major grant funding or tenured men *without* major grant funding.

[7] An example is *Communications of the ACM*, which changed its editorial mission several times. It now seeks to publish more academic papers from member conferences (such as SIG MIS CPR), in contrast to its practitioner focus for the last 15 years.

of increasingly higher "journal impact factors" over time. This is due to the creation of more new venues for publishing academic research over time (which, in turn, provide a larger base of articles that cite previous articles), combined with the demise of very few journals.[8] The newly-created journals publish papers which, in turn, cite the earlier work in more established journals, thus leading to the result of established journals having ever higher "impact factors" as time goes on. If citations from the newer venues *are* counted, then the average citation rates to articles published in older journals will increase over time.[9] For example, the impact factor for *MIS Quarterly* – which measures the mean number of citations to a given paper in *MIS Quarterly* for a given time interval – consistently increases year after year, largely due to other new journals being founded. Thus, year of a paper's publication (which, in turn, is a proxy for the total set of journals published in a given field) is a key covariate to include.

For instance, if women published just 5% of papers in *ISR* in 1995 but women published 15% of papers in *ISR* in 2005, then the higher average impact factor for *ISR* in 2005 than in 1995 (which is, in turn, based on a larger set of IS journals that are available to cite *ISR* papers after 2005), may lead to the result that women's papers in *ISR* are cited more often – and thus of apparent higher quality than papers by men. It is thus critical to control for year of publication when analyzing the citation rates of papers published years apart, even for papers published in the same journal. To capture such covariates, we posit that:

H4: Papers published in recent years will have higher citation rates (citations per year after publication) due to the artifact of more journals becoming available to cite them. To the extent that women publish their work in some or all journals at rising *proportions* over time, then this artifact of the rising "impact factor" of journals over time will positively affect women's citation rates.

4. RESEARCH METHODS

For this study, we analyzed papers published from 1992 to 2007 in the AIS Senior Scholars' "Basket of Six" list of journals. Of the six journals included in the AIS Senior Scholars' "Basket of Six,"[10] we omitted *Journal of the Association for Information Systems* because citation data to its papers were not available until 2009 (and then only for papers published in 2008). We analyzed the remaining five IS journals in the "Basket of Six." For each paper, we coded each author's gender.[11] We recorded citation data from ISI/Reuter's *Web of Science* database, which tracks citations in "Social Science Citation Index" and "Science Citation Index."

In order to compute the outcome variable (citations rate), we coded the month and year of each article's publication date,[12] and used this to identify the "amount of time elapsed" – which was the denominator we used to compute each paper's citation rate. Web of Science initiated its online version in 1992, which indexes the citations to all AIS "Basket of Six" journals starting in 1992 (for *MIS Quarterly*),[13] or in subsequent years.[14] We truncated our search as of 2007 because our own prior work revealed that it takes at least five years for papers published in these leading IS journals to reach their maximum citation rate [9]. This means that a paper published in 2011 would not start to receive its maximum rate of citations until at least 2016. We limited our analyses to papers published before 2007 – so our dataset encompasses 1992 to 2006.

With the help of several research assistants, we coded the citation data for over 800 papers published in these journals. For coauthored papers, we recorded author data, including gender, on separate rows of our spreadsheet. Next, we calculated descriptive statistics for each journal with regard to the outcome variable (citation rate per year), and we conducted simple T-tests (ANOVA) with gender as the predictor variable.

Table 1. IS Journals Analyzed		
Title	**Start Date**	**End Date**
EJIS	January 1995	October 2006
ISJ	January 1995	October 2006
ISR	March 1994	December 2006
JMIS	Fall 1999	Winter 2006/07
MISQ	March 1992	December 2006

We also used the non-parametric test, Mann-Whitney U-test, to analyze the effect of gender on citation rate, allowing for the possibility that citation rate data are non-normal.

We completed our analysis by creating a consolidated dataset for all five journals. We used multiple regression on the

---

[8] Similar to population growth, if the "birth rate" of new journals exceeds the "death rate" (discontinuation of older journals), then there will be a larger total number of journals – and papers in them – available to cite prior articles.

[9] Of course, the newer venues may not be indexed by the citation indexing services (e.g., ISI's Web of Science).

[10] The journals include *European Journal of IS, Journal of MIS, Information Systems Journal, Journal of Association for Information Systems, MIS Quarterly, Information Systems Research*

[11] This results in 1% missing data, mostly for authors of papers in European journals (*Information Systems Journal* and *European Journal of Information Systems*) for whom we were unable to locate author website containing photographs.

[12] As mentioned above, several journals now provide pre-publication copies of papers on their website to subscribers – in an attempt to begin accruing citations even before the paper is officially published. Since some citation indexing services (e.g., Google Scholar) count citations from unpublished dissertations and working papers, then the citations from various sources to the not-yet-published papers on publisher's websites can increase the citation counts to these papers (and in turn, raise the journal's impact factor). While this is a concern when using Google Scholar, it is not an issue for ISI's *Web of Science* (which only tracks citations from published papers *to* other published works). This limits the problem of counting citations to unpublished papers, but also introduces major time delays.

[13] For papers published before 1992, it is possible to search for citation data using a specific "cited reference search," but only the first author of each paper was tracked for these papers published before 1992.

[14] Web of Science began indexing other journals later: in 1994 (*Information Systems Research*); 1995 (*European Journal of IS* and *Information Systems Journal*); 1999 (*Journal of MIS*), 2008 (*Journal of Association for Information Systems*). We excluded JAIS, since we analyze papers published before 2007.

consolidated data using separate "dummy codes" to represent each journal. We also included "publication year" as a covariate to test our last hypothesis.[15] After adding the journal dummy variables and year, we included gender as a predictor, and we identified the change in the proportion of variance explained (R^2 change) by gender, as well as the associated p-value.

When differences in the number or rate of citations occur for distinct groups of authors (e.g., men vs. women), it may be because the topics that one group studies are more popular (i.e., have larger numbers of scholars working in them) relative to the topics studied by the other group. For example, in their study of legal research, it was necessary for Ayres and Vars [3] to control for topic using standardardized topic categories to show that papers published on "jurisprudence" and "constitutional law" are cited more often than average. To the extent that women are more likely to publish papers on popular topics (e.g., jurisprudence), their work is more likely to be cited later on. If women are more likely to be authors of "unpopular" topics (international law), the opposite outcome would occur To allow for the analogous effects of IS papers on popular and unpopular topics, we specified the fraction of papers by men and women on various topics, using a typology by Sidorova et al [28].

5. RESULTS

H1: Journal papers published by women authors will be more frequently cited than those of men.

When we analyzed each journal individually, we were unable to identify any journal in which men or women had higher citation rates (at p< .05), before controlling for topic or year of publication. We found a weak, non-significant effect for three journals: *Information Systems Journal* (p< .10), *EJIS* and *ISR* (both p = 0.11) where women had higher citation rates, before controlling for topic. These values are summarized in Table 2.

When we consolidated the data for all journals and controlled for each journal using dummy codes, there was a weak gender effect (p < .10), with women's papers receiving higher citation rates than those men (by 0.9 citation per year). This was a very weak effect, accounting for less than 0.5% of the variance in citation rates. This weak effect was much larger and significant when we omitted *MIS Quarterly* from the analysis, in which case, the effect became significant (p < .001). The difference was equal to 1.3 citations more per year for papers by women.

H2: There is no difference in the probability of women publishing on a given topic relative to men.

In this analysis, we analyzed the fraction of women's papers on a given topic, vs. the analogous fraction of men's papers on the same topic. Contrary to our null hypothesis, we found three out of 13 topics for which women were *less* likely than men to publish papers (relative to men's and women's representation among authors overall). Using the topic category labels from Sidorova et al [26], the significant differences we found in the proportion of papers are as follows for men (M) and women (F):

- Topic 1: IS Development: 2.9% (M) vs. 1.6% (F) (p < .01)
- Topic 3: Value of IT: 5.2% (M) vs. 3.3% (F) (p < .05)
- Topic 5: IT and Markets: 3.1% (M) vs. 1.9% (F) (p < .05)

These percentages are all small in absolute terms (in part, because these topics were all among the less-frequent topics, in terms of overall prevalence). In relative terms, men were 60%-70% more likely to publish on such topics compared to women.[16]

We performed a similar topic analysis for each journal separately. We found that the gender effect for Topic 1, above, was attributable to *Information Systems Research*; moreover the gender effect for Topic 3 was attributable to both *Journal of MIS* and *MIS Quarterly*. The other effect we mentioned above (Topic 5) cannot be attributed to any single journal (based on separate journal analyses we conducted). For *Journal of MIS*, we found a weak effect, where women are more likely to publish on Topic 11: Virtual Collaboration: 2.1% (M) vs 3.1% (F) (p < .10).

Although these differences are small in absolute terms, we believe that they account, in part, for the observed effect that papers published by women are cited more often than ones by men. In particular, for Topic 1 (IS Development, which includes "design science" research), papers on this topic in published in *ISR* are cited significantly less often than papers on other topics in *ISR*.[17] Since men are far more likely than women to publish papers on this topic – and since such papers are cited much less often, this is one identifiable reason for women's higher citation rates. Likewise, in *Journal of MIS*, papers on Topic 5 ("IT and Markets") were cited less often than papers on nearly all other topics. Since men were more likely to publish papers on this topic – and since such papers are cited less often, this contributes to women's higher citation rates overall. The Appendix lists some examples of papers corresponding to Topics 1, 3, and 5. In contrast to women's lower fraction of papers on Topics 1, 3, and 5, women are more likely to serve as authors for Topic 11 ("Virtual Collaboration") in *Journal of MIS*; however, this topic was not related to higher or lower citation rates in any journal.

Overall, the results for the relative prevalence of papers by men and women on certain topics indicate that women's (slightly) higher citation rate – of 0.9 more citations per year – across the set of journals is due to the fact that women rarely publish papers on two topics ("IS Development" and "IT and Markets") which are cited less than average in certain journals (i.e., *ISR* and *Journal of MIS*). These are the topics for which male authors predominate and which we found to be cited less often than papers on other topics. This effect also contributes to women's higher citation rates.

---

[15] When including publication year, we also allowed for higher-order terms (squared and cubed), in case the impact factor of a given journal changed in a non-linear manner over time. For instance, a journal may have experienced a very large increase in its impact factor from 1995-2002, then a leveling off later on. Conversely, a journal's impact factor may have increased rapidly, then declined drastically after 2004 (*ISR*).

[16] In contrast, the most prevalent topics in these journals exhibited no significant gender difference in the likelihood of men and women publishing on them: Topic 4 ("IT Adoption and Use"), Topic 7 ("Development and Validation of Measurement Instruments"), or Topic 8 ("IS Discipline Development" – which includes papers on qualitative research or epistemology).

[17] Papers on "IS Development" in *ISR* were among the least-cited topics. The three other least-cited topics in *ISR* were Topic 11 (Virtual Collaboration), Topic 10 (Human Resource Issues), and Topic 2 (IS Management).

H3: There is no difference in the fraction of papers in the highest-quality IS journals by men and women (compared to the ratio of papers by men and women in a larger set of journals).

Next, we compared the fraction of papers women published across the set of five journals (which was 19.8%) to the fraction of papers they published in each journal. While, of course, we expected some variation, we had no reason to suspect that the fraction of papers women published would vary significantly from one journal to another. Our analysis shows that we were wrong! The fraction of papers that women published varied greatly from the overall mean of 19.8% for four journals – all except for *Information Systems Journal*. The ratio of papers by women was highest in *MISQ* (24.9% of papers by women), but far lower in *Journal of MIS* (14.7%), *ISR* (17.3%), and *European Journal of IS* (17.7%). Relative to their fraction in the overall dataset, women were over-represented in *MISQ* (24.9%) but under-represented in *Journal of MIS, ISR*, and *EJIS*. Since *MIS Quarterly* is the journal with the highest citation rate – by far – women's over-representation among MISQ authors contributes to their overall higher citation rate. Likewise, the fact that the three journals in which women are under-represented have average citations rates of 40%-70% lower than citation rates for papers in *MISQ*, also contributes to women's higher citation rates.

Finally, we analyzed data corresponding to our hypothesis that incorporates other artifact to determine whether women are more highly represented in early or later years of our dataset.

H4: Papers published in recent years will have higher citation rates (citations per year after publication) due to the artifact of more journals bec available to cite them. To the extent that women publish their work in some or all journals at rising *proportions* over time, then this artifact of the rising "impact factor" of journals over time will positively affect women's citation rates.

Consistent with our expectation, we found that papers published in more recent years (i.e., 2007 was the last year in our dataset) exhibited higher citation rates in several journals, compared to papers from earlier years. This was true for all five journals; however, we found no evidence of a higher or lower fraction of papers published by women in any journal in the most recent years, compared to in earlier years. Thus, the year of publication (and the fact that most journals have a higher impact factor in more recent years) was not a factor that contributed to women's higher citation rates in any journal. When we controlled for year of publication, however, we found a statistically significant result, whereby papers by women were cited more than papers by men. This result is significant for the combined dataset of all five journals, as well as in the two European journals (*EJIS* and *Information Systems Journal*). In the various analysis, gender explained 0.5%, 0.8%, and 2.5% of citation rate in the combined data, in *European Journal of IS* and *Information Systems Journal*, respectively. In contrast, papers published by women were not cited either or more or less often in the North American journals, after controlling for time.

6. DISCUSSION AND CONCLUSIONS

We provide the following figure to summarize the drivers we identified for women's higher citation rates. The most important

effect is the fact that that women publish a higher fraction of papers in MISQ (24%) than their average fraction of papers in the set of five journals overall (19.8%), and MISQ is, by far, the journal with the highest citation impact. In addition, there were two additional, minor effects that contribute to women's higher citation rates. Women are less likely than men to publish papers on two topics – "IS Development" and "IT and Markets" – that are poorly-cited in *ISR* and *Journal of MIS*, respectively. Since men are more likely to publish papers on these topics (as well as on "Value of IT"), such papers have the effect of suppressing men's average citation rates, because such papers are cited less than papers on most other topics. There was just one topic on which women were more likely to publish papers than men ("Virtual Collaboration") in *Journal of MIS*, but papers on this topic had just an average citation rate in *Journal of MIS* (rather than a higher- or lower-than-average rate).

Similar to other disciplines in which the number of citations per paper or citation rate have been compared for men and women, our analysis identified an overall gender effect such that papers by women were cited more often on a yearly basis. There are three primary reasons we identified for this result: First, women publish a much higher fraction of papers in *MIS Quarterly* than in any other journal in our dataset; since papers in *MIS Quarterly* have a much higher citation rate than papers in the other four journals, this boosts the average citation rate of women's publications. Second, women publish a smaller fraction of papers in three journals (*EJIS, ISR*, and *Journal of MIS*), relative to their overall representation. These journals have citation rates that average just 25%-40% of *MISQ*. Finally, women are less likely to publish on three unpopular (i.e., under-cited) topics – "IS Development," "IT and Markets," and "Value of IT." The first two of these are cited less often in one or more journals, relative to other topics. We believe that such topics are under-cited as a result of having fewer scholars working – or at least, publishing – in these areas. In a future study, we plan to consider the interaction between gender and coauthorship (i.e., number of coauthors), in terms of how they jointly affect citation rates. (For a related study about gender and coauthorship, refer to [9]).

7. REFERENCES

[1] Adya, M. and Kaiser, K. "Early Determinants of Women in the IT Workforce: A Model of Girls' Career Choices," *Information Technology & People*, 18, 2005, 230-259.

[2] Aksnes, D., Rørstad, K., Piro, F. and Sivertsen, G. "Are Female Researchers Less Cited? A Large-scale Study of Norwegian Scientists," *Journal of the American Society for Information Science & Technology*, 2010.

[3] Ayres, I. and Vars, F.E., "Determinants of Citations to Articles in Elite Reviews," *Journal of Legal Studies*, 29, 2000, 427-450.

[4] Beyer, J.M., Chanove, R., and Fox, W. "The Review Process and the Fates of Manuscripts Submitted to Academy of Management Journal," *Academy of Management Journal*, 38, 1995, 1219-1260.

[5] Borrego, A., Barrios, M., Villarroya, A. and Olle, C. "Scientific Output and Impact of Postdoctoral Scientists: A Gender Perspective," *Scientometrics*, 83, 2010, 93-110.

[6] Cole, J. and Zuckerman, H. "The Productivity Puzzle: Persistence and Change in Patterns of Publication of Men

and Women Scientists," *Advances In Motivation and Achievement*, 2, 1984, 217-258.

[7] DeSanctis, D. "The Social Life of IS Research: A Response to Benbasat and Zmud's Call for Returning to the IT Artifact," *Journal of the Association for Information Systems*, 4(1), 2003, 16.

[8] Dwyer, P. "Gender Differences in the Scholarly Activities of Accounting Academics," *Issues in Accounting Education*, 9(2), 1994, 231-246.

[9] Gallivan, M.J. and Ahuja, M. "A Longitudinal Analysis of the Antecedents and Consequences of Coauthorship in IS Research," *Journal of the Association for Information Systems*, 2012, forthcoming.

[10] Gallivan, M.J. and Benbunan-Fich, R. "Examining the Relationship between Gender and IS Research Productivity," *Proceedings of ACM SIG MIS Conference*, Claremont, CA, 2006, 103-113.

[11] Gallivan, M.J. and Benbunan-Fich, R. "Exploring the Relationship between Gender and Career Outcomes for Social Scientists," *Information Technology & People*, 21(3), 2008, 178-204.

[12] Ginther, D.K. and Hayes, K.J. "Gender Differences in Salary and Promotion in the Humanities," *American Economic Review*, 89(2), 1999, 397-402.

[13] Ginther, D.K. and Kahn, S. "Women in Economics: Moving Up or Falling Off the Academic Career Ladder?" *Journal of Economic Perspectives*, 18(3), 2004, 193-214.

[14] Joshi, K.D. and Kuhn, K. "Examining the Masculinity and Femininity of Critical Attributes Necessary to Succeed in IT," *Proceedings of 2005 ACM Conference on Computer Personnel Research*, Atlanta, 32-35.

[15] Joshi, K.D. and Kuhn, K. "What It Takes to Succeed in Information Technology Consulting: Exploring the Gender Typing of Critical Attributes," *Information Technology & People*, 40, 2007, 400-424.

[16] Judge, T., Cable, D., Colbert, A. and Rynes, S. "What Causes a Management Article to be Cited – Article, Author, or Journal?," *Academy of Management Journal*, 50(3), 2007, 491-506.

[17] Kimery, K.M., Rinehart, S., and Mellon, M. "Gendered Patterns in Academic Authorship: Examples from the MIS Discipline," *Proceedings of 9th Americas Conference on Information Systems*, 1567-73.

[18] Lariviere, V.; Vignola-Gagne, E.; Villeneuve C., "Sex Differences In Research Funding, Productivity and Impact: An Analysis of Quebec University Professors," *Scientometrics*, 87(3), 2011, 483-498.

[19] Long, J.S. "Measures of Sex Differences in Scientific Productivity," *Social Forces*, 1990, 1297-1315.

[20] Mangold, W., Bean, L. and Cummings, M. "A Cohort Analysis of the Changing Gender Composition of MIS Faculty," *Journal of Computer Information Systems*, 39(1), 1998, 7-13.

[21] Markus, M.L. and Lee, A. "Special Issue on Intensive Research in Information Systems: Using Qualitative, Interpretive, and Case Methods to Study Information Technology," *MIS Quarterly*, 23, 1999.

[22] Medoff, M. "Collaboration and the Quality of Economics Research," *Journal of Labour Economics*, 10, 2003, 597-608.

[23] Payton, F.C. and White, S. "Views from the Field on Mentoring and Roles of Effective Networks for Minority IT Doctoral Students," *Proceedings of ACM SIG CPR Conference*, Philadelphia, PA., 2003.

[24] Peñas, C.S. and Willett, P. "Gender Differences in Publication and Citation Counts in Librarianship and Information Science Research," *Journal of Information Science*, 32(5), 2006, 480-485.

[25] Riemenschneider, C., Armstrong, D.J., Allen, M. and Reid, M. "Barriers Facing Women in the IT Work Force," *Database for Advances in Information Systems*, 34, 2006.

[26] Sidorova, A., Evangeloupolos, N., Valacich, J. and Ramakrishnan, T. "Uncovering the Intellectual Core of the Information Systems Discipline," *MIS Quarterly*, 32, 2008, 467-482.

[27] Straub, D.W. "Editor's Comments: Type II Reviewing Errors and the Search for Exciting Papers," *MIS Quarterly*, 32, 2008, i-vi.

[28] Straub, D.W., Hofman, D., Weber, B. and Steinfield, C. "Measuring e-Commerce in Net-Enabled Organizations: Introduction to the Special Issue," *Information Systems Research*, 13, 2002, 115-124.

[29] Trauth, E.M., Adya, M., Armstrong, D.J., Joshi, K.D., Kvasny, L., Riemenschneider, C., Quesenberry, J. "Taking Stock of Research on Gender and the IT Workforce," Vancouver, Canada, 2010.

[30] Trauth, E.M., Quesenberry, J. and Yeo, B. "The Influence of Environmental Context on Women in the IT Workforce," *Proceedings of 2003 ACM SIGMIS Conference on Computer Personnel Research*, Philadelphia, PA., 24-31.

[31] Trauth, E.M., Quesenberry, J.L. and Huang, H., "Cross-Cultural Influences on Women in the IT Workforce," *Proceedings of the 2006 ACM SIG MIS Conference on CPR*, St. Louis, MO, 2006.

[32] Valian, V. *Why So Slow? The Advancement of Women*, Cambridge, MA: MIT Press, 1998.

[33] Woszczynski, A.., Beise, C., Myers,, M., and Moody, J. "Diversity and the Information Technology Workforce: An Examination of Student Perceptions," *Proceedings of the 2003 ACM SIG CPR Conference*.

[34] Xie, Y. and K. Shauman. "Sex Differences in Research Productivity: New Evidence about an Old Puzzle," *American Sociological Review*, 63(6), 1998, 847-870.

Table 2: Citation Rates for papers Published by Men and Women

Journal Name	Citation Rate Overall mean (s.d.)	Citation Rate for Men mean (s.d.)	Citation Rate for Women mean (s.d.)	% Higher for Women	ANOVA p-value	Mann-Whitney p-value
EJIS	2.035 (1.586)	2.013 (1.383)	2.308 (1.911)	+14.7%	p = .109	p = .583
ISJ	2.164 (1.600)	2.066 (1.361)	2.577 (2.300)	+24.7%	p = .079$^+$	p = .143
ISR	7.828 (7.286)	7.489 (6.902)	9.274 (8.671)	+23.8%	p = .111	p= .128
JMIS	4.401 (3.312)	4.316 (3.240)	4.933 (3.743)	+14.3%	p = .287	p = .142
MISQ	11.600 (13.27)	11.709 (14.00)	11.274 (10.91)	- 3.7%	p = .785	p = .819

Legend: $^+$ p < 0.10; * p < 0.05

Figure 1: Conceptual Model of Results

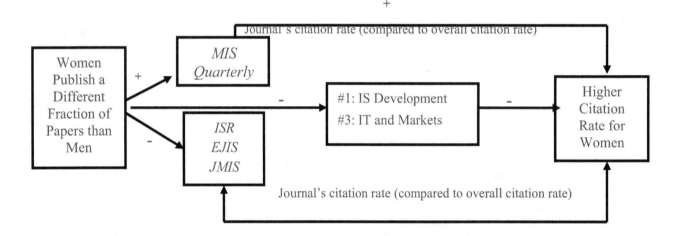

Exploring Gender and Job Embeddedness in Information Technology Professionals

Sherry D. Ryan
University of North Texas
1155 Union Circle #311160
Denton, TX 76203-5017
1-940-565-3106

sherry.ryan@unt.edu

Gina Harden
University of North Texas
1155 Union Circle #311160
Denton, TX 76203-5017
1-940-565-3174

gina.harden@unt.edu

ABSTRACT
Despite the current difficulties in the economy, the demand for information technology (IT) workers is expected to grow substantially in the next several years. The need for talented IT workers is exacerbated by the looming retirement of many IT professionals. Thus, it is becoming increasingly important for organizations to find ways to retain their valuable and skilled IT employees. One construct that has been introduced to assess reasons employees choose to stay in their current position is job embeddedness. This paper explores the effect of gender on the three dimensions of job embeddedness: an employee's fit with the organization, the potential sacrifice they would make if they left their job, and links or connections they have to others in their organization. This research-in-progress paper hypothesizes that there are differences between males and females in in each of the embeddedness dimensions.

Categories and Subject Descriptors
K.6.1 [**Management of Computing and Information Systems**]: Project and People Management; K.7.0 [**The Computing Profession**] General

General Terms
Management

Keywords
Job embeddedness, gender, turnover intention.

1. INTRODUCTION
Attracting, developing and retaining skilled employees are critical issues for organizations, especially when those employees include skilled workers in areas such as information technology (IT). Organizations that rely on IT workers must consider the growing number of baby-boomers that are set to leave the workforce in growing numbers, taking with them critical amounts of "tacit knowledge, operational heuristics, stories and organizational history," [8, p. 908]. Aggravating these staffing challenges for the organization is a growing number of positions for technology

Permission to make digital or hard copies of all or part of this work for personal or classroom use is granted without fee provided that copies are not made or distributed for profit or commercial advantage and that copies bear this notice and the full citation on the first page. To copy otherwise, or republish, to post on servers or to redistribute to lists, requires prior specific permission and/or a fee.
SIGMIS-CPR'12, May 31–June 2, 2012, Milwaukee, Wisconsin, USA.
Copyright 2012 ACM 978-1-4503-1110-6/12/05...$10.00.

professionals that has not been matched by a similar growth in IT talent [13].

While traditional turnover models (e.g., [10]) address why some people choose to quit an organization, they do not specifically address why some employees are reluctant to leave [11]. Findings in management literature show that "commitment systems" that are designed to elicit behaviors and attitudes that enhance the psychological links between organizational and employee goals leads to decreased turnover and increased performance [26]. One factor that has been identified as a way to explain how employees become psychologically and socially enmeshed in both their organization and their community – thereby explaining why employees remain in an organization – is "job embeddedness" [11]. There has been evidence that job embeddedness significantly affects turnover intention [18]. However, there has been a paucity of studies in the Information Systems literature evaluating embeddedness and none that we are aware of examining the relationship between gender and embeddedness. This research begins to fill this gap.

Another concern for the organization is the underrepresentation of females in the IT profession. The gender gap in the IT sector has been investigated in many studies [1, 14, 20, 21]. Suggested explanations for this imbalance between males and females in the IT profession include biological differences as well as differences in socialization to technology for men and women [14].

Studies have shown that not only is there a gender gap, but that the imbalance is increasing with the number of females reaching 34.9 percent of the American IT workforce in 2002 and falling to 32.4 percent in 2004 [21]. Also, women who do enter the IT workforce were found to be more than 2.5 times more likely to leave it than men, were employed at lower levels, and made less money [25]. Other obstacles to women in the IT workforce have been identified as conflicts between work and family interests, and an even more pronounced gender gap at higher managerial levels [12].

With the positions for technology professionals continuing to grow at a rate that is not matched by a similar growth in IT talent [13], there is a need to understand why there is an under representation of women in the IT workforce. As the IT field deals with the unique challenges of employment and turnover within the profession, researchers must explore the under representation of women in the IT workforce to better understand how to attract and retain women in IT positions. The focus of this study is on gaining a better understanding of the role that gender plays when investigating the job embeddedness of IT professionals, and how gender moderates the relationships between job embeddedness and other important variables such as turnover intention, job satisfaction and perceived pay equity.

2. LITERATURE REVIEW AND HYPOTHESES

2.1 Job Embeddedness

Prior research distinguished the level of relationship ties as being somewhere between arm's-length and embedded [24]. The exchanges that occur among those with embedded ties are based on their social attachments and affiliations which foster enhanced levels of trust and shared norms. This can result in in an environment where actions are learned and become internalized through socialization, thus creating motivations to share private information with these trusted others [24].

Job embeddedness is theorized to influence the employee's decision to remain with the organization. The individual aspects of job embeddedness are 1) fit: the degree of congruity that employees perceive between their self-concept and the environment that they live and work in, 2) sacrifice: the consideration of what they would forfeit if they would leave their jobs, and 3) links: the number and level of associations a person has to other people or activities [11]. Each of these aspects has both organization-related (on-the-job) and community-related (off-the-job) characteristics. These authors conceptualized the connections associated with each of these dimensions as forming a complex web of relationships and attachments [11]. The more elaborate the web is, the more lines that connect the individual to the many aspects of his or her work and community life. Thus, the greater the number of connections, the more dense the web becomes. As the web grows more elaborate and dense, the more an employee becomes "embedded" or stuck in the web, and the harder it becomes for the individual to detach or leave the organization. Each of these embeddedness dimensions are discussed in more detail below.

2.2 Fit

Fit refers to how well employees perceive their jobs and communities are similar to or fit with the other aspects of their life and environment. Fit is distinguished with two types: 1) Organization-related fit is essentially an individual's cognitive assessment of compatibility with his or her organization, and 2) Community-related fit includes the individual's level of enjoyment from leisure activities that are offered and wanting to be a part of the community in which they live [11]. The more congruent an employee's career goals, personal values, knowledge, skills and abilities are with the demands of the job and culture of the organization, the greater the fit.

2.3 Sacrifice

The sacrifice dimension of embeddedness refers to an individual's perception of financial and psychological benefits that may be lost by leaving a job. Organization-related sacrifices include tangible items such as loss of health benefits or vacation time as well as psychological sacrifices such as leaving an interesting project or seniority. Researchers suggest that job stability and advancement possibilities are important potential sacrifices an employee risks by quitting a job [17]. Community-related sacrifices are mainly an issue if one has to relocate. Sacrifices might include leaving a safe or desirable neighborhood or moving from a town in which the individual is respected.

2.4 Links

Links are conceptualized as the formal or informal connections people have to other people or the organization. Organization-related links are those psychological or social connections that the employee has with other employees within the organization through such activities as being involved in work teams or groups. Community-related links are those connections that are established in the community through such activities as owning a home or developed with family or friends in the community [4].

Researchers found that employees with a greater number of links to coworkers are more motivated than those employees with fewer links and found that organization-related embeddedness was a significant predictor of both in-role and extra-role job performance [9]. The employees who were embedded were more highly motivated to remain in their current positions, making them more motivated to perform well in order to do so [6].

Additionally, research has shown that job embeddedness was positively and significantly related to innovation-related behaviors [15]. These authors suggest that as creativity is a key factor in achieving pay raises and promotions, it can thus lead to greater innovation for embedded employees who want to stay with the organization. Other researchers noted that the factors of job embeddedness could vary across people and certain characteristics such as age [11]. The current research suggests that gender may also affect job embeddedness.

2.5 Gender

Gender has been theorized from two main approaches in much of the literature, the essentialist perspective and the social constructionist approach [20]. The essentialist viewpoint sees gender as leading to certain traits that are inherent in men and women and therefore explain the IT profession as one that is male dominated. Essentialism views gender as a fixed, biological variable that can be examined with positivist methodologies. In contrast, the social constructionist viewpoint is one that sees the emergence of the IT profession being a male domain as the result of a social shaping of attitudes. This viewpoint not only examines the differences between men and women in the IT profession, but also the ways in which those differences have occurred.

Researchers found explanations for the imbalance between males and females in the IT profession included both biological differences as well as those due to differences in socialization to technology for men and women [14]. Additionally, it was suggested that organizational ideas of effectiveness are focused on masculine models where competence may be related to traits of toughness or self-promotion [3]. However, it is possible that women who act more masculine and strong may be judged harshly and therefore still encounter difficulty being declared effective within the organization [3].

2.6 Research Model and Hypotheses

Stage 1 of this research will explore what effect gender has on the three dimensions of job embeddedness. Various studies have found differences between genders based upon work environmental influences, organizational culture, the availability of mentors, work-life balance issues, and social interaction between employees [5, 2]. These issues are captured in the three dimensions of embeddedness.

The fit dimension of embeddedness refers to the congruence between an employee's career goals, personal values, knowledge, skills and the competing demands of the job and culture of the organization. It incorporates ideas such as the perceived similarity of the individual with his or her coworkers, as well as the ability to meet his or her goals for professional growth and development. Prior research has shown that if women view their work environment as male-dominated and hostile they are less likely to remain on the job [2]. Research has also highlighted the lack of female role models in IT as a significant concern [19]. While mentors do not necessarily need to be of the same gender, role models, with the same identity characteristics are important [22]. As gender differences have been identified in the literature based upon organizational culture and availability of mentors, the following hypothesis is proposed:

H1: There is a significant difference between the perceived organizational fit experienced between males and females

The sacrifice dimension of embeddedness refers to the employee's perception of financial and psychological benefits that may be lost by leaving a job. The sacrifice dimension incorporates issues such as the compensation that would be lost if one leaves the organization, health care, retirement, and other benefits, as well as the psychological benefits obtained from the job such as respect. Organizational benefits are often viewed differently by men and women. For example, a woman who is a mother may value on-site childcare more highly than her male counterpart. Flexibility in terms of work schedule and sick leave policy may hold different appeal based upon work-life balance issues. While there are stage-of-life and individual differences among females, past research has found that family-career balance is important, and lack of workplace flexibility can sometimes be a limiting factor for the continuing employment and advancement of women [16]. Therefore, the following hypothesis is proposed:

H2: There is a significant difference between the perceived organizational sacrifice experienced between males and female

The link dimension of embeddedness refers to the formal or informal connections people have with others. Research suggests that informal behaviors such as "gendered exclusion from social networks" can have a negative effect on women [22, p. 477]. One female interviewee gave an example in which the men in her workplace often went to lunch together but the women were not usually invited, thus creating a perception of "a good 'ole boy's club." In terms of formal connections, females without influential mentors may be less likely to be chosen for high visibility teams or committees. As gender differences have been identified in the literature based upon formal and informal organizational characteristics, environmental influences, organizational culture, and the availability of mentors within the organization, women might not develop the same type of organizational relationships as men. Therefore, the following hypothesis is proposed:

H3: There is a significant difference between the organizational links of males and females

The research model is shown below in Figure 1. Stage 2 of this research will evaluate a model in which gender is a moderator between job embeddedness and turnover intention and job embeddedness and job satisfaction. This is not discussed further for sake of brevity.

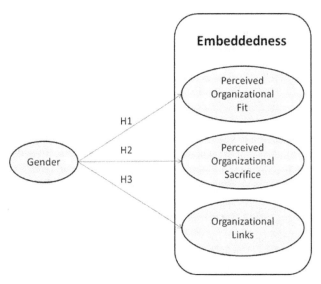

Figure 1 Conceptual Model

3. RESEARCH METHOD

An electronic survey was used to collect data from a large federal government agency's employees. The present research is part of a larger study. The current instrument is based on validated scales that to measure three embeddedness dimensions: organizational fit, organizational sacrifice, and organizational links [11]. Due to the restrictions of the organization, the authors were only able to gather data regarding the organizational-related aspects of embeddedness, and not the community-related aspects. Organizational fit was measured with nine 7-point Likert scale items ranging from Strongly Agree to Strongly Disagree. Examples of items include: "My coworkers are similar to me," and "I fit with the company's culture." Organizational sacrifice was measured with ten 7-point Likert scale items ranging from Strongly Agree to Strongly Disagree. Examples of items include: "The benefits are good on this job," and "I feel that people at work respect me a great deal." The organizational links was measured with seven fill-in-the-blank format. Examples of items include: "How many coworkers do you interact with regularly?" and "How many work teams are you on?"

A pilot study was conducted with 27 working professionals from the agency to review the survey instrument for format, appearance, instruction clarity, and item wording. Written and oral feedback was provided and modifications to the survey were made. Two additional rounds of pilot testing ensured that technical issues surrounding the online survey were resolved, and the final survey was created.

Supervisors emailed their subordinates, provided the URL for the electronic survey, and requested they complete the survey. A letter from the chief information officer was included. Reminder emails were sent two weeks after the initial announcement.

We plan to test the hypotheses using multivariate analysis of variance (MANOVA). This is an appropriate procedure to investigate whether the independent variable has a significant effect on the dependent variables.

4. CONCLUSION

The underrepresentation of women in the IT profession is a concern. Thus, minimizing the voluntary turnover of females IT professionals is important. Job embeddedness has been shown to be an important predictor of turnover intention, yet its relationship with gender remains unexplored. This research examines gender in relation to the dimensions of job embeddedness, which consists of 1) the fit that employees perceive between themselves and their organization 2) the sacrifices that employees would have to make if they resigned from their job, and 3) the links that employees have to other coworkers and activities.

The results of this study have implications for research as well as practitioners. For the literature on gender in the IT workforce, this research helps fill the gap on the effect of gender on job embeddedness, which is an important predictor of job turnover. For practitioners, the results of the study could indicate that if the organizational fit isn't good for women, there may be some reason that they are feeling stymied in their professional growth. If something as obvious as adequate mentoring or training presents a challenge for women reaching their goals, the organization should consider how to provide these..

Next, if organizational sacrifices aren't viewed equally by men and women, it could indicate that women and men value the benefits that organizations provide differently. Third, if the organizational links aren't perceived as strongly by women as men, then once again, maybe women don't feel as highly visible or as crucial a part of their teams and work groups as their male counterparts. If making changes to counter these effects on job embeddedness can result in the reduction of turnover in the IT field, it is imperative for academics to continue their investigation and understanding of these effects. It is also imperative for organizations to not only understand these effects, but implement measures to counter these effects.

5. REFERENCES

[1] Adam, A. 2002. "Exploring the gender question in critical information systems," *Journal of Information Technology*, (17), pp. 59-67.

[2] Ahuja, M. 2002. "Women in the information technology profession: a literature review, synthesis and research agenda," *European Journal of Information Systems* (11), pp.20–34.

[3] Callister, R. R. 2006. "The Impact of Gender and Department Climate on Job Satisfaction and Intentions to Quit for Faculty in Science and Engineering Fields," *Journal of Technology Transfer*, (31:3), pp. 367-375.

[4] Cohen, A. 1995. "An examination of the relationships between work commitment and nonwork domains," *Human Relations*, (48), pp. 239-263.

[5] Hewlett, S. A.; Luce, C. B., Servon, L.J. 2008. "Stopping the exodus of women in science," *Harvard Business Review*, (86:6), pp. 22-24.

[6] Hom, P.W., Tsui, A.S., Lee, T.W., Ping Ping F., Wu, J.B., Zhang, A.Y., and Li, L. 2009. "Explaining Employment Relationships With Social Exchange and Job Embeddedness," *Journal of Applied Psychology*, (94:2), pp. 277-297.

[7] Igbaria, M. and Chidambaram, M. 1997. "The impact of gender on career success of information systems professionals," *Information Technology & People*, (10:1), pp. 63-86.

[8] Jackson, P. 2010. "Capturing, Structuring, and Maintaining Knowledge: A Social Software Approach," *Industrial Management and Data Systems*, (110:6), pp. 908-929.

[9] Lee, T.W., Mitchell, T.R., Sablynski, C.J., Burton, J.P., and Holtom, B.C. 2004. "The effects of job embeddedness on organizational citizenship, job performance, volitional absences, and voluntary turnover," *Academy of Management Journal*, (47:5), pp. 711-722.

[10] March, J. G., and Simon, H. A. Organizations. New York: Wiley, 1958.

[11] Mitchell, T.R., Holtom, B.C., Lee, T.W., Sablynski, C.J., and Erez, M. 2001. "Why people stay: Using organizational embeddedness to predict voluntary turnover," *Academy of Management Journal*, (44:6), pp. 1102-1122.

[12] Moody, J. W., Beise, C. M., Woszczynski, A. B., & M E Myers. 2003. "Diversity and the information technology workforce: Barriers and opportunities," *The Journal of Computer Information Systems*, 43(4), 63-71.

[13] Moore, J. E. 2000. "One road to turnover: An examination of work exhaustion in technology professionals," *MIS Quarterly*, (24:1), pp. 141-168.

[14] Morgan, A., Quesenberry, J., & Trauth, E., 2004. "Exploring the Importance of Social Networks in the IT Workforce: Experiences with the 'Boy's Club,'" *AMCIS 2004 Proceedings*. Paper 165.

[15] Ng, T.W.H. and Feldman, D.C. 2010. "The Impact of Job Embeddedness on Innovation-Related Behaviors," *Human Resource Management*, (49:6), pp. 1067 – 1087.

[16] Riemenschneider, C.K., Armstrong,D.J., Allen, A.M., Reid, M.F. 2006. "Barriers Facing Women in the IT Work Force," *Database for Advances in Information Systems*, (37:4), pp. 58-78.

[17] Shaw, J., Delery, J.E., Jenkins, D.G., and Gupta, N. 1998. "An organization-level analysis of voluntary and involuntary turnover," *Academy of Management Journal*, (41:5), pp. 511-525.

[18] Tanova, C., & Holtom, B. C. 2008. "Using job embeddedness factors to explain voluntary turnover in four European countries," *International Journal of Human Resource Management*, (19:9), pp. 1553-1568.

[19] Tapia, A.H., Kvasny, L., and Trauth, E.M. 2004. Is there a retention gap for women and minorities: the case for moving in versus moving up. In Strategies for Managing IS/IT Personnel (Shyo, C., ed.), pp. 143-164, Hershey, PA, Idea Group, Inc..

[20] Trauth, E. M. 2002. "Odd girl out: An individual differences perspective on women in the IT profession," *Information Technology & People*, (1:52), pp. 98-118.

[21] Trauth, E. M., & Howcroft, D. 2006. "Critical empirical research in IS: an example of gender and the IT workforce," *Information Technology & People*, (19:3), pp. 272-292.

[22] Trauth,E.M. Quesenberry, J. L., and Huang, H.2009. "Retaining women in the U.S. IT workforce: theorizing the influence of organizational factors," *European Journal of Information Systems*, (18:5), pp. 476-497.

[23] Wardell, M., Sawyer, S., Mitory, J., & Reagor, S. 2006. "Gender and IT professionals in the United States: A survey of college graduates," *Labour & Industry*, (16:3), pp. 39-58.

[24] Uzzi, B., & Lancaster, R. (2004). Embeddedness and Price Formation in the Corporate Law Market. *American Sociological Review*, 69(3), pp. 319-344.

[25] Wardell, M., Sawyer, S., Mitory, J., & Reagor, S. 2006. "Gender and IT professionals in the United States: A survey of college graduates," *Labour & Industry*, (16:3), pp. 39-58.

[26] Wheeler, A., Harris, K., & Harvey, P. 2010. "Moderating and Mediating the HRM Effectiveness - Intent to Turnover Relationship: The Roles of Supervisors and Job Embeddedness," *Journal of Managerial Issues*, (22:2), pp. 182-196

Observations Regarding the History of the Study of Computer Personnel

Fred Niederman
Saint Louis University
3674 Lindell Blvd.
St. Louis, Missouri 63108
+1-314-977-3878
Niederfa@slu.edu

Svetlana Krasteva
University of Missouri – St. Louis
240 Express Scripts Hall
St. Louis, Missouri, 63121
+1-314-516-6626
skrasteva@umsl.edu

ABSTRACT

The goal of this study is contrast the original concerns regarding computer/information systems personnel from the early days of computing with emergent concerns reflecting the accumulation of evolution of both computing technology and IS management in the subsequent years. Our approach to this is to review the proceedings of the Computer Personnel Research group, by analyzing the very first proceedings (1962), analyzing the first five proceedings (1964 to 1969), and the last five proceedings (2006 to 2011). Our intention is to present a broad picture of trends and we use observations of particular studies to this end.

For this study we selected three perspectives that highlight changes from the earliest days to the present. The first is based on a close reading and consideration of the first "conference" in 1962 and the discussion it generated. The second considers the themes and topics of articles in the first five conferences running from 1964 to 1969. Finally we identify and comment on the array of themes and topics that the CPR conferences have addressed in the most recent five years.

Categories and Subject Descriptors

H.0 Information Systems, General

General Terms

Management, Performance, Human Factors

Keywords

IS personnel, computer personnel, hiring, performance evaluation, retention, global IS personnel, training, diversity, curriculum, IS workforce

1. INTRODUCTION

"Those who cannot remember the past are condemned to fulfill it."

This quotation attributed to George Santayana, has become a maxim for the value of understanding history. Much is written about the history of computing technology – who created the first

machines? How these have been marketed over the years? And what can be done with them? It is our objective to focus in this essay on the history of the professionals who work most closely with computing.

The study of computing can logically trace its history to the invention of the computer in the 1940s and subsequent rapid evolution ever since. We might trace "pre-computing" back to the inventions of binary mathematics and early computational engines. In any case it was not long after the initial spread of computers that people were working to design new applications and keep the big machines running. As machines grew more numerous, the number and diversity of people working with them also increased.

The goal of this study is contrast the original concerns regarding computer/information systems personnel from the early days of computing with emergent concerns reflecting the accumulation of evolution of both computing technology and IS management in the subsequent years. Our approach to this is to review the proceedings of the Computer Personnel Research group, by analyzing the very first proceedings (1962), analyzing the first five proceedings (1964 to 1969), and the last five proceedings (2006 to 2011). Our intention is to present a broad picture of trends and we use observations of particular studies to this end.

For this study we selected three perspectives that highlight changes from the earliest days to the present. The first is based on a close reading and consideration of the first "conference" in 1962 and the discussion it generated. The second considers the themes and topics of articles in the first five conferences running from 1964 to 1969. Finally we identify and comment on the array of themes and topics that the CPR conferences have addressed in the most recent five years. This discussion is based on materials presented in the Proceedings of the CPR conferences but recognizes that much additional knowledge and understanding of CPR overall is found in diverse locations including other IS and management sources. We chose this categorization scheme because we believe this type of structure (very first proceedings, first five immediately following the first one proceedings, and the very last five proceedings) would highlight the contrast of early and more recent issues and understandings in the field thus increasing our understanding of how research topics evolved over time.

Following consideration of each of these three perspectives, we will discuss contrasts of the early with later concerns in the field and provide our view of implications for the future. We conclude with acknowledgement of limitations and presentation of future research recommendations.

THE FIRST ASSEMBLY: NOT JUST A MEETING NOT QUITE A CONFERENCE

"I don't conceive of this group being much larger than it is now or with much different representation [25]."

Thus began the first CPR conference, originally called the Computer Personnel Research Group, in 1962. This first conference was convened by the RAND Corporation and its client, the US Air Force, to consider human resource management problems pertaining to what were called computer personnel or more specifically programmers and systems analysts. We don't have a definitive list of those who attended, but the proceedings refer to 12 people in the room, though at other times it seems there were some people arriving and leaving. Seemingly all of the participants in this first session were practitioners, though at least one is a psychologist by training and familiar with some of the emerging literature and tests for job candidate selection and personnel evaluation. It is sobering to consider that the first CPR conference occurred before the invention of the personal computer, the electronic spreadsheet, relational databases, the cell phone, the internet, open source, electronic commerce, function points, ITIL, ERP and on and on.

The first "proceedings" is presented as a partial transcript of the discussion of the first meeting. In many ways the transcript rambles, some topics are noted, the conversation veers from topic to topic. It is perhaps the original "spaghetti code". Emergent from the discussion are many interrelated issues, questions, suggestions, and even organizational business.

To simply draw up a list of the array of problem areas that the group discussed wouldn't adequately capture their awareness of how interlinked these issues are. For example, without defining the tasks of a programmer, how do you know what selection criteria to use for hiring? Without defining expectations, what is the basis for performance evaluation? One discussion thread addresses issues of what came to be called "end-user computing" in terms of how to manage scientists or engineers programming their own 'smaller' problems. One firm's representative reports that this problem is solved by providing one week of training for a scaled down version of FORTRAN and requiring discussion with an IT person before resources are assigned for use.

Another participant raises the issue of dealing with what we now look at as one aspect of project risk. What happens if you assign a problem to a programmer and six months later there is still no answer? Or if the solution is to a different problem, one that no longer looks the same. Along these lines, the question of how you assign programmers to particular tasks also comes up. This triggers consideration of different types of programmers, ones who can work on a large problem over months and others who do better on a series of short problems. Of course, one of the delegates mentions the classic ultimate decision rule for task assignment: "Who is available?" These questions raise the logical follow up: "How do you check on progress?" Of course we still ask this question framed in terms of the constant search for IS metrics and addressed with increasingly complex approaches such as "real-options" theories. Without naming it, the discussants intuitively began to approach the idea that problem solving and coding known problem solutions are distinct tasks, though sometimes the same people do them, sometimes they do them simultaneously, and sometimes it doesn't add much value to break them into discreet pieces. Many of the issues raised during this conference are still of interest today, for example, "programmer

selection" and "evaluation" reflect the broader theme of the difficulties of early managers in identifying, selecting, and then evaluating good candidates, which has evolved into today's research on IT Workforce Development, Management, and Recruitment and Retention of IT Workforce.

The participants seemed partially aware of how general HR issues like selection, training, and promotion quickly give way to unique IS issues reflecting the particularities of the job and its specific required skills, not to mention the personality types and work tendencies that differentiate IS personnel from others and, when well-managed, may lead to more successful engagement. A generic selection test or evaluation method is not viewed as sufficiently helpful without addressing the distinct characteristics of IS work and people. Seeming dilemmas such as needing individual concentration and problem solving versus interaction with clients to solve the right problems are also noted. However, it seems that during the 1960s most of the leadership in the field derived from the non-programmers, thus raising the question about programmers' leadership qualities and the training they were provided at that time. Programmers were seen as "non-leaders" and as people who "do not like to work on their own problems".

Several themes that have been of recurring concern for the last 50 years are already identified. These include balancing quickness and accuracy, optimizing knowledge of a particular system versus transferring knowledge to other systems, and assessment of problem solving versus generation of code related skills. Last but not least, the degree to which we might say creativity is an attribute to the programmers was discussed.

The group is also concerned with defining its own mission. There is a tension between members doing their own research and pooling common research to increase the "N" and decrease the bias of either selecting respondents from a particular organization or focusing on only one type of respondent resident in a particular organization. Much of this discussion revolves around the potential design of collaborative research studies most particularly regarding the sort of test that should be validated for selection of programmers. It also addresses reducing the number of questions to a manageable number while still providing a validated study. Participants observed that practitioners aren't going to spend a lot of time taking personality tests. The ability to interact with and garner practitioner support for research has been an on-going challenge for IS researchers.

A summary of the mission discussion is presented [16] as the following three items: (1) to identify and discuss common needs among computer users in the areas of selection, development, and evaluation of computer programmers and analysts and to encourage research on the associated problems; (2) to collect, integrate and disseminate research information on these problems; and (3) to coordinate the participation of programmers and analysts in such research.

THE EARLY YEARS: LOTS OF QUESTIONS (1964-1969)

In this second portion of this paper we will present observations about the topics raised in the early conferences (see Table 1) and note the addition of discussion in some new areas. After the first meeting in 1962 no meeting was conducted in 1963. For the first two conferences there were no formal sessions in place. The

Table 1. Emergence of Issues during the Early Years (Topics presented in 5 years are highlighted).

Issue	1962	1964	1966	1967	1968	1969
Contrasting computing supervision with other management		X				
Defining professionalism in computer personnel		X		X		
Defining variation in programming needs	X					
Effects of evaluation on salary	X					
Evaluating new languages	X					
Evaluation/ Instruments	X	X	X			X
Extension of interest from programmer to system analyst				X	X	
Job analysis/design	X					X
Listing skills and measures of each	X					
Predicting programmer performance		X	X	X		
Privacy invasion					X	
Problems faced by computing managers		X		X		X
Programmer career development					X	X
Programmer selection/tests	X	X		X	X	X
Promotion	X					
Retention/turnover						X
Supervisor selection	X	X				
System design for the human factor					X	X
Training/learning	X		X	X	X	X

initial sessions focused on raising questions, organizing the problem space, and to a lesser extent exchanging initial findings or products (e.g. job descriptions) that would be of help to the group. It is worth pointing out that the acceptance rate for the Only 4 out of the 12 papers included in this proceeding were authored by academic researchersfirst 5 conferences is 100%. Papers submitted were highly practitioner oriented and focused on immediate problem solving.

The 1966 conference was the first meeting to have formal sessions in place however the researchers were still predominantly from industry and government. Of 10 papers presented, 4 were authored by practitioners and 2 by representatives of U.S. government agencies. During this meeting the first empirical reports and the first instrument validation paper was presented [6].

Another striking observation from 1966 proceedings can be best summarized by quoting one of the participants who "…find it difficult to believe that there is an academic base for a computer profession. I can think of only one course of study that truly belongs to the computer programmer -- I would say that is information theory. Everything else, it would appear to me, already belongs to another profession, so that the best you can get is a person who knows a lot of things about a lot of areas, and therefore can contribute in the computer area as a specialty, not as a profession."

During the 1967 conference the issue of privacy invasion was raised for the very first time. Privacy may be emerging as a topic of conversation in the larger public space as a result of growing awareness of computing in society, or that this represents the initial insight about the relationship between computer professionals and ethical issues like promoting and protecting privacy. Although the issue of personal privacy was only mentioned once, in one paper presented in 1964, their recommendations are worth mentioning. We believe they are still applicable today. We present below a portion of that presentation that we consider to be of contemporary as well as historic interest:

"First, we should assume that not everyone is as honest and trustworthy as ourselves--but is just as diabolically clever. Second, that the only time that the fundamental safeguards that we seek can often be applied is at the time of the initial system design. Third, that laws can be helpful in only two ways: First, laws outlawing certain practices will be of minor help in increasing the price of the act and making its commission less flagrant, and second, that laws can be written so that potentially weak systems cannot be built unless adequate safeguards are incorporated throughout for the protection and accuracy of the information stored. And finally, that statutory regulations be established governing the confidentiality of all information of any nature held by the Federal Government and/or the private sector pertaining to individuals. Implicit in this would be something along the lines of a "Writ of Erasure" which would guarantee to the individual the right to be made cognizant of the information collected about him and to have the right to protest through the courts as to accuracy and relevancy of this information. No responsibility of our Government or all our nation's citizens will be greater than the preservation of privacy and the protection of our fundamental human values. It is time now to reflect on how far we have come and where we are going before we drift onto a course that is beyond our capacity to navigate."[13].

The 1968 conference introduced the issues of system design for human factors (p.112), and man-computer communication [27]. Over time this issue has tended to migrate to specialized Human Computer Interaction (HCI) groups differentiating the content of IS employee activity from issues dealing with their status as employees per se.

For first time, during this conference, research originated outside of the USA was presented [3]. This was presented by a British researcher from Rolls Royce Corporation and his take on global CPR was largely as follows:

I do not think that in the United Kingdom we have any problems significantly different from those encountered in the United States or in other countries who have had some years' experience of the design, development and operation of computer based systems. We have shared, proportionately, the same tremendous increase in the number of computers installed during the last five years. We have made the same mistakes and have reaped the same benefits from computer based systems. We have suffered from the same problems of recruiting and training and retaining competent staff. We have had the same discussions with our colleagues in other departments, we have learned to talk the same jargon and even shared the same jokes about computers.

In the following year a paper on computing in Bolivia was presented [22] and ever since, the conference has embraced a small but steady flow of international submissions. Although this discussion highlighted the commonalities of IS personnel research around the world, many later studies have also considered the differences, both as a source of richness and impediments to smooth technology implementation.

In 1968 the State of California presented its selection and training program, and their representative emphasized the need for continuous training and self-development. They applied the same program for both their own graduates [from programming training they offered] and external candidates. During the most recent 5 years, a new list of "skill gaps" was reported. Among lacking skills were leadership skills, general business knowledge, communication skills, and technical skills, especially those related to programming, analysis, security and hardware. Authors reported that one of the reasons for this skills gap is the fact that MIS programs fail to prepare students adequately. In 2008 a study reported that a likely solution for the selection issue would be

creating job descriptions by specifying the people companies they want to hire in terms of the artifacts they will be expected to contribute to"[11], in other words "competences are useless, unless they are described in behavioral terms". It was ultimately concluded that qualified staff is still rare [12] due to the demographic situation worldwide and that companies could benefit from using e-recruitment systems.

Although not as targeted a subject of research in the early days, retention of key personnel was already appearing as one of the concerns of the field. One particularly intriguing study showed that large proportion of the programmers was selected from within the organization, which led to reduced attrition rate (6%) vs. programmers transferred from outside the organization (38%).[10] this study might have raised issues of programmer loyalty to firm versus to profession and the relative value of market competitive programming skills versus acceptable programming skills but with specific company attachment. It is interesting to consider the broader changes in society and growing tendency of individuals to have multiple careers and rare long term tenure with particular employers more generally in the past few years relative to prior eras.

THE MOST RECENT YEARS: A BROADER SPECTRUM OF ISSUES AND STAKEHOLDERS (2006-2011)

We identified the following twelve topics noted below. Naturally some studies address multiple topics. An example is one paper that explores CSFs for global software classroom work which crosses both global and IT curriculum issues. In this case the author [1] reported 4 levels of factors: faculty, student, technological, and class constructs each of which showed important areas of concern for successful e-learning and a positive classroom experience. Our focus is not to develop a flawless classification scheme but rather to provide reasonable categorization as a basis for discussion of the various topics and themes as presented below.

Table 2. Themes in Most Recent CPR Proceedings Years (Topics presented in 5 years are highlighted).

		2007	2008	2009	2010	2011
1	Diversity and Cultural Issues of IT Workforce	X	X	X	X	X
2	Global/Cultural	X	X	X		
3	IT and Recruitment/HRIS			X	X	
4	IT Careers, competencies, training	X	X	X	X	X
5	IT Workforce Development		X		X	X
6	IT Workforce Education/Preparation	X	X	X	X	X
7	IT Workforce Management	X	X			X
8	Performance					X
9	Project Outcomes			X		
10	Recruitment and Retention of IT Workforce	X	X	X	X	X
11	The Nature of IT Work	X				X
12	The Practice of IT			X	X	

Diversity and Cultural Issues of IS Workforce. This topic deals with the array of issues pertaining to the demographics of the IS workforce and the variations in attitude among IT workers that can be described as cultural. This was not a topic found in the initial five years of CPR. Several studies focused on the role women play in the IS workforce [2, 7, 8, 15]. Somewhat counter-intuitively Joseph [17] suggests that job shadowing tends to impede IS as a career choice, while experimental (learning by doing) training aids student in making transition from school into the IS profession.

Global/Cultural. This topic deals with the array of issues pertaining to similarities and variances based on national identity. Note that this pertains both to issues such as blending people of different ethnicity in offshoring work groups but also in terms of how different ethnic or national groups react to varied HR policies or technical issues. This is a topic not addressed during the first five years of CPR, though as noted earlier, the first submission from outside the US did appear during that time frame. However, we noticed that data has been collected in relatively few countries. Most studies focusing on international samples of IS workers report findings from either China or India, with sporadic reports from other countries (Venezuela, Botswana, Australia). This leaves much room for continuing work to address exactly in what ways all IS workers exhibit the same patterns and where they differ by location and ethnicity. Of course, the differing types of IS work (e.g. a preponderance of receiving offshored work in India, a preponderance of security and entrepreneurial IS in Israel) makes for a natural confounding of IS workers with different types of IS work that present thorny methodological challenges for CPR researchers.

IS and Recruitment/IIRIS. This topic pertains to the role of information systems in support of general HR activity. Specific studies may target the use of Internet delivered electronic recruiting systems as well as IS support for traditional HR activities including hiring, monitoring, and evaluating within organizations. This topic illustrates the duality of how IS can support work areas that in turn are used by IS. For example, information technologies are used as a set of tools to support HR in general, selection/recruitment, benefits/compensation, and evaluation are applied to IS workers while at the same time information systems and computing tools support each of these processes in many if not most organizations. As a result, it is unfortunately easy to become vague in specifying topics being addressed.

IS Careers and enrollments. This topic pertains to individuals in their choice of IS as a career, what skills are needed to enter the field, and what added skills enhance their career opportunities. Studies, for example, considering the effect of certifications on long term career goals and achievements would be a central example of this sort of topic. We also see studies regarding the skills sets that employers seek with the implication that these ought to be ones that we teach. Most such studies reinforce the importance of soft skills such a project management, leadership, communication and business skills. Of course [5] and [29] remind us that "programming skills are still needed..." as well.

IS Workforce Development. This topic pertains to active efforts and passive responses to environmental factors that shape the collection of IS workers taking part in the IS workforce. Much discussion focuses on issues around enrollment in IS programs around the world and, on the one hand what can be done to increase such enrollment and on the other whether or not the pipeline will be sufficient for those in industry who which to hire IS workers.

IS Workforce Education/Preparation. This topic pertains to educational curriculum and techniques that aid students in developing skills, knowledge, and abilities to enter the IS workforce. This is another areas of duality where IS uses education and is in turn used for education. IT is used as a set of tools to support education in the classroom and distributed through e-learning. At the same time, education is a prime mechanism for students to develop IS skills in preparation for an IS career and for those in the workforce to enhance their skills as organizational needs change. Studies that we view falling in this category range from evaluation of particular learning techniques such as e-learning.

IS Workforce Management. This topic pertains to managerial interventions that improve or retard successful organizing and deployment of IS workers. An example of such a topic is telework and its potential for aiding IT workers. By extension this relates to efforts of firms to take advantage of IT tools made available across the workforce to enhance productivity and/or worker benefits. Another example of a topic is the effects of layoffs and outsourcing on the remaining IS workers.

Performance/Project Outcomes. This topic focuses on factors related to enhancing (or that inhibit) the successful outcomes of IS workers. One track specifically looked at project outcomes. This includes concern for metrics as well as the study of interventions and their results. Overall, in our view, performance is perhaps the most understudied of the topics both in the initial and most recent time periods. Early studies showing vast differences in programmer abilities have become viewed as doctrine or dismissed by those who are not really concerned about individuals writing lines of code. However, assessment of IS department, work unit, and individual outcomes remains difficult with best practices unclear and differences of opinion unresolved. In practice simple and sometimes simplistic approaches are used such as setting goals and checking off their completion, supervisor intuitive assessments, and lack of complaints.

Recruitment and Retention of IS Workforce. This topic focuses on factors that encourage and inhibit IS workers from remaining with a particular employer. Job turnover is yet another well studied topic largely focusing on intentions to leave (e.g. Wang, Teo, and Yang, 2010) and their precursors such as lowered job satisfaction and lack of organizational commitment.

One interesting study considers the role ethnicity plays in students' intention to stay in IT programs (Lewis, Smith, & Hall, 2008). Their findings suggest that "the strength of one's ethnic identity explains significant variance in a student's intent to stay in IS. However, while ethnic pride can help students maintain happiness when faced with stress, it may not help students stay in IT programs." On the same note, a 2009 study of Botswana IT personnel reports that "life style does not feature as a significant career anchor in Botswana. The dominant career anchors include organizational stability (security) and sense of service (service)." [23].

The Nature of IS Work. This topic focuses on the shifting roles and responsibilities of IS workers. With the growing range of IS products that support an increasingly vast array of user functions, the range of IS tasks and how they are organized for workers continues evolving. For example, virtual teams and the way globally distributed groups collaborate in IS development has been an important topic during the last five years (e.g. Trauth & Huang, 2007). The nature of IS work is of much interest because as computing has spread throughout the organization and society, the need for an IT function to manage large scale infrastructure, information policies and practices (e.g. compliance and utilization), and services continues. However, as technologies and organizational practices have evolved, what elements of the IS work requirements or task have remained constant and which have emerged?

The Practice of IS. This topic focuses on what IS workers actually do and what they ought to do. This topic considers better approaches IS workers can adopt for particular tasks such as working in virtual teams or moving through stages in software development. This is another understudied area of CPR, though perhaps because it is addressed in other areas of the IS community. Workplace practices can affect productivity and performance evaluation, thus would have a potentially strong impact on retention and job satisfaction.

Of course a topic or two naturally don't fit in any standard category. We found two papers, [18, 19] focused on the potential for "evil" that may arise from a technical rational paradigm supporting the creation of systems that embody administrative evil. Unlike the typical notions of harm created by malevolent and unethical individuals, the processes and structures that create administrative evil rely on good people acting within their professional roles to design the systems where the evil is latent in the unintended impact of these systems.

DISCUSSION

Contrasting content and concerns expressed in the initial versus the most recent years' proceedings shows significant changes in four areas:

(1) the total volume of work is several times larger in recent years, for example in 1968 the total number of papers presented was 9 plus a keynote talk whereas in 2008 the total number of papers was 31 including research, panels, and research in process;

(2) the tendency in early years is to raise questions and provide some tentative suggestions regarding directions and initial empirical efforts contrasts with the presentation of more formal research studies largely based on behavior science techniques and approaches;

(3) the participation shifted from predominantly industry to nearly exclusively academic scholars – which perhaps explains the shift in topic from how to staff the IS function to broader understanding of IS employees in their many roles and perspectives; and

(4) the preponderance of topical interest focused on within firm application of HR processes to IS employees (e.g. recruiting, selection, job design, evaluation, promotion, and retention) whereas the range of topics now includes concern for careers from the employee perspective, the nature of the workforce with some emphasis on managerial programs and external effects, and the nature of education and preparation of students to become members of the workforce.

Among the topics emergent in the later years, the issue of gender disparity among computer professionals has been consistently researched during the more recent time period. Female IS professionals were mentioned only once in 1967, where it was reported that authors found no difference between males and females in systems analysis proficiency. From a study exploring the issue of women underrepresentation (2007) three key findings emerged: "First, technical competence and managerial competence are mutually exclusive. Second, a combination of career anchors for a given individual can be found. Third, career anchors vary in terms of temporal characteristics." Another study [4] reported that "female IS managers were particularly highly satisfied" with their career choice. Yet another study reported that"…the work identity of female IT professionals is noticeably different from their male counterparts. Females show a stronger relationship to job satisfaction but a weaker relationship with intent to leave, relative to males in the IT field," [8].

Another trend emerging in both time periods pertains to IS/IT education and training. During the 60s the idea of specialized CS/IS curricula emerges, and remains very much a topic of concern today. We still struggle with problems of attrition in IT academic programs and difficulties attracting students. In 1969 one of the papers presents experiences in self-selection of disadvantaged people into a computer operator training program, and this is a topic which we could see discussed much later in time as well [14]. Another study discusses teaching techniques and quality education/training for the "disadvantaged". In showing how some topics persist over time, [14], as well as [9] discuss opportunities for people with physical disadvantage in computing. This is followed up many years later by [28] in studying students with disabilities writing that:

"…educational institutions may unwittingly foster separate educational tracks for disabled Vs. non-disabled students; while simultaneously paying mere lip service to the notion of "making reasonable accommodations" for their disabled student population as required by law. In this research project, we intend to use our current understanding of how humans learn in technology enabled environments and findings in cognitive neuroscience, to develop and assess the effectiveness of online course materials that will be made inclusively accessible to both disabled and non-disabled students"

It is always enlightening to reflect on predictions that have not come to pass. We observed on [26] the following opinion that IS curriculum has no future and there will be no practical benefits of implementing one (in hindsight this may be less about whether computer programmers need skills than about whether they need a separate department or field for acquiring these):

"Question: I find it difficult to believe that there is an academic base for a computer profession. I can think of only one course of study that truly belongs to the computer programmer -- I would say that is information theory. Everything else, it would appear to me, already belongs to another profession, so that the best you can get is a person who knows a lot of things about a lot of areas, and therefore can contribute in the computer area as a specialty, not as a profession"[24]

In the same proceedings another scholar called for the need of implementation of undergraduate programs in computer science as noted below:

"Moreover, a curriculum along the lines of the ACM Curriculum Committee report, even with its imperfections, is likely to fulfill a need in the educational system not currently met by any other curriculum. A well-balanced computer science program is likely to produce graduates who have the training attitudes of mind, and mental agility, appropriate to academic, administrative and technological careers in the computer age." [32]

In contrast, during the second time period of our interest a study concluded that:

"...informal professional development activities had no effect on organizational tenure and career satisfaction, while formal professional development activities contributed most to the progress of an IT career."[21]

Numerous papers emphasize the need of online learning communities (informal online networks, online courses etc.). Some of them report their findings, supporting the claim that students greatly benefit from such learning facilitators. Thus, we can observe how our field shifted from "there is no need to implement academic program in computer science" to "we need to help our students learn better, because they're unprepared for real work life challenges".

This leaves us with the difficult questions: "Where will the field go in the future?" It is always risky to speculate about the future, however, we would envision two primary forces at work toward the continued evolution CPR. First we would see a continued "filling in" of knowledge regarding core topics. We would see studies considering the similarities and uniqueness of IS workforces around the world. We would like to see, for example, some illustrations of principles that may apply generally to all IS workers, some of the dimensions along which they are likely to vary, and some knowledge of the drivers of that variation – for example can we make predictions about the workforce where a national IS presence is predominantly software package creators (e.g. like Microsoft) versus consultants (e.g. like Deloitte and Touche) versus industry support (e.g. like Boeing or Nestle). We would anticipate additional clarity in terms of the techniques that work or do not (or where they work) to encourage enrollment in IS programs; in terms of the factors that make application of IS in general education successful (e.g. with e-learning in its myriad formulations); and in terms of how jobs are changing as a result of new technologies like mobile computing (and more generally are there principles by which IS jobs have been reacting to technology shifts wave after wave).

Second, we see the trend of a broadening of CPR concerns beyond core HR issues also accelerating. As computing has become ubiquitous throughout the world, we have all become computer personnel to varying degrees. As such our constituency has changed from workers in IS departments to workers using IS in organizations (e.g. training end users). Increasingly, our focus will come to include all folks using computing equipment for performing work, educational, recreational, and other life tasks. What has been learned about IS for more constrained groups may provide a seed of knowledge for furthered understanding of the role of computing as it manifests anywhere.

CONCLUSION

Over time the concerns of CPR have broadened from how to apply HR techniques in the management of IS personnel and functions to consideration of the tradeoffs facing individual workers pertaining to their careers and to the placement of organizations in larger IS workforce communities. As educators we may be looking at how to enroll and retain more individuals in IS programs while organizations are looking at how to best compete with one another to assimilate those individuals or alternatively from where to source them. Overall, we think this is a very healthy development for the CPR field as we have a broader array of stakeholders and their concerns to address. While this presents challenges reconciling findings pertaining to one stakeholder group with those of another, it also presents the opportunity for each to learn from the insights of others with whom there must be contact and integration of effort.

Some topics have come to significance since the originators of the CPR discussion began. For example, the topic of global IS was not yet of particular significance. We now have IS companies such as that sell products globally (and have done for decades now). We also have the offshoring phenomenon and its accompanying issues of global and virtual teams. This topic has implications for teaching students about to enter the field skills that pertain to distributed computing and also to interacting with people of varied cultural and ethnic background.

We would anticipate and call for continued research (1) in the topics that have declined in popularity like selection and evaluation particularly as new knowledge in management suggests innovation for IS practitioners and as specific technologies and practices require revision in these practices; (2) in the topics that have been continual in prompting research such as retention and training where much economic benefit/cost is at stake and complexity of the variety of individuals and situations may create many contingencies that need to be accounted for; (3) in the emerging topics particularly diversity, global workforce, and extensions of computing and the labor that accompanies it outside the traditional organizational boundaries. We would also call for continued examination and considerations of trends in IS personnel including potential confirmation, elaboration, or rejection of the patterns and explanations we've proposed, as well as the potential, for such patterns to prove consistent or at odds with theories of change and evolution.

Readers should of course keep in mind the limitations of this study. By focusing on the proceedings of the CPR conferences, we have underrepresented much excellent knowledge that has appeared outside of this setting. We would argue, though, that many if not all of the researchers represented in the proceedings incorporate knowledge from a wide variety of sources so that key materials from top IS and management journals tend to indirectly find their way into the conference content. Most importantly, this writing represents the observations of patterns and trends that are idiosyncratic to the authors' perceptions and values. Other scholars might come to different conclusions based on the same set of underlying content. The observations and opinions presented herein should, therefore, be taken as possible rather than validated and proven trends and tendencies.

We believe that there is positive value in understanding the origins of the CPR field and how these have influenced the current understandings and practices that we observe today. This essay has attempted to describe the first "conference", some of the themes of the first five conferences as well as the most recent five conferences, and present some observations regarding how we anticipate the field will move forward in the future.

REFERENCES

[1] Adya, M. (2007). Bringing Global Sourcing into the Classroom: Experiential Learning via Software Development Project. *Human Factors*, 20-27.

[2] Adya, M. P. (2008). Work Alienation among IT Workers: A Cross-Cultural Gender Comparison. *Human Factors*, 66-69.

[3] Allan, J. C. C. (1968). The selection and training of computer personnel in the United Kingdom. *Computer Personnel Research Group* (pp. 64-80).

[4] Ballou, D. J., & Huguenard, B. R. (2008). Personal and situational predictors of IS professionals' career choice satisfaction. *Proceedings of the 2008 ACM SIGMIS CPR conference on Computer personnel doctoral consortium and research - SIGMIS-CPR '08*, 50. New York, New York, USA: ACM Press. doi:10.1145/1355238.1355250

[5] Benamati, J. "Skip." (2007). Current and future entry-level IT workforce needs in organizations. *Proceedings of the 2007 ACM SIGMIS CPR conference on 2007 computer personnel doctoral consortium and research conference The global information technology workforce - SIGMIS-CPR '07*, 101. New York, New York, USA: ACM Press. doi:10.1145/1235000.1235024

[6] Benjamin, R. S., & Lederer, J. L. (1964). A data systems intern program. *Computer Personnel Research Group* (pp. 42-59).

[7] Berkelaar, B. L., Kisselburgh, L. G., & Buzzanell, P. M. (2008). Locating and Disseminating Effective Messages: Enhancing Gender Representation in Computing Majors and Careers. *Design*, 106-108.

[8] Buche, M. W. (2008). Influence of Gender on IT Professional Work Identity: Outcomes from a PLS Study. *Measurement*, 134-140.

[9] DeLegall, W.A. (1969). "Teaching techniques and quality education/training for the "disadvantaged" Proc*eedings of the seventh annual conference on SIGCPR - SIGCPR '69*, 91-94. New York, New York, USA:.

[10] Dickson, C. M. (1969). In-house recruiting---one answer to programmer force losses. *Proceedings of the seventh annual conference on SIGCPR - SIGCPR '69*, 120-127. New York, New York, USA: ACM Press. doi:10.1145/800163.805188

[11] Downey, J. (2008). An artifact-centric method for creating software job descriptions. *Proceedings of the 2008 ACM SIGMIS CPR conference on Computer personnel doctoral consortium and research - SIGMIS-CPR '08*, 12. New York, New York, USA: ACM Press. doi:10.1145/1355238.1355243

[12] Eckhardt, A., Stetten, A. V., & Laumer, S. (2009). Value Contribution of IT in Recruiting – A Multi-National Causal Analysis. *Methodology*, 1-6.

[13] Gallagher, C. E. (1964). The computer and invation of privacy. *Computer Personnel Research Group* (pp. 108-114).

[14] Gilbert, J. P., & Mayer, D. B. (1969). Experiences in self-selection of disadvantaged people into a computer operator training program. *Proceedings of the seventh annual conference on SIGCPR - SIGCPR '69*, 79-90. New York, New York, USA: ACM Press. doi:10.1145/800163.805183

[15] Guzman, I. R., Joseph, D., Papamichail, K. N., & Stanton, J. M. (2007). RIP - Beliefs about IT culture: Exploring National and Gender Differences. *English*, 217-220.

[16] Jones, J. P. (1964). Data processing management: Is it unique? *Computer Personnel Research Group*.

[17] Joseph, D. (2008). Increasing the Number of Entrants into the IT Profession: The Role of Experiential Training. *Information Age*, 8-10.

[18] Landry, John R. (2008). Can computing professionals be the unintentional architects of evil information systems? *Proceedings of the 2008 ACM SIGMIS CPR conference on Computer personnel doctoral consortium and research - SIGMIS-CPR '08*, 76. New York, New York, USA: ACM Press. doi:10.1145/1355238.1355256

[19] Landry, John Reid. (2009). Analyzing the London ambulance service's computer aided despatch (LASCAD) failure as a case of administrative evil. *Proceedings of the special interest group on management information system's 47th annual conference on Computer personnel research - SIGMIS-CPR '09*, 167. New York, New York, USA: ACM Press. doi:10.1145/1542130.1542163

[20] Lewis, T. L., Smith, W. J., & Hall, W. (2008). Determining Students ' Intent to Stay in IT Programs: An Empirical Model. *Computing*, 5-11.

[21] Mahatanankoon, P. (2007). The effects of post-educational professional development activities on promotion and career satisfaction of IT professionals. *Proceedings of the 2007 ACM SIGMIS CPR conference on 2007 computer personnel doctoral consortium and research conference The global information technology workforce - SIGMIS-CPR '07*, 9. New York, New York, USA: ACM Press. doi:10.1145/1235000.1235003

[22] Mehlis, M.O., (1969). "Data processing in Bolivia," Proc*eedings of the seventh annual conference on SIGCPR - SIGCPR '69*, 114-119. New York, New York, USA:.

[23] Mgaya, K. V., Uzoka, F.-M. E., Kitindi, E. G., & Shemi, a P. (2009). Examining career orientations of information systems personnel in an emerging economy context. *Proceedings of the special interest group on management information system's 47th annual conference on Computer personnel research - SIGMIS-CPR '09*, 41. New York, New York, USA: ACM Press. doi:10.1145/1542130.1542139

[24] Orden, A. (1966). An emergence of a profession. *Computer Personnel Research Group*.

[25] Reinstedt, R. N. (1964). Summary report on nationwide testing effort, 1-8.

[26] Rosove, P. E. (1969). Training requirements for computer programmers in relation to system development phases. *Proceedings of the seventh annual conference on SIGCPR - SIGCPR '69*, 65-76. New York, New York, USA: ACM Press. doi:10.1145/800163.805182

[27] Sackman, H. D. (1968). Man-computer communication: experimental investigation of user effectiveness. *Computer Personnel Research Group* (pp. 93-105).

[28] Shayo, C. (2008). The role of technology and authentic task contexts in promoting inclusive learning for disabled and non-disabled college students. *Proceedings of the 2008 ACM SIGMIS CPR conference on Computer personnel doctoral consortium and research - SIGMIS-CPR '08*, 109. New York, New York, USA: ACM Press. doi:10.1145/1355238.1355266

[29] Sumner, M., & Yager, S. E. (2002). An Investigation of Preparedness and Importance of MIS Competencies: Research in Progress. *Information Systems*, 97-100.

[30] Trauth, E. M., & Huang, H. (2007). Cultural Influences and Globally Distributed Information Systems Development: Experiences from Chinese IT Professionals. *Communications of the ACM*, 36-45.

[31] Wang, X, Teo, H-H, and Yang, X. (2010). "Turnover Intentions of IT Employees in non-IT Organizations: Effects of Organizational and Professional Identification, "SIGCPR conference on Computer personnel research - SIGCPR '66, Vancouver, B.C., Canada 100-104.

[32] Wegner, P. (1966). Undergraduate programs in computer science. *Proceedings of the fourth SIGCPR conference on Computer personnel research - SIGCPR '66*, 121. New York, New York, USA: ACM Press. doi:10.1145/1142620.1142633

Embracing Intersectionality in Gender and IT Career Choice Research

Eileen M. Trauth
The Pennsylvania State University
330C IST Building
University Park, PA 16802
1.814.865.6457
etrauth@ist.psu.edu

Curtis C. Cain
The Pennsylvania State University
307G IST Building
University Park, PA 16802
1.814.865.8952
caincc@psu.edu

K.D. Joshi
Washington State University
440B Todd Building
Pullman, WA 99164 USA
1.509.335.5722
joshi@wsu.edu

Lynette Kvasny
The Pennsylvania State University
329C IST Building
University Park, PA 16802
1.814.865.6468
kvasny@ist.psu.edu

Kayla Booth
The Pennsylvania State University
307GC IST Building
University Park, PA 16802
1.814.865.8952
kmb5445@ist.psu.edu

ABSTRACT

Results of an examination of with-gender variation in gender stereotypes about the skills and knowledge in the IT profession demonstrates the value of applying an intersectionality perspective in the study of under represented groups in the IT field. Focusing on gender or ethnicity, alone, is insufficient to explain the under representation of women and minorities in IT careers. Rather, we believe that stratifying the population in a more nuanced manner, such as by gender within ethnic group, provides deeper insights into the phenomenon of under representation. Hence, this research approaches the topic of gender and the IT profession from the perspective of intersectionality of gender and ethnicity. Within-gender analysis reveals variation in gender stereotyping by gender-ethnic group. White females and minority males (i.e. Black and Hispanic males) exhibited the most masculine stereotyping of IT skills. In contrast, White males and minority females (i.e. Black and Hispanic females) exhibited the fewest. Three themes emerge from this research. First, the skills that will be increasingly important in the future in distinguishing equivalently credentialed IT professionals were not absorbed into the "masculine" category. Second, hegemonic masculine traits appear to be deeply entrenched in the next generation of IT professionals. Third, when peering more deeply into the gender stereotyping of skills by respondent demographics, what emerges is a pattern that emphasizes the critical role of intersectionality in gender analyses of the IT profession.

Categories and Subject Descriptors

K. Computing Milieu, K.3.2 Computer and Information Science Education, K.7 The Computing Profession, K.7.1 Occupations

Keywords

Career choice, ethnicity, gender, gender stereotypes, individual differences, IT professional, IT skills, IT workforce, race

1. INTRODUCTION

For half a century ACM has sponsored conference devoted to the topic of computer personnel research, which has presented work related to factors affecting the supply of information technology (IT) professionals. More recently, the topic of the gender imbalance has been introduced as a topic of examination. As shown in the Appendix, over the past 50 years 43 papers that have gender and the IT workforce as a central theme have been presented at this conference. Of these papers, only ten have considered the topic of multiple identity characteristics. Eight papers examined gender with nationality or culture [1][33][54][64][65][66][80][89]. Two other papers dealt with the topic of gender and ethnicity. Of these, Gallivan et al. [31] focused on recruitment and retention strategies to address the under representation of women and ethnic minorities as two separate populations in the American IT workforce. But only one paper -- Kvasny [53] -- has examined the intersectionality of gender and ethnicity as a means of explaining the under representation of certain groups in the IT field. Rather than examining identity characteristics such as race, ethnicity, gender and class in isolation, intersectionality considers how these interact to mutually construct one another [20].

At this transition point in the history of the conference, as we look backward and forward, it is important to consider how CPR research into gender will need to change in the future. In the United States, changing population demographics will necessarily influence gender research. For example, current population statistics show 47.8 million Hispanic Americans in 2010 with a projected Hispanic population of 102.6 million in 2050 [87]. The projected demographic shifts in the USA call into question the value of continuing to view "males" and "females" as homogeneous groups that do not take into account other identity characteristics such as race, ethnicity, class and sexual orientation. Hence, our point of departure in this paper is that focusing on gender or ethnicity, in isolation is insufficient to explain the under-representation of women and minorities in the IT field. We believe that stratifying the population in a more nuanced manner, such as by gender within ethnic group, will provide valuable insights into the phenomenon of under representation. Hence, this paper approaches the topic of gender and the IT profession from the perspective of intersectionality of gender and ethnicity. We begin by reviewing the literature of sex roles as it relates to the IT profession. We then describe our theoretical perspective, methodology and results. Finally, we discuss the findings and implications for research and practice.

2. LITERATURE REVIEW

The social constructionist theory of gender is often used to explain stereotyping of skills and knowledge required to succeed in IT careers. In this view gender is perceived as a socially constructed script that prescribes different values, attributes, and activities for men and women [2][26][51][71][91]. According to the social constructionist perspective, the social perception that feminine attributes are commonly female-owned traits and masculine attributes are commonly male-owned traits are socially constructed, accepted and internalized. In other words, men will be socially perceived to be well suited to perform stereotypically masculine roles whereas women will be viewed to fit well in stereotypically feminine roles. These social prescriptions of gender-based roles put pressure on men and women to conform to prescribed normative roles. While conformance to the gendering process may be resisted by certain individuals, the constructivist view holds that the cultural and social roles and norms ascribed to their gender nevertheless shape the majority of individuals' world views [91].

A meta-analysis of a decade's worth of gender studies has reported gender differences in job attribute preferences in the general population (see [51] for a comprehensive review). Many job attributes can be connected to gender roles and stereotypes, and differences in self-concept and self-presentation may cause women and men to value job attributes differently. For example, it is assumed in many quarters that men are socialized to be more concerned with a job's pay, prestige, and power. Indeed, research has shown that men are more likely to initiate negotiations for higher pay [7]. Similarly, parts of society hold the assumption that women are socialized to place more importance on aspects such as social interactions and relations with co-workers, customers, and working with people. These assumptions have, in turn, been linked to masculine stereotypes of dominance and exhibition and feminine stereotypes of nurturance and affiliation. For this reason theories of gender roles, gender stereotypes, and gendered social structures have been used to explain differences in what men and women most desire from their work [51][92].

However, the results of Kuhn and Joshi's [52] recent examination of gender similarities and differences in IT job attribute preferences among graduating seniors challenge these assumptions. Participants evaluated a series of multi-attribute job descriptions in a policy-capturing design. Overall, their results showed that male and female aspiring IT professionals are more similar than different in their performances of job attributes. This observation runs contrary to underlying assumptions about gender that have been reflected in past research, thereby challenging the applicability of commonly accepted stereotypes. However, the results also demonstrate that although male and female aspiring IT professionals have similar work values and desire the same types of job attributes, there remain subtle gender differences in the weight placed on these factors in evaluating potential jobs. For instance, women, on average, were less attracted to jobs described as mainly coding and testing of systems, and preferred job descriptions which had a higher level of social interaction. However, contrary to the hypothesis of gender differences, both men and women were more attracted to jobs described as service-oriented than to the more technical description, suggesting that an increased emphasis on social-orientation in IT work may be attractive to both genders.

While there is evidence of a trend towards feminization of certain IT careers paths [35][88][93], this trend is not observable in the IT consulting career paths [45][46]. Joshi and Kuhn [45] captured multiple stakeholder perceptions from a large international IT consulting firm to assess prototypes of a "top" consultant. They found that most critical skills used to characterize a top IT consulting performer at all job levels (entry, mid and upper levels) are significantly more masculine-typed rather than feminine-typed. This stereotypic perception was stronger when viewed through the lenses of "others," (subordinates, supervisors, and clients). Within this other group, male participants identified significantly more feminine typed skills to characterize top IT consultants, whereas the converse was true for women. That is, women participants identified significantly more masculine traits to describe a prototype of top consultant.

As this evidence shows, there is considerable interest in understanding gender norms and stereotypes as they apply to specific behaviors. And, despite contrary findings such as those described above, unilateral perceptions of gender differences continue to be asserted [25]. Women are stereotypically perceived to be more expressive: building relationships; nurturing and concerned with emotions. Men, on the other hand, are thought to be more instrumental: assertive and focused on getting a job done or a problem solved [9]. Cognitive abilities such as being analytical and quantitatively skilled are perceived as more masculine, whereas verbal skills and creativity are typed as feminine [15]. Woodfield's [93] interviewees revealed that skills such as building credible relationships with clients are often viewed as feminine-typed attributes whereas an attribute like technical competency is associated with men. Although there is some evidence change over time in these stereotypes, with traditionally masculine traits seen as more acceptable for women, the basic pattern is still observable [6][15][32][39][45][47][90]. Overall, the research literature indicates that business students are more likely to rate masculine traits as more applicable to successful managers than feminine traits [6][90]. Cejka and Eagly [15] found that students rated feminine attributes as more important to success in female-dominated occupations, and masculine attributes as more important to success in male-dominated occupations. However, higher prestige and higher earnings were associated with occupations thought to require masculine attributes. Greening [32] examined gender typing among computing students, and Hull and Umansky [39] found that male accountants tended to devalue female accountants who displayed "masculine" leadership traits. Personality measures based on self-reports also reflect these stereotypes [21]. The ascription of different traits to men and women has pervasive, although often subtle, effects on how people perceive both their and others' capabilities which in turn determines occupational choice of men and women.

But in all of this research, what remains critically unexamined is a deeper level of analysis about masculine and feminine traits. That is, the intersectionality of gender with other identity characteristics such as race, ethnicity, sexual orientation, gender identity or socioeconomic class are not taken into account when gender stereotyped behavior is examined. The purpose of this paper it to introduce a finer grained analysis of gender stereotypes about behavior in technical fields such as IT by examining the effect, if any, of gender intersectionality. Hence, the research question addressed in this paper is the following: Does the intersectionality of gender and ethnicity affect gender stereotypes about the skills and knowledge in the IT profession?

3. METHODOLOGY

In conducting this research we sought a theory that could provide the conceptual tools to examine variation in perceptions about the IT field based on the intersectionality of gender and ethnicity. That is, we sought a theory that accounts for both social constructionist influences (such as those described in the literature review) and within-gender variation due to influences such as racial and ethnic identity. Hence, the theory chosen to guide this research is the Individual Differences Theory of Gender and IT [75][76][84]. This theory originated out of the effort to explain factors that accounted for within-female variation in participation in the IT field [81][86]. This theory is comprised of three constructs. The individual identity construct consists of two sub constructs: personal demographics (e.g. age, race, nationality, socio-economic class, and parenthood status); and career items (e.g. the type of IT work in which one engages). The second construct, individual influences, consists of the personal characteristics sub construct (e.g. educational background, personality traits and abilities); and the personal influences sub construct (e.g. mentors, role models, and significant life experiences). Finally, the environmental influences construct consists of four sub constructs: cultural influences (e.g. national, regional or organizational attitudes about women or about women and IT); economic influences (e.g. cost of living, availability of IT employment); policy influences (e.g. laws about gender discrimination and maternity leave); and infrastructure influences (e.g. existence of childcare facilities). The individual differences theory of gender and IT argues that, taken together, these constructs can explain the under representation of women in the IT field b[1]y identifying differences among women in the ways they relate to the IT field, experience gendered discourses about IT, and respond to them [82].

In this research the environmental influences construct accounts for social constructivist influences described in the literature review above. The individual identity construct is used to introduce intersectionality by accounting for the influence of race and ethnicity.[1] Because of its focus on within-gender variation that results from a combination of individual and group effects, this theory has already been used to explore within-gender variation related to the intersectionality of gender and other identity characteristics such as race and ethnicity. Kvasny et al. [56] applied this theory in an examination of variation among African American women with respect to their engagement with IT and participation in the IT profession.

Intersectionality is explored in this paper through examination of gender differences among contemporary Black, Hispanic and White male and female college students with respect to gender stereotypes they hold about the IT field. Undergraduate students enrolled in IT courses at 12 public institutions were surveyed during 2010 and 2011 to explore gender stereotypes about the skills and knowledge of the IT field. Three of these institutions are classified as predominantly White institutions (PWI), four are classified as Hispanic serving institutions (HSI) and five are classified as historically Black colleges and universities (HBCU).

Students participated in this study on a volunteer basis; in some cases, instructors offered extra credit for participation in the survey. Using a five-point Likert scale (1 = feminine, 3 = gender neutral, 5 = masculine) students were asked to assign gender norms to a list of 39 skills that are considered to be part of the IT professional toolkit that were d[2]rawn from previous research [36][78][79]. To avoid sequencing bias these skills were presented to each participant in a randomized fashion.

4. FINDINGS

Out of a total number of 4523 survey participants the distribution of participants by ethnicity and gender category is shown in Table 2.[1]

Gender / Ethnicity Category	Number
Male	2679
Female	1453
White	2171
Black	768
Hispanic	346
White Male	1557
White Female	611
Black Male	377
Black Female	390
Hispanic Male	206
Hispanic Female	139
Total	4523

Table 2. Respondent Numbers by Gender / Ethnicity Category

Data was analyzed using standard deviation (x) from the median. The median in this survey was 3: the gender-neutral point. The means were taken across each trait in the survey. If deviation existed that was greater than $+0.1$ ($x > 0.1$) that trait was classified as trending masculine. Conversely if deviation occurred that was less than -0.1 ($x < -0.1$) that trait was classified as feminine. For any trait in which deviation existed between -0.09 and $+0.09$ ($-0.09 < x < 0.09$) that trait was identified as gender neutral. A two-sample T-TEST determined that the differences between Black, White and Hispanic males and females were statistically significant ($p < .05$). Using the standard deviation from each trait, the following Venn diagrams were developed to visually represent the findings of our investigation of the influence of the intersectionality of ethnicity and gender on gender stereotypes about the IT field.

---

[1] While the research study from which this paper is written includes qualitative data collection that accounts for the third construct (individual influences), that construct is not addressed in this particular paper.

[2] The variation in categories is due to nonresponses by some survey participants about gender and / or ethnicity.

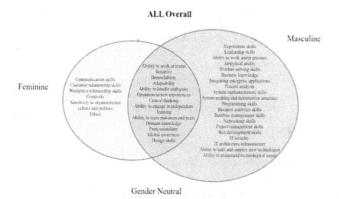

Figure 1: ALL Ethnicities Overall Venn Diagram

Figure 1 represents the responses of all participants in the study with respect to gender stereotyping of IT skills. This Venn diagram is included here to provide a basis for comparison in tracking changes in these responses by specific gender/ethnic groups. As might be expected, stereotypical feminine traits, or "soft" skills, such as sensitivity and customer relationship skills are considered to be feminine. Similarly, stereotypical masculine traits such as programming are listed as masculine or "hard" skills, as are several business and management skills. Interestingly, creativity is listed among the feminine skills even though design, something heavily dependent upon creativity, is listed as gender neutral, and problem solving is listed as masculine. This finding is also noteworthy in view of the current emphasis on innovation in the IT field, insofar as it might be thought that males would want to claim this newly powerful trait as masculine.

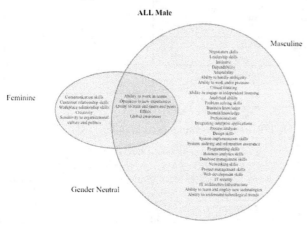

Figure 2: ALL Male Overall Venn Diagram

Figure 2 represents the responses of all participants who identified themselves as males.[3] In comparison to Figure 1, we begin to notice a shift between "soft" IT skills, such as communication skills and customer relationship skills, and "hard" IT skills, such as programming skills and networking skills. The skills that men describe as masculine are a representation of typical stereotyping of males as more inclined to be skilled in business knowledge and skills that are perceived to require in-depth thought. However, as noted, there is a disconnect with respect to creativity and innovation. Men placed creativity into the feminine category even though c[3]reativity is necessary to spur innovation, many of which

---

[3] Respondents who identified as transgender were excluded from this analysis as were those who declined to indicate their

traits are categorized as masculine. Reflecting the fact that males outnumber females in our survey by a ratio of nearly two to one, the Male Overall diagram represents a stark contrast to the Overall diagram in Figure 1 with respect to the movement of skills from feminine and gender neutral to masculine.

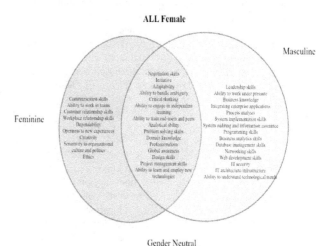

Figure 3: ALL Female Overall Venn Diagram

Figure 3 represents the responses from all survey participants that identified themselves as female. In comparison to the Male Overall diagram in Figure 2, females were much more likely to rate traits as being gender neutral than their male counterparts. Like the males, females also viewed the more traditional "soft" IT traits of communication skills and customer relationship skills as feminine. Females also rated creativity as being a feminine trait. The "hard" IT skills, such as programming and networking skills remain as masculine. The trend of "soft" skills being feminine and "hard" skills being masculine reinforces conventional gender stereotyping of these skills. In comparison to the All Overall diagram in Figure 1, there was a movement by females to classify more IT traits as gender neutral and feminine.

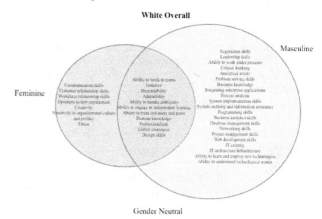

Figure 4: White Overall Venn Diagram

Figure 4 displays the White Overall inclusive of male and female ratings of IT skills. Figure 4 is similar to the diagram in Figure 1. In view of the fact that Whites outnumber non Whites in the survey nearly three to one, this is not surprising. Ratings of "soft"

---

gender. A separate paper on gender nonconforming respondents is in development.

skills such as customer relationship skills and ethics appear as feminine while "hard" skills such as programming and IT security appear as masculine. Since White males outnumbered White females in the survey by a ratio of nearly 2.55:1, for traits to appear in the feminine category, a significant number of males had to have rated the trait as feminine. Thus, it appears that many White males associate some IT skills as non-masculine. However, the traits that appear as feminine are those which are mostly stereotypically viewed as "soft" IT skills.

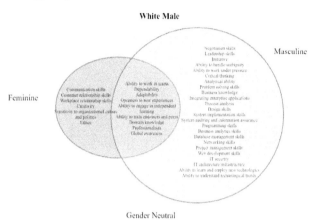

Figure 5: White Male Venn Diagram

Figure 5 shows how White males rated IT skills. The White male diagram is most similar to the White overall diagram due to the fact that White male survey respondents greatly outnumbered White females. However, White males ranked IT soft skills as feminine, which included communication skills and customer relationship skills, while ranking hard skills, such as programming and networking skills, as masculine. White males rated skills such as openness to new experiences and the ability to work in teams as gender neutral. In comparison to the White overall diagram in Figure 4, no trait moved from masculine over to feminine or gender neutral.

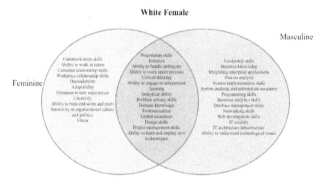

Figure 6: White Female Venn Diagram

Figure 6 shows White females' representation of IT skills. Females tended to rank more skills as feminine, such as dependability and adaptability. The White female Venn diagram closely resembles the female overall diagram in Figure 3. White females rated more skills, such as analytical ability and critical thinking, as gender neutral. However, in comparison to the White Overall diagram in Figure 4 and White Male diagram in 5, White females continued to rank IT soft skills such as communication skills and customer relationship skills as feminine, and IT hard

skills such as IT security and programming as masculine. The continued rating of traditional IT soft and hard skills as feminine and masculine is indicative of how deeply entrenched are these gender stereotypes about the IT field, even by those who are negatively impacted by them.

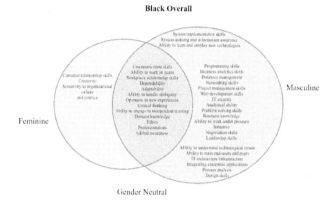

Figure 7: Black Overall Venn Diagram

Figure 7 represents the gender stereotyping of IT skills by those participants who identified themselves as Black. This diagram shows a shift in skills that were represented in Figure 1 as feminine, such as workplace relationship skills and ethics, to the gender neutral category. This shift shows that Black participants classified more skills as gender neutral and masculine and fewer as feminine. It is noteworthy that while creativity remained in the feminine classification, design skills shifted from gender neutral (in Figure 1) to masculine (in Figure 7). "Soft" skills, such as communication skills and customer relationship skills remained feminine. Conversely, "hard" skills, such as programming skills and IT security, remained masculine.

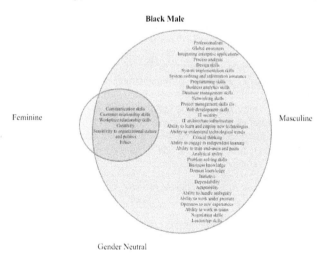

Figure 8: Black Male Venn Diagram

Figure 8 represents the results from survey participants who identified themselves as Black males. These participants represent the starkest contrast of any gender/ethnic group to the overall responses shown in Figure 1. Black males identified no IT skill or knowledge area as being feminine, even those that have been found elsewhere in the literature and in this survey to be stereotypically feminine, such as communication skills and customer relationship skills. Interestingly, Black males shifted every trait that appeared in the overall diagram of all ethnicities in

Figure 1 as feminine to gender neutral and every trait that appeared as gender neutral in Figure 1 to masculine. The shift noticed in the Black male diagram might suggest that they do not view the IT domain as one that necessitates a female's "soft" skills. Another view may be that Black males do not view the IT field as one that is welcoming to women. To the extent that the Black male view is representative of the majority of individuals working in IT, this finding might help to explain the over representation of males in the IT profession.

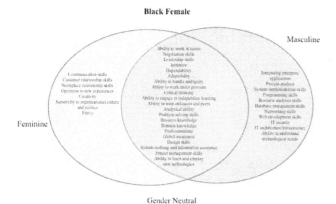

Figure 9: Black Female Venn Diagram

Figure 9 depicts the responses of survey participants that identified themselves as Black females. Black females' conceptualization of feminine IT skills is nearly identical to that in Figure 1. The only exception is "openness to new experiences," something that was classified as gender neutral in Figure 1. An interesting finding was that Black females were much more likely to identify a trait as being gender neutral instead of masculine or feminine. Skills that were masculine in Figure 1 and Figure 8, such as negotiation skills and leadership skills were classified as gender neutral by Black females. This shift from masculine to gender neutral may suggest that Black females do not believe that IT skills that are traditionally categorized as masculine should be classified as such. However, some of the more stereotypical feminine skills, such as communication skills and customer relationship skills, remained within the feminine domain. Another interesting finding for Black females is that most of the "hard" skills did not shift from being masculine. Perhaps the biggest indication that technology remains male centric is that "ability to understand technological trends" has remained masculine in Figures 1, 7 and 8.

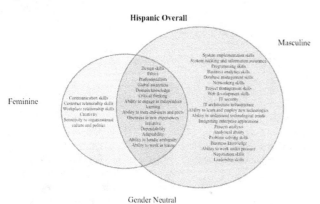

Figure 10: Hispanic Overall Venn Diagram

Figure 10 depicts the responses of survey participants that identified themselves as Hispanic. This diagram shows the separation of "soft" skills being categorized as feminine and "hard" skills being categorized as masculine. Compared to the White Overall diagram in Figure 4 and Black Overall in Figure 7 the Hispanic Overall diagram more closely resembles the Black Overall diagram. Hispanics were more likely to rate skills as masculine or gender neutral than feminine. In comparison to the overall diagram in Figure 1, the Hispanic Overall diagram bears a close resemblance and a small shift between skills.

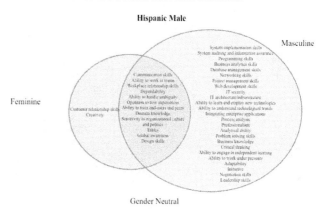

Figure 11: Hispanic Male Venn Diagram

Figure 11 represents the results from survey participants who identified themselves as Hispanic males. Our Hispanic male participants represent the second starkest contrast to Figure 1 of any gender/ethnic group after Black males as seen in Figure 8. Hispanic males identified only two IT skills as being feminine: "customer relationship skills" and "creativity". Those traits that have been found elsewhere in the literature and in this survey to be stereotypically feminine, such as communication skills and workplace relationship skills, are rated as gender neutral by Hispanic males. Similar to Black males, Hispanic males shifted all but two traits that appeared in the overall diagram of all ethnicities in Figure 1 as feminine to gender neutral and every trait that appeared as gender neutral in Figure 1 to masculine.

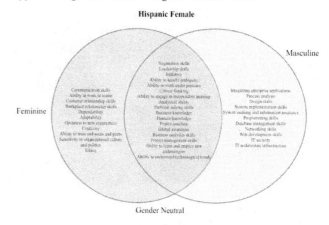

Figure 12: Hispanic Female Venn Diagram

Figure 12 depicts the responses of survey participants that identified themselves as Hispanic females. Hispanic females' conceptualization of feminine IT skills is similar to that in Figure 1, which reflects the responses from all survey participants. An interesting finding was that Hispanic females were much more likely to identify a trait as being gender neutral instead of masculine or feminine than their Hispanic male counterparts. The Hispanic females' representation of IT skills closely resembles that of Black females. Skills that were masculine in Figure 1 and Figure 11, such as negotiation skills and leadership skills were classified as gender neutral by Hispanic females. Some of the more stereotypical feminine skills, such as communication skills and customer relationship skills, remained within the feminine domain. Similar to Black females and White females, most of the "hard" skills remained masculine.

5. DISCUSSION

The results shown in the previous section clearly demonstrate the need for CPR researchers to consider the intersectionality of gender and ethnicity when investigating issues related to the gender imbalance in the IT field. As these data show, the intersection of gender and ethnicity appears to be a significant factor influencing gender stereotypes held by current university students about the skills and knowledge of the IT profession. It can be expected that these gender stereotypes will, in turn, affect both the students' own career decisions and their interactions with IT professionals who possess different demographic characteristics than theirs.

In this regard, we would like to focus on three themes. First, the skills that will be increasingly important in the future in distinguishing equivalently credentialed IT professionals were not absorbed into the "masculine" category. The skills that can give an individual a competitive advantage in a crowded employment field were classified as gender neutral or feminine. These include such traits as initiative, dependability, adaptability, critical thinking, global awareness, comfort with ambiguity and new experiences, and ability to engage in independent learning. It is particularly noteworthy that despite the fact that innovation is touted as a key economic driver of virtually every sector, "creativity" was categorized as a feminine attribute by all the respondents except Black males (who didn't identify any traits as feminine). The implication of these findings is that to the extent that the IT field is stereotyped as a masculine field, the demasculinization of these traits might coincide with devaluing them – to an IT professional's peril. Further research is needed to relate the gender stereotyping of these traits to the value placed upon them. Second, hegemonic masculine traits appear to be deeply entrenched in the next generation of IT professionals. Whereas the gender boundary separating human and domain skills into feminine, gender neutral and masculine appears to be porous, the stereotypically masculine technical skills appear to remain impervious to change. Third, when peering more deeply into the gender stereotyping of skills by respondent demographics, what emerges is a pattern that emphasizes the critical role of intersectionality in gender analyses of the IT profession.

We can see this by examining within-gender variation in gender stereotypes. Within the context of hegemonic masculine traits deeply entrenched in the IT profession, White females exhibited sex role stereotypes to a greater extent than did their Black or Hispanic counterparts. They classified 14 skills as masculine, 14 as gender neutral and 11 as feminine. In contrast, minority women rated only 11 skills as masculine and shifted other masculine skills into the gender neutral category. We find it noteworthy that Black women classified 21 of the 39 skills as gender neutral and Hispanic women classified 17 as gender neutral.

One interpretation of these results is that Black Women, historically, have worked outside the home and have been socialized to work in the formal economy. Arguably, Black Women, as a group, have had considerably more experience with handling discrimination and assumptions that they are not smart or only have a position because they are "an affirmative action hire." This interpretation of the data flows from the intersectionality argument that White women and women of color have different notions of womanhood and relationship with work. Whereas women of all ethnicities are victims of the feminization of poverty, and are often exploited and underpaid in the service economy, White women have historically enjoyed an ethnic privilege that gives them advantages in the workplace. In contrast, the work of Black and Hispanic women – until quite recently -- has consisted of domestic labor (for upper and middle-class white women), factory work and migrant farm labor. For instance, Davis [23] points out that historically, virtually all African American women were workers. African American women and men worked side by side in the fields during slavery. Following slavery, Black women struggled to be economically successful in a society that greatly limited the opportunities for both African Americans and women. Domestic service in white households was one of the few jobs that society offered African-American women. In 1940, 60 percent of Black women in the labor force were household workers; in 1960, one-third were still in domestic service - and their employers were White women [23].

With respect to the gender stereotypes assigned by Hispanic women, understanding differentiations in their pre-college experience may provide some insight. In immigrant households, which includes many but certainly not all Hispanic families, adolescents may take on the role of "brokering," which encompasses interpreting language, culture, and media and then translating these understandings for their parents or caregivers to integrate the family into a community. This happens most frequently when children of immigrant parents are the primary English speakers in the household. Female adolescents are most often brokers, something that gives them experience in interpretation, problem solving, and communication. This, in turn, may bolster their confidence in their abilities as well as reinforce an association between being female and being capable with these sets of skills. In addition, Hispanic females are more inclined to be bilingual, able to successfully communicate both in their family's language of origin, as well as in English. This may also fuel comfort and association with communication skills [50]. The combination of both exposure and association may indicate why some Hispanic females, who may have or are currently brokering for their families, associate skills such as communication, negotiation, and problem solving as either strictly feminine or gender neutral.

The identity internalized by Black and Hispanic women stands in contrast to the idealized gender identity of White women. The notion of womanhood as pampered, spoiled and elevated on the invisible pedestal was never extended to women of color. hooks [37] argues that Black women, from the seventeenth century to the present day, were and are oppressed by White men, Black men and White women. Caraway [12] states that this history continues to shape women's work identities and serves as a potent legacy that should not be underestimated.

This historical tension between White women and women of color is played out through the social construction of ethnicity and class in the context of gender. While White women may suffer under gender oppression, they also benefit from a privilege system based on ethnicity. This line of reasoning is consistent with the criticism of American feminism as a "White female" phenomenon. The argument is that since a women of color has always needed to work and has not been able to rely on a man to support her, the issues around the female dilemma of working outside the home versus working in the unpaid labor force does not resonate with her. Hence, she might be less influenced by societal sex role stereotypes applied to the IT field.

With respect to male gender stereotyping of IT skills, relative to other male groups, White males classified the least (24) as masculine and the most (6) as feminine. This contrasts with Black males by whom no traits were classified as feminine and only 6 as gender neutral, and Hispanic males who only classified two traits as feminine and 12 as gender neutral. One interpretation of these findings is that in an ethnically stratified society (which accompanied European settlement and only began to be dismantled in the mid1960s) Black men have not had equal access to the central components of masculinity, i.e. patriarchal power and authority. Hence, they now pursue the conventional routes to masculinity, as evidenced in the gender stereotypes revealed in these findings. According to Harris [34], Black males have redefined White male patriarchal notions of masculinity to emphasize sexual promiscuity, toughness, thrill seeking, and the use of violence in interpersonal interactions as a means of asserting masculinity. According to hooks [38], part of the hypermasculine identity is to make manhood synonymous with domination and control of others. This interpretation applied to our data would mean that these cultural forces motivate Black men to reject and distance themselves from feminine roles.

bell hooks [38] views the Black male identity – as constructed by Black males - as being largely nonexistent. She views Black male identity as largely the creation of white culture. Racial identity development as applied to African American males is a concept that psychologists have studied intensely [14][17][19][28]. In harmony with hooks' assessment of African American male identity, Jackson [41][42] voices the observation that Black male identity is largely a white media construction. This is particularly the case when it comes to characterizations of Black males by academic systems that have stereotyped them as being intellectually inferior to White students and disinterested in learning [18][28]. This stereotype has been challenged by scholars who have contended that African American students are intrinsically highly motivated and that their motivation is not related to how they perform academically or to their academic self-concept [14][17][18][19]. Margolis et al. [58] posits that Blacks' lived experiences equate to struggles with a stratified intellectual class system for which there are unintended consequences of well-intended policies at every level. We posit that this competing mix of projected and internalized ethnic identities has produced a hypermasculine IT identity being adopted by Black males.

A study by Saez et al. [70] of cultural and ethnic definitions of masculinity can also provide insights into why Hispanic men rated IT skills as predominantly masculine. They found that Hispanic men who strongly identified with their ethnic identity were also more likely to identify with traditional masculine ideology, which emphasizes characteristics such as aggressiveness, assertiveness, and patriarchal values. This study also found Hispanic men tending to endorse ideologies similar to their fathers and other men from the environments in which they were first socialized. Hence, this idea of hypermasculinity defined as an "exaggerated form of traditional masculinity ideology" [70, p. 116] might explain why Hispanic men rated almost all IT skills as masculine, fewer as gender neutral, and only two as feminine.

A desire to perceive oneself as dominant and successful, as possessing traits often associated with the traditional masculine gender role, may have influenced Hispanic male respondents'

interpretation of IT skills as not being feminine. If skills necessary for success in their chosen field are classified as masculine, an identity with which males often seek to align themselves, then they may more easily perceive themselves capable of succeeding and therefore fulfilling their masculine roles. It may be threatening to patriarchal values, towards which males aspire in public career spaces, that skills men are required to use daily may be feminine, thereby threatening a sense of career success or dominance over their female counterparts. Finally, Saez's study points out that hypermasculine men are often less willing to acknowledge differences among individual males, something that may explain their polarized views and the adherence to strict, unbending views of what it masculine.

These results suggest empowerment for underrepresented Black and Hispanic women insofar as their gender stereotypes are more in alignment with their gender identity than is the case for White women. However, these results also point to the challenges they might well encounter in the workplace due to the overall hegemonic masculine stereotypes held by all men. The more extreme hegemonic masculine stereotypes held by Black and Hispanic males suggests that these women may encounter within-ethnic group barriers associated with differences about sex roles and the IT field. But while White men revealed fewer hegemonic masculine stereotypes, they have historically held more power in IT organizations. Hence, minority women might experience the effects of these gender stereotypes even more from White males than from Black and Hispanic males.

6. CONCLUSION

The findings of this research have implications for both theory and practice. They reinforce our theoretical position that analyses of gender under representation benefit from examination of within-gender variation. In this paper, within-gender variation was examined through the lens of gender-ethnic intersectionality. When peering more deeply into the gender stereotyping of skills by respondent demographics such as gender and ethnicity, what emerges is a pattern that emphasizes the critical role of intersectionality in gender analyses of the IT profession.

One of the limitations of this research is the imbalance in the respondent categories. There were approximate 10 times more White males than Hispanic females in the study. Efforts are currently underway to increase the response rates of Black and Hispanic participants. The results presented in this paper also represent only part of the story of intersectionality and the gender imbalance. Further research is being conducted in order to see the relationship between gender stereotypes about IT skills and the importance placed upon them. Research is also being conducted into the connection between gender stereotypes and gender-based differences in self-efficacy related to these skills. The ultimate objective of this research is to link perceptions about gender stereotypes, skill importance and self-efficacy in a model that can predict intention to become and IT professional.

There are implications from these findings for both research and practice. The implications for research lie in the support for intersectionality in gender research and the value of using theories that enable finer-grained analysis of underrepresented groups in the IT profession. The implications for practice are that efforts to address the gender imbalance must take into account the varying gender stereotypes held by specific groups in the population. Despite the ubiquity of digital technology in use by today's youth, our finding show that gender stereotypes about who should develop the digital world remain entrenched.

7. ACKNOWLEDGMENTS

This work was supported by a grant from the National Science Foundation (0733747). Any opinions, findings, and conclusions or recommendations expressed in this paper are those of the authors and do not necessarily reflect the views of the National Science Foundation.

8. REFERENCES

[1] Adya, M.P. 2008. Work Alienation Among IT Workers: a Cross-cultural Gender Comparison. *Proceedings of the 2008 ACM SIGMIS CPR conference on Computer personnel doctoral consortium and research* (SIGMIS CPR '08), ACM, New York, NY, USA, 66-69.

[2] Adya, M., and Kaiser, K. 2005. Early Determinants of Women in the IT Workforce: A Model of Girls' Career Choices. *Information Technology and People*, 18,3, 230.

[3] Ahuja, M.K. 1995. Information Technology and the Gender Factor. *Proceedings of the 1995 ACM SIGCPR conference on Supporting teams, groups, and learning inside and outside the IS function reinventing IS* (SIGCPR '95), Olfman, L (Ed.), ACM, New York, NY, USA, 156-166.

[4] Ahuja, M., Robinson,J., Herring,S., and Ogan, C. 2004. Exploring Antecedents of Gender Equitable Outcomes in IT Higher Education. *Proceedings of the 2004 SIGMIS conference on Computer personnel research: Careers, culture, and ethics in a networked environment* (SIGMIS CPR '04), ACM, New York, NY, USA, 120-123.

[5] Armstrong, D.J., Riemenschneider, C.K., Reid, M.F., and Nelms, J.E. 2011. Challenges and Barriers Facing Women in the IS Workforce: How Far Have We Come? *Proceedings of the 49th SIGMIS annual conference on Computer personnel research* (SIGMIS-CPR '11), ACM, New York, NY, USA, 107-112.

[6] Atwater, L. E., Brett, J. F., Waldman, D., DiMare, L., & Hayden, M. V. 2004. Men's and Women's Perceptions of the Gender Typing of Management Subroles. *Sex Roles, 50*, 3/4, (Feb. 2004), 191-199.

[7] Babcock, L., Laschever, S. 2003. *Women Don't Ask: Negotiation and the Gender Divide*. Princeton University Press, Princeton, NJ, USA.

[8] Beise, C., Chevli-Saroq, N., Andersen, S., and Myers, M. 2002. A Model for Examination of Underrepresented Groups in the IT Workforce. *Proceedings of the 2002 ACM SIGCPR conference on Computer personnel research* (SIGCPR '02), ACM, New York, NY, USA, 106-110.

[9] Bem, S.L. 1981. Gender Schema Theory: A Cognitive Account of Sex Typing. *Psychological Review*, 88, 4, 354-364.

[10] Berkelaar, B.L., Kisselburgh, L.G., and Buzzanell, P.M. 2008. Locating and Disseminating Effective Messages: Enhancing Gender Representation in Computing Majors and Careers. *Proceedings of the 2008 ACM SIGMIS CPR conference on Computer personnel doctoral consortium and research* (SIGMIS CPR '08), ACM, New York, NY, USA, 106-108.

[11] Buche, M.W. 2008. Influence of Gender on IT Professional Work Identity: Outcomes from a PLS Study. *Proceedings of the 2008 ACM SIGMIS CPR conference on Computer personnel doctoral consortium and research* (SIGMIS CPR '08), ACM, New York, NY, USA, 134-140.

[12] Caraway, N. 1991. *Segregated Sisterhood: Racism and the Politics of American Feminism*. University of Tennessee Press, Knoxville, Tennessee, USA.

[13] Carayon, P., Hoonakker, P., Marchand, S., and Schwarz, J. 2003. Job Characteristics and Quality of Working Life in the IT Workforce: the Role of Gender. *Proceedings of the 2003 SIGMIS conference on Computer personnel research: Freedom in Philadelphia--leveraging differences and diversity in the IT workforce* (SIGMIS CPR '03), ACM, New York, NY, USA, 58-63.

[14] Carter, R.T. and Goodwin, L. 1994. Racial Identity and Education. *Review of Research in Education*, 20, 291-336.

[15] Cejka, M. A., & Eagly, A. 1999. Gender-Stereotypic Images of Occupations Correspond to the Sex Segregation of Employment. *Personality and Social Psychology Bulletin*, 25, 4 (April 1999), 413-423.

[16] Clayton, K.L., von Hellens, L.A., and Nielsen, S.H. 2009. Gender Stereotypes Prevail in ICT: a Research Review. *Proceedings of the special interest group on management information system's 47th annual conference on Computer personnel research* (SIGMIS CPR '09), ACM, New York, NY, USA, 53-158.

[17] Cokley, K.O. 2002. Ethnicity, Gender and Academic Self-Concept: A Preliminary Examination of Academic Disidentification and Implications for Psychologists. *Cultural Diversity and Ethnic Minority Psychology*, 8, 4, 379-388.

[18] Cokley, K.O. 2005. Racial(ized) Identity, Ethnic Identity, and Afrocentric Values: Conceptual and Methodological Challenges in Understanding African American Identity. *Journal of Counseling Psychology*, 52, 4, 517-526.

[19] Cokley, K.O. 2003. What Do We Know about the Motivation of African American Students?: Challenging the 'Anti-Intellectual' Myth. *Harvard Educational Review*, 73, 4, (Winter 2003).

[20] Collins, P.H. 1998. It's All in the Family: Intersection of Gender, Race, and Nation. *Hypatia*, 13, 3, 62-82.

[21] Costa, P. J., Terracciano, A., & McCrae, R. R. 2001. Gender Differences in Personality Traits across Cultures: Robust and Surprising Findings. *Journal of Personality & Social Psychology*, 81, 2, 322-331.

[22] Cukier, W. 2003. Constructing the IT Skills Shortage in Canada: the Implications of Institutional Discourse and Practices for the Participation of Women. *Proceedings of the 2003 SIGMIS conference on Computer personnel research: Freedom in Philadelphia--leveraging differences and diversity in the IT workforce* (SIGMIS CPR '03), ACM, New York, NY, USA, 24-33.

[23] Davis, A. 1983. *Women, Race and Class*. New York: Vintage Books, New York, NY, USA.

[24] Davis, J., and Kuhn, S. 2003. What Makes Dick and Jane Run?: Examining the Retention of Women and Men in the Software and Internet Industry. *Proceedings of the 2003 SIGMIS conference on Computer personnel research: Freedom in Philadelphia--leveraging differences and diversity in the IT workforce* (SIGMIS CPR '03), ACM, New York, NY, USA, 154-156.

[25] Eagly, H., & Wood, W. 1991. Explaining Sex Differences in

Social Behavior: A Meta-analytical Perspective. *Personality and Social Psychology Bulletin,* 17, 306-315.

[26] Eagly, A. H., Wood, W., & Diekman, A. B. 2000. Social Role Theory of Sex Differences and Similarities: A Current Appraisal. In Eckes, T. and Trautner, H.M. (Eds), *The Developmental Social Psychology of Gender*, Mahwah, NJ: Lawrence Erlbaum, 123-174.

[27] Enneis, W.H., Palormo, J.M., & Sorenson, W.W. 1971. Current perspectives on selection testing. Panel in *Proceedings of the ninth annual SIGCPR conference* (SIGCPR '71), Willoughby (Ed.), ACM, New York, NY, USA, 54-74.

[28] Franklin, A.J. 1999. Invisibility Syndrome and Racial Identity Development in Psychotherapy and Counseling African American Men. *The Counseling Psychologist*, 27, 6, 761-793.

[29] Gallivan, M. 2003. Examining Gender Differences in IT Professionals' Perceptions of Job Stress in Response to Technological Change. *Proceedings of the 2003 SIGMIS conference on Computer personnel research: Freedom in Philadelphia--leveraging differences and diversity in the IT workforce* (SIGMIS CPR '03), ACM, New York, NY, USA, 10-23.

[30] Gallivan, M.J., and Benbunan-Fich, R. 2006. Examining the Relationship Between Gender and the Research Productivity of IS faculty. *Proceedings of the 2006 ACM SIGMIS CPR conference on computer personnel research: Forty four years of computer personnel research: achievements, challenges \& the future* (SIGMIS CPR '06), ACM, New York, NY, USA, 103-113.

[31] Gallivan, M., Adya, M., Ahuja, A., Hoonakker, P., and Woszczynski, A. 2006. Workforce Diversity in the IT Profession: Recognizing and Resolving the Shortage of Women and Minority Employees. *Proceedings of the 2006 ACM SIGMIS CPR conference on computer personnel research: Forty four years of computer personnel research: achievements, challenges \& the future* (SIGMIS CPR '06), ACM, New York, NY, USA, 44-45.

[32] Greening, T. 1999. Gender Stereotyping in a Computer Science Course. *Proceedings of the 1999 ACM SIGCSE technical symposium on Computer science education* (SIGCSE '99), New York, NY, USA, 203-207.

[33] Guzman, I.R., Joseph, D., Papamichail, K.N., and Stanton, J.M. 2007. RIP - Beliefs About IT Culture: Exploring National and Gender Differences. *Proceedings of the 2007 ACM SIGMIS CPR conference on Computer personnel research: The global information technology workforce* (SIGMIS CPR '07), ACM, New York, NY, USA, 217-220.

[34] Harris, S. 1995. Psychosocial Development and Black Male Masculinity: Implications for Counseling Economically Disadvantaged African American Male Adolescents. *Journal of Counseling & Development,* 73, 3, 279-287.

[35] Hazzan, O., and Levy, D. 2006. Women, Hi-tech and the Family-Career Conflict. In Trauth, E. (Ed.), *Encyclopedia of gender and information technology*, Hershey: Idea Group Inc, 7-12.

[36] Huang, H., Kvasny, L., Joshi, KD., Trauth, E., and Mahar, J. 2009. Synthesizing IT Job Skills Identified in Academic Studies, Practitioner Publications and Job Ads. *Proceedings of the ACM SIGMIS Computer Personnel Research Conference* (Limerick, Ireland, May 2009), 19-25.

[37] hooks, b. 1999. *Aint I a Woman: Black Women and Feminism*, Boston: South End Press, Boston, MA, USA.

[38] hooks, b. 2004. *We Real Cool: Black Men and Masculinity*, New York: Routledge, New York, NY, USA.

[39] Hull, R. P., & Umansky, P. 1997. An Examination of Gender Stereotyping as an Explanation for Vertical Job Segregation in Public Accounting. *Accounting, Organizations and Society,* 22, 6, 507-528.

[40] Igbaria, M., and Chidambaram, L. 1995. Examination of Gender Effects on Intention to Stay Among Information Systems Employees. *Proceedings of the 1995 ACM SIGCPR conference on Supporting teams, groups, and learning inside and outside the IS function reinventing IS* (SIGCPR '95), Olfman, L. (Ed.). ACM, New York, NY, USA, 167-180.

[41] Jackson, R. L. 2006. *Scripting the Black Masculine Body: Identity, Discourse and Racial Politics in Popular Media.* SUNY Press, Albany, NY, USA.

[42] Jackson, R. L. 1999. *The Negotiation of Cultural Identity.* Praeger Press, Westport, CT, USA.

[43] Joshi, K.D., and Kuhn, K. 2005. Examining the Masculinity and Femininity of Critical Attributes Necessary to Succeed in IT. *Proceedings of the 2005 ACM SIGMIS CPR conference on Computer personnel research* (SIGMIS CPR '05), ACM, New York, NY, USA, 32-35.

[44] Joshi, K.D., and Kuhn, K. 2001. Gender Differences in IS Career Choice: Examine the Role of Attitudes and Social Norms in Selecting IS Profession. *Proceedings of the 2001 ACM SIGCPR conference on Computer personnel research* (SIGCPR '01), Serva, M. (Ed.), ACM, New York, NY, USA, 121-124.

[45] Joshi, K. D., and Kuhn, K. 2007. What It Takes to Succeed in Information Technology Consulting: Exploring the Gender Typing of Critical Attributes. *Information Technology and People* 20,4, 400-424.

[46] Joshi, K. D., Kuhn, K., & Niederman, F. 2010. Excellence in IT Consulting: Integrating Multiple Stakeholders' Perceptions of Top Performers. *IEEE Transaction of Engineering Management,* 57,4, 589-606.

[47] Joshi, K. D. and Schmidt, N. 2006. Is the Information Systems Profession Gendered? Characterization of IS Professionals and IS Careers. *DATABASE for Advances in Information System*, 37, 4, 26-41.

[48] Joshi, K.D., Schmidt, N.L., and Kuhn, K. 2003. Is the Information Systems Profession Gendered?: Characterization of IS Professionals and IS Careers. *Proceedings of the 2003 SIGMIS conference on Computer personnel research: Freedom in Philadelphia--leveraging differences and diversity in the IT workforce* (SIGMIS CPR '03), ACM, New York, NY, USA, 1-9.

[49] Katz,S., Aronis, J., Allbritton, D., Wilson, C., and Soffa, M.L. 2003. A Study to Identify Predictors of Achievement in an Introductory Computer Science Course. *Proceedings of the 2003 SIGMIS conference on Computer personnel research: Freedom in Philadelphia--leveraging differences and diversity in the IT workforce* (SIGMIS CPR '03), ACM, New York, NY, USA, 157-161.

[50] Katz, V. S., 2011. *Children Being Seen and Heard: How Youth Contribute to their Migrant Families' Adaptation,* Publidisa, Spain, 29-32.

[51] Konrad, A. M., Ritchie, J.E., Lieb, P., & Corrigall, E. 2000. Sex Differences and Similarities in Job Attribute Preferences: A meta-analysis. *Psychological Bulletin*, 126, 593-641.

[52] Kuhn, K. and Joshi, K. D. 2009. The Reported and Revealed Importance of Job Attributes: Implications of Gender Differences Among Information Technology Students. *DATABASE for Advances in Information System*, 40, 3, 40.

[53] Kvasny, L. 2003. Triple Jeopardy: Race, Gender and Class Politics of Women in Technology. *Proceedings of the 2003 SIGMIS conference on Computer personnel research: Freedom in Philadelphia--leveraging differences and diversity in the IT workforce* (SIGMIS CPR '03), ACM, New York, NY, USA, 112-116.

[54] Kvasny, L. 2006. Let the Sisters Speak: Understanding Information Technology from the Standpoint of the 'Other'. *The DATA BASE for Advances in Information Systems*, 37, 4, 13-25.

[55] Kvasny, L., Payton, F.C., Chong, J., and Mbarika, V. 2006. Information Technology Education and Employment for Women in Kenya. *Proceedings of the 2006 ACM SIGMIS CPR conference on computer personnel research: Forty four years of computer personnel research: achievements, challenges \& the future* (SIGMIS CPR '06), ACM, New York, NY, USA, 114-119.

[56] Kvasny, L., Trauth, E.M. and Morgan, A. 2009. Power Relations in IT Education and Work: The Intersectionality of Gender, Race and Class. *Journal of Information, Communication and Ethics in Society (*Special Issue on ICTs and Social Inclusion*)*, 7, 2/3, 96-118.

[57] Lending, D., and Kruck, S.E. 2002. What Predicts Student Performance in the First College-level IS Course?: Is it Different for Men and Women? *Proceedings of the 2002 ACM SIGCPR conference on Computer personnel research* (SIGCPR '02), ACM, New York, NY, USA, 100-102.

[58] Margolis, J., Estrella, R., Goode, J., Holme, J.J., Nao, K. 2008. *Stuck in the Shallow End: Education, Race, and Computing*. The MIT Press, Cambridge, MA, USA.

[59] Myers, M.E., and Beise, C.M. 2001. Nerd Work: Attractors and Barriers Perceived by Students Entering the IT Field. *Proceedings of the 2001 ACM SIGCPR conference on Computer personnel research* (SIGCPR '01), Serva, M. (Ed.), ACM, New York, NY, USA, 201-204.

[60] Myers, M., Woszczynski, A., and Shade, S. 2005. Opportunities for Women in IT Security. *Proceedings of the 2005 ACM SIGMIS CPR conference on Computer personnel research* (SIGMIS CPR '05), ACM, New York, NY, USA, 36-39.

[61] Newton, S., LeRouge, C., and Blanton, J.E. 2003. The Systems Developer Skill Set: Exploring Nature, Gaps, and Gender Differences Research in Progress. *Proceedings of the 2003 SIGMIS conference on Computer personnel research: Freedom in Philadelphia--leveraging differences and diversity in the IT workforce* (SIGMIS CPR '03), ACM, New York, NY, USA, 150-153.

[62] Niederman, F. and Sumner, M.R. 2001. Job Turnover Among MIS Professionals: an Exploratory Study of Employee Turnover. *Proceedings of the 2001 ACM SIGCPR conference on Computer personnel research* (SIGCPR '01), Serva, M. (Ed.), ACM, New York, NY, USA, 11-20.

[63] Nielsen, S.H., von Hellens, L.A., Beekhuyzen, J., and Trauth, E.M. 2003. Women Talking About IT Work: Duality or Dualism? *Proceedings of the 2003 SIGMIS conference on Computer personnel research: Freedom in Philadelphia--leveraging differences and diversity in the IT workforce* (SIGMIS CPR '03), ACM, New York, NY, USA, 68-74.

[64] Nielsen, S.H., von Hellens, L.A., Greenhill, A., and Pringle, R. 1997. "Collectivism and Connectivity: Culture and Gender in Information Technology Education," *Proceedings of the 1997 ACM SIGCPR conference on Computer personnel research* (SIGCPR '97), Niederman, F. (Ed.), ACM, New York, NY, USA, 9-13.

[65] Nielsen, S.H., von Hellens, L.A., Greenhill, A., and Pringle, R. 1998. Conceptualizing the Influence of Cultural and Gender Factors on Students' Perceptions of IT Studies and Careers. *Proceedings of the 1998 ACM SIGCPR conference on Computer personnel research* (SIGCPR '98), Agarwal, R. (Ed.), ACM, New York, NY, USA, 86-95.

[66] Nielsen, S.H., von Hellens, L.A., Greenhill, A., and Pringle, R. 2000. People, Business and IT Skills: the Perspective of Women in the IT Industry. *Proceedings of the 2000 ACM SIGCPR conference on Computer personnel research* (SIGCPR '00), ACM, New York, NY, USA, 152-157.

[67] Quesenberry, J.L. 2006. Career Anchors and Organizational Culture: a Study of Women in the IT Workforce. *Proceedings of the 2006 ACM SIGMIS CPR conference on computer personnel research: Forty four years of computer personnel research: achievements, challenges \& the future* (SIGMIS CPR '06), ACM, New York, NY, USA, 342-344.

[68] Quesenberry, J.L., and Trauth, E.M. 2007. What do Women Want?: an Investigation of Career Anchors Among Women in the IT Workforce. *Proceedings of the 2007 ACM SIGMIS CPR conference on Computer personnel research: The global information technology workforce* (SIGMIS CPR '07), ACM, New York, NY, USA, 122-127.

[69] Roldan, M., Soe, L., and Yakura, E.K. 2004. Perceptions of Chilly IT Organizational Contexts and Their Effect on the Retention and Promotion of Women in IT. *Proceedings of the 2004 SIGMIS conference on Computer personnel research: Careers, culture, and ethics in a networked environment* (SIGMIS CPR '04), ACM, New York, NY, USA, 108-113.

[70] Saez, P. A., Casado, A., Wade, J.C. 2009. Factors Influencing Masculinity Ideology among Latino Men. *Journal of Men's Studies*, 17, 2, 116-128.

[71] Smith, J. 1997. *Different for Girls: How Culture Creates Women*. Chatto and Windus Press, London, England.

[72] Sumner, M.R., and Werner, K. 2001. The Impact of Gender Differences on the Career Experiences of Information

Systems Professionals. *Proceedings of the 2001 ACM SIGCPR conference on Computer personnel research* (SIGCPR '01), Serva, M. (Ed.), ACM, New York, NY, USA, 125-131.

[73] Tapia, A.H. 2003. Hostile_Work_Environment.com. *Proceedings of the 2003 SIGMIS conference on Computer personnel research: Freedom in Philadelphia--leveraging differences and diversity in the IT workforce* (SIGMIS CPR '03), ACM, New York, NY, USA, 64-67.

[74] Tapia, A.H., and Kvasny, L. 2004. Recruitment is Never Enough: Retention of Women and Minorities in the IT Workplace. *Proceedings of the 2004 SIGMIS conference on Computer personnel research: Careers, culture, and ethics in a networked environment* (SIGMIS CPR '04), ACM, New York, NY, USA, 84-91.

[75] Trauth, E.M. 2002. Odd Girl Out: An Individual Differences Perspective on Women in the IT Profession, *Information Technology and People*, 15, 2, 98-118.

[76] Trauth, E.M. 2006. Theorizing Gender and Information Technology Research. *Encyclopedia of Gender and Information Technology*, Trauth, E.M. (Ed.), Idea Group Publishing, Hershey, PA, 1154-1159.

[77] Trauth, E.M., Adya, M., Armstrong, D.J., Joshi, K.D., Kvasny, L., Riemenschneider, C.K.,, and Quesenberry, J. 2010. Taking Stock of Research on Gender and the IT Workforce. *Proceedings of the 2010 Special Interest Group on Management Information System's 48th annual conference on Computer personnel research on Computer personnel research* (SIGMIS-CPR '10), ACM, New York, NY, USA, 171-178.

[78] Trauth, E.M., Farwell, D.W., & Lee, D. 1993. The IS Expectation Gap: Industry Expectations versus Academic Preparation, *MIS Quarterly*, 17, 3, 293-307.

[79] Trauth, E., Joshi, K.D., Kvasny, L., Chong, J., Kulturel, S, & Mahar, J. 2010. Millennials and Masculinity: A Shifting Tide of Gender Typing of ICT? *Proceedings of the Americas Conference on Information Systems*, Lima, Peru, (August 12-15, 2010).

[80] Trauth, E.M., Quesenberry,J.L., and Huang, H. 2006. Cross-cultural Influences on Women in the IT Workforce. *Proceedings of the 2006 ACM SIGMIS CPR conference on computer personnel research: Forty four years of computer personnel research: achievements, challenges & the future* (SIGMIS CPR '06), ACM, New York, NY, USA, 12-19.

[81] Trauth, E.M., Quesenberry, J. and Huang, H. 2008. A Multicultural Analysis of Factors Influencing Career Choice for Women in the Information Technology Workforce. *Journal of Global Information Management*, 16, 4, 1-23.

[82] Trauth, E.M., Quesenberry, J.L. and Huang, H. 2009. Retaining Women in the U.S. IT Workforce: Theorizing the Influence of Organizational Factors. *European Journal of Information Systems* (Special Issue on Meeting the Renewed Demand for IT Workers), 18, 476-497.

[83] Trauth, E.M., Quesenberry, J.L., Huang, H., and McKnight, S. 2008. Linking Economic Development and Workforce Diversity through Action Research. *Proceedings of the ACM SIGMIS Computer Personnel Research Conference*, ACM, New York, NY, USA, 58-65.

[84] Trauth, E.M., Quesenberry, J.L., and Morgan, A.J. 2004. Understanding the Under Representation of Women in IT: Toward a Theory of Individual Differences. *Proceedings of the 2004 SIGMIS conference on Computer personnel research: Careers, culture, and ethics in a networked environment* (SIGMIS CPR '04), ACM, New York, NY, USA, 114-119.

[85] Trauth, E.M., Quesenberry,J.L., and Yeo, B. 2005. The Influence of Environmental Context on Women in the IT Workforce. *Proceedings of the 2005 ACM SIGMIS CPR conference on Computer personnel research* (SIGMIS CPR '05), ACM, New York, NY, USA, 24-31.

[86] Trauth, E.M., Quesenberry, J. and Yeo, B. 2008. Environmental Influences on Gender in the IT Workforce. *The Data Base for Advances in Information Systems*, 14, 4, 8-32.

[87] US Census 2010, http://www.census.gov/population/www/socdemo/hispanic/hispanic_pop_presentation.html

[88] Vaas, L. 2000. How to Beat the Odds. *EWeek*, 17, 61.

[89] Von Hellens, L.A., Nielsen, S.H., and Trauth, E.M. 2001. Breaking and Entering the Male Domain: Women in the IT Industry. *Proceedings of the 2001 ACM SIGCPR conference on Computer personnel research* (SIGCPR '01), Serva, M. (Ed.), ACM, New York, NY, USA, 116-120.

[90] Willemsen, T. M. 2002. Gender Typing of the Successful Manager - A Stereotype Reconsidered. *Sex Roles*, 46, 11/12, 385-391.

[91] Wilson, M. 2004. A Conceptual Framework for Studying Gender in Information Systems Research. *Journal of Information Technology*, 19, 81-92.

[92] Wood, W. and Eagly, A. H. 2002. A Cross-Cultural Analysis of the Behavior of Women and Men: Implications for the Origins of Sex Differences. *Psychological Bulletin*, 128, 5, 699-727.

[93] Woodfield, R. 2002. Woman and Information Systems Development: Not just a Pretty (Inter)Face? *Information Technology & People*, 15, 2, 119-138

APPENDIX. Gender Research at CPR Conferences

Reference	Topic
Armstrong et al. [5]	Investigates challenges and barriers women in the IT field experience within the workplace.
Trauth et al. [77]	Current research in the SIGMIS community on women's participation in the IT workforce.
Clayton et al. [16]	Effect of gender stereotypes on girls' participation in ICT work and education.
Adya [1]	Comparison of Asian and American cultures about factors affecting IT workplace alienation.
Berkelaar et al. [10]	Effect of messages on recruitment and retention of women in computer science programs.
Buche [11]	Gender influences on IT professional's work identity.
Guzman et al. [33]	Cross-cultural examination of IT field / career cultures and occupational commitment.
Quesenberry and Trauth [68]	Women's career anchors within the IT workforce.
Trauth et al. [80]	Cross-cultural influences on women's experience in the IT field.
Gallivan and Benbunan-Fich [30]	Gender differences in IS scholarly publication rates.
Quesenberry [67]	Interaction of organizational culture, career anchors, career satisfaction and retention of women in IT.
Gallivan et al. [31]	Investigates the underrepresentation of women and minorities within the IT workforce, focusing on attracting and retaining both populations.
Kvasny et al. [55]	Kenyan women in university ICT programs, and seeking, and maintaining employment.
Trauth et al. [85]	Effect of environmental context on underrepresentation of women within the IT workforce
Joshi and Kuhn [43]	Relationship of masculine perception of characteristics, skills, and roles in IT workforce to retention of women in IT field.
Myers et al. [60]	Opportunities and retention of women in the information security and assurance part of the IT field.
Roldan et al. [69]	Effect of organizational context on retention and promotion of women within the IT field.
Trauth et al. [84]	Theory based on the individual differences of women to explain their underrepresentation within the IT field.
Ahuja et al. [4]	Factors contributing to women's success within the IT field from examination of 5 IT degree-awarding institutions.
Tapia and Kvasny [74]	Examines retention strategies for women and minorities in the IT field.
Joshi et al. [48]	Gendered perceptions held by potential IS professionals.
Gallivan [29]	Adaptation of men and women in IT field to technological innovations in the workplace.
Cukier [22]	Effect of institutional definitions of an IT professional in creation of barriers to women within the IT workforce.
Carayon et al. [13]	Role of satisfaction and job strain to explain underrepresentation and turnover rate of women within the IT field.
Tapia [73]	Behaviors of male employees within software development companies that created a hostile work environment for women during the dot com era.
Nielsen et al. [63]	How women discuss dualisms and contradictions that reinforce preconceived notions about the IT field.
Kvasny [53]	Impact of race, class, and gender on perceptions of IT and need for further research on intersectionality in diverse populations.
Newton et al. [61]	How social gender constructs affect IT job selections for systems developers.
Davis and Kuhn [24]	Investigation of long term plans of men and women to remain in IT careers.
Katz et al. [49]	Performance, based on gender, of potential CS and IS students during a programming tutorial.
Lending and Kruck [57]	A method to address gender disparity in IS degree recipients by predicting academic success during introductory level IS courses.
Beise et al. [8]	Factors encouraging and discouraging women with interests in IT.
Niederman and Sumner [62]	Factors in IT turnover including gender, job satisfaction and salary.
Joshi and Kuhn [44]	Explores what causes men and women to be attracted to the IS field.
Sumner and Werner [72]	Gender differences effect on IS career success and experience.
Myers and Beise [59]	Factors that encourage and discourage pursuit of IT career, including gender age, etc. from students in a standard introductory-level programming course.
von Hellens et al. [89]	How women in Australian IT field view masculinity of the IT industry.
Nielsen et al. [66]	How Australian women view necessary IT skills, the skills they bring to the industry, and how those skills affect their career.
Nielsen et al. [65]	Role of culture and gender on students' perceptions of IT to explain fewer students choosing to study IT.
Nielsen et al. [64]	Which cultural factors in Australia encourage female Asian students to pursue careers in IT.
Ahuja [3]	Barriers women face to entering the IT field with respect to three separate life stages.
Igbaria and Chidambaram [40]	How women and men in the IS workforce were differentiated in terms of commitment, satisfaction, and a desire to remain in the field.
Enneis et al. [27]	Implications of legislation prohibiting employment discrimination based on sex.

Author Index

NOTES

www.ingramcontent.com/pod-product-compliance
Lightning Source LLC
Chambersburg PA
CBHW080406060326
40689CB00019B/4154

* 9 7 8 1 4 5 0 3 1 1 1 0 6 *